Conditions of Identity

A Study in Identity and Survival

———

ANDREW BRENNAN

CLARENDON PRESS · OXFORD
1988

Oxford University Press, Walton Street, Oxford OX2 6DP
Oxford New York Toronto
Delhi Bombay Calcutta Madras Karachi
Petaling Jaya Singapore Hong Kong Tokyo
Nairobi Dar es Salaam Cape Town
Melbourne Auckland
and associated companies in
Beirut Berlin Ibadan Nicosia

Oxford is a trade mark of Oxford University Press

Published in the United States
by Oxford University Press, New York

British Library Cataloguing in Publication Data
Brennan, Andrew
Conditions of identity: a study in
identity and survival.
1. Identity
I. Title
111   BD236
ISBN 0-19-824974-8

Library of Congress Cataloging in Publication Data
Brennan, Andrew.
Conditions of identity.
Bibliography: p.   Includes index.
1. Identify. 2. Metaphysics. 3. Identify
(Psychology) I. Title.
BC199.I4B74   1988   110   87-28237
ISBN 0-19-824974-8

Set by Cotswold Typesetting Ltd, Gloucester
Printed in Great Britain by Biddles Ltd, Guildford and King's Lynn

Conditions of Identity

Preface

PHILOSOPHY is a communal activity in more than one way. Although it can claim to be one of our species' oldest intellectual preoccupations, it cannot advance far without the existence of a global community of philosophers who support, stimulate, and encourage research in the subject. That kind of community itself has links with larger and smaller communities in turn. On the one side there are the smaller, local communities of philosophers supported by their societies in one way or another. On the other side society itself supports philosophy and other intellectual activities because of the value that the study of philosophy, and its practice, is deemed to bring to the community at large. Conscious of this, I have tried to write this book in such a way that, while addressing current concerns in the theory of identity, it is not so technical as to be inaccessible to the non-specialist reader. To some extent, the pursuit of clarity is at odds with the pursuit of accuracy and precision, as many others have noted before me. When faced with a choice, however, I have tried, unashamedly, to err on the side of clarity.

I have benefited in preparing this book from the support and assistance of both my local and the wider philosophical community. Over the years at Stirling, I have been fortunate to enjoy the stimulation and encouragement of lively colleagues and friends. They have made contributions to the book in many ways, in some cases long before its preparation was undertaken. As I write this preface, I am acutely aware of the many debts I owe, and of the impossibility of giving them due acknowledgement. The wider community of philosophers also contains many people who have helped me understand both my own, and other people's, views better. Particular gratitude is owed to those colleagues and friends who have gone through the entire manuscript in its draft version, offering suggestions and help without which the book would be a poorer one. Although it is impossible to mention everyone who has helped in this way, I would like to record my special thanks to Jonathan Lowe, Murray MacBeath, Alan Millar, Harold Noonan, and George Schlesinger, each of whom has made a significant impact on the final version of the work. Thanks also to Elspeth Gillespie for her efficient typing and revision of the manuscript.

There are several passages in the book that are based on work that has already appeared in print. I am grateful for permission to reproduce material from the following of my articles:

'Survival', in *Synthese*, 59 (D. Reidel, 1984);

'Amnesia and Psychological Continuity', in R. Copp and J. J. McIntosh (eds.), *New Essays in the Philosophy of Mind* (*Canadian Journal of Philosophy*, Supplementary Volume II, 1985);

'Best Candidates and Theories of Identity', in *Inquiry*, 29 (Norwegian University Press, 1986);

'Discontinuity and Identity', in *Nous*, 21 (Indiana University Press, 1987).

I am also grateful to MIT Press for permission to use the epigraph from *Word and Object* and to Russell Hoban and Pan Books for permission to quote Eusa 33 from *Riddley Walker*.

A.A.B.

Contents

Contents

Eusa 33

Eusa sed, How menne Chaynjis ar thayr? The Littl Man
sed, Yu mus no aul abowt that I seen yu rite thay Nos.
down in the hart uv the wud. Eusa sed, That riting is
long gon & aul thay Nos. hav gon owt uv my myn I doan
remember nuthing uv them. Woan yu pleas tel me how
menne Chaynjis thayr ar? The Littl Man sed, As menne
as reqwyrd. Eusa sed, Reqwyrd by wut? The Littl Man
sed, Reqwyrd by the idear uv yu. Eusa sed, Wut is the
idear uv me? The Littl Man sed, That we doan no til yuv
gon thru aul yur Chaynjis.

RUSSELL HOBAN, *Riddley Walker*

The dividing of reference consists in settling conditions
of identity: how far you have the same apple and when
you are getting onto another.

W. V. QUINE, *Word and Object*, §24

Introduction

PHILOSOPHY is a voyage of a very special kind. In it the traveller is subject, for the most part, to constraints which would be intolerable to the social scientist, literary critic, or historian. For the appeal of much contemporary philosophy is to those of a highly rational temperament with a great respect for logical consequence. One rather irritating consequence of all this is the appearance, on occasion, of pedantry, a tendency to literalness, and a close attendance to the details of language reminiscent of the fabled Vermonters. Smullyan reminds us of the story about Calvin Coolidge visiting a farm with some friends. When his group encountered a flock of sheep, someone remarked that the sheep had just been shorn. 'Looks like it from this side,' was the president's reply. In keeping a diary of my explorations of identity in the following pages, I have not lived up to the standards of Coolidge. Rather, I have tried to convey some of the excitement and interest of the topic by taking a relaxed approach to it. Although I deal with many of the topics that are of central concern to the theory of identity, I have kept technical matters to an absolute minimum.

There is, however, more to say by way of introduction than this. Despite some respect for the three L's (attend to the Literal, to Language, and to Logic) any work in philosophy needs to be prepared to engage in theorizing. Everyone, of course, theorizes some of the time—even off-duty philosophers. But in this book I have presented a sustained example of philosophy as theory-construction, and have done so at the risk of occasionally not showing tremendous respect for the three L's. Theorizing in philosophy is not constrained by the techniques of science. For instance, there are few references to objective, repeatable experiments, except in the chapter dealing with some psychological issues. But there are many sorts of perfectly respectable kinds of theorizing which are responsive to the everyday and scientific knowledge which we possess, and some of these have a place in philosophy. To the extent, then, that this book succeeds as a piece of philosophy, it is a vindication of my view that theory construction, and certain kinds of speculative endeavours, are a genuine part of the business of philosophy.

These remarks are not meant to exhaust the story of what philosophy is, or indicate any limitations on its scope. As our oldest academic subject, philosophy is also, perhaps, the most polymorphic. Further, contemporary philosophy as practised in most universities in the UK and North America is, for all its diversity, just one style of philosophy among others. It is not easy for dedicated practitioners of a certain style of philosophy to take this last remark seriously. However, I regard it as a limitation on my own work that my training and skills only permit me to write one kind of account of the sights I have encountered.

To the extent that theorizing is an attempt at giving explanations, the notion that philosophy involves theorizing—at least for some of the time—suggests that philosophy is concerned with explaining things. And given the connections between explanation and understanding, philosophy will be concerned with understanding. My initial question is: in what, if anything, does the identity or unity of a persisting thing consist? Related to this general puzzle are more specific ones, dealing with whether identity is, or is not, primitive and indefinable, and concerning whether the identity of different kinds of thing is itself different. Occasionally, although epistemology is not my main concern here, I also have to consider questions of how unity is determined or discovered. In answering the initial question, I produce a theory that is meant to yield understanding of what the unity of a persisting thing involves, and an understanding of how we are able to recognize such unity. It is clear, then, that unlike some other contemporary thinkers— Nozick, for one—I do not restrict attention solely to questions of how something or other is possible. If the reader is convinced that some discoveries of interest are described in the following pages, then this will perhaps make plausible the claim that there can be systematic theorizing outside the sciences which does not descend into merely idle speculation.

Someone who does dabble in philosophical theorizing is liable to fall foul of those austere souls who fear that too much speculation and too many thought-experiments lead us far from reality and, ultimately, into fairyland. The label *analytical* helps to suggest that philosophy is concerned with uncovering the nature of our existing beliefs and concepts rather than with developing new ones. If all the analysts were after was a reminder of the need to hold fast to Russell's concern that we do not lose touch with the real world, then their worries would be perfectly justified. However, I hope to show that some flights of fancy simply help focus our thoughts on problems that are already real. The use of thought-experiments is no more than an enjoyable means for working on issues that even the soberest of analysts must recognize as important, and as demanding solution. At various points in the book I return to this issue, indicating in a conciliatory vein the relation between a particular flight of fancy and a real problem of analysis.

In a less conciliatory vein, we might also observe that some enemies of thought-experiments simply reveal an astonishing degree of conservatism about what they will and will not discuss. Should we, for example, be constrained in our philosophizing by restricting our attention only to those theories which have the stamp of approval from contemporary science? Suppose that apparently sincere persons tell me that they know someone who is the *reincarnation* of a person long dead. Our best current science provides nothing which would enable us to make sense of such a claim in terms of physical or chemical models. But that science cannot vindicate the claim does not mean that we cannot make any sense at all of it, nor that we cannot investigate what difference it would make to our views if it turned out that reincarnation did occur. To refuse to think about phenomena lying beyond our present scientific ken is to adopt a stance that is not only blinkered but is ultimately alien to the very spirit of inquiry that drives science and philosophy forward.

It is worth noticing that even the most sober of analytical philosophers are capable of occupying positions that are entirely alien to common sense. Quine is a notable example. For him, science is no more than an extension of common sense, and psychology is a branch of science. The theory of knowledge is, moreover, no more than a sub-department of psychology. So what does this sober analyst have to say about our knowledge of physical objects? These, Quine tells us in his early work, are not the basic items we might have thought. Rather, we have a theory that the world around us contains enduring physical things, and these things are themselves no more than the entities of theory—posits. As some kind of reassurance, Quine urges us to remember that to call a posit a posit is not to patronize it.

Like all good philosophers, Quine shows commendable consistency in following his view to its logical conclusion. But in urging us to accept that enduring physical things are merely theoretical entities he has, in my view, left common sense, and any sense of reality, far behind. By contrast, the theories of identity put forward in this book are, I would maintain, far closer to the scientific, common-sense world-view (if there is such a thing) than the theories of Quine, or those of rival identity theorists. The reader who is initially hostile to my approach may like to bear this point in mind. Such a reader I would also urge to give careful consideration to my claims about, and examples of, conceptual development. If I am right in thinking that what is done under the label of *conceptual analysis* is often quite a different enterprise, then it is high time that this enterprise was recognized for what it is.

1
Identity and Continuity

1.1. IDENTITY AND SIMILARITY

Most students of philosophy are familiar with the dictum that you cannot step twice into the same river. In the two thousand odd years since Heraclitus (or whoever) made the observation, we have seen disappointingly little progress in solving problems about identity. My claims in the present work are fairly modest. One is to show how we can give a plausible account of identity that will cover some— even if not all—of the interesting cases. This will yield us a theory which gives us the identity conditions for many sorts of objects; for trees, mountains, and perhaps cats, even if not for bicycles and other artefacts. Some of the questions posed about identity, have no determinate answer. Of this kind are some questions about fairly humdrum objects and also some of the puzzles about *personal* identity. In some of these cases, at least, we can make practical decisions about what to do, hope for, expect, and think, even while leaving the question of identity unsettled. Showing just how we can do the latter constitutes a further aim of the work.

It may seem that such a view is deflationary. For if we can come to practical decisions while leaving questions of identity unresolved, how can identity be what matters in such situations? We will see that, despite this deflationary possibility, identity does not become entirely discredited in my theory. Indeed, one large aim will be to show how identity is established in some cases, and in what identity then consists. Why identity matters, though, is that it is regularly associated with other things that matter. Such a view is bound to shock those who believe that identity itself is something of fundamental importance, a feature of the world that underpins, for instance, our naming and referential practices. I can only appeal, at this point, to such readers to keep an open mind for the time being. They will soon discover that the theory explained in this work has the virtue of resolving many otherwise intractable puzzles. Then they can judge for themselves whether this benefit is worth the cost of giving up the view that identity itself is too basic ever to be capable of elucidation or definition in other terms.

Identity, as defined in the majority of philosophical treatments of the notion, is related to another puzzling notion, that of *similarity* (or, sometimes, *qualitative identity*). We can reveal the connection between the two notions in informal terms thus:

> *Similarity*: If *a* is similar to *b* then something true of *a* is also true of *b*.
>
> *Identity*: If *a* is identical with *b* (that is, *a*=*b*), then everything true of *a* is also true of *b*.

Instead of making the distinction in terms of truth and falsehood, we can make it—equally informally—in terms of properties (and relations):

> *Similarity*: If *a* is similar to *b* then some property of *a* is also a property of *b*.
>
> *Identity*: If *a* is identical with *b* (that is, *a*=*b*), then every property of *a* is also a property of *b*.

Here, since we are talking loosely and pre-theoretically, *a* has a property if it has true of it some sentence ascribing a property or indeed one that assigns a relation between it and another thing. Understood in this way, similarity is a pretty broad notion. I do not normally regard my coal-scuttle as being at all similar to the still life that hangs in the sitting-room. However, both are similar, by the above account, through sharing the property of being in the sitting-room. Later, we will try to construct a more plausible notion of similarity, although this is no easy matter.

Similarity is an important notion in the theory of knowledge. Our knowledge of the world is dependent on our ability to identify similarities among things. There are different views about what we should say about similarity. Perhaps, as Quine has suggested, we have some kind of innate 'similarity space', which enables us to classify the Heraclitean flux of experience into categories. Thus we are able to determine, for a newly encountered item, whether or not it is of the same *sort* as items we have met with previously. And, certainly, if we could not thus classify objects into *sorts* or kinds, it is hard to see how even the most elementary form of communication regarding our environment could get under way. Quine's theory of similarity spaces, however, is not the only, or the best, account of our similarity skills. As I will argue later, the world we live in may itself be the provider of similarities to us in the first place, and the existence of such similarities may be an important factor in making it intelligible to us. Whatever account we give of similarity, its importance is undeniable.

Identity, likewise, seems to be a fundamental notion, one which—like similarity—combines this importance with diverse theories about how it is to be elucidated and what our standards of identity are. Some examples will reveal its claimed significance. Suppose, for a very simple case, I am telling a story about an incident I witnessed last week. One person who figures in the story is a woman in a stained trench coat whose name I do not know. However, to add vividness to the story I give her the name 'Amanda'. Now I can tell you various things about what Amanda did, where she was, and how she came to be, let us suppose, arrested. You can ask me if Amanda put up a struggle against the police, or whether her behaviour was such that she really ought to have been arrested. Here, each time either you or I have used the name 'Amanda' and its correlated pronoun, we have taken these terms to refer to *one and the same person*. And to speak in this way about 'one and the same person' is to use the notion of identity: identity is, we might say, the property of *being one and the same*. Not just proper names and pronouns, but arbitrary symbols and certain descriptive phrases get used quite regularly in this way: so that each time the same expression is used, one and the same thing is referred to. So it seems that our very apparatus of naming things, and referring to them subsequently, presupposes the existence of identity, and involves the concept of identity.

For the time being, let us allow the strong claim that the reference of names and descriptions does in fact require this presumption of identity, and continue to look at the sort of argument that tries to establish the centrality of the notion. Think again of individual things, objects. As already pointed out, the objects we talk about in daily life belong to well-established sorts or kinds—trees, goats, fields, bicycles, desks, cranes, fence posts, swifts, and so on. Each of the nouns used in the list given seems to apply to items which we can count. So, as well as calling such nouns *sortals*, or *terms of divided reference*, we could also call them *count-nouns*.[1] Terminology here is

---

[1] Griffin defines count nouns thus: 'A general term, "*T*" is + count if "There are *n* *T*'s . . ." makes sense, where "n" is a variable taking numerals as values; otherwise "T" is − count.' (Griffin [2], p. 23.) Although such a characterization would no

various and—without wanting to impose one nomenclature on the reader—I will mainly use the term 'sortal' to apply both to the nouns and to the related concepts. The important thing about sortal general terms, and the associated sortal concepts, is that their exercise seems to be associated with principles for counting and individuating the items to which they apply. So the items associated with a sortal (term. or concept) thus constitute a collection of things that may be counted, things like goats, trees, and cows, where it is fairly clear, therefore, where one such thing ends and another begins.[2] Whatever we call such terms, someone who could not tell a swift from an eagle, or from a fir-tree, would show a poor grasp of the use of the term 'swift'. More significantly, someone who could not distinguish one swift from a flock of them, or who thinks that a flock of swifts is just another swift, would be someone who has not grasped the use of the term 'swift' (nor the associated concept). And such a person would never learn to count swifts, if unable to grasp the conditions of identity for swifts—the conditions under which one swift ends and another begins. Of course, grasp of the sortal 'swift', and the ability to count may not go hand in hand. We can imagine someone whose best attempt at differentiating swifts went 'One, two, several, many, lots and lots . . .', and this would not be a person skilled in counting. But such an example does not undermine the claim that sortal terms do have principles of counting associated with them. Sortals in fact have all kinds of interest for the identity theorist, and we will be looking at some aspects of this in due course.

doubt be roughly adequate for defining *sortals*, Griffin prefers to distinguish the latter from count-nouns, giving this modification of a criterion originally due to Sheehan: 'A term "*A*" is sortal if there *can* be cases in which "*A*" provides, without further conceptual decision and without borrowing other principles of individuation, principles adequate for counting *A*'s.' (Griffin [2], p. 43.) Thus 'thing' is a count-noun, by these definitions, but not a sortal. As is clear in the text, I am happy to accept that sortals, rather than count-nouns, are of interest to theories of identity. Sortal and count terms show an interesting difference from *mass* terms, the latter being, in Hirsch's terminology, *dispersive*: 'A term like 'wood' is dispersive because any stretch (quantity, bit) of wood will extensively overlap numerous other stretches of wood that make it up.' (Hirsch [2], p. 42.) Hirsch is thus able to define sortals as *nondispersive* terms.

[2] As stated in the epigraph from Quine [2], § 24. Although it may not seem necessary to distinguish *sorts* from *kinds*, I treat sorts as forming the more general category. Thus, one important variety of sortal terms is the set of *natural kind* terms.

Not only is our understanding of identity, of someness and difference, associated with our understanding of the world as containing individuals, themselves of various sorts, it is also associated with other concerns. One of the most significant of these, perhaps, is our concern with *persons* and our care about their future, their pasts, and their responsibilities. Some people, late in life, still feel troubled by guilt about actions they carried out when children or teenagers. Others, often religiously inspired, claim an interest in a future that continues after their bodily death. Our punishment of offenders, our criticism of our own, or others', moral failings are based on an understanding of *personal identity* which goes unchallenged for the most part. Yet as soon as we ask the right questions, we can find ourselves puzzled. Am I the same person I was as a child? How could I be the same person I am now after the destruction of all my body? If I had a brain transplant after committing a crime, would 'I' (if it is still me that we are talking about) deserve punishment for that crime? Not only has this topic attracted a literature all to itself, but it poses problems that seem almost as great once we have studied other cases of identity as they seemed when we first started. One virtue of the theory of identity ventured here is that it makes some of the questions about personal identity seem easier to answer than we might have thought. Unfortunately, for some of the problems, as we shall see, there remain no determinate answers nor is there—I would argue—hope of achieving determinacy.

Let us conclude this introductory section by looking at the formal principles of identity. Two of these suffice for all the logic of identity. The first, the principle of relexivity of identity, simply states that everything is identical with itself, in symbols.

Reflexivity: $\forall x[x = x]$

The second simply repeats the informal statement already given: that if x is identical with y, then everything that is true of x is also true of y. This principle is given many names in the literature, two of the most common being *Leibniz's Law*, or *the principle of indiscernibility of identicals*. In symbols, we have

Indiscernibility: $\forall x \forall y \forall F[(x = y) \supset (Fx \supset Fy)]$

I have given this in its second-order formulation partly because it seems natural to do so, and partly because it avoids certain formal niggles.[3] In this form, we can use the two principles to derive a third, important principle. Unlike the uncontroversial fact that identity is symmetric (if $x = y$ then $y = x$) and transitive (if $x = y$ then $y = x$) and transitive (if $x = y$ and $y = z$ then $x = z$), this further principle states the *identity of indiscernibles*, and is controversial enough to have been dismissed by Peirce as 'all nonsense'. The principle tells us that if everything true of x is also true of y, then x is one and the same as y, in symbols:

Identity of Indiscernibles: $\forall x \forall y [\forall F(Fx \supset Fy) \supset (x = y)]$

It is tempting to suggest, in view of the difficulty some people have in accepting the third principle, that classical second-order logic enriched with identity is in much the same position as first-order logic given the Boolean definitions of the conditional and conjunction. The system, in each case, works well. But enough questions are raised to point to a discrepancy between the logical systems we use on the one hand and the system of reasoning encoded in our natural language on the other. Fascinating though such a topic is for investigation, I ignore it in this work.

1.2. IDENTITY AND CONTINUANTS

It is one thing to know the logic of identity, another to look for those conditions of identity that apply to the case of correctly reidentifying objects. Theorists who accept the principles of reflexivity and indiscernibility have fallen by and large into two distinct camps

---

[3] For example, we do not need to consider the problems posed by adding indiscernibles (which may be distinct) to a first-order theory. For further comments on the formal principles, see the standard treatments by Wiggins and Griffin. Ishiguro [1] gives more information on Leibniz's Law. Sometimes indiscernibility is expressed in either of the following forms, where the schemes are valid for all instances:

(i) $(x = y \ \& \ Fx) \supset Fy$
(ii) $x = y \supset (Fx \equiv Fy)$

(i) is obviously equivalent by truth functional logic to the version in the text. (ii) is easily derived from that version given the principle of reflexivity. For suppose that $x = y$, but $\sim(Fy \supset Fx)$. Substitution for F yields $\sim(x = y \supset x = x)$, that is, $x = y$ while $\sim(x = x)$, which latter is a contradiction. Hence $x = y \supset (Fy \supset Fx)$, which establishes (ii).

Interestingly, as Quine shows in Quine [3], we can derive all the properties of identity from one principle, Wang's Law: $Fy \equiv \exists x(x = y \ \& \ Fx)$.

over the matter of how to reidentify objects—we can call them *continuity theorists* and *indiscernibility theorists,* respectively. The problems come about due to a phenomenon known to, and celebrated by, Heraclitus himself: *change.* If doors that were painted red never changed their colour, if bodies didn't change their cells, if rivers never changed their water or their course, if cameras, bicycles, and houses never needed new parts, then we would have a duller world and far fewer problems about identity. Luckily, though, the world is not dull. Change is with us all the time, and this is the source of a great many problems.

Perhaps, whatever the logical laws of identity state, an important feature for the identity of one persistent thing is its continuity in time and space. The continuity theorist can point here to the celebrated case mentioned by Hobbes, supposedly about the ship of Theseus.[4] After sailing from Athens, this ship finds itself gradually subject to replacement: plank by plank, nail by nail, sheet by sheet, the entire hull, masts, rigging, and so on are replaced by new versions which themselves look fairly similar to their originals. In the end, not a single dowel, not a single strand of hemp survives from the original ship. Yet all the time, the ship has been plying its trade, going to sea, colliding with jetties—in short, functioning normally as a ship throughout the period of replacement.

What is the right thing to say here! Has Theseus' ship been *repaired* or *replaced*? If the latter, then when did the original ship go out of existence—when the very first repair occurred, or only after a certain amount of the original material had been replaced? If it has not been replaced, but has stayed the same all along, then it seems that one and the same thing can be two quite different collections of masts, spars, planks, and sails. Pondering on this question, we see that, for a start, the logical principles already given do not settle the matter of identity for this kind of case. This may seem a disappointment, until we recognize that logical principles seldom supply legislation for conceptual puzzles: their ability to codify agreed inferences makes them hospitable to the expression of divergent theories. Thus those who think that the replacement of parts leads to the existence of two distinct ships can agree with those who think that one ship survives all the changes: indeed, failure to

---

[4] The puzzle originated in Hobbes [1], pt. II, ch. 11, although, as Wiggins observes, Hobbes no doubt found the idea in Plutarch (see Wiggins [9], p. 92).

agree on principles like Leibniz's law and indiscernibility would make the disagreement about sameness and difference assume a new character. It would become, at least in part, a disagreement about the meaning of the term 'identity'.

Faced with the problem of change, a theorist wedded to the notion of *continuity* may point out that typically the concrete objects surrounding us are persisting things—*continuants,* to use Wiggins's word. The term 'concrete' is used in the last sentence in the philosopher's, not the builder's, sense. In the next chapter, more will be said about what this sense is. Persisting things can change; some changes are greater than others. But the changes to Theseus' ship are not such as to turn it from a ship into something that is not a ship. So perhaps the best thing to say here is that we have witnessed spatio-temporal continuity of one enduring ship. On this approach, we can still distinguish the ship at one time from the ship as it is at other times. Such a *stage,* or *temporal part,* of the ship will differ from other stages in terms of the collection of planks constituting it. Thus, one same thing, the persisting ship, has a number of different stages we can allocate to it. Let us suppose that we can make these stages long or short in duration, but that relative to the total history of the object such stages are pretty short-lived. The replacement of any part of the ship by a new part could be the point we choose for transition from one stage to the next. We could then think of the ship as a series of stages each one of which is itself a distinct collection of ship-parts. We can make this clear on a standard space-time diagram depicting a portion of the ship's history (Fig. 1). Notice, of course, that this is only one of indefinitely many ways of partitioning the ship into stages. And there will still be changes during the stages: chips and dents and scratches, weathering, flaking of paint and tar, not to mention a host of minor changes all the way down to molecular and atomic levels. However we select our stages, we have here an attractive way of dealing with sameness and difference. The ship itself is more than one collection of parts. Moreover the collection of parts that constitutes the ship changes from time to time. The differences among stages plot the visible changes in the history of one enduring and continuous thing—the ship.

Looking at the case of the ship in this way starts to make some sense of our second principle—that of indiscernibility. It is because we can trace continuants through time, and assign diverse stages to

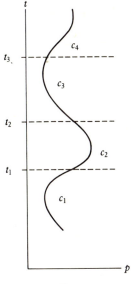

Fig. 1.

one and the same persisting object, that we can both allow for the phenomenon of change and at the same time insist that if a is the same as b then any property of the one is likewise a property of the other. In the case of our one ship, being constituted of collection c_1 at one time and of c_3 at a later time are properties true of it and nothing other than it. Sameness and change thus become incorporated into a comprehensible account of the ship's history.

1.3. CONTINUITY AND INDISCERNIBILITY

The continuity account is not the only one we can give here. As already pointed out, there are two different camps into which people divide on this issue; if one camp contains the continuity theorists, the other contains theorists who take indiscernibility as a *sufficient* condition of identity. Of course, these indiscernibility theorists are justified by our third principle; they even take it as the fundamental law of identity, rather than as a consequence of the others. Our newly introduced theorists deny that continuity has any central role in settling identity questions. Even though they admit that our world consists of relatively enduring and changing objects, they find continuity alone neither necessary nor sufficient for identity. Let us give some content to this disagreement by considering another space-time diagram (Fig. 2).[5] This time we are tracing the history of an entity called—quite arbitrarily—'Bill'. After coming into existence, at all times up to and including t_1 Bill is fairly stationary in the region of p_1. Immediately after t_1, however, Bill makes a sort of instantaneous 'quantum jump' to p_2 where he remains for the rest of his life. Bill's history appears to be discontinuous in space (though not in time); and—of course—we are not used to such happenings in regard to objects in the macroscopic world. None the less, we seem to be able to make sense of the idea that we should assign these lengthy discontinuous stages to the history of just one thing.

To complicate things, we can consider the history of some other entity, perhaps the Amanda of our earlier example. Oddly enough, Amanda occupies position p_2 for some time right up to t_1, whereupon she makes a quantum jump to place p_1. We can thus

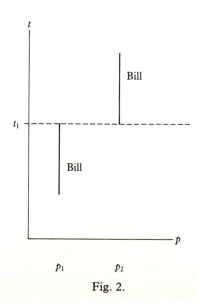

Fig. 2.

[5] My version of the indiscernibility theorist's case is based on the discussion in Brody [3].

complete our earlier diagram with the lifeline of Amanda, recognizing that her discontinuous existence in no way prevents us from assigning both life segments to the one entity (Fig. 3).

Now consider what the continuity theorist has to say about this case. There are two continuous space-time paths shown on the diagram. The one at p_1 has a Bill phase followed by an Amanda phase, while the other has an Amanda stage followed by a Bill stage. If continuity in space and time is what really counts for identity, then, however different the properties of Bill and Amanda, we have to recognize that one same thing can begin its career with a Bill phase and then continue for the rest of its history with an Amanda one.

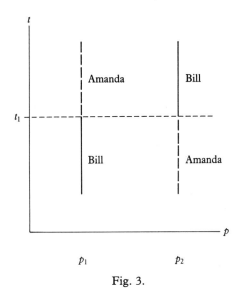

Fig. 3.

Put in these sketchy terms, the continuity view of the matter seems distinctly implausible. So perhaps it would be wise to look at another example to see if we can sharpen our intuitions. However, the best cases for this purpose are—to put it mildly—somewhat fictionalized. One that we can try to explore concerns an unfortunate dog. Rover, who is supposedly the victim of a NASA experiment. The plot is as follows.[6] Having been sent on a pioneer mission to Mars, our terrier returns to earth where, to everyone's surprise, a nasty and untoward effect of Martian radiation begins to show itself. In the isolation unit in which he is kept under continuous observation, Rover begins to manifest a number of slow changes. Over the weeks he gradually transforms, rather like a caterpillar in its pupa stage—only to a far greater extent. Within months our dog has been transformed into a mass of cells, totally without structure. Within the cells, even the constitution of chromosomes has changed so that the lump of matter that remains does not even have any of Rover's original DNA. Using a new name to designate the amorphous mass into which Rover has been transformed, let us call the blob 'Clover'.

Unlike the preceding case, we are not here faced with instantaneous change. And Marjorie Price, in putting forward this grisly story, is taking a line in favour of continuity. Her claim is that the example poses a difficulty for those who maintain that what is required for identity is *continuity under some same sortal*; for Clover has none of the interesting sortals true of it that were originally true of Rover. The mention of 'interesting sortals' is meant to preclude the objection that Rover and Clover are both *things, objects, occupiers of space*; none of the latter are what Wiggins would call 'substance sortals', and certainly those who make much of sortal-covered continuity do not have such uninformative sortals in mind.[7] So Price's view is that Rover and Clover are indeed identical, although they are not the same dog, the same animal, or the same anything else of an interesting sort.

---

[6] So writes Marjorie Price in Price [1]. For a thorough discussion of the case, Brody [3] is worth consulting.

[7] For Wiggins, sortals provide the most privileged and fundamental answers to questions of the form: what is *x*? As well as obvious cases where sortals apply to an individual throughout its entire history—such sortals being, in Wiggins's treatment, *substance concepts*—there are two special cases worth noting. First, there are restrictions of some underlying sortal, where the restriction is concerned with a phase in the history of an item: thus we have 'child' as a restriction of the substance concept, 'human'. Second, there are concepts and terms that seem to lack individuative force, and are thus too unspecific to count as interesting sortals, or even as sortals at all. Examples are 'entity', 'thing', 'space-occupier', and so on. 'Uninteresting' sortals, however, seem just to be extreme cases of fairly obvious disjunctive sortals (e.g. 'spouse' as meaning 'husband or wife'; 'insect' as meaning 'wasp, or bee, or dragonfly, or . . .'). The most sensitive discussion of these tricky matters is to be found in Wiggins's work, especially Wiggins [9].

The example, however, serves well enough to show how those not committed to continuity as a sufficient condition of identity can argue that Rover and Clover are distinct things despite their continuity. Rover and Clover do, of course, sit on segments of one continuous world line: so does a living butterfly and the remains of its skeleton; so did Bill and Amanda. The indiscernibility theorist can argue in some, or all, of these cases that distinct things sit on these segments, notwithstanding the continuities. And the basis for the claim of distinctness is the lack of common properties: Rover and Clover are discernible; they are thus two rather than one. And the indiscernibility theorist can maintain this while admitting that there is no clear way of knowing just when Rover ceased to exist and when Clover started to exist.

It has not been my intention thus far to defend one or another of these positions. As the theory of identity unfolds in later chapters, we will see that there are interesting things to be said about continuity and about discontinuity. At the moment, I am concerned to impart the flavour of some of the central puzzles in the area, and to establish the sorts of positions that can be taken towards these puzzles. Later, we will see that some of the puzzles are more apparent than real, and that what appear at first to be quite baffling problems will yield to essentially simple treatment.

1.4. IDENTITY AND SURVIVAL

In 1971 Derek Parfit published a defence of the claim that *survival* may often be more important than identity.[8] What does he mean by 'survival'? Is it not just identity under another label? In Parfit's early treatment, we can think of survival as a kind of *default option*: it is the feature we default to when conditions for identity are satisfied but something else rules out an identity claim, or when the matter of identity itself is indeterminate. It is clear that we can ask of

[8] See Parfit [1] and [2]. Although I borrow the term 'survival' from Parfit's early work, he subsequently dropped it. In *Reasons and Persons* he simply writes of *psychological continuity and connectedness* as being the relation that matters for psychological unity. This is convenient, for my own account of survival may well not be one that Parfit would endorse. In subsequently reconstructing his view on persons, I will continue to use the term 'survival', understanding it in the way defined in the present book. I hope this terminological device does not cause unnecessary confusion.

Theseus' original ship whether or not it *survives* the replacement of its parts; and we can likewise ask if Rover *survives* as Clover. Parfit's point is that we can make sense of survival even where identity is out of the question (for example, where the original ship survives twice over), or where we are unable to determine the right thing to say about identity. We can thus have survival without identity, even though we may not have identity without survival.

That we cannot have identity without survival is rather easily established provided we accept the logical principles already introduced and make the assumption that everything *survives as itself*. Suppose, now, that $a = b$; then, it must be true, by our assumption, that b survives as b; so, by the indiscernibility of identicals, the very same thing—surviving as b—must be true of a. So if a is one and the same as b, a survives as b. It is therefore more interesting to examine the converse case.

Let us start with a case of the second kind mentioned above—one where we are unsure what to say about identity, but still seem able to make a claim about survival. Parfit considers the intersting case of resurrection.[9] Although personal identity is a topic for special treatment later, we can dwell for a moment on this case without raising all the special considerations demanded by study of persons. Suppose, then, that we think of the Great Day of Judgement in the following terms: God creates *replicas* of all those who have ever lived, in order to pass judgement on them. These replicas, let us suppose, are accurate down to the finest level of biological and biochemical description. Given that an enormous number of years may intervene between an individual's death and subsequent replication, we can see that there is a real problem over whether to count the replicas as identical with the originals. If I am numerically one and the same as the replica God makes of me, then, of course, it will be I, and no other, who stands judged on that fateful occasion. On the other side, if I am not identical with my replica, then it is not I who stand to be judged, but someone extremely similar to me, who is judged in my place.

Suppose, at least for the argument, that we cannot decide between thse two situations: we just don't know how to cast our vote on the identity question. Parfit's interesting suggestion is that we should just forget this problem, and concentrate on the survival

---

[9] The discussion in the text is based on Parfit [2].

question instead. An item can not only survive as itself but can survive *as or in something else*. Given our understanding of genetics, for instance, it is no wild metaphor to suggest that parents may survive in their children: parental genes do indeed get passed on to offspring. With this in mind, we can start to see how Parfit is able to prise the identity question from the survival question. If identity is the important thing for survival, then our puzzlement over the right answer in the resurrection case leaves us puzzled over what to say about survival in that case. But shift the focus, and see survival as the crucial thing, and we can start to think of resurrection by replication as being as good as survival.

There is no doubt that many people find Parfit's account of survival obscure. One reason for this is that we think that answering identity questions is a way of getting clear about survival. His suggestion, correct in my view, seems to be that survival may be the more primitive notion. Indeed, as will become clear, I think that on one approach we can use survival to explicate identity, just as Tarski found that the apparently primitive notion of truth could be explicated by a still more primitive relation of satisfaction.[10] Moreover, the analogy with Tarski has a further feature. Survival, in what we may call its *genuinely relational* sense, underpins and explicates identity, where identity is not genuinely relational. By 'genuinely relational', I mean some relational feature that links *distinct* things, whereas identity as a congruence relation simply links one thing with itself. Likewise truth seems to be a non-relational property of sentences or propositions while satisfaction, as understood by Tarski, is a relation between quite distinct things—open sentences, say, and sequences of objects.

For those who do think identity is the primitive, or fundamental idea, with survival depending on it, a great deal of charity is needed to make sense of Parfit's radical alternative. The case of resurrection is not by itself going to swing their intuitions into some new alignment. In the third chapter, I will give a quite precise account of what it is for one thing to survive in or as another, but for now I will

---

[10] This can be found in Tarski [1]. There is a certain air of hocus-pocus about Tarski's definition of truth, since it depends on a technical trick involving a truth-like notion: satisfaction, after all, is simply the relation of *being true of*. My account of identity involves no formal tricks of the sort Tarski plays—and so, as it seems to me, gives a *satisfying* account of identity in some cases. For a helpful introduction to the Tarski machinery, see Wallace [1].

make do with some further intuitive examples which may—I hope—establish at least the plausibility, if not the correctness, of Parfit's line. Think, for example, of the hope that authors entertain of immortality through their works. Here there can be no question of identity between author and work, yet we can make sense of survival to some extent. Notice that, unlike identity, survival comes in degrees. We could never talk of identity *to some extent*: items are either self-identical or not (only items like the empty set are not self-identical); if '*a*' and '*b*' are different names, then '*a* = *b*' is either true or not (but not true to a degree).

Switching from people to other sorts of things, we can talk about the relative survival of buildings, paintings, pieces of music, and so on. How much of Vivaldi, we can ask, survives a transcription by Bach, or a subsequent transcription to synthesizer? After an ambitious series of conversions and extensions, very little of an original house may survive, but that little which does survive may be of importance to the occupiers. So even survival to a small degree can be of significance in certain circumstances. Those who perhaps have qualms about the resurrection case may, by considering cases like these, start to feel that talk of survival does make sense at least some of the time where talk of identity would be inappropriate.

We can now elaborate the case of Theseus' ship to provide an example of a case where we know identity is out of the question. Here we are looking at a case of fission, and the point concerns the existence of rivals for identity with some original. In honour of the champion of flux, let us christen the ship that originally set sail from Athens the *Heraclitus*. That good ship stayed afloat throughout its various refurbishings, and by the end of its career, we find it more or less structurally the same as the sparkling original, although a deal shabbier and mouldier. Now imagine that while the repair work was under way, some eccentric of the ancient world set about collecting together every item discarded during the repair process. Over the years our plank-hoarder, no doubt at great difficulty and at some expense, built up an increasing collection of original parts from the old *Heraclitus*. At least, the project of constructing the *Heraclitus* as she originally was can be realized: a ship grows on the stocks, not only structurally identical to the *Heraclitus*, but consisting of all the original materials. Eventually, this extremely shabby replica puts to sea, competing for the honour of identity with the original. Just to keep our minds minimally clear, let us name the plank-hoarder's ship the *Heraclides* (after an obscure head of the Academy). We can imagine a time when both ships lie at anchor together: for those who sympathise with Parfit, we can use the vocabulary of survival: the old *Heraclitus* seems to have survived twice over. The identity theorist, of course, is interested in the question of which ship we are to identify with the original: the *Heraclides*, for all its tattiness, can claim a pretty pure pedigree; while the *Heraclitus* has shown continuity under the name and throughout the various refurbishments.

It is clear that although the *Heraclitus* may have survived twice over, she is not identical with both surviving ships. For two things cannot be one thing. It is perhaps best to consider this problem by comparing the situation just described with two others. We can think of the cases in terms of a diagram (Fig. 4). The dotted lines in situations (a) and (b) represent collections of ship stages during the repair process, while the alternate dots and dashes represent the plank-hoarder's ship. Our natural response might be this. We think in case (a) that the *Heraclitus* is the same throughout the repair process: the figure represents the life of one ship. In (c) the *Heraclitus* seems to be the same ship as the *Heraclides*. In this case, the ship in question has undergone what we might call a *functionally discontinuous* existence. This is a common kind of life for some artefacts—tents, collapsible boats, garden sheds, and so on are often constructed so that they can be disassembled. Big ships seldom are these days, although many of the steamers of inland Africa were made in this way. So we can probably make sense of the *Heraclitus*

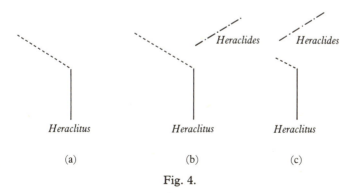

Fig. 4.

ceasing to function as a ship for some time, and then being rebuilt to undertake its functional life once more.

The case in the middle, case (b), is the one that gives us the greatest headache. For here we do not seem to know what to say. Of course, we can try to come to an identity decision in such a case. And such a decision can be important (for settling legal matters about insurance or ownership, for example). Parfit's position here is to deploy the notion of survival independently of our identity decision. Suppose that we give the judgement for identity in favour of the continuously functioning ship (from solid to broken line). Then Parfit can still point out that the original *Heraclitus* survives as the *Heraclides* although not identical with it. And this seems entirely right. Our eccentric has assured a double success, a success which is not captured by our verdict on identity.

1.5. INDETERMINACY

We have a stubborn tendency to think that all sorts of problems will yield to suitably dedicated thinking. Thus it comes as something of a surprise to find that in some of the examples we have so far considered, the issue of identity may stay forever unresolved. This is not the case in all of them. For example, it is easy enough to think of the Theseus ship case as one in which we can probably be persuaded to give our verdict in favour of the continuously functioning ship. In the resurrection case, by contrast, it is not easy to decide for or against identity. Of course, if what is important for practical decisions is survival rather than identity, we lose one fairly significant incentive for worrying about the identity question. In the third chapter, we will look again at Theseus' ship with the issue of importance in mind. In the fourth chapter, we will defend the informal account sketched here in which the presence or absence of rivals seems to make a real difference to our verdict on identity. At the moment, it suffices to point out that importance is relative. When asking whether or not identity is important, we want to know the answer to the question: important *for what*? As we will see, survival can be important for identity itself!

Let us suppose, however, that we are satisfied enough by the survival story, so that we lose interest in the matter of identity in some cases. We may thus come to regard the identity issue as indeterminate. It is not necessary to take a strong line on the matter of indeterminacy here. One legacy of Quine's work is that many contemporary philosophers regard genuine indeterminacy as a real possibility. But we need not commit ourselves at this stage to any kind of Quinean indeterminacy about identity (which would involve admitting the existence of ontological relativity).[11] Rather, we can just keep things at an epistemological level: suppose we do not *know* what the answer to the identity question is when faced with situation (b) in Fig. 4. Then whether our ignorance be due to some inscrutability in the very notion of identity itself is not something about which we need currently venture an opinion.

Nor should we make the mistake of regarding our knowledge about survival as always more determinate than our knowledge about identity. In the case of Theseus' ship, we certainly seem to be able to speak about the Fig. 4(b) case as one in which the original ship survives twice over. But we may not always be so lucky. There may well be occasions where our ability to pronounce on the survival question is no greater than our ability to pronounce on questions of identity.

1.6. CONDITIONS OF SURVIVAL

The conception of ordinary things as continuants makes sense of one prevalent feature of our experience. This is that how a thing is at one time very much depends on what happens to it at others. Objects carry their history on them in various ways. High-level items, like persons, not only carry the scars of cuts and broken bones, but also have memories as depositories of their history. But the scratches on my desk, or the old ink-stains that have never quite faded, are themselves a testimony to the desk's past existence: it is an object with a history.

Let us think of things now in terms of their *stages*. Each extended object (extended through space and time) consists, so we suppose, of successive stages. This supposition, of course, is open to question: Hume regarded our belief in persisting objects as a vulgar confusion on our part between the ideas of relation and of identity.

---

[11] Quine's accounts of these matters are to be found scattered through Quine [2] and [7].

But let us not give in to such doubts at the moment. So the successive stages of my desk (however we choose to divide it into these) will show a regular pattern of relation to each other. Suppose, for example, we think in terms of hour-long stages. It would be wholly baffling if from one hour to the next the desk gained or lost legs in a random way; if scratches present at ten in the morning had disappeared by lunch-time, but reappeared by tea-time; if the large drawer on the left had changed places with the small drawer on the right an hour after we had checked their position, and so on. Of course, we could tell a story to make sense of all these happenings. For example, maybe someone takes great care to make scratches on the desk every morning, notes their position, polishes them out, and then makes them again in the afternoon. Or maybe a carpenter modifies the drawers and their housings at regular intervals. These explanations would immediately demystify the situation. Why is this?

The reason is that, without such accounts, we would be in a genuine difficulty when trying to explain the sort of changes imagined. Scratches do not appear, disappear, and reappear without some responsible causal agency. The story of the compulsive scratcher and polisher supplies just such a suitable causal account. Nor do desks gain or lose legs, or have their structure modified in other ways without our being able to assign appropriate causal explanations. If my desk is clean and unmarked in the morning, I expect it to remain so—unless something happens to it. If I return to my office at lunch-time and find scratches and ink-stains on it, I do not just suppose that somehow the desk-stage I witnessed earlier in the day has, fortuitously, given way to a desk-stage of a scratched and stained kind. Rather, I presume that something has happened in the interim. What all this amounts to can be expressed as follows:

(1) The stages of a persisting object succeed each other in a lawful and regulated manner.
(2) If a later stage manifests certain differences from an earlier stage, then something has affected the earlier stage, or some intervening stage, and that thing, whatever it is, is responsible for these differences.

The differences and changes here are, of course, not *merely Cambridge* differences. In the 'Cambridge' sense, my desk has undergone a change if, say, a certain car is now further away from it than it was a few moments ago. That is, a Cambridge change occurs simply if some proposition about my desk changes in truth value. Such changes affect objects all the time: but they are not the sorts of changes we can discern just from inspecting the object concerned in isolation from everything else. It is a philosophically difficult matter to give an account of properties and changes which captures just what is involved in a 'real' rather than a merely 'Cambridge' change. But this problem is not one for tackling here. All my talk of properties and changes, unless explicitly qualified, should be taken to be about 'real' properties and changes.

Our observations, or rules of change, (1) and (2) above, go some way towards meeting Hume's scepticism about identity and relation. For the hypothesis that objects trace extended continuous paths through space and time seems to be the simplest one that accounts for the general coherence underlying (1) and (2). None the less, as we shall see in Chapter 4, it is possible to imagine a more Humean world in which (1) and (2) are satisfied while objects fail to be continuous. Leaving this to one side, however, let us consider the related question of survival. Is there, in one persisting object, survival of any of its stages in, or as, others? As we have already seen, survival of one thing as itself may be trivial, while survival of one thing as something other than itself is non-trivial and possible. Think again of the case of the parent and the child. When we say that the parent survives in the child, what do we mean? And would our account here be able to throw any light on the question of the survival of one stage of a persisting object as a later stage? We can take these questions in turn.

When we say that a parent survives *in* a child, we suggest, by our use of the term 'in', that the survival is not to as high a degree as is possible. Likewise, suppose I wake up one day with the memories of someone else—Jane Austen, for example. Then we would tend to say, if we made a survival claim at all, that Jane Austen survived *in* me, but not that she survived *as* me. Remember that survival comes in degrees, and we can have survival of one thing in another thing to a pretty low degree. So when would we be likely to say that one item survived *as* another item? We can construct clear cases of this. For example, a child designs a marvellous bridge using a plastic construction set. Her brother, inspired by her work, models the bridge exactly using wooden blocks and glue. The original bridge is thereafter taken apart and the plastic components of which it was made are used for the next creation. Has the child's original bridge survived? The answer to this question is that it has survived *as* the wooden bridge.

Those who are happy with the terminology and already feel that they can make sense of *survival as* in these terms will need no reassurance from further examples. But the fact that it seems natural to me to speak of survival in this way may be simply eccentric. So this example may be taken, by those who cavil over my use of language, as stipulative. Likewise, the same readers can take my remarks about *surviving in* as equally stipulative if they find my linguistic intuitions out of step with theirs.

The example of the toy gives us all we need for sketching an account of conditions for survival. Note that the following two conditions are satisfied in the situation described:

> *Structure condition*: the brother's copy is structurally the same as the original; that is, it has components of the same size and shape as those of the original arranged in the same relative positions;
> *Causal condition*: the causal account of how the brother's model was constructed makes reference to his sister's original model; in particular, his version was obtained from hers by being copied, albeit in a different material.

There are clearly features of these conditions that require more investigation. For example, in the structural condition what do we mean by 'component'? And what difference does relative *size* of the components make to survival? Would topological deformations also preserve structure? Of the causal condition, we can ask about the varieties of appropriate causal story, or about how accurate the copying process need be, and so on. We will tackle these detailed questions in due course. In the meantime, we might wonder if there is anything more to survival than these two conditions. We might ask if there are prospects for the survival of the original model that would result in an even higher degree of survival for it than in the imagined case (stopping short of preserving the original itself).

Clearly a higher degree of survival would be obtained if the brother used the same sort of plastic bricks for his model that his sister used in the original. Of course, they need not be exactly the same bricks: indeed, we would face ourselves with a decision on identity if we imagined that the original model was taken apart, then the same bricks used in the same positions for constructing a bridge. One natural way of describing this latter case would be to say that the bridge had been dismantled and then put together again. What we are looking for is a case where there is no identity claim to be made, but none the less a really high degree of survival. Use of similar bricks in the same arrangement gives us this case. Thus we can suggest a third condition on survival that takes account of material similarity:

> *Matter condition*: one item survives as another when, in addition to the conditions on cause and structure being satisfied, the item as which the original survives is made of material similar to the original.

In both this and the structure condition, it does not really seem to matter whether we speak of the *same* matter or structure or of *similar* matter and structure. This is because sameness of such things itself can come in degrees (for example, we can speak of 'much the same matter' and 'almost the same structure'). The conditions obviously prompt questions. What happens if we vary them to certain degrees: do we then give an account of survival to various degrees? Does the reference to sameness of structure and sameness of matter mean that survival depends ultimately on identity—albeit identity not of objects but of more abstract things? Even at the moment, we can suggest that, of our three conditions, only the two concerning structure and cause are *necessary* for survival. For, since one thing can survive as another, we can hardly insist even on similarity of matter in all such cases. Further examples in Chapter 3 will show that this proposal is along the right lines.

By contrast, all three of the conditions taken together seem to constitute a set of *sufficient* conditions for survival. If one item possesses lots of material similar to that possessed by another, if the second item has that material structured in the same way as it is in the first, and if the first item participated causally in bringing about this sharing of structure and matter, then the first item survives as the second. As the theory of survival unfolds in the following chapters, we will tackle the questions raised here in the hope of answering enough of them to show that the theory is interesting.

Looking now to the case of the parent surviving in the child, we can start to get some idea of how our conditions fare under various kinds of weakening. If the model bridge case is a paradigmatic example of survival under optimum conditions, the parent–child case is probably one of the weakest cases of survival recognized in literature and common sense. Parents who think they will not wholly die thanks to the preservation of their characteristics in their offspring believe something we can all make some sense of. In terms of our conditions, we can try to make clear just what this hope for survival is based on. The *structure condition* suggests that parental structure is preserved in the offspring. Can we make sense of this? We need to think of two sorts of structure here: first, structure as a physical characteristic, and, second, structure in a more extended sense. As to physical characteristics, it is clear that offspring bear various resemblances to their parents: these structural characteristics are coded for by genes and therefore to be expected; and even those bits of structure normally hidden from casual inspection—location and size of the liver, for example, or pattern of blood-vessels supplying the retina—will be genetically determined.

More difficult to deal with are those characteristics of personality, mood, and behaviour which parents recognize both in themselves and in their children. Here we need to think about the structure of personality and of mind—something that requires an extended notion of structure to be deployed. Later, I will suggest that it is particularly helpful to think of the mind as having a structure, just as a physical object has a structure. Just as the structural invariances in someone's facial features enable us to recognize him or her after a change in hair-style, after gain or loss of weight, or after changes due to ageing, so structural invariances in mind and personality will also provide a means of identifying someone as being someone we know.

The causal condition has already been used implicitly in what has so far been said about the parent–child case. For it is the mechanism of genetics that explains those structural similarities between parents and their children on which survival claims are to be based. Genetics thus gives us just the right kind of causal account. Incidentally, note that I am not defending any sort of extreme genetic determinism here. There is no suggestion that *all* a person's physical and behavioural characteristics are a parental legacy: the development of disease, the acquisition of agility and fitness, the possession of a sour or an optimistic personality, are things that may well depend on environmental and developmental factors. Indeed, my suggestion is the modest one that since some features of physical morphology and personality are genetically determined, then parents can make a claim to survive to the extent that such heriditary characteristics in fact appear in their offspring. Much bolder is the notion in T. H. White's children's novel, *The Master*, where the central character hopes to avoid wholly dying by kidnapping someone else's children and passing on to one of them his lore and values.[12] Here the Master's survival depends on the changes in behaviour and values that he can induce in others by teaching, indoctrination, and other such means. Although I think we can make sense of even this sort of case, and illuminate it by use of the three conditions, we would need to look carefully at it in terms of the account of mind and personality developed later.

And what of the third condition, the one concerning *matter*? Thanks to the remarkable features of animal reproduction, we again see in the parent–child case a clear example of similarity of matter from parent to child, this similarity being explained by the mechanisms studied by genetic theory. As we will discover, the term 'matter', is not always clear: suffice it to say here that in terms of matter, understood at a fundamental biological level, parents and their offspring are constituted of just the same sort of matter—cells with certain structures, these depending in turn on the properties of a limited number of types of organic molecules. So our case of the parent–child survival can be described in terms of our three conditions, albeit recognizing that only *some* parental structures will reappear in any offspring, and that the reappearance of these structures and the fact that they utilize the same sort of material can be plausibly explained by reference to current biological theory.

Notice, by the way, that although current biological theory gives good support to what is said here, it is by no means necessary to the

[12] The Master's attempt to survive through other people unrelated to him reminds us that the transmission and preservation of culture and values may be just as important to survival as the (more currently fashionable) transmission of genes. At various places in the text I do depend on the naturalness of the idea that the passing on of genetic material is of significance, given certain conceptions of survival. It is worth noting explicitly at this point, however, that I would just as happily have used examples concerning the transmission of culture, political and moral values, religious or other myths, and so on. Complications about the kind of survival involved in these, and the genetic cases, will be explored later. In White's story, when the Master finds one of the 'detained' children is suitable for education, he says: 'Non omnis moriar' (*I shall not wholly die*). (T. H. White, *The Master*, London: Jonathan Cape, 1957.)

account of survival. It is easy to imagine ancient Egyptians believing that they survived *in* their children; and superficial structural features and similarity of matter would underpin these claims. Anthropologists have reported, so I understand, that in some societies there is thought to be no causal connection between sexual intercourse and pregnancy. In such societies, if my proposals are roughly right, we would not expect fathers to believe they survived in their children. Alternatively, if they did hold such a belief, they would also hold some associated beliefs about appropriate causal relations between themselves and their mates' offspring (though these beliefs would be very different from our own). So nothing in what is proposed here ties the philosophical theory of survival to acceptance of particular scientific theories.

We can now turn to the other question we raised, namely, whether the account of survival can be applied to the survival of one stage of an object in or as some later stage of the same object. It should be clear that the prospects for doing this are quite good. Objects of various sorts change their material from time to time. Thus the mammalian pancreas has a complete change-over of cells roughly every twenty-four hours, yet in healthy organs this replacement is structure-preserving (and hence function-preserving). Small trees with thin stems grow into large trees with thick trunks; in this case we have structural as well as material changes. Again, though, we can look for the survival of one tree stage in some later stage: the geometry of leaf distribution shows some consistency over time, so that we can envisage the shape of the later stage by inspection of a stage of the immature tree. Likewise, later stages carry the historical evidence of pruning and damage suffered by earlier stages of the tree.

In discussing plants and other such organisms, we have to note the biological distinction between the unitary and the modular. A unitary organism has a highly determinate structure, with the number and location of limbs and organs determinate (within the range of genetic variability). Human and other animals are clear examples of such organisms. By contrast, modular organisms are characterized by a post-zygotic phase in which a module of construction is developed which itself develops further modules, and so on. Modular organisms typically branch, and their growth and development depends strongly on their relationship to the environment. A tree will thus reveal not only the history of past pruning but, to the knowing eye, also the story of the mineral deposits in the surrounding soil and the direction of prevailing winds and available sunlight. As recent ecological work has noted, modular organisms show differential response to predator attack and invasion by disease organisms. Thus a tree behaves in some respects more like a community of modules than like a single particular. An extreme case of environmental influence on the development of a modular organism is that of bonsai cultivation, where perfect miniatures of trees and shrubs are grown in deliberately impoverished environments.

Artefacts of certain sorts do not generally show such dramatic changes over their histories. A paintbrush tends to keep pretty well most of its material as long as it is able to function at all. Upon finding a brush that I had used when new, and which now bears the scars of a long working life, I may recognize both the constancies and the changes. If the bristles have clogged with paint, I may regret that its ability to hold paint and apply it smoothly has been lost; but it may still be a good width for painting certain awkward spots. Here I both recognize the survival of the earlier stage to some extent, and—at the same time—regret that it has not survived better! Of course, we normally just speak of this in terms of the properties of the brush itself. The point being laboured here is that we can readily translate into talking of survival of earlier stages in— or as—later stages.

In this chapter, identity has been distinguished from similarity. The formal principles of identity reveal it to be a congruence relation, that is, it is reflexive, symmetric, and transitive. Leibniz's Law (the indiscernibility of identicals) has generally been taken as less controversial than the converse principle of the identity of indiscernibles.

Although it is natural to explicate the identity of a persisting thing in terms of spatio-temporal continuity, some theorists have preferred to appeal to indiscernibility as elucidating identity because of the existence of cases where more than one thing occupies portions of the same path through space-time. Continuity theorists deal with the same cases by explicating identity in terms of sortal-covered continuity.

A relation of survival was then provisionally defined. Although suggested by the work of Parfit, the definition of the concept involves conditions concerning structure, matter, and cause which are not explicit in his treatment. The definition given can be taken as stipulative.

Although the three conditions given appear to be sufficient for survival, only two of them—the cause and structure conditions—seem to be necessary. Since survival can hold to a degree, it is not surprising that sameness of structure and matter can also be a matter of degree. The nature of the causal condition requires more study, as does the scope of the structure condition. The programme for the immediately following chapters is the elucidation of survival and a consideration of its relation to identity. More consideration will also be given to the question of spatio-temporal continuity.

2
Metaphysical Problems

Philosophy is often concerned with theory-construction. Not all philosophers recognize this as a proper description of their work but if it is taken seriously, then my concern here is with theories of identity. We have already undertaken, in the first chapter, the sketch of a theory of survival, a theory which will have a significant role to play in the theory of identity.

But to approach the identity or unity of a persisting object through the study of survival in the way implied in the first chapter is to take a certain view on what a unified object is. We can call this the *chain theory* of unified objects. On this conception, itself highly theoretical, a unified object, like a table, or cat, is a chain of temporal parts, all neatly linked to each other. The temporal parts, or stages, do not, of course, have the spatial property of interlocking: but we may expect them to be in some sense 'tied' in to each other.

If an enduring, or persisting, object is like a chain of stages, then we can think of such stages as being *links* in the chain of its life. This immediately suggests that we should make a clear distinction between enduring things and their temporal parts. For although a chain is composed of links, no link on its own constitutes a chain. Rather, only a collection of interlocking links makes up a chain. Just so, we might think, a suitable collection of time slices 'glued' together according to our three conditions will constitute an enduring object. But the object is one thing of a kind; the temporal part is something of a different kind.

Viewed in this way, the suggestions sketched in the previous chapter look like moves in a decent reductionist programme. We are puzzled, let us suppose, by the notion of *persisting thing*: what is a unified spatio-temporally *broad* object? What is a *body*, to use Quine's term? The answer is that such a unified broad object is nothing more than a suitably connected sequence of object-stages (each of which survives as its successor); so a table is a suitably connected sequence of table-stages and a person is a suitably connected sequence of person-stages. Since stages are links, bodies are chains, and links are of a different kind from chains, then we have explained the nature of one thing in terms of something else. Maybe we can even *define* a unified, persisting thing as a maximal *S-related* sequence of object stages. Here, stages are *S*-related if and only if they are sequentially linked according to our three proposed conditions.

However attractive this approach seems, it encounters several difficulties. One of these is that we have still to decide whether or not temporal parts of things are items *of the same kind* as the larger things supposedly constituted out of them. Links, as we have noted, are never chains. But it is not so clear that table-stages are never tables. After all, a table-stage is simply a table-at-a-time, and surely *that* is a *table* (at a time)! But if table-stages are tables, then our reduction of tables to sequences of connected table-stages is not so impressive.

We will look in more detail at this worry later. For the moment, let us note a further appealing feature of the programme associated with the chain theory. Suppose that we use the term 'individual' in the *mereological* sense. The mereologist is someone who prefers, often for reasons of metaphysical austerity, to work with individuals instead of such 'abstract' objects as sets. In fact, the notion of *abstract* is just as bedevilling as its opposite, the notion of *concrete*. It is odd how many terms of art there are which can be readily acquired by students, used by professionals, dropped impressively into everyday conversations, and yet prove embarrassingly difficult to define or explicate. 'Concrete' and 'abstract' are good examples of just such terms. One way in which things can be concrete is by having effects or being acted on by causes. My desk and I are concrete by this account, for we causally act on one another (or, to be more precise, we are ingredients of events which are causally related to each other). My unit set and my desk's (the set whose sole element is the desk) are not causally interactive at all and thus abstract. Again, perhaps alternatively, to be concrete is to be 'in' space and time. Thus a concrete object may be something that is in a one–one correspondence with a set of points in space-time. As Kripke points out, such an identification would mean that no two objects could be in the same place at all times. On this account of the concrete, numbers are abstract for they, like sets, lie outside space and time.

Goodman's well-known account of *mereology* (the calculus of individuals) in *The Structure of Appearance* relies on the following nominalist tenet: 'entities differ only if their content at least partially differs'.[1] Individuals are precisely what satisfy this tenet, but—it turns out—they can be 'abstract' in a certain sense. For our purposes, we can start from this same conception of individuals, and let the worry about abstractness go. As we will see later, it is quite easy to slip into 'abstract' conceptions of objects without using any set-theory. The appealing feature of chain theory is the following. Suppose we think again about Theseus' ship (Chapter 1.4). If stages are individuals, collections or fusions of stages are individuals as well. This follows from a happy feature of the mereology: if x and y are individuals, however disparate, then x together with y is also an individual. So suppose we represent the ship case as shown in Fig. 5. Here we take A, B, and C to be names of collections of individual stages. This is a departure from our practice in the previous chapter where the name 'Heraclitus', for example, designated the broad continuously functioning ship consisting of $A + B$ in the first two situations. Since each stage is an individual, then a collection of such stages will also be an individual. And, of course, $A + B$, $A + C$ and so on, will also be individuals. So in our three diagrams, how many individuals are represented? The answer to this question is quite unclear. For we do not know how

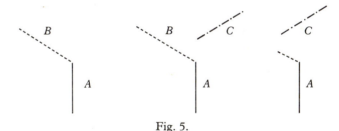

Fig. 5.

[1] See Goodman [1], p. 36. Goodman tries to clarify his understanding of nominalism in the following passage: 'If no two distinct *entities whatsoever* have the same content, then a class (e.g. that of the counties of Utah) is different neither from the single individual (the whole state of Utah) that exactly contains its members nor from any other class (e.g. that of acres of Utah) whose members exactly exhaust this same whole. The platonist may distinguish these entities by venturing into a new dimension of Pure Form, but the nominalist recognises no distinction of entities without a distinction of content.'

many stages are in each of A, B, and C. But we can answer the question: how many individuals constructed out of A, B, and C are represented in the diagrams? For the answer to this is: three—$A + B$, $A + C$, and $B + C$.

Now, although each of these collections or fusions of A, B, and C are individuals, it does not follow that each is a unified enduring object, let alone a persisting ship. Take $B + C$, for example. They coexist in the situation depicted in the middle diagram, and constitute together one individual, but this individual is not something that we would recognize as itself constituting any *one thing of a kind or sort*. Likewise, my desk-top and a rat in Bali constitute one individual, but we lack any generic title for such a combination. Thus, there are more individuals—a great many more—than there are unified objects of sorts we recognize. The chain theory therefore confronts the following interesting problem: since we can construct any number of chains from the links available, what features make certain of these chains stand out, so to speak, as unified, persisting objects of a sort? The problem here is no more (and no less!) than the temporal analogue of a similar problem concerning spatial parts. Some collections of spatial parts stand out as unified objects, as we have seen, and some do not.

The proposal in Chapter 1 was to use the idea of survival in the account of chain construction. The crude idea, applied to Theseus' ship, would be that those stages belonging to B—indeed which constitute B—have suitable survival relations to each other. Each stage in B survives as its neighbour in the chain of links constituting the large individual, B. But no stage of B survives as a stage of C. So we have no grounds, based on survival, for linking the stages of B together with those of C into a unified individual $B + C$.

By contrast, any stage of A survives as some stage of B and also as some stage of C, in the cases where C is present. We can construct plausible sequences of stages, then, which would allow us to count each of $A + B$ and $A + C$ as unified objects. A worrying question, which we defer for the moment, concerns the conditions under which we can allocate such unified objects to kinds or sorts: in the situation where both B and C coexist, it has seemed to some that $A + C$ cannot be a ship, even if all the stages of A and C are themselves ship-stages.

Leaving this tricky matter aside for the moment, we can ask whether, from the point of view of chain-builders, there is any alternative account that would supply the unification of A and B in the leftmost case of our diagram, of A and C in the rightmost, and yet make no appeal to survival. One standard account does attempt to do this—the account in terms of spatio-temporal continuity.

It is a virtue of the chain theory that it allows us to formulate the question of unity in terms of stages or temporal parts: what properties does a collection of stages have to possess in order to constitute the links in the history of one unified thing? The continuity theorist is able to give an apparently straightforward answer to this question in terms of a sortal-covered, continuous path through space time.

It is not clear, however, why an enduring or persisting item should not be episodic, that is, have gaps in its spatio-temporal history. This possibility is to be explored in the fourth chapter. However, it will become clear from simple examples to be discussed in the third section of this chapter that continuity is not an easily defined notion. Worse, the problem of Kripke's disc—to be discussed in the fourth section of the chapter—shows that the links, conceived as momentary things, will not give us the basis for constructing an account of moving bodies.

Kripke's work on identity forces us to confront the issue of primitiveness, an issue that will recur in various forms later in the book. Although objects or particulars are distinct from their trajectories or histories in space time, this does not mean that the unity of particulars is ultimate or primitive. Particulars are not restricted to three dimensions; as will be argued in the fifth chapter, there are ways of thinking about particulars as three-, four-, or even five-dimensional. In the present chapter, I will be trying to show that in giving an account of the unity of one sort of thing, we are able to take the unity of other sorts of things as primitive; primitiveness is relative to the explanatory exercise.

More objections to continuity theories will come in the fourth chapter. For three-dimensional theorists, as I will suggest later, it is hard to phrase the unity question at all, while ignoring the distinction between metaphysics and epistemology would simply make the unity issue even more confused.

2.2. CONTINUITY

We have already seen (in Chapter 1.2) how some theorists take the notion of a persisting thing to be a notion of an item which traces a

continuous path through space and time. And at first sight, the
notion of a continuous path of this kind seems useful, provided a
certain number of problems can be overcome. In Chapter 1.3 we
saw how continuity and indiscernibility theorists could come to
different views on the Rover/Clover case. This time, of course, we
are taking the continuity theorist as engaged in tracing the history of
a broad object by following the history of successive and continuous
stages.

One alternative suggestion for dealing with the Rover/Clover
case is that the path starting with a Rover-stage, although
continuous with one ending with a Clover-stage, is not one that can
be traced throughout *under the same sortal*. Although we mentioned
this manœuvre earlier, we did not then pursue in detail the
difficulties with it. The most profound of these is not whether a
sortal still applies to an item when, for example, it is dismantled.
There seems no problem about pointing to a bundle of nylon fabric
and a pile of aluminium poles and saying 'That's our tent.' Many
artefacts are designed for regular dismantling—gliders, sailing
dinghies, inflatable boats, tents, many kinds of gun, and so on. Even
those that are not meant for leading such *functionally discontinuous*
lives, can be taken apart for repair and reassembled. Thus an
automobile engine can still be traced under a sortal while scattered
over the garage floor. The dismantling, we may say, prevents its
functioning as an engine, without thereby leading to its ceasing to
exist as an engine.

Some theorists—Hirsch and Quinton, for example—take functional discontinuity as a case of going out of existence.[2] For them,
the disassembled works scattered over the garage floor do not
constitute an engine at all. Rather the engine goes out of existence
when dismantled and comes back into existence when reassembled
(provided enough of the same components go back in without being
replaced). Now this difference of perspective is nothing to get hot
under the collar about. Very little, other than terminological
conventions, depends on whether we adopt my way of speaking
about functional discontinuity, or their way of speaking about
lapses of existence. The important thing for a continuity theorist is
that, even if the engine is said to go out of existence when
dismantled, there is spatio-temporal continuity of enough of its

---

[2] See Hirsch [2], ch. 1, and Quinton [2], pp. 63 ff.

parts to sustain the claim of identity upon reassembly. We can call this the requirement of *compositional* continuity, and let us suppose for the time being that we can come up with some reasonable standard for this.

So a continuity theorist can take two lines on this question of dismantling. One is to treat the space-time path as still continuous and still the path of that object (this is the advantage that comes of talking about functional discontinuity). For this kind of view, there is a separate issue to confront, of course, in the case of dismantling, as also in the case of things which can survive renewal of their parts. This is the quite general question of how tolerant an item is to replacement of its parts, and since it is an involved question, we defer it for the moment. The second line the continuity theorist can take in the present case is to recognize discontinuities in the existence of objects under certain descriptions, but supplement the continuity story in such cases by appealing to continuity of (enough of) their parts. Clearly either line might still permit us to think of a continuous path traced though space-time by objects and their parts.

So where are the more profound difficulties with the continuity view? It looks as if it has a certain advantage over the survival account. For it is surely *simpler* to regard the Theseus' ship case in terms of continuities among the stages of *A* and *B* and of *A* and *C* (but not of *B* and *C*!) than in terms of our more cumbersome conditions on survival. The two big problems for this account arise in connection with the phrase 'sortal-covered continuity'. The first problem is to say what it is for a stage of an object to *fall under* a sortal. And, secondly, we have to ask if we can give a satisfactory account of spatio-temporal continuity which does justice to what we usually *count* as continuities in an object's history. The first big problem has already been mentioned earlier in the chapter and will be mentioned in subsequent chapters before we get round to discussing it properly. Even then, in our discussion of possible worlds and possible things, we will end up with only a tentative conclusion.

The second problem will be dealt with now. In subsequent chapters we will be exploring the survival account in more detail, and so an explanation is owed at this point to those who think of spatio-temporal continuity as a clear and helpful adjunct to the theory of identity.

2.3. PROBLEMS WITH SPATIO-TEMPORAL CONTINUITY

If, like David Wiggins, we take identity as a primitive notion, we might wonder why we should talk about it in terms of indiscernibility, spatio-temporal continuity, survival, or anything else. My own view here is that we take the identity of *some items* as primitive in our theory construction; in terms of these primitives we can give an account of the identity of *other items* in any terms that seem appropriate. Thus, for example, our account of the identity of a table in terms of certain relations among table-stages, presupposes that we have an understanding of what it is to be *one and the same table-stage*. But the account gives us no way of explaining the presupposed identity. For this reason, as several theorists have noted, it would be better if we dropped the term 'identity' from treatments of this topic.[3] Instead, we might talk about the problem of the *unity* of tables, lakes, engines, or whatever.

It is important to recognize this problem about primitiveness, for it is a source of confusion to many people. If identity is *always* primitive, then of course there is little point in a theory of identity for any sort of thing. Wiggins emphasizes that his notion of the primitiveness of identity 'in no way excludes discursive elucidation in collateral terms'.[4] And one of the ways he suggests giving such elucidation is through recognition of the fact that what organizes our method of determining identity is the idea of a continuous path

[3] Compare Perry's remarks in Perry [7], for example. He writes: 'Let us say that stages of a single human being are H-related. . . . Our speculation is that . . . H-related stages are, at least for the most part, related by some other relation (or at least by a relation that, for all we know, may not be the H-relation), and their being related by that other relation explains the effect of the earlier stages on the later. This new relation . . . is my candidate for the analysis of personal identity. That is, it is the *unity relation* for persons . . .' Even if dropping the term 'identity' is going too far, it is certainly valuable to reconstrue thoughts about identity as thoughts about unity.

[4] Wiggins [9], p. 49. If we take identity as a congruence relation, namely that relation holding between a thing and itself, it becomes hard, as Frege pointed out, to distinguish between interesting identity statements, of the form '$a = b$', which can add to our knowledge, and trivial statements of the form '$a = a$'. For, where '$a = b$' is true, it says that a is the same thing as itself. This led Frege to a semantic account of how the two kinds of statements differ; see 'On Sense and Reference' in Geach and Black [1]. For discussion of the interpretation of identity statements, see Morris [1]. The semantics of identity statements is not of particular importance to the present study. For those who take identity as being primitive, there is no more to be said about the unity of particular things except that they are unitary. The semantics of identity statements will, for them, be the natural focus of study in this area.

in space and time. We will return to the issue of primitiveness at the end of the chapter, so let me concentrate just now on the 'elucidation' in terms of continuity.

One point that Wiggins makes clear is that any notion of continuity or gappiness we use must be appropriate to the kinds of object we are studying. We have seen already that some things are expected to lead *functionally discontinuous* lives. But we need to be sure at this point that, in other cases, we do not confuse continuity with some other relation between objects or their stages. There is a Hollywood sense of 'continuity' which has a certain vogue in these discussions, and we must be wary of confusing this with spatio-temporal continuity. In the Hollywood sense, two sequences in a film show continuity provided a number of conditions are met. These include similarity of clothing and make-up worn by those on screen, similarity of lighting conditions (so that a sequence in which a car stops in broad daylight is *not* followed by one in which the occupants get out in pitch darkness) and so on. Observance of strict continuity standards is essential to fooling the audience. For it ensures that the audience views sequences that have been shot separately and often non-consecutively as if they form one unbroken stretch of action.

Robert Nozick has introduced the idea of a *close continuer* into discussions of identity, where this is something like the Hollywood idea. On Nozick's account:

to be something later is to be its closest continuer. . . . To say that something is a continuer of x is not merely to say its properties are qualitatively the same as x's, or resemble them. Rather it is to say they grow out of x's properties, are causally produced by them, are to be explained by x's earlier having had its properties, and so forth.[5]

Nozick illustrates what he means by an ingenious experiment using a screen. Suppose we view the situation in Fig. 6. If x disappears behind the screen moving right, and y comes out appropriately later, at a slightly different angle but looking like x (same shape, colour, and so on) and moving at the same velocity x had, then we will, according to Nozick, see y as the same object as x, deflected by collision with something behind the screen. However, if—in competition with y—an item z emerges, again with a suitable

[5] Nozick [1], pp. 33–5.

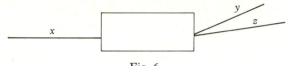

Fig. 6.

delay, and looking and moving just like x—then we will tend to identify z with x if the track of z is closer to x's original track. In this case, y is a *close continuer* of x, but z is a *closer continuer*.

Here we have a nice vocabulary for applying to the Theseus' ship case. For our problem there is how to pick out *the closest continuer*: the closest continuer of the original ship, A, will deserve our vote for being Theseus' ship. The trouble here is not so much Nozick's approach to the unity question, but his choice of vocabulary. For, of course, in the screen experiment, there need be no spatio-temporal *continuity* between x and either y or z. For all an observer with limited information might know, x just stops dead behind the screen and some completely new object is launched on an appropriate trajectory. The continuity here, then, might very well be of the merely Hollywood sort. We will look in Chapter 4 at more cases like this, where identity is discussed in relation to episodic objects.

The important lesson we should learn at this stage is that cases of unity may be envisaged where a single object can be supposed to have gaps in its spatio-temporal history. But then such objects would not be things that trace a *continuous path* in space-time.

So what, then, is a continuous path through space and time? This question is rather harder to answer than we might at first have thought. For we seem to have, on the one hand, a clear notion of what such continuity is; but when we consider even mathematically naive formulations of the notion, we run into severe difficulties. If, following Hirsch, we define the *place* of an object at some time as the region of space coinciding with the object at that time, we can say that places overlap if they have a part in common. Now one notion of continuous spatio-temporal change is that if we take successive times t and t' at both of which an object exists, then we can make the extent of overlap between the places of the object at t and at t' as great as we like by taking t' suitably close to t.[6] Negatively, we can

---

[6] Hirsch [2], pp. 15–21.

put the same point in the way Kripke does it in his lectures on identity. If we take two successive volumes of space occupied by an item then we can make the extent of *non*-overlap of the two volumes arbitrarily small if we make the times arbitrarily close.

One big problem with this simple version of the mathematical notion of continuity is that it fails to do justice to those continuities we recognize in daily life. Hirsch shows this by taking the example of a tree. Suppose we lop a large branch off the tree. Now, although, as we cut, the branch may slowly move downwards, it is still attached to the tree until, with the last stroke of the saw it is completely severed. But then there must be an *instantaneous* change in the tree from the volume it occupied when the branch was attached to the volume it occupies once the branch has gone. In other words, the continuity of the tree is compatible with a real discontinuity in its volume from one moment to the next.

Hirsch suggests one way we could try to patch things up here. Maybe the notion of continuity we want is one like this. Take any two successive volumes occupied by an object. Then we can still maintain a moderate degree of continuity if we let the extent of overlap between the volumes be greater than the extent of non-overlap.[7] Thus, we cannot instantaneously deprive a tree of branches accounting for more than half its volume, on this view, without thereby destroying the tree.

Obviously, we could go for even weaker kinds of continuity. Maybe we could permit objects to have discontinuous changes provided there is always *some* overlap between successive volumes occupied by the objects. It is clear that we would need to take the weakest view of continuity if we were to allow that items like rockets can stay the same while shedding their various stages. Consider, for example, exactly what happens when a multi-stage rocket jettisons its first stage. This large piece of equipment, being mainly a massive fuel tank with motors attached, may well account for an enormous share of the total volume of space occupied by our original rocket. its instantaneous jettisoning thus accounts for a loss of volume that prevents us saying the history of the rocket is any more than weakly continuous.

However, we cannot rest content with weak continuity in Hirsch's sense as a general account of what we mean by saying that

[7] Hirsch [2], pp. 10–14.

objects trace continuous paths through space and time. As Kripke points out in his lectures, if we were to watch the motion of a rolling ball that was merely weakly continuous then we would see not continuous movement but a series of jumps or jerks in its behaviour which—however appropriate to subatomic particles—is hardly what we expect from macroscopic objects like balls. Just as Locke remarked that identity is suited to the idea, so we might want to say that standards of continuity have to be made appropriate to the objects under investigation. But any such admission seems to threaten the simple view that the notion of a continuous path through space and time is intuitively clear and mathematically definable.

As if this were not a big enough problem, our attachment to continuity is liable to be threatened by a further one. We could take a stab at it by asking: what is it we are judging continuity of? Here I am, looking at a tree. And over there is the tree. It doesn't move, so it shows more than moderate continuity from moment to moment. Even if it sways gently in the wind, it still shows more than moderate continuity. For the closer I take the successive volumes it occupies, the greater the overlap between them. But there are lots of other continuities here too, although we are not usually inclined to recognize them. For example, there is a high degree of continuity between the tree just now and the tree a few seconds later when trimmed of a few millimetres all round. And between that diminished tree and the tree diminished by a further few millimetres all round there is also continuity. Of course, we don't normally recognize the existence of such continuities: but those individuals are all there even if we don't see them. For the continuous path of the undiminished tree there are thousands of alternative paths of diminishing and growing objects, also highly continuous. So why do we pick the one we do?

Hirsch's tentative solution to this problem is that we trace the tree as a continuous object and ignore all the alternative possibilities because to do so *minimizes change*. Indeed, he takes sortal-covered continuity to be a refinement of this more primitive notion of change-minimizing continuity. And this looks plausible. For certainly a Papuan who had never before seen a car could no doubt trace the history of a car for a certain time as the history of one thing even though lacking the appropriate sortal vocabulary and the associated concept. But this is no more than a plausible suggestion.

We are left with the feeling that we cannot talk about change minimizing continuity unless we know just what our frame of reference is. Relative to *what*, in other words, is change to be minimized?

Related to this problem is the epistemological question of how anyone could start from the links, taken as momentary slices of objects, and build up from them continuous and continuously changing broader objects. Kripke has focused this issue for us by discussing the problem of a rotating disc, and to that we now turn.[8]

2.4. KRIPKE'S DISC

It is helpful, in coming to understand this problem, if we follow Kripke in thinking about what I have called the 'chain theory' in a slightly different light. Recall that the chain theorist is trying to give an account of broad objects in terms of connections among their temporal parts. At the moment, we have two accounts of how this is to be done. On the *survival* account, whole objects are constituted of temporal parts—object-stages—suitably linked according to our three conditions on survival. On the *continuity* account, the links between stages consist of appropriate spatio-temporal overlap of the stages, the degree of overlap standardly depending on the nearness in time of the stages in question.

Kripke suggests that we think about the links in our chains as follows. Each link is part of an enormous, three-dimensional

---

[8] Kripke's lectures are unpublished, but widely circulated in manuscript form. The disc example is just one of several that pose a problem about spatio-temporal continuity. For a detailed discussion of it and for further references, see the article 'Identity, Properties and Causality' in Shoemaker [6]. In the same article, Shoemaker provides examples that cast doubt on whether spatio-temporal continuity is even sufficient for identity. I had long ago tried to argue for the same conclusion as Shoemaker, using the example of a projected picture. If we could agree that the identity of the projected picture was determined by the identity of the slide in the projector, then continuity of projected picture would be compatible with difference of picture (for projection of one slide can be stopped at the same time as projection of a different slide was commenced). Although Shoemaker's example is more fanciful than this one, it is perhaps more convincing. He imagines that we have machines that bring tables into existence and which can also cause them to dematerialize. But, given such machines, a continuous series of table-stages may well be stages of different tables—for a given table is made to materialize by the table-producing machine at just the very time and place that another table was destroyed by the table cancelling machine.

photograph of the world at a time. We could call such a freeze frame a *hologram* of the universe at that moment. The important thing is that we be able to read off from the hologram the complete state of the world at the given time *without prejudice to whether successive holograms are showing the same or different objects.* An analogy with experience may help here. Clearly, I can have two experiences separated by, say, ten seconds. I look at a cat in the corner of the room, close my eyes for ten seconds, and then look again. Clearly, my visual experience when I look again can be so described as not to prejudge the question of whether I am seeing *the same* cat again or simple a different, but extremely similar, cat. The holograms imagined by Kripke are likewise to be thought of as having all the information we need about the state of any items in the world, but *not* information about their numerical sameness with items depicted in earlier or later holograms.

Now we imagine a thinnish, circular disc about which we have just such information. In hologram after hologram we glean the information that the disc is apparently sitting there in the same location. So let us try to track the disc's history. One way is to say that the disc just sits there. Each time we inspect the hologram, we put a blob on part of the disc, or shine a light, or whatever. So in Fig. 7 is one tracing of the disc's history through time: the spot in each case is meant to mark the same part of the disc each time. But equally continuous is the track of the disc's history seen in Fig. 8. We can ensure that this mode of tracing is continuous according to our earlier accounts: if we shorten the time between successive holograms then we move the spots closer together. Moreover, each

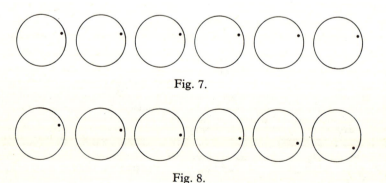

Fig. 7.

Fig. 8.

time, we are not only tracing continuously but tracing under the same sortal (provided we can apply sortals to instantaneous stages). So, how can we decide—at least on continuity grounds—between these two modes of tracing the disc?

One tempting reply to this question does no good at all. According to it, the answer is to be found in Hirsch's notion of *minimizing change*. For surely, of the two proposed accounts, the former is to be preferred simply because it does minimize change. But this won't do at all. The case of the disc is significantly different from the case of the tree where minimizing change looked like a good idea. For we have no information, so far, as to whether our disc is rotating or not. Our successive pictures will be the same from instant to instant whether the disc is rotating or at rest!

Here is the real trouble with the freeze-frame approach to the description of the world: it just cannot provide us with the information we need in order to know if the disc is rotating or not. Kripke points out that it must follow from this example and similar cases that the hologram view of the world is completely flawed, certainly so if we thought that from a sequence of such holograms we could *deduce* facts about the identity or otherwise of objects. Nor is the deduction theory saved by attempting to construct suitable counter-factuals. We might say, for example, that the disc is rotating if, were we to paint a white spot on it, the spot would show up in different positions in successive holograms. This would hardly save the day. For surely we cannot *define* rotation by this means. The changing position of the spot would, of course, be evidence of rotation, but the rotation would be the independently specifiable fact that *explains* the movement of the spot.

What conclusions can we draw from this case? It might be thought that a Quinean move is attractive here. As we have seen, Quine distinguishes bodies (unified, broad objects) from physical objects (which are any old mereological individuals we care to take). Now, for the Quine of *Word and Object*, bodies are posited by us; or, more accurately, we learn the body theory as we grow up because bodies were posited by our ancestors in an inspired bout of theorizing.[9] Theorizing—in Quine's view—is not to be taken

---

[9] See Quine [2], § 6. Quine's view on posits and reality is modified in his later work: see Quine [9], where, as noted in the text, he comes round to a position closer to Hirsch's on body-mindedness (see Hirsch [2], ch. 8).

lightly. 'To call a posit a posit,' he cautions us, 'is not to patronise it.' So we could try defending the hologram model of the universe from Kripke's attack by claiming that the features and unities of bodies are postulated on the basis of the freeze-frames as data. In the case of the rotating disc, the data permit the generation of alternative theories. And in this case we are as likely to come to the wrong theory as to the right one. Luckily, though, the universe is not stocked entirely with uniform symmetric objects for which the rotation puzzle arises. So in most cases, we come to theories about bodies that are not in competition with close rivals.

The idea that our body-mindedness is the result of this kind of theorizing seems an attractive response to Hume's problem about the continued and independent existence of external things. Our access to the world is, clearly, partial and incomplete. Empiricist theories of knowledge and perception have often used the notion of *inference* in an inappropriate way. If we are to infer the existence of bodies from our experience then it has seemed that a dilemma must be faced. Either there is more to the nature of bodies than is given to us in experience—in which case the inference cannot be logically or deductively justified—or bodies are themselves in some way constructions out of experience—in the way phenomenalists, for example, have claimed objects to be logical constructions out of sense-data. But in the second case, the empiricist seems driven into a kind of idealism—of the sort found in Berkeley.

The theory of knowledge is not, of course, a central concern of this study. But we cannot dwell long on problems about identity without these leading us into other central areas of philosophy. We will not be able to solve some of the problems we face without further excursions into the theory of knowledge. Hirsch, interestingly, finds himself facing the problem of body-mindedness too. For him, our 'sense of unity', as he calls it, is itself an innate endowment. I think there is quite a gap between Hirsch and other empiricists here, although Quine has come round to thinking in terms of body-mindedness. Even on Quine's earlier views, the theory of bodies needs some help from our innate abilities. However, what Quine thinks is innate in us is a kind of biased spacing of qualities, an ability to treat objectively similar situations as in fact dissimilar. In our later discussion of objective similarities we will see how Quine has solved a problem that some would dismiss as unreal. For it requires us to take seriously the existence of objects as mereological individuals, a requirement that can be dismissed by opponents of what in Chapter 7 I call *the extensionalist myth*.

Returning to Kripke, we can ask if the suggestion that we have a *theory* of bodies solves the immediate difficulty. Unfortunately, it doesn't. For what Kripke seems to be arguing is that the *motion* of bodies deserves to be among the basic facts from which any further theories are generated. Why should we rest content with an entirely artificial picture of how we come to our views about unity? If I cannot tell, in a given case, whether a disc is rotating or not, I can always put out my hand and touch it. Of course, if I am looking at an expensive piece of equipment, or a dangerous one, there may be good reasons for not poking around in the works. But, in many cases, such an option is available to me: even if I can't decide by looking, I *can* decide by feeling, whether the disc is rotating or not. If we insist on restricting ourselves to instantaneous cross-sections of the universe, we cannot include motion among the data. And Kripke's arguments are fatal to the suggestion that motion can be inferred from instantaneous descriptions.

Of course, Kripke's disc example is not fatal to the idea that enduring bodies are theoretical posits. So we have to be clear that, where we are worried about *conclusive* arguments, his example does not seem to mark the end of bodies as posits. But we can perhaps appeal to good sense here. Quine is right to suggest that we can draw the dividing line between theory and data virtually anywhere we like. But it would be perverse, unless initiated by very compelling reasons, to draw it in such a place as to rule out motion in objects as part of the data used in constructing theories of the world. So let us agree with Kripke that we can identify things as displaying changes of motion without having to infer, or theorize, this motion on the basis of instantaneous data.

This granted, though, it does not seem to follow that the concept of an enduring or persisting thing is primitive and irreducible. Motion is a form of change which affects an object. Kripke seems to think that if change of this sort is admitted as a datum, then we have to accept the primitiveness of broad, enduring things. But how long-lived need something be for us to detect its motion? Of course, if we look at a freeze-frame photograph, we will not detect motion, either of the camera or of the object, *provided our shutter-speed was fast enough*. But at shutter-speeds of one-thirtieth of a second it is usually easy to tell if the camera, or object being photographed, was in motion or not. At exposures of one or two seconds, it is yet easier to give such verdicts.

So we have to note that Kripke's motion example does not force us into accepting as primitive objects that are very broad. Of course, for some rare elements, a lifetime of one or two seconds would be long indeed. But in the history of people, rivers, mountains, and planets, a slice of one or two seconds is a miniscule portion. It would be odd, in fact, to approach the question of object-stages with instantaneous stages in mind—although we might have to bring instantaneous stages into our story in order, for example, to give an account of continuity. But, as we have already seen earlier in this chapter, there is no general, intuitively compelling account of spatio-temporal continuity which matches the changes in persisting objects. And, as we will see in Chapter 4, it is relatively easy to imagine a world (perhaps one with different physical laws from this one) in which a sequence of genuinely discontinuous stages can all be allocated to one object. That example, together with the comments in this chapter, establish fairly conclusively, I think, that a persisting thing need not have a spatio-temporally continuous history. And this is an important result, for it may be that human beings, and other animals, are precisely items of a sort whose mental histories are discontinuous in this way.

In mounting the defence of the chain theory against Kripke's arguments, I have accepted his example, without querying its plausibility. However, it is clear that some difficult issues would need to be resolved before we can rest content with the example as given in his lectures. Suppose the disc of the example is not isolated from other physical systems, but, like the turntable of a record player, is connected causally to surrounding objects. In this case, although our holograms would not reveal obvious changes in the disc itself from moment to moment, they would reveal changes in motors, drive belts, speed-controlling devices, and the like, which are linked mechanically to it. Remember that the holograms give us as much information as we want to have about the state of the universe at the time in question. From all this information, it would be possible to infer that the disc is indeed rotating. Alternatively, think—in case this is what Kripke has in mind—of the disc as constituting a relatively isolated physical system, alone in deep space. Now we have the problem of specifying the frame of reference relative to which we are to make sense of the disc's rotation, and of doing so in a way that leaves undecided the fact of its actual motion.

I have not explored these kinds of problems here because I am happy to keep epistemology distinct, for the time being, from metaphysics. The metaphysical significance of the chain theory is that it gives an account of what it is for an item to be a single, unified, persisting thing. From such an account of the nature of things, nothing follows immediately about how we come to know their properties. So, a defender of the chain theory can accept Kripke's point about the impossibility of deducing motion from freeze-frame photographs. Further, even conceding that the individuation of a stage involves essential reference to the object whose stage it is does not threaten the theory that persisting things are chains of suitably linked stages. Not until Chapter 7 will the issue of the links between metaphysics and epistemology be explored. In that chapter, I will attempt to forge at least one link between the two domains by proposing some tentative explanations for how we come to recognize the world as containing items belonging to sorts.

2.5. THE PRIMITIVENESS OF IDENTITY

We have come up with a number of suggestions in this chapter. One is that continuity in space and time is not as clear a notion as we might have expected it to be; another is that the concept of enduring things which change may be as primitive as any other concept used in constructing our theory of the world. Further, it has now been suggested that enduring things may themselves enjoy discontinuities in their histories. Yet we have stopped short of saying that everyday broad objects—tables, trees, dogs, or human beings—are primitives in our scheme of things. Instead, we have admitted that the slices or stages of such things with which we start will typically be at least of several seconds' duration, and it may be that stages spreading through several years are just as significant for our theorizing.

Those who are familiar with Kripke's lectures may still not know to what extent I share his views on the primitiveness of identity. Therefore, some clarification of the primitiveness issue will be undertaken in this section. For Kripke, the identity of broad objects is primitive and irreducible, while it is clear that on my approach there is a theory of their unity to be given. But this disagreement may not be as great as it appears. Moreover, it is important to recognize what is right and what is wrong in the widespread belief that the identity of persisting things is itself something that is ultimately fundamental. On the wrong reading of this belief, it is hostile to the entire project of this work; while on its correct reading, it simply records a feature of experience.

We have to take care that we do not get into a position that is hostile to explanatory and theoretical endeavours. Desks are solid, and support books, lamps, elbows, and sandwiches. Diamonds are hard, and make impressive scratches on glass and other materials. Yet—although both of these could be said to be pretty basic facts of experience—we should not rule out the possibility of explaining the solidity of desks or the hardness of diamond. Indeed, both of these things are perfectly well explicable given even a slight acquaintance with the science of materials.

So I am happy to admit that persisting things, like solid and hard things, are fundamental ingredients of our experience. But if we are not debarred from explaining hardness or solidity by appeal to the interrelations of the components, or parts, of things, why should we not attempt to explain the persistence of things by reference to the interelations of their parts? In the latter case, of course, the parts in question will be temporal, not spatial, parts. In general, those who are doubtful of the enterprise of explaining four-dimensional persistence are so because of qualms they have about temporal parts and the associated chain theory of objects. Let me now look at a number of worries that are commonly expressed, and give some reassurance to those who may require it.

First, a point made by Kripke in his lectures is the worry that any four-dimensional view of objects may rule out the possibility that two different things can occupy the same place and the same times. Think of Hirsch's example of a tree and its trunk.[10] Although trees are not trunks, if we forget about the roots and think of a tree with all its branches removed, we can envisage a case where—for some considerable time—the tree and the trunk may occupy the same places and times. Likewise, in Gibbard's well-known case of a

---

[10] 'When the space-time paths associated with objects partly coincide and partly diverge we have a case in which two (strictly) different objects occupy the same place at one time . . .' (Hirsch [2], p. 61.) cf. Lowe [2].

statue formed from clay, we can think of a lump of clay which comes into existence at the same time as the statue it constitutes and which ceases to exist at the same time as the statue.[11] Surely the statue and the lump of clay are two distinct things. Yet, looked at from a mereological, four-dimensional viewpoint, the tree and the trunk are, for a time, the same sum of stages; likewise, the statue and the lump of clay are the same sum of stages and thus indistinguishable.

This concern is not unique to four-dimensional approaches. Anyone who thinks that a statue—or a lump of clay—is wholly present at a time, but who then goes on to describe the statue as being simply an aggregate of clay particles, is faced with a similar difficulty. For precisely the same aggregate of clay particles constitutes the statue and the lump of clay. One response to this difficulty is to maintain that statues, and indeed lumps of clay, are distinct from the aggregates of particles that constitute them. After all, if we smash the statue, we will still have an aggregate of clay particles (where 'particle' is not being used to refer to any fundamental portion of matter). Likewise trees, and tree trunks, are distinct from the aggregate of cells that constitue them. Applied four-dimensionally, this solution would mean distinguishing objects from their life histories, or trajectories, in space-time.

As we will see in Chapter 5, there are very good reasons indeed for making just such a distinction. A unified object, or persisting thing—what I will be officially calling a *particular*—is not, on my account, bound either to three or to four dimensions. So I agree with those who maintain the distinction of objects from their life histories, but I do this for reasons that are quite different from those generally given. Hugh Mellor, for example, writes: 'a thing's trajectory, like Churchill's life, can itself only be identified by appeal to the persisting identity of the thing whose trajectory it is. Not every timelike path in space-time, whose parts are all occupied by events, is the trajectory of a thing.'[12] Although I agree that we

---

[11] See Gibbard [1]. Noonan has recently defended the claim that in the case described, the statue and the lump of clay are one and the same. This predilection for concreteness on his part forces him into a strange position. Since the predicate 'might have been squeezed into a ball and not destroyed' is true of the lump of clay but false of the statue, this—like other modal predicates—must signify a different property when concatenated with singular terms differing in sense (see Noonan [8]). Luckily, I am not wedded to concreteness in this way; as is shown in Ch. 5, persisting things are not to be identified with their actual paths through space-time.

[12] Mellor [1], p. 286. Mellor's paper is a critical response to Nerlich [1].

need to distinguish things from their trajectories, and also agree with one reading of Mellor's claim about identification, this does not force me to give up the attempt to explain the unity of a thing by reference to the relations among its temporal parts. Moreover, considering the spatial analogue of my temporal claims will give further support to them.

Consider, then, the spatial analogue of Mellor's identification principle in the above remark. We can think of the spatial extent of an item as being similar to its temporal extent. Not every region of space whose parts are all occupied by things is itself a region occupied by a unitary thing. Because we know the typical spatial extent of things like bicycles, dogs, and bridges we are usually able to identify the spatial extent of something once we know what kind of thing we are looking at. But now consider an attempt to give an account of the spatial unity of a desk along the following lines. We claim that the desk consists of certain parts, or matter, placed in certain structural relations and with certain kinds of causal dependence exhibited among them. The causal story will involved showing that, for example, the top and the sides, stand in certain relations of support to each other that do not hold between the components of the desk and other things. Moreover, if we apply a suitable force to one side of the desk, the other side will move. Changes affecting one part of the desk thus have consequences on other parts. We thus explain the independent movability of the desk and thus why it has an extent which is the extent of a thing, while the desk and the floor—although entering into some causal relations—do not constitute one spatially unified thing.

Now readers may make up their own minds whether they think there is any merit in such an approach to the question of spatial unity. The moral to observe here is that, even though spatially unified items are pretty fundamental in our experience, there is no reason why an account of spatial unity along the above lines should not be ventured. Moreover, if I were to propose such an account, I could do so while maintaining that desks are distinct from the sum of their parts and while admitting that identifying a certain portion of space as being occupied by a sum of desk parts requires me to have the concept of a desk. Likewise, my account of the temporal unity of an object is not to be seen as denying any epistemological claims about concept exercise; nor should I be accused of failing to distinguish items from their histories or trajectories.

As already mentioned, there are very good reasons for distinguishing objects from either their three- or four-dimensional extents. Even those, like Mellor, who think that objects are in some way more fundamental than events, are prone to think that to talk about an object, or a persisting thing, is to talk, essentially, of something three-dimensional. On my account, however, there is no good reason for taking up this stance—and rather good grounds against it. The fundamental grounds for adopting the view that objects can be regarded as three-, or four-, or even as five-dimensional will be given in Chapter 5, and I will save most of my positive suggestions until then. In the meantime, largely negative arguments will be used to wean away those who are devoted to the three-dimensional conception of objects.

A second objection to a four-dimensional treatment of persistence is related to the first. Since an object, conceived four-dimensionally, is really just a long event (or a chain of events), the four-dimensional treatment threatens the very distinction between object and event. Yet surely, the objection goes, this is wrong. Objects are what participate in events, or changes. A world of unchanging objects is not impossible, and such a world would have no events. Thus objects are metaphysically prior to events, for a condition of the latter existing is that the former exist.

There are two responses to this objection. The first is to challenge the metaphysics. There is no reason, independent of a particular theory, to think that either the category of events or other categories (of objects, properties, or whatever) will turn out to be fundamental. Although I favour such a challenge, I will not defend it here, for it should be clear that a second response can be made in the light of what was said to the first set of difficulties. Since a unity theorist can make the distinction between an item and its life history without giving up the enterprise of explaining the unity of broad things, this second objection can be bypassed. An object's life history is a sequence of events; the chain theory is concerned with the issue of which sequences of events constitute the histories of particulars— unified, persisting things—and which do not. But, as we have already seen, a particular is not to be identified either with its spatial components or with its spatio-temporal spread.

In effect, both of these objections have been answered by distinguishing constitution from identity—a distinction that is familiar to identity theorists.[13] As will become clear in the fifth

---

[13] See e.g. Wiggins [2], Wiggins [9], and Hirsch [2], ch. 2.

chapter, constitution and identity will be distinguishable in ways that have not so far been recognized by most theorists. Let it be noted, however, that a difficulty confronts the theorist who would maintain that objects are distinct from their components, yet are in some fundamental way three-dimensional. Mellor, for example, has maintained that the three-dimensionality of things is so fundamental that, supposing the general theory of relativity entailed the denial of this, we would have to give up that theory.[14] A theorist like Mellor can give some account of the spatial unity of things—either along the lines suggested above, or along quite different lines. Since any unified object is wholly present, on his view, at any given time, we can at least make sense of the question of what its unity consists in.

But if an object is wholly present at a given time, it is not clear what sense can be made of the unity questions I have been asking so far. How can there be a real question of unity over time for an item that is completely present (and thus present as a unified item) at a given time? Remember that the three-dimensional unity theorist gives an account of spatial—and only of spatial—unity. Here are all these regions of space occupied by particles, or other things. Some of these regions sum into regions occupied by larger, spatially-unified things (desks, bridges, sandwiches, and so on). Even if the three-dimensionalist thinks that there is not interest or merit in theories of spatial unity, such theories make sense in that the puzzles they answer can be expressed in terms acceptable to the three-dimensionalist. But if we limit ourselves to the three-dimensional conception of objects, we cannot even give voice to the unity puzzle. The parallel question asks us to think of all the time-slices of objects occupying space-time. Many of these slices sum to unified, four-dimensional things, and many do not. The chains which are constitutive of objects cannot even figure in the three-dimensional account, for as long as we restrict ourselves to three dimensions, there just are no such chains.[15]

[14] Mellor's protestations remind me of another Cambridge philosopher's claim that if the quantum theory delivered results contary to common sense then that theory would have to be abandoned. See Mellor [1], p. 285. The issue of things and dimensions is explored in more detail in Ch. 5 of the present work.

[15] It can be argued that three-dimensional objects can endure through time. Something like this seems to be Mellor's position. But if we observe that what are usually called 'temporal' parts of objects are in fact *spatio-temporal* parts of them, we can begin to see the oddness in that position. If an item has *only* spatial parts, then the

This inability to pose the question typically forces those committed to the three-dimensional conception of objects into two further dogmas. One is the dogma of denying that certain puzzles actually arise. Wiggins, for example, considers that a certain kind of fission puzzle for persons might be tackled using a four-dimensional, mereological approach. However, rather than deal in mereological unintelligibilities, he is prompted to question whether the fission case described really is a conceptual possibility.[16] Here, I suggest, is a clear case of letting philosophical predilections carry too much weight. The fact that the fission puzzle can best be tackled mereologically will, after all, reassure the confirmed four-dimensionalist that the three-dimensional account of objects is inadequate.

A second dogma of three-dimensionalists is the often repeated claim that identity is primitive and irreducible. It is thus incapable of explanation. I do not, as has been already explained, deny the primitiveness of identity. But what I recommend is that we explain the unity or identity of some things, and in explaining this we accept the unity or identity of certain other things. Relative to any theorizing we engage in, there will be a distinction between the primitive and the non-primitive. But there is nothing, as far as I can see, to show that identity is always primitive. It would be monstrous to maintain that the identity of certain theoretical or social

question of its extent in time does not arise, for time is not one of three spatial dimensions. Minkowski space-time is *not* simply Euclidean three-space with an extra dimension attached, as Lucas observes: 'Minkowski geometry is markedly different from Euclidean geometry—as we have noted, a line in Minkowski geometry can be at right angles with itself . . . Moreover the $(3+1)$ dimensional geometry of space-time is very different from a $(2+2)$ dimensional geometry (two space-like and two time-like). It is therefore dangerously misleading to speak as though time were just a fourth dimension of space.' (Lucas [1], p. 205.) cf. the disagreements in Nerlich [1] and Mellor [1]. Nicholas Measor takes a similar line in unpublished work, where he suggests that an item cannot, strictly speaking, be in both spaces. However, my own line here is more cautious. What we have to recognize, as argued in Ch. 5, is that items may be viewed either three-dimensionally or four-dimensionally. But there are no good grounds for the claim that a particular thing is 'really' three- or four-dimensional. cf. also Lewis [6], ch. 4.2.

[16] Perhaps I am too crude in attributing this move to Wiggins. Here is how he puts it: 'The conceptual possibility of a delta in the stream of consciousness jogs our whole focus on the concept of personhood. But, rather than jump to the conclusion that we have no idea at all of what we are about . . . let us go back to the beginning and ask: Is such a delta really a conceptual possibility?' (Wiggins, [9], p. 169.) Measor is in no doubt, however, that Wiggins's strategy is as I give it.

constructs—say ecosystems, income groups, social classes, or groups bound by certain kin relations—is primitive and incapable of definition. The objection to four-dimensional accounts of unity is thus not motivated by any general principle as to the universal primitiveness of identity or unity. Rather, it is a dogma applied to persisting things because of the fear that any explanation of their unity will involve four-dimensional notions.[17]

None of this, then, is a denial on my part of the primitiveness of identity. Relative to properties, taken as primitive, we can try to give an account of objects as bundles or clusters of properties. If we instead take objects as our primitives, then we can try to explain properties as sets of objects. There is no final way of settling the question: but which is the real primitive, objects or properties? Rather, we could try to adjudicate between object-based and property-based theories and ask: which is, for the time being, the better theory? Just so is it with identity. We will give the survival theory a run for its money in the next few chapters. But that means that stages will be our primitives, and so the identity of stages will be used in giving an account of the identity of broad objects. Of course, we could take broad objects as primitives and use them, as suggested already, in constructing a theory of stages. And then we could argue about which theory worked better, and which we should prefer. Either way, we are taking the *identity of some things* as primitive. Perhaps in this way, we can best appreciate the truth that identity itself is a primitive; though appreciation of this truth in no way diminishes the interest of constructing a theory of the unity, or identity, of persisting things.

2.6. CONTINUITY, EXPERIENCE, AND UNITY

Since so many theorists of identity speak, entirely naturally, of 'continuity', this term is bound to crop up later in my treatment. The problem, we now see, is how to understand it. For we have just discovered how *conceptual development* (as I will call it) can lead us

---

[17] To be fair to some of my opponents here, it is worth noting that some of them champion the primitiveness of identity on general grounds: they are what I later call *foundationalists* about identity, holding that at least some identities must be primitive in order that non-primitive unities do have grounding. For a discussion of their position, see Ch. 8.9.

into a bind. If we develop the notion of continuity in a mathematically precise way, we get a concept that does not apply to many of the changes we normally count as continuous. However, if we develop the concept so as to embrace Hollywood-style 'continuity', then we can no longer distinguish the spatio-temporally continuous (whatever *that* means!) from the discontinuous. This finding is enormously gratifying to one who, like me, believes that we frequently operate with concepts that are extremely unclear, perhaps even incoherent (in the way Dennett suggests our concept of pain is) and yet tremendously useful *for all that!*[18] The term 'continuity' will be used in what follows to mark some intuitive notion of a continuous path in space-time which we cannot, at the moment, make clear in any mathematically precise way.

This chapter has not, however, finished off continuity theory for good. In addition to the attacks on it made in this chapter, some time will be spent in Chapter 4 showing that a continuous path in space-time (whatever *that* is) is not necessary for the unity of an object. Even such obviously persisting things as mountains can be unitary, while discontinuous. The considerations in that chapter really do put paid to the continuity account. However, it is worth avoiding a common pitfall in philosophical theorizing. We often try to establish the plausibility of one theory or account in a rather indirect way. First of all, the major rivals to the favoured account are shown to be false, implausible, incoherent, meaningless, or whatever. Having obtained by this strategy a relatively clear field for the favourite, no argument at all is given on its behalf. It is presented as self-commending given the failure of the rivals. In this work, I try to do rather more than this. As well as showing the implausibility of any continuity version of the chain theory, I also try to show that there are independent reasons for favouring a version of the chain theory using the account of survival already sketched.

Of course, one thing we must remain clear about is the distinction between epistemological and metaphysical, or ontological, questions. What I mean is the distinction between our basis for judgements about things in the world on the one hand, and the way the world has to be if such judgements are true on the other. We

---

[18] See the article 'Why You Can't Make a Computer that Feels Pain' in Dennett [1].

must be very careful about how we put this matter. We might think we could phrase the identity or unity question like this:

(1) I perceive a desk in my office at 3 p.m.
(2) I perceive a desk in my office at 5 p.m. the same day.
(3) Are the desks I perceive the same or not?

It is quite remarkable how many theorists who ought to know better fall into this kind of trap when putting forward their analyses of identity. Wiggins writes, for example: 'If one locates each of the particulars *a* or *b* (under covering concept or concepts) and . . . traces *a* and *b* through space and time . . . one must find that *a* and *b* coincide'[19] as the truth condition for '*a* = *b*'. But if *a* = *b* then there can be no question, strictly speaking, of locating '*each* of the particulars *a* and *b*'. For there is only *one* persisting thing to be located, called '*a*', and also called '*b*'. Wiggins's mistake—an entirely natural one—is to talk in terms of two objects, instead of dealing with the case as one in which there is but a single object with two names.

Our above case is similar. If I perceive a desk in my office at 3 p.m., then there is a desk in my office at that time and I perceive it. Likewise for the five o'clock case. But either there is one desk there all the time, in which case there is no question of *desks* being the same, or the desk I saw earlier has been replaced by another. In the second case, there is no question of the *two* desks being the same in the numerical sense, no matter how similar they may be.

So how are we to phrase the matter? From the point of view of our experience, we can talk about *experience-of-a-desk*, where the experience in question is indifferent to the identity of the object in the world producing it. Suppose my experiences-of-a-desk in the office are both produced by a desk (though this is not to deny that I could have an experience-of-a-desk produced by something that is not a desk). Then we can ask: was the same desk responsible for producing both experiences, or were they produced by more than one desk? And, again, if we wished to complicate the issue even further, we could even ask if the experiences were produced by things other than desks. But let us keep to the simple cases for the moment.

So we can now get clear on the epistemological issue. Our

---

[19] Wiggins [2], p. 45.

experiences of the world are many, and usually short-lived. Of course, I have been working at my present desk for many years now: so I have had thousands of desk-experiences. My theory of the way the world is allocates to just one desk the role of having produced these many experiences. Incidentally, given university policies on furniture renewal, my theory may be quite false. For, on reflection, I realize that there have been opportunities over the years for my institution to have given me a different desk *without my having noticed*. Luckily, such occasions have been relatively rare: yet, of course, the slight probability remains that my judgement about the furniture is wrong, and not wrong for any *philosophical* reason.

What, then, are the philosophical problems? Well, there are two. The first one can be put fairly vaguely. How is it, that on the basis of our hotchpotch of experiences we have constructed a picture of the world as consisting of relatively stable, persisting things whose changes are predictable and ordered? The answer to this great question is liable to have something in it about the nature of the world and the nature of we who experience it. Secondly, there is the question: what is it we are judging when we say that one persisting object has been esponsible for all my experiences-of-a-desk in my office, and a quite different object has been responsible for some other set of different experiences, and so on? Our business is to answer this second question by saying something about the unity of things; but our answer is bound to have some relevance to the first great question as well. Because empiricist philosophers these days often say strange things about our knowledge of the world, Chapter 7 is devoted to correcting some current myths about this. In that chapter, I argue that the world is structured in such a way as to make our knowledge of it possible.

In terms of our second question, we have set out to discover if what we are saying about the world when we say it contains my desk is that it contains a sequence of desk-stages connected by the survival relation. It will not do to cast survival aside and opt instead for spatio-temporal continuity; for, in terms of problems, we have not so far encountered—nor will we encounter—difficulties with the survival relation to match those encountered in explaining continuity.

3
Structure and Survival

Three points were sketched out in Chapter 1. First, we noted that survival can occur as a relation between distinct things. Second, it was suggested that the causal and structure conditions are each necessary for survival, while the matter condition added to the other two yields a trio of jointly sufficient conditions for survival. And thirdly, it was argued that for cases in which survival claims seem natural, our conditions are plausible.

In this, and the following, chapter, we look at some distinctly non-normal cases. These are cases which do not arise; indeed, they may some of them be impossible to realize. We are thus engaging in an activity that is still fairly common in philosophy: the construction of thought-experiments. However, it is important to recognize that such experiments are not without risk. One rationale for using them is that we thereby employ concepts in ways that put demands on them far in excess of those made in daily life. Just as engineers subject mechanical components to strain tests that far exceed any strains likely to occur in their normal situations, a thought experiment supposedly enables us to expose concepts to loads not normally encountered. One problem, however, is that whereas the engineer can pronounce on tensile stength after the strain test, it is not clear what properties of concepts can be discovered from thought-experiments.

The trouble is that in looking at significantly unusual cases we stray away from conceptual *analysis* and move towards what might be called *conceptual development*. For an every day example of what this phenomenon involves, think of how blind people describe their examinations of objects, or their meetings with people. Anyone who has a blind friend or relative will be aware of his or her use of 'see' in what strikes a sighted person initially as a quite inappropriate way. Yet, in time, it becomes quite natural to use the word in a way that is related to our ordinary, daily use of it, but significantly different, for it records investigatory successes without involving visual perception. This is a simple example of conceptual development, for our concept of *seeing* is not so well determined that we cannot develop it in this new way.

Now, my suspicion is that analytical philosophers practise conceptual development more often than is usually admitted. Given the indeterminacy, and vagueness, in our concept of a person, for example, what is meant to be an analytical study of personal identity may end up proposing one particular development of the concept over various rivals. The competing conceptions of personhood may fail to uncover one agreed core of doctrines for the very good reason that there may be no such core. Applying this thought to the case in hand, it is necessary to realize that I shall be arguing for particular conceptual developments in this and the following chapter. In Chapter 4, for example, I will argue for a specific development of the concept of *physical object* in the face of certain imagined oddities. So any confirmation for my proposed conditions that emerges from these experiments is itself conditional upon acceptance of the plausibility of the conceptual development in what follows.

It can be helpful to think of conceptual development in terms of what we might call *the Eusa problem*. In Hoban's novel, the Eusa story is venerated by the primitive folk who are remote descendants of the survivors of a nuclear holocaust. The story itself is a strangely garbled mixture of terms drawn from the nuclear physics and politics of our day incorporated into a narrative expressing the predicament of these sorry survivors. The epigraph quoted on the flyleaf nicely represents the worrying circularity we face when dealing with either conceptual analysis or development.

Eusa asks the little man (a mysterious figure in the story) how many changes there are, the response being that there are as many as required by the idea (we might say *concept*) of Eusa. Logically enough, the next problem is to find out what this concept or idea is—but this we will not know till we have seen all the changes. The exchange here reminds us of Aristotle's definition of substance as what admits of change. The point is that the changes appropriate to Aristotelian substances permit them to continue falling under the same concept.[1] We recognize that there are principles of change for many sorts of natural thing: indeed change is mandatory for trees

---

[1] For Aristotle, 'sensible substance is changeable', while the substratum which persists though change is what he calls 'matter' (*Metaphysics* 1k).

and mammals if they are to be properly counted as trees or mammals at all. The principles of development and growth for living things, incidentally, are the sort that would enable us to arrange a collection of Kripkean holograms into correct chronological order—for example, puppy-stage before adult dog-stage.

But the changes that items undergo, or have undergone so far in our human experience, in this world, do not seem to exhaust the entire repertoire. It seems that we can readily enough imagine possible worlds in which things would still count as trees even if they behaved somewhat differently from trees as we know them. The concept of tree is indeterminate, or open-textured, enough, to allow it to apply in these other situations. We have seen just such a phenomenon in the case of the concept of seeing in relation to the blind. So this means that we could develop a concept from our presently vague concept of a tree which would apply to things (in some other world) whose behaviour is significantly different from the behaviour of trees as we know them. One thing the Eusa passage reminds us of is the difficulty of *knowing where to stop*. Philosophy must be different from science fiction. But it is hard to state just where in an exercise in conceptual development it is time to stop. A sensible methodological principle is that we do not continue conceptual development beyond the point at which it ceases to have value for our account of how things are *in the real world*. All philosophical theorizing—even that which involves quite different possible worlds—must keep its centre of interest in the one world in which we live and on which our curiosity is ultimately focused.

A further insight we can derive from the Eusa problem is this. When tackling philosophical topic of a general kind, we tend to restrict our thinking to a particular range of cases. Then we simply project, or generalize, our findings from this range over cases we have not dwelt on. Alternatively, we just do not think about the other cases at all. So we must be wary of coming up with theories of identity or of survival that are fine for relatively unchanging things—like many artefacts, or mountains, or works of art—but which make the identity of much more changeable things mysterious. Locke was well aware of this difficulty, and insisted that identity was suited to the idea of the thing in question.[2] It follows

---

[2] Locke [1], II. 27: 'It being one thing to be the same *substance*, another the same *Man*, and a third the same *Person*, if *Person*, *Man* and *Substance*, are three Names standing for three different *Ideas*; for such as is the *Idea* belonging to that name, such must be the *Identity* . . .'.

that an account of identity or survival for mountains may well not be suitable for persons, or vegetables. What is true of accounts of identity is also true of accounts of *change*. So Locke would agree with the little man that we need to know the changes an item is liable to go through before pronouncing on the principles of its identity. In terms of talk about kinds, or sorts, we can maintain that different possibilities of change are associated with different kinds of thing. The Eusa insight will be very much with us throughout this work. Even in this chapter, we will be speculating on the identity of daffodils—a topic strangely neglected by identity theorists for, if I am right, attention to daffodils will help us in the end resolve some of the problems of personal identity!

3.2. TELECLONING

The case to be studied in the present chapter involves a remarkable imaginary piece of technology which Dennett has called the *teleclone*. In essence, teleclone machines permit transport of people and their belongings to distant corners of the universe without any movement of their physical stuff. How can this be? In its simplest form, the machine consists of two parts—a 'sender' unit and a 'receiver'. The sender unit dismantles the bodies of potential interstellar travellers swiftly and without pain into their molecular and submolecular components. During this process, however, the unit makes a blueprint detailing the structure and arrangement of every molecule and atom in the subject's body. When complete, this blueprint is beamed at the speed of light to the distant receiver unit where carbon based molecules are cleverly combined in accordance with it so that an exact replica of the traveller is constructed. Thus the teleclone differs quite significantly from the 'normal' transporter beam beloved of science-fiction authors.

When thinking about the teleclone in this form, many people are inclined to accept that those who 'travel' in this way *survive* the experience. Of course, the machine can just as readily be regarded as what Dennett calls a 'murdering twinmaker'.[3] But it may be that talk of *murder* in this context draws attention to the lack of identity between the original traveller and the telecloned replica. It is easy to

---

[3] See the introduction to Hofstadter and Dennett [1]. Parfit calls the same machine a 'teletransporter' (see Parfit [4], ch. 10).

see how the machine could be modified so that a sender unit transmits blueprints simultaneously to two distant receiver stations in quite different places. In this case, the process would lead to the production of *two* replicas—a kind of fission by teleclone. For obvious reasons (mentioned in our earlier discussion of Theseus' ship), we could not count the original traveller as *identical* with both replicas. But then, we might argue, identity is not present in the simple case either. This argument relies on a principle called the 'only *x* and *y* rule' and has been deployed to good effect by Bernard Williams. We will discuss it in the next chapter, when considering the role of rivals in establishing identity claims. For the moment, let us accept the Williams point. If we would not want to count the traveller identical with both replicas in our latest case, then let us take this as showing that the traveller is not to be counted as identical with the replica in the original case, noting that all that distinguishes the two cases is the presence of a rival for identity in the latter one.

None of this, of course, counts against the *survival* claim. As we have already seen, interesting cases of survival occur in relating *different* things. In the first case of telecloning, the traveller may seem to survive as the replica; in the second case, the traveller may seem to survive twice over. Of course, we can hardly accept this reasoning just as it stands. For we might wonder if it is right to make even a survival claim in this case. Would we have any sympathy for someone who viewed telecloning as something to be avoided if at all possible? What the teleclone does, after all, is produce a *replica* of me. Such a person will be indistinguishable in all respects from me as I am at the time I enter the teleclone sender unit. But what comfort does the production of a replica afford *me*? It may be good news for those near and dear to me that someone indistinguishable in all physical and psychological respects will emerge at the other end (assuming, of course, that nothing goes wrong with the process). But should any of this afford me comfort? It seems quite plausible to maintain that our attitude to ourselves may be very different from our attitude to our pets, our favourite music, our friends, or even our loved ones. The thought that my replica will shortly be around on some distant planet, and that a replica of that replica will in five years be back here on earth may prove unconsoling to me no matter how high the quality of reproduction.

Part of the trouble here is that we are handling a complicated case before we have even become clear on the simple cases. It may be that in the end we have to admit to permanent puzzlement over the prospects for personal survival. This would not in any way inhibit us from examining the question of whether less complicated, lower-level, items might survive the teleclone. And notice, too, that remaining agnostic about the question of the survival of a person does not mean that we could never decide about whether to teleclone or not to teleclone. An agnostic might encounter a situation in which telecloning is undoubtedly the sensible choice. Indeed, even if I thought that death was a certainty for me in the sender unit I might very well choose to teleclone if I happen to be facing certain death in any case, stranded in some far-flung corner of the galaxy. I might consider the sending of the blueprint and the production of a replica a last act of kindness to those who care about me.

What adds complexity to the situation is that we feel comfortable with the notion that high-level objects—like persons—have the sorts of properties that can survive destruction of their physical embodiments. No doubt, this kind of view is a legacy of our Christian-Platonic concept of the *soul* and its Cartesian development in the concept of *mind*. Nowadays, with analogies to computers in fashion, we are maybe tempted to think of persons as a kind of software: the package that constitutes the *real* me can perhaps be run on different hardware. What the blueprint carries in all its detail about my brain and central nervous system structures is a program which can be run on any suitable machine. Attractive though this way of thinking is, my strategy will be to suspend judgement on this matter for the moment and instead to concentrate on getting clear on the issue of survival for lower-level items. However, those who already find the idea of persons surviving the teleclone congenial should find my argument that lower-level items also survive it quite easy to accept.

3.3. THE IMPORTANCE OF STRUCTURE

Let us turn, therefore, to the case of simple things, like stones, models, shoes, shrubs, and typewriters. Any of these that can be accommodated inside the sender unit can be telecloned and can survive as their replicas. Why should we say so? Every scratch on the stone, every detail of the model, every ripple on the sole of the shoe will be reproduced by the telecloning process, and reproduced in exactly similar material, let us suppose, to the original. Just as in our case of the brother who copied his sister's model bridge, we seem to have clear grounds for making a survival claim. What more, we might wonder, could there be to the notion of survival?

Of course, there are those who see no sense in talking about my survival unless by this we mean *my survival as myself*. Just as in the first chapter, I have to ask for such readers to treat my remarks on survival as stipulative, and hope that my analysis of identity by means of survival eventually convinces them that there is a use for the notion, however bizarre it seems to them. But a different objection may come from quite another source. For there may be those who are happy to concede that identity and survival are distinct. Further, they admit that it makes sense to talk of a person surviving the teleclone. But they deny that anything other than something that lives can survive the procedure. I and the rose-bush may survive; but my typewriter and my shoes do not.

What motivates this new objection is a kind of Lockean distinction between living things and mere 'masses of matter'. For Locke, non-living things are 'mere cohesions of Particles of Matter any how united'. By contrast, living things are a 'disposition of particles' together with an organization of parts suitable for receiving and distributing nourishment and for continuing the life (vegetable or animal) of the thing in question. What telecloning does is replicate this life-supporting organization, or structure; but such replication is what goes on in the normal course of events all the time inside living bodies. My pancreas renews its cells roughly every twenty-four hours; what keeps my pancreas the same throughout the changes is the replication each time of the previous cellular structure.[4]

Although Locke is one of the most interesting historical writers on identity, his distinction here seems to be misconceived. Suppose he happens to be wrong about the animate versus the non-animate. We can easily imagine discoveries in physics that tell us that crystals of quartz, despite their apparently fixed and stable structure, undergo frequent renewals of their subatomic parts. This new turn to science would effectively put living and non-living things on just

---

[4] The reference is again to Locke [1]. II. 27.

the same footing as far as structure and organization are concerned. But we do not even have to go as far as this kind of speculation to establish Locke's errors. For he is wrong about how things are, given our current orthodoxy. Very few inanimate objects are, as a matter of fact, completely without internal structure and absolutely amorphous. It is the highly organized structure of materials like steel and iron that make them so suitable for industrial use and artefact manufacture. Different kinds of steel, for example, not only differ in respect of the amount of elements, like carbon, that they contain, but also in the alignment and arrangement of their atoms and molecules. Processes like annealing and tempering are specially designed to induce specific crystalline structures that give metals their useful and distinctive properties.

But we can stop short of this fine level of description and still make the point about structural arrangements. The child's model bridge is hardly a cohesion of particles 'any how united', nor is even so simple a thing as a wooden carving. The pattern of the grain in the latter, like the arrangement of the blocks in the former, may be entirely distinctive. If the teleclone succeeds in reproducing such patterns and arrangements, then why should we deny that a model, or a carving, survives as its replica? What the Lockean objection has done, in fact, has been to bring to our attention the importance of our structure condition to survival. To the extent that structure is preserved in our replication process, then we have partial grounds for a survival claim. Of course, the teleclone satisfies our other conditions as well. We get replicas made in similar material to the originals, and we also have a straightforward causal account of why structure and matter are thus preserved.

3.4. TYPES AND TOKENS

It may have occurred to some readers that an item and its replica seem to be good candidates for being tokens of the same type. This is indeed the case, provided the standard of replication is high enough. Of course, many people have suggested that the type–token distinction can be made to apply to persons. As we will see later, Parfit's account of what he calls 'q-memory' gives us a good example of the applicability of the distinction to psychological items, and Bernard Williams has previously suggested a way of understanding the idea of *person-types*.[5] Since at this stage of the investigation we are trying to avoid dealing in any detail with complicated cases, let us continue to restrict our attention for the time being to simple physical things.

The type–token distinction is commonly used in linguistic contexts. For example, we distinguish utterance, word, or sentence tokens from utterance, word, or sentence types. In the last sentence, for example, the type word 'utterance' has two token occurrences. If we say that the one word 'utterance' has occurred twice, then our reference is to the *type*. If we say two different words have occurred in the sentence, even though they have just the same form, then our reference is to word *tokens*. Clear though the distinction appears to be, it is by no means easy to state it precisely, nor to give a formal specification of what a *type* is. One possible benefit of the account given here is that we can approach the definition of types and tokens by way of the theory of replicas.

As I have argued elsewhere, *artefacts* are not only amenable to the type–token distinction, but in our conversations about them we consistently fudge just this very distinction.[6] This fudging on our part may partly explain why the distinction is so hard to state precisely. Such *referential opportunism*, as I call it, aids and abets the normal flow of conversation by letting us avoid over-specificity in discussions about cars, bicycles, cameras, or clothing. If I tell my friend that I am going to buy the same car again, then it is very likely that I would be construed as referring to a car type. This is not to deny that in some circumstances, we find ourselves buying the same artefact token more than once! We can think of my present car, then, as a token of a certain car type. In the case of Theseus' ship, we can think of the continuous ship and the plank-hoarder's product as both of them being tokens of one and the same ship type.

Applying this distinction to the case of Theseus' ship suggests that some of the problems raised by it may not be so acute as we

[5] See his essay 'Are Persons Bodies?' in Williams [5].
[6] For more details, see the original treatment in Brennan [3]. If what is argued later about the case of persons is correct, then we are similarly opportunistic in our discourse about them. Sometimes, in our valuations of persons, it appears that we are concerned with features of the token: I like someone's smile because it is the smile of *that* person. In other cases, I like someone's smile because I like smiles of those kinds or types. One difference between our valuings of persons and of cars is that it is easier to become aware of the existence of opportunistic referential practices in the latter case.

thought. Many artefacts are, as we might say, *replaceable*. If I break a part of my bicycle, or a piece of cooking equipment, then I will generally be satisfied if I obtain a replacement which is a fairly exact replica of the broken component. This is not, of course, always the case. Human beings can grow attached to, and fond of, even inanimate things. Thus nostalgia can make us reluctant to part with an old camera, or replace a tried tennis racket with a new model. In general, however, artefacts show a kind of replaceability which is not displayed by animals or other living things. (This last remark is controversial as far as some moral philosophers are concerned, namely those who would maintain that *only* persons are irreplaceable and that even animals are replaceable. Their views strike me as simple human chauvinism, but this is not the place to argue the point.)

As far as the fuctioning of an artefact is concerned, the substitution of one artefact for another identical in structure and material should make no difference to the execution of the task in hand. Let us apply this thought, then, to the ship case. Suppose we have the two rivals before us: the *Heraclitus* and the *Heraclides*. Although they very likely differ in condition from each other, the ships may well look as if they have both been produced according to the same set of plans. And in a sense they have. When manufacturing large and expensive artefacts—say aircraft—it is not unusual for one, or several, *prototypes* to be built. These prototypes enable important aspects of the new design to be tested in real situations, away from the limitations of wind-tunnels and drawing-boards. If the design is a success, then the plans that enabled the prototype to be built will also enable further items exemplifying the same design to be assembled. But the prototype artefact itself can be regarded as a kind of codification of a certain set of plans. And we can regard the *Heraclitus* in very much this way. Its repair and the associated construction of the plank-hoarder's ship is a kind of manufacturing process, albeit slow and inefficient.

In a normal manufacturing case, we will know for sure which artefact is the prototype and which is the first of the production run. This is, of course, not the case with Theseus' ship, at least, not as long as we are unclear about the identity issue. But in the case of normal production processes, I can be interested in acquiring a certain sailing dinghy, let us say, while being indifferent as to whether I am buying the prototype or the first of the production run. Indeed, if the prototype is in good condition after its trials, and is offered at a substantial discount, I may prefer it to the first of the production run. Likewise, if my interest in Theseus' ship is in getting a trip on a ship of its *type*, I may be indifferent as to choosing the *Heraclitus* or the *Heraclides*. If my interest is in purchasing one of them, and assuming that both offer much the same by way of seagoing qualities, accommodation, and so on, then I may choose the one which offers the best value for money. In each of these cases, my interest has been in the *type*, we might say, rather than in a specific *token*.

Are there situations in which we might be interested in one specific token? It is possible to imagine that many circumstances require us to choose one token ship rather than the other, but even here there are surprises. Let us consider briefly the matter of insurance claims, or tussles over ownership. These legalistic situations seem to require a verdict on *identity*. Theorists who have given consideration to this sort of case generally opt for a decision in favour of the continuously functioning ship: it is, and stays, the *Heraclitus*. There are good reasons for such a verdict. For example, it is easier to establish *possession* of a spatio-temporally continuous object (using the notion of *continuity* in the intuitive way); also, money invested in its maintenance and upkeep is lost if anything should happen to it (thus it is no compensation when the *Heraclitus* has been destroyed by fire if the insurers maintain that their cover in fact extended only to the *Heraclides*). These are, of course, simply pragmatic reasons for going along with the identity verdict. But it is worth noting that to go along with the identity verdict in favour of the continuously functioning ship is not to have settled all questions of interest when tokens are under scrutiny.

For example, suppose that in the refurbishment of the *Heraclitus* over time it turned out that certain materials were replaced with different materials; some methods of construction were changed; new forms of jointing and caulking were tried; the rigging and sails were modified, and so on. All this is perfectly familiar in the case of artefacts like ships that require repair and refurbishment over a long working life. Now we imagine that long after both ships have sunk to the bottom of the Mediterranean, a naval archaeologist has the opportunity to raise one, or the other, but not both. Here is a case where a token has to be selected. But even if the verdict on identity has been given in favour of the continuous ship, our archaeologist may find more of interest about the original methods of construction by lifting the *Heraclides*. When we think about this fiction, we can begin to see that we have a double success—as far as survival is concerned—in this case. This double success allows us very interesting choices—choices which can be independent of the decision, whatever it may be, on identity.

3.5. REPLICATION

It is likely the case that whenever we have highly successful replication, we can talk of types versus tokens. Thus a good recording of a recording yields another token of that recording type: in this way pirate videos and other recordings are made. We have to take care, though, and not just about matters of copyright infringement. Suppose someone were to tape a record: the resulting tape might reproduce the *performance* on the original record, but it is not another token of the *record*, for tapes are not records. Records, viewed from the perspective of information theory, contain a recipe for the production of certain sounds given appropriate technology; this recipe is contained in the microgrooves cut into the plastic medium. Tapes can store equivalent information, this time in the form of patterns of magnetized particles. It is clear that the record–tape relation is much more complicated than other cases of replication we have so far considered.

But one case we have looked at seems to cry out for the application of the type–token distinction. Surely, when we teleclone a stone, or a rosebush, we produce thereby another token of the same type. Here is a result that gives us pause. For we do not normally think of the ordinary denizens of the physical world as types at all. Yet, if I had a teleclone machine, with sender and receiver units suitably close together, I could produce new tokens of any given object as readily as write new tokens of any given word. The introduction of the teleclone thus threatens to extend the duality of type and token to everything in the physical universe.

Limitations on size would make it unlikely that telecloning could ever work for mountains and planets. But even they are not exempt from our reflections. So we have to contemplate the idea that a huge teleclone device could yield a replica of Mount Everest from the original. Now imagine modifying the machine so that although the object in the sender unit is scanned, and a blueprint made, it is not thereby destroyed (or perhaps it is disassembled and then quickly reassembled). Telecloning thus does not consist simply in the production of a sequence of tokens one after the other; it can allow the original to be retained, while more and more tokens are produced. Our ability to produce new objects of some same type is now much closer to our ability to produce further tokens of some type word. In the next section, we will consider an even more dramatic modification of the teleclone, but for the moment let us see if we can sort out the implications of this latest fantasy.

We seem to have three things to deal with: replication, survival, and types and tokens. Let us see how far we can get using the notion of survival to yield an account of what it is for two items to be tokens of the same type. This will involve trying to use survival as an ingredient in the theory of replication. One consequence of this is that we may be able to render talk of *types* fairly harmless. This would be a move in the spirit of Peirce and many who have followed him in declaring that types just do not exist. To talk of two tokens being of the same type, after all, is simply to indicate some relationship between them, rather than to make the ontologically bold claim that some further thing exists which they both instantiate. We will find that we can make a certain limited headway on the matter by trying to construe the relation between tokens as one of *survival*.

We have already noted the importance of the structure condition in contexts of survival. It, together with the causal one, seems to suggest a mode of dealing with the type–token problem. Survival comes in degrees, and in some cases we can find a very high degree of survival between one item and another. Indeed, the brother's replica of his sister's bridge, or the new recording tape obtained from copying another precisely similar tape, are good examples of one item surviving as another to such a high degree that we are able to talk of *replication*. Just what do we mean here by talking in this way? A good example is found by studying natural replicators, like crystals and genes. In genetic replication, each replica of a gene is itself a gene, that is, it has the same kind of material in the same structural relations as the original; and it has been produced by a causal mechanism of which we have some dim understanding. Interestingly, genetic replication itself involves transfer of chromosomal material each time a new copy is made: this transfer helps to keep the replicating process highly accurate. But we can imagine causal mechanisms for producing replicas, whether teleclones, or digital recording devices, which would also be highly accurate yet in which there would be no transfer of material of this sort.

Let us consider, then, whether we might not give an account of replication purely in terms of survival. When one item survives to a suitably high degree as some other item then the latter is a replica of the former. Further, when one item is a replica of another, they are both describable as tokens of the same type. Will this do? Unfortunately, attractive though the suggestion seems at first, there are a number of counter-examples which prevent this tidy assimilation occurring. The existence of these counter-examples is highly instructive; for it reminds us that the fit between theory and reality is often a messy business. First, let us take *replication*. We could only maintain the account of replication in terms of survival to a high enough degree if we were to use the term 'replica' in a somewhat artificial way. For example, a model aircraft assembled from plastic components would normally be regarded as a replica of the real thing, provided it was an accurate scale model of some real aircraft. So there are cases of replication that do not live up to our requirements. Worse cases are in store, however, when we consider the issue of types and tokens.

3.6. PRODUCTION AND COPYING PROCESSES

Since our account of survival involves a *causal* condition, we apparently cannot use survival at all in giving a general account of types and tokens. For there is no reason why, for two items to be tokens of the same type, they should be causally related. Thus, I may doodle on an envelope here, while simultaneously, someone unknown to me on the far side of the planet produces another token design which coincidentally matches mine. Our two designs are thus tokens of the same type although neither was causally obtained from the other. It may be thought that the example is strange. After all, we do know of perfectly ordinary cases where we can produce marks on paper that match those produced by others unknown to us. What I type, for example, will contain word, sentence, and certainly letter tokens that match those produced by others busy at their machines. And even though my tokens are not causally productive of yours, yet there is a good causal story that explains the agreement among typewriters and word-processors about what tokens of English letters should look like. We could say in such a case that all the tokens thus produced lie on the same causal tree. The same goes, of course, for handwritten tokens.

But none of this will do to explain the doodle case. Doodling is not taught like handwriting, and it is hard to see why we would even start to look for any causal explanation of the adventitious replication were it not for a theoretical interest in using the notion of survival in the account of replication. Besides, suppose we find a lump of quartz on Neptune that exactly replicates one here on earth. The behaviour of silicon and oxygen atoms no doubt explains in both cases why the lumps have the crystal structures they do: but we are not forced to trace both lumps back to some common ancestor, or otherwise locate them on some same causal tree. Although I have already used the term, reflection may make us doubt whether such adventitious matching should be described as 'replication' at all.

In fact, it is not clear what to say about usage here, and the attempt to impose theory on the matter may itself arouse legitimate suspicions. Here are some suggestions. One reason, I conjecture, why we are suspicious of calling our bits of quartz *replicas* of each other is that we tend to take a replica as something produced by a *copying process* (about which more in a moment). Now, in the case of the matching doodles, we can make sense of these being said to replicate each other because we can envisage circumstances such that the one *could* have been copied from the other. Again, printing can be copied, as can handwriting. So when we look at two printed documents which contain some of the same letter tokens we can again speak of replication to the extent that one set of tokens *could* have been copied from the other set of tokens.

Think now of type and token cars. Since production cars are reproducible, they can also be copied (although, as we will see in a moment, they are normally produced by a process that is quite different from a copying process). Only the introduction of the teleclone, however, has made mountains, trees, lumps of rock, and the like reproducible. We don't normally think of two voles as tokens of the same type or as replicas of each other—no matter how similar they seem to be. Barring processes like cloning, mammals are just not reproducible: two very similar voles are just two very similar members of the same species. We are only able to think of the Neptunian quartz example in terms of types and token because, I suspect, we had already prepared the ground for this by speculating about telecloning. But without that background we would not have thought of the lumps as anything other than two very similar (in ordinary talk, 'identical') lumps of quartz.

If all this is accepted, then it seems to make sense to apply our account of survival to the type–token issue. If we go along this route, we part company with much contemporary wisdom on the issue, according to which type–token talk is simply understood to apply to similarity of pattern.[7] It is a problem, of course, for this current wisdom, to explain why your last inscription of an 'e' and mine, although not very good replicas of each other, still count as tokens of the same type, while 'identical' badgers or 'identical' panes of glass do not. Perhaps, then, we can agree that there is more to two items being tokens of the same type than simply similarity of structure. The problem remains over how to specify the missing ingredient in the story.

We could start by trying the following three conditions as *sufficient* for x to be a token of the same type as y (that is for them to be replicas of each other). First, x must possess a structure that is highly similar to y's. Second, x is *materially* similar to y. And, thirdly, it is *possible* to obtain one of them using a process in which the other has a suitable *causal* role to play. Intuitively, the most likely such causal role is that one acts as the prototype, model, or original from which the other is copied. These conditions obviously cover the case where one is in fact causally obtained from the other. In such situations, where one thing is in fact produced using the other, we have survival in our sense. So the proposed modification to deal with adventitious replication looks quite simple. We are saying two items are tokens of the same type where one survives to a suitably high degree as the other or where one *could have been the survivor* of the other (to a suitably high degree).

We can now close this section by looking at some counter-examples to the theory of types just given. The first deals with personal survival, and we can look briefly at this even though we are not yet officially in a position to deal with such complicated cases.

---

[7] There are a number of *Analysis* papers on this topic, including Simons [1] and Goldstein [1].

On a remote planet, in a distant star system, there is a person who is an exact replica of someone—let us call her *Beatrice*—who lives here on earth. Indeed, if telecloning existed (which in this story it doesn't) Beatrice's twin is exactly just what the teleclone might have produced, as far as superficial appearance is concerned. Beatrice dies tragically young. But her replica lives on. According to the theory just given, we seem to be able to make sense of Beatrice having a replica, but apparently have to deny that Beatrice survives as that replica. For although Beatrice's twin *could* have been produced by teleclone, she wasn't. But should we not perhaps think again? Is it not plausible to suggest that in this case Beatrice does, after all, survive? The objection, therefore, suggests that we need to modify the account of survival. Instead of saying that in some cases of replication, one item could have been the survivor of the other, we now say that all cases of replication are cases of survival. And our causal condition on survival now requires a modal clause in it: if x survives as y then it is *possible* to obtain y using an appropriate process in which x has a *causal* role to play.

Now this objection may have the thought underlying it that if, *per impossibile*, Beatrice's twin could be transported to earth, those who had known Beatrice might be fooled. And, once they knew the circumstances, they might still want to regard Beatice as surviving as her twin. There is, no doubt, some force in this worry. But the objection is not conclusive. If Beatrice's twin had been produced by the teleclone, then Beatrice would have survived as her twin. But she was not so produced. We seem faced, then, with a choice between maintaining a strict, non-modal account of survival, which will make that relation incompatible, on occasion, with replication, or weakening our account of survival, so that survival and replication simply coincide. A decision either way is likely, in the end, to be stipulative. For, interestingly, we are faced, even within our theory, with the possibility of *development*, rather than analysis, of the concept of survival.[8]

But we need not turn to science fiction to find cases where replication is incompatible with survival. For we need to notice that

---

[8] This development would, of course, threaten our strong causal ingredient in survival; since survival can be regarded as constitutive of identity in some cases, then the proposal also threatens the claim that unity is a causal notion. For some people, this would be good news. See the discussion of Schlesinger's objection in Ch. 8, n. 29.

there are in fact two distinct ways in which causal processes may be involved in the obtaining of replicas. We can dub these *copying processes* and *production processes* respectively. And only in copying processes do survival claims seem appropriate. In a copying process what happens is that a certain item is a model, original, or prototype from which a replica is made. By contrast, in a production process, a number of replicas are produced simply by going through the same causal process (often on similar material) a number of times. The last six stitches made by the sewing machine, for example, will be replicated by the next six so long as we do not change the thread or adjust the stitch. length or needle swing. The earlier stitches, however, do not participate directly in the production of later ones. They thus do not survive as the later stitches. Again, notes produced on a piano, or jam jars in the factory, replicate each other provided the *producing causes* are not varied too much.

In this way we can get a whole range of cases of replication that are rather different from the photocopying, tape-recording, and telecloning cases we have studied so far. And, like our cases of adventitious matching, the existence of such cases threatens the role of survival in the general account of types and tokens. The safe conclusion thus seems to be that we can still avoid the Platonism that was threatening our earlier account of objects as types. But the story of how to avoid this Platonism is getting increasingly complicated. In the case of copying processes, to say that two things are tokens of one type is to say that one survives to a suitably high degree as the other. In the other cases—those where production processes are involved—items that are tokens of the same type are items of similar structure and (usually) matter produced by some same causal process. In this second case, we can have replication without survival.[9]

None of this is to say that the fact that two items match each other

---

[9] To try to deal with the modal cases of replication, we might wonder if two adventitiously produced tokens are of the same type when either (1) one could have been the survivor of the other by virtue of some *copying process*, *or* (2) one could have been *produced* by the same causal process that produced the other. It is not clear that even these conditions will do for handling the Beatrice case. But they do offer the prospect of handling many of the cases of type and token talk that are common in the literature. To forestall a misunderstanding, it is worth observing that production processes may be involved in copying processes themselves. Moreover, a real production process (e.g. in a factory) may well involve both copying and production processes.

may not be of interest even when one does not survive as the other. We have seen with the Beatrice case, that a replica of Beatrice might be almost *as good* as a survivor, even when Beatrice does not survive as her replica. Likewise, I may want to choose a replica that is as similar as possible to the broken statue, even where the broken one plainly fails to survive in, or as, the replica. If both statues are reproductions of some original, then the rationale for such a choice is clear: for the original will have survived as both (at least in ideal cases). The rationale for the decision in Beatrice's case is perhaps less clear. But we will return to this problem when we come to the study of personal identity.

For just now we will stick with the austere conception of survival. However, note the cost that our austerity incurs. Instead of introducing strange entities, we have had resort to talk about possibilities and possible worlds. To some empiricists, then, our victory over Platonism hardly seems significant. For them, we have jumped out of the frying-pan of Platonism into the fire of Aristotelian essentialism.[10] For those, however, who see resort to possible worlds as harmless—at least when it is undertaken in a suitably modest spirit—our proposals may have some merit.

The conclusion of this discussion is that we must withdraw our support for the use of the theory of survival in giving a general account of types and tokens, and of replication. What looked at first a good idea has turned out to be fraught with problems. However, obtaining a decent, austere account of type–token language would have been, at best, an incidental benefit of the theory of survival. More significant for the project in hand is the discovery that the use of type–token language in some instances of replication is easily glossed using our account of survival: the tokens resulting from telecloning and other high-quality copying processes will certainly be new items of the same type as their originals.

3.7. PSEUDOMORPHISM

Pseudomorphism is a quite astonishing natural phenomenon. As is well known, most materials occurring naturally, and nearly all the

---

[10] In the light of what is said about *real possibilities* (Ch. 5), this worry might be thought to be somewhat overscrupulous.

materials we use in industry (with glass as a notable exception), have a well-organized crystal structure. A crystal is built up by repetition of certain basic structures—the so called *unit cell of the crystal*. Of course, these basic structures come in a fair variety of arrangements. The patterns displayed by solids on the surface of the earth are the results of the cooling of the earth from an earlier, liquid form. And in this slow cooling, atoms of the various elements had time to arrange themselves into a finite number of stable patterns.

Under high pressures, and over time, changes in the distribution of atoms and electrons in a solid can still occur. Indeed, the ability of materials to change their crystal structure when far from their molten state is exploited in common industrial processes. Annealing, for example, consists in heating a metal to a temperature between a third and one half of its melting point. At this temperature, significant migrations of atoms can occur and new crystal structures form.[11] Pseudomorphism is one such change in nature, whereby, for example, the atomic ingredients of fluorite (calcium and fluorine) are replaced gradually by atoms of oxygen and silicon (the ingredients of quartz). Although the unit cells of quartz and fluorite are slightly different, the overall shapes of the crystals of both materials are much the same. Thus pseudomorphism is an example of preserving overall structure while seemingly changing constituent matter.

With such a natural phenomenon as a model, it is not hard to dream up a modified teleclone machine that does the same kind of thing for lots of materials. After all, we can maintain the large structures of an item while producing a copy of it in material which has a very different fine crystal structure. So, if nature can change fluorite to quartz, while maintaining overall shape and dimensions, can we not imagine a teleclone that transmutes an object of one material into a replica of quite different material? Instead of using the teleclone as dubious transport over interstellar distances, we can use it for transmuting things here on earth into replicas in new material. Do you fancy transforming your rusty old car into one made of pure titanium (recognizing that, of course, it will no longer run)? Or how about seeing that bronze statue in gleaming silver? Even natural objects, like pieces of rock, can undergo wonderful

---

[11] See Ian Wilson [1], 7.7. Pseudomorphism is described in Ames [1].

changes in their material stuff. The modified teleclone is no less than the Philosopher's Stone!

The question we have now to face is whether particular things could be said, properly, to survive this new telecloning procedure, 'telemutation', to give it a name. Presumably, the new machine works on similar principles to the old ones. Let us suppose that objects placed inside it are destroyed, as in the original model described by Dennett. Computer crystallography, and goodness knows what all else, enables us to produce at the receiver terminal replicas with new atomic components arranged in appropriate crystal structures. So long as we have a large enough supply of atoms at the receiver terminal, and avoid nasty chemical incompatibilities, we can carry out the sort of transformations described. And surely we have not lost the old objects completely. They may have been destroyed. But they survive as, or at least in, their replicas, and—if we can agree on this—it confirms a significant discovery already suggested in the first chapter. For it is clear that structure is more important than matter when it comes to survival. This conclusion will be reinforced by our Chapter 6 discussion of structure and stuff.

We have perhaps now reached the limits of conceptual development in our study of the teleclone. It has prompted us to reach certain conclusions—conclusions that we might have reached by more sober, less fantastical, thinking. However, it has been more fun getting to these conclusions by the present route. Thinking about the teleclone has enabled us to get clearer on the type–token issue. Using the vocabulary of types and tokens in the case of Theseus' ship has helped us see that identity is not—for many purposes—what matters. What matters, rather, is *survival*. And thinking about the varieties of telecloning has enabled us to reinforce our earlier proposal that preservation of structure is of fundamental importance to survival. Survival, of course, is still itself something of a vague notion. It comes in degrees and although we might have thought we could give an account of it in terms of matter, structure, and cause our latest thought-experiment has cast some doubt on the necessity of the matter condition. Preservation of matter may only be necessary for survival that is higher than a given degree.

Those who are suspicious of thought-experiments and science fiction in philosophy might care to reflect on how we could have reached these conclusions without them. In particular, it is worth noting that our latest use of the teleclone fantasy was simply a device for eliciting verdicts on cases that are parallel to a natural one. Here is a crystal of fluorite, with a determinate shape, a certain number of facets, in contact with minerals which, over the years, will exert the right effects to induce pseudomorphism. In time, our crystal of fluorite will be destroyed, as atoms migrate to be replaced by quite new ones. But, after its demise, our crystal survives in the new crystal, this time of quartz, which has taken its place and preserved its overall structure. Our teleclone fantasy simply allows us to corroborate this verdict. In this case, as elsewhere, our fantasies do not interfere with our sense of the real. Rather, they act merely as heuristic flavourings, adding spice to our analytical diet.

4
Identity and Discontinuity

In the present chapter, there is an attempt to achieve two goals that are of significance for the work as whole. First, I try to discredit the claims of the continuity version of the chain theory, thus leaving the survival story with a clear field. Second, I argue that identity or unity is a causal notion. These results encourage the hope that we can give some account of unity in terms of a chain of stages linked by the survival relation. Although such an account may appear to be reductive, I will try to show that the account does not force us to give up deep intuitions about the primitiveness of some unity concepts—in particular certain notions about the concept of a person. However, dealing with the issue of reductionism is not easy.

As suggested earlier, there is more than one way of thinking about particulars. The recognition that this is so is itself a powerful consideration against reductionism. Any account we give of, let us say, the three-dimensional unity of a particular in no way reduces all talk about particulars to discourse in purely spatial terms. At the start of the present chapter, a last attempt is made to convince those wedded to three-dimensional conceptions of things that there are perfectly proper four- and even five-dimensional ways of thinking about objects. A useful corollary of this result is that for theoretical purposes we may draw upon whichever conception of particular is most useful at a given time.

The chapter continues by delivering a powerful attack on continuity theories, an attack based on the argument that particulars might be discontinuous in space and time without this preventing our assigning stages to larger, unified wholes. What supports the assignments of stages to a persisting particular in a world of discontinuities is precisely the causal nature of the unity relation.

Some objections to the proposed case are considered, the most worrying of which involve the notion that causal mechanisms could not operate in the case of discontinuous objects. This objection is not disastrous, and the Humean account of causality is argued to have application to these unusual cases.

Next, there is a brief anticipation of the later application of the results on episodic objects to mental states. For those not attracted by the claim that one enduring particular may have a discontinuous existence, it is shown that the version in terms of survival supports an alternative account of the discontinuity cases. This account seems more cumbersome than my preferred one, but is possible. On either account, it is clear that the theory of survival has an important role to play.

The most beguiling objections to best-candidate theories of identity are then studied, and it is shown that these do not force the abandonment of the claim that rivals can make a relevant difference to identity. However, important relations—like the survival relation—are to a certain extent independent of identity. If we make a clear distinction between constitution and identity, we can avoid the identification of particulars with their histories or their paths through space and time.

Finally, the chapter concludes by following up the Eusa insight. Different possibilities of change are associated with different kinds of thing. Additionally, it is shown that different parts and components are of varying importance to the determination of survival.

4.2. THREE- AND FOUR-DIMENSIONAL VIEWS OF THE WORLD

We started with a straightforward commitment to a four-dimensional view of the world, at least as far as our theories were to be concerned. The chain theory took objects as collections of temporal parts, themselves items with four dimensions—three in space and one temporal. Yet in the last chapter we used examples of survival that were not in keeping with the chain theory at all. We took the teleclone to be something that worked on one broad object—a person, table, or car—to produce another broad object. So the survival claim we made was not that a stage of a table survived the teleclone as a stage of (some other) table. Rather, we maintained that a table undergoing telecloning survived as *another table*.

We have already distinguished holders of the chain theory from those who maintain that a complete particular thing (chair, person, or vole) is present at any given time. The three-dimensionalist, in Wiggins's words, never uses terms like 'boy' so that they '. . . denote either "phases" of entities or (if that were different) the entities themselves frozen at an instant. They denote the changeable changing continuants themselves, the things that are *in* these phases.'[1] A natural development of this view, as we have seen, is to hold that in some way a whole object can be before me at a time. Thus, on such a view, all of my desk is in the room just now as I write. It is not clear that Wiggins wants to go as far as this, but some three-dimensionalists certainly do.[2] For such a thinker, not all of my desk would be in the room just now if, a few moments ago, I had carried one of the drawers into the room next door. By contrast, the chain theorist insists that, even if all the spatial parts of my desk are in the room just now, only a small temporal part of it is.

The three-dimensionalists have apparently got common sense on their side. Yet the chain theory has numerous theoretical advantages. For example, it is very easy to put our unity question in an unconfusing way as: under what circumstances do a number of different stages belong to the history of one object? There is no comparably easy way for the three-dimensionalist to put the unity question. At first, it might look as if we could put it as follows. Given that one object (my desk, say) is wholly in the room just now, and given that one object (my desk) was wholly in the room last week, what circumstances ensure that it was the same object on both occasions? But this is no way to put the question that puzzles us. For the very form of the question suggests that it is my desk which was in the room on both occasions. If, as an alternative strategy, we try to put the question in terms of the relation between my-desk-last-week and my-desk-this-week, we get no further. For, although there are two ways of understanding this formulation, neither is very helpful to the three-dimensionalist.

First, we could take 'my-desk-last-week' as designating a temporal slice of my desk. But this precisely what the three-dimensionalist finds a puzzling notion. Moreover, if we take it that there are such things as slices, or stages, of objects, then last week's

---

[1] Wiggins [9], p. 26.
[2] See Mellor [2], ch. 8. Mellor does, in fact, allow that there are genuinely four-dimensional things, e.g. events. But he balks at counting ordinary physical particulars as being genuinely four-dimensional.

slice of my desk is not the same thing as this week's slice of it. A great deal has been written about identity through time, or 'diachronic identity', in apparent indifference to this simple point. Of course, we know what the chain theory can say about the relation between these different desk slices—but to say this is to resort again to our familiar four-dimensionalist strand of theory.

Alternatively, we could take the phrase 'my-desk-last-week' as designating nothing other than my desk *as it was last week*. This successfully avoids problems about stages, but only at the cost of not allowing us to say anything about the identity of the desk except in terms of the identity relation itself. For my desk as it was last week can be none other than my desk as it is now (or any other time), and the relation here is simply identity. Yet it is precisely this relation—identity, sameness, unity—which we are trying to explicate.

In an ambitious series of unpublished arguments, Nicholas Measor has gone rather further in making life difficult for the three-dimensionalist.[3] He has tried to show that identity over time—diachronic identity—poses a significant problem for the three-dimensionalist. For if there are relations that are *criterial* of such identity over time, he argues, they are bound to lack properties that the three-dimensionalist assigns to relations that could be criterial for classical identity (properties like transitivity, for example). Thus, in the literature on personal identity, Parfit has made a great deal of relations like psychological connectedness and continuity (relations we will be discussing in detail later). Measor's argument is that since such relations lack transitivity, they cannot constitute criteria of identity on any stringent, three-dimensional view of persons.

I am not sure that pressing these kinds of point would really impress the three-dimensionalist. Nor does it help to dwell on technical points—for example, the fact that Minkowski space-time is not simply a Newtonian three-space enriched by the addition of a further Euclidean dimension. The impact of this particular finding is, of course, dramatic. It means that items in Newtonian absolute space cannot be truly said to be *in* Minkowskian space-time at all. For those liable to be influenced by such considerations, the

---

[3] The arguments here are additional to Measor's arguments in his 'Four Dimensional Man' (see Ch. 2, n. 15).

discussion and references in note 15 to Chapter 2 contain enough material, I hope, to help them make up their minds. I have to confess to a certain reluctance to make my philosophical theorizing depend too strongly on accepting any specific scientific view. This is not because I wish to deny that philosophy involves a posteriori theorizing—for it undoubtedly does. Rather, I want to continue to talk of space and time in a relatively informal way, while ensuring that what I put forward is not incompatible with our best attempts to understand the world in terms of current physical theory.

As suggested in Chapter 2.5, the issue is not whether *objects, continuants, persistents, particulars, things* are really three-dimensional or not. On my account, there is a certain ambiguity in each of these terms. If we want to know how much space an object occupies, then we can consider it as three-dimensional. If we want to know how much space-time it occupies, then we regard it in four-dimensional terms. And these considerations do not exhaust all we may be interested in knowing about an object. A balloon, for example, might have been blown up larger, or burst sooner, than in fact it did. We can contrast its actual three-and four-dimensional extent with other, possible, extents it might have had. A parent may regret the wasted potential of the child who might have been a brain surgeon: the possible careers of their offspring often loom just as large in the minds of parents as the actual careers.

This issue of alternative possible histories will be discussed further in the next chapter. By then, it should be clear why unified objects, or particulars, in some ways transcend their parts, their dimensions, and their life histories. This very transcendence makes them rather elusive things. At first, nothing seems clearer than the idea of a unified, concrete, specific thing—like the lamp sitting on my desk. Yet as we begin to recognize that it has three-dimensional extent, four-dimensional extent, and possibilities that may never be realized, we can start to become worried about what the lamp itself really is. Is it something abstract, rather than concrete? Is it something that is the bearer of properties, while distinct from the properties it bears?

We can avoid the resort to bare particulars and other metaphysical snares fairly readily. It is important to recognize that unitary objects—particulars—need not be the source of any special puzzlement if we are clear on the dimension-relativity of what is true of them. Let us go back to Gibbard's example of the statue and the lump of clay (mentioned in Chapter 2.5). Although these are distinct things, they can both be described as constituted of clay bits. How, then, can we describe the difference between the statue and the lump of clay?

One obvious difference involves structure. To be a statue is to be structured in a way that a lump of clay need not be; for the same lump of clay can take up many forms, while a statue is destroyed if its structure is significantly changed. For a lump of clay to constitute a statue, then, it has to have components that are organized in relation to each other. Indeed, one mistake Gibbard makes is to identify the statue and the lump of clay, while it seems clear that although the lump constitutes the stuff of the statue it is by no means one and the same thing as the statue.[4] Taken three-dimensionally, then, there is no more to the statue than its components and their structure. To say this, of course, is by no means to deny that the statue is distinct from the aggregate of clay pieces constituting it. The lump of clay, however, taken three-dimensionally, is no more than the aggregate of clay pieces constituting it (provided that by 'aggregate' we mean 'collection of suitably joined clay pieces'). Nor is the life history of a lump of clay anything other than the life history of an aggregate of clay pieces.

Taken four-dimensionally, the statue is more than just a structured assemblage of components (themselves structured aggregates of clay pieces). Over time, the statue may lose a hand, or have a damaged leg replaced, while remaining the same statue (I simplify here: more doubt and less dogmatism will attend the discussion of artefact identity in Chapter 6.4). If the view urged later in this chapter is accepted, the statue over time will be a chain of stages linked according to the conditions on survival. But, taken as an item that might have had different histories from the one it in fact had, the statue is still more than a chain of structured statue slices. For this reason, we have to distinguish the statue as it *actually* is (which is a chain of slices, each of which is a structured

---

[4] Resistance to my claim here is liable to be based on too 'concrete' a conception of objects or particulars. Notice how misleading it is to describe a figurative statue as simply 'a lump of clay'. Of course the statue is, constitutively, made of that very clay and no other; but this is by no means to establish that it is a 'mere' lump of clay. Misleading, or false, descriptions, incidentally, are not always infelicitous. If the intention is to denigrate, then it is perfectly proper (pragmatically) to refer to a statue as a lump of clay, or to a car as a heap of rust.

assemblage of components) from the statue *as it might have been.* So although the statue actually is a chain of slices, it might have been a chain of rather different slices.

Viewed from the perspective of alternative possible histories, the humble lump of clay is more than a mere aggregate of clay bits. For the lump might have endured for longer or less long than it actually did. Even lumps have unrealized potential. So although the actual lump of clay can be identified with a certain chain of lump slices (themselves simply aggregates of the same clay pieces) the lump of clay viewed as something with a number of possible histories is distinct from the chain that constitutes its actual history. Thus, as suggested previously, I can make the distinction between an item and its dimensions, its extent, its components, its trajectory or its life history, though for a rather different reason from that usually advanced. In an old piece on spatializing time, J. J. C. Smart comes close to representing what I think is the sensible view here: 'What we can achieve with a four dimensional logic, ordinary language achieves by using words like "cricket ball" with neither a three dimensional logic nor a four dimensional logic, but with a hybrid between the two. That is, it uses "cricket ball" with a three dimensional logic modified by the use of concepts like "change", "alteration", "staying the same".'[5] Smart stops short of thinking about a five-dimensional account—one which we will explore in the next chapter.

It should now be clear that a purely three-dimensional conception of particulars can only be maintained at some considerable cost. One of these costs might be a denial that the project followed in this book is possible at all. I have so far resisted saying much about criteria of identity, though they will be the subject of some later discussion. By the end of the present chapter, however, it will be clear that the search for conditions of identity is not only possible, but profitable and illuminating. That in itself will show a considerable advantage in the four-dimensional treatment of particulars.

As a kind of reconciliationist move, I would point out that I have so far been happy to speak with the three-dimensionalist, even though theorizing with the chain theorist. This is a simple consequence of the fact that nothing is *wrong* with either the three-

---

[5] Smart [1], p. 165.

or four-dimensional treatment of particulars. Indeed, it is important to the methodology of the treatment here that we can take the survival claims of the last chapter at face value. Our success in talking about the survival of particular things (from the three-dimensional point of view) can be taken as a basis for projecting this talk over the four-dimensional treatments. Our theory of identity and survival has to coexist, in the end, with the common sense way of putting things, even if—as happens elsewhere in the sciences—our official view involves some correcting of our ordinary way of expressing ourselves. In this way, conceptual development can lead to conceptual *correction* as well. Later in this chapter, we will see that the problems posed by the treatment of discontinuous things might lead us to reinterpret our everyday ways of speaking about identity.

The present chapter, then, extends the theory of survival by showing the role it has to play in the unity of particular objects. We also choose a case that is intolerably difficult for the continuity theorist to handle, thus enabling us to focus on the importance of survival without the distraction of continuity considerations. As a result, the case for the view that survival is what is important to unity will be strengthened.

4.3. EPISODIC OBJECTS AND CONTINUITY

'A single object', wrote Hume, 'plac'd before us and survey'd for any time without our discovering in it any interruption or variation, is able to give us a notion of identity' [*Treatise*, I. iv. 2]. Such a claim might fit well with the notion that the basic furniture of the world consists of objects displaying spatio-temporal and qualitative continuity. It is hardly surprising, then, that Hirsch should say: 'there is the most intimate connection between our concept of the identity of a specified sort of body and the idea of a spatiotemporally and qualitatively continuous succession of body-stages of that sort.'[6] But what if—astonishingly—a new finding were to suggest the existence of a gap between our concept of identity and the way objects 'really' are, a gap associated, ironically enough, with a certain gappiness in objects themselves?

---

[6] Hirsch [2], p. 235.

Among macroscopic phenomena, there seem to be few examples of concrete, but discontinuous, objects (using 'concrete' to apply to items that occupy determinate volumes of space). Admittedly, pains and certain other 'inner' states, letters (that is, epistles), plays, television serials, and the like apparently exhibit identity along with spatio-temporal discontinuity. Yet none of these items is concrete, and the periodic nature of such astronomical curiosities as pulsars, variable stars, or transients is thought to result from the vagaries of observation. Thus, for example, a star in a binary system may appear to wink off at regular intervals, but only because the earth lies on the plane of the orbit of the two bodies, so that the invisible partner eclipses the other from our point of view.

Perhaps, though, we are looking in the wrong place. Maybe pain *tokens* and tokens of mental states in general are concrete, while the types that correspond to them are not. This view would be taken by those who regard the concrete as that which can enter into causal relations with other things (recall our previous distinction between senses of 'concrete'). Numbers, on this conception, are non-concrete, while thought-tokens are concrete. In the end, we may want to agree that mental events of many sorts are episodic, and concrete in just such a sense. But it is safer, for the nonce, to work with items of a somewhat low-level kind, namely those things that are uncontroversially space-occupiers, and ignore the duality of hardware versus software.

It might seem that such things as orchestras and committees have determinate physical location and the sort of gappiness displayed by radio serials. But we must not confuse the episodic with the functionally discontinuous. Whatever reservations attach to the label 'functionally discontinuous', it is meant to pick out a class of things which admit disassembly while the components show continuity in space and time. Garden sheds, gliders, and even steamers, as we have seen, can be discontinuous in this way. When an orchestra disperses after rehearsal, or a committee after a meeting, we have a process similar to artefact disassembly. But committee members and orchestral players presumably show as much (or as little) continuity in space-time as the components of these other artefacts.

So, for radical discontinuity, let us resort to fantasy. A series of studies involving high-speed photography and so on has been carried out, let us suppose, in order to check for brief discontinuities in ordinary objects. Amazingly, one of the hills adjacent to the Stirling campus has been established to 'flicker' occasionally. The hill (called 'Dumyat' incidentally) runs steadily, so to speak, for 167 hours, winks off for approximately $\frac{1}{1000}$ of a second, runs for a further 36 hours, winks off briefly again, returns to the 167-hour cycle, winks off again, and so on. Many simple tests, let us further suppose, have established that the hill is not simply invisible during these brief flickers. Projectiles, for example, can pass through the place normally occupied by the hill provided they traverse it in the requisite $\frac{1}{1000}$ of a second; otherwise, of course, they become lodged deep in its interior. So there are times when the hill, however briefly, is just not there at all. Walkers, and the rest of us, however, are quite unaware of these changes, even though it means that on some occasions I may have been standing unsupported for those brief instants many hundreds of metres above the nearest solid ground!

We may suppose that only a few such gappy objects have been found. The discovery suggests, though, that for all we know every physical thing is subject to regular even if brief discontinuities. Unfortunately, the continuity theory of identity seems no match for such a possibility.

Whatever else is true of the Dumyat case, our experiments have revealed the existence of a number of objects successively inhabiting the location of Dumyat. Diagrammatically, the situation is like that seen in Fig. 9. Our problem is to relate our beliefs about

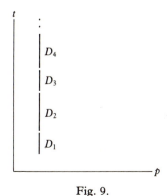

Fig. 9.

Dumyat to the succession $D_1, D_2, D_3, \ldots D_n$. Were we dealing with a person rather than with a hill, one tempting suggestion would be that each D_i is an *embodiment* of Dumyat. But it is not easy to see how to separate hills and their physical stuff in the way that some would say persons are distinct from their physical stuff. The trouble is that hills do not seem to have appropriate high-level properties, for example memories, intentions, beliefs, and ambitions. For a person to survive a change of body we might look for persistence of such high-level properties. And of course replacement of a person's body by another exactly similar body is indeed a change of body. The Dumyat case is thus like a change of body without persistence of the mind.

A better option, perhaps, is to claim that each D_i is an extended stage of some same object in just the way that momentary stages of objects are stages of objects. But of what kind of object are we thinking? If we stick with the notion that our hill is a concrete continuant, then—unlike the usual situation in such cases—it fails to exhibit continuity among its stages. So have we here some special sort of continuity—continuity that allows little gaps?

As we have already seen, there is a Hollywood sense of 'continuity' which is just right for the job here. But if we leave that sense of the term aside, we are left with the various kinds of continuities discussed in Chapter 2. We observed there, by looking at the tree and rocket examples, that some of the continuities exhibited by objects in their everyday careers are pretty weak. For instance, successive volumes occupied by a multi-stage rocket do not always show a high degree of overlap. But in the present case, unlike that of the rocket, we cannot even speak of *weak* continuity.

There is in fact *no* overlap between the place occupied by any D_i just before a gap and the place of its successor in the very next $\frac{1}{1000}$ of a second. For it has no successor then, and coincides with no place at all in that interval. As a desperate remedy perhaps we should allow the temporal jump, taking it as no more than a special case of the partial discontinuities already discussed. But this looks most odd—as if we are trying to allow discontinuity as a special case of continuity. Some of the oddness of this course of action is perhaps reduced if we recall an ambiguity in the notion of continuity itself. For although Hirsch's conception is entirely natural if we are thinking in terms of a continuous path traced by an item through space-time, not everyone has just this notion in mind when they use the term 'continuity'. Consider, for example, Parfit's, Lewis's, and others' accounts of psychological continuity.[7] None of these authors is unaware of the episodic nature of consciousness. Rather, what they mean by 'psychological continuity' is that each new mental episode goes on where its predecessor left off, whether or not any temporal gap separates the episodes in question. This is, again, our familiar Hollywood sense of 'continuity', and I do not intend to follow these authors in using the term in such an extended way. Rather, I will restrict the notion of continuity to what seems to be a perfectly natural conception even though, as we have already seen, we lack a satisfactory mathematical account of it. Using this very notion, then, it is clear that the Dumyat example is not a case of some rather weak continuity; rather, it is a case of something entirely different.

4.4. SCATTERED OBJECTS AND STAGES

Perhaps we should consider assigning each D_i to Dumyat in much the way that each instalment of *The Archers* can be assigned to one and the same radio series. We have already noted that many sorts of episodic object seem to be non-concrete. But it would be simply question-begging to move from this observation to the conclusion that any discontinuous thing must be nonconcrete. So just what is the relation between discontinuity and concreteness?

In dealing with functionally discontinuous things, I have taken it that after dismantling, the things persist, albeit in a somewhat scattered fashion and with some of their normal functions suspended. But some authors, like Hirsch and Nozick, find it natural to regard an item that is taken apart for repairs as going out of existence for a while and then coming back into existence upon reassembly. As already noted, not much would be gained by arguing about whether their description of such cases is preferable to mine. However, accepting their view for the moment, it is interesting to think about the conditions that have to be met for a newly assembled item to be numerically the same item as one previously disassembled. One such condition, drawn from what Quinton calls 'compositional theories', might be that the item in

---

[7] See Parfit [1], [3], and David Lewis [3].

question should contain the majority of the same components in much the same arrangement as in the original.[8] Another condition might be that some same sortal be true of both original and reassembled items.

Still holding the matter of sortals in abeyance, it should be clear that the compositional criterion is of no help to us in the present case. Even if we suppose that a watch taken apart for repairs does go out of existence for a time, there is no suggestion that its parts could in turn undergo similar disassembly, and the components thus revealed undergo further disassembly . . . and so on. For if such a process were carried on long enough we would have no components upon which a compositional criterion could plausibly operate. Molecules probably and atoms certainly would not yield identity conditions of the sort needed by the compositional theorist. The information that some object contains just the same atoms as some original object would not incline us, in the absence of other considerations, to count the two objects as the same. The compositionalist wishes to allow discontinuity of the watch along with *continuity* of its parts. So the identity of the parts themselves—or of a fairly significant proportion of them—is required to underpin the later identification of the repaired watch as the same as the original. Such an identity of components is just what we do not have in the hill case. Each D_i, of course, has much the same structure as its immediate predecessor (with due allowance for erosion, quarrying, and landslip). But whether the parts participating in the structure of a given D_i are the same as those in its immediate predecessor or successor is something that the hill's discontinuity prevents us deciding. So even the compositional theorist cannot come to our help here, and we are still faced with the problem of the relation between spatio-temporal continuity and concreteness.

Let us then return to the conception of each D_i as an extended Dumyat-stage and think about the relation of momentary stages to the larger concrete continuants of which they are stages. In Quine's familiar example, each momentary stage of the Cayster is a concrete object, while the river itself is also 'a single concrete object extended in space and time'.[9] On this account, momentary stages are *parts* of

---

[8] Hirsch discusses this proposal in Hirsch [2], ch. 2. See also Quinton [2], p. 63.

[9] 'Identity, Ostension and Hypostasis', in Quine [1].

continuants. Viewed in this way an object is (improperly) a part of itself. Moreover, there will be objects—an abundance of them—manifesting spatio-temporal discontinuity; it just happens that we, with our limited resources, lack the terminology, time, or patience for singling out such items. Thus Goodman deals with *possible* entities by speaking not of new, non-actual entities, but by speaking instead about actual, scattered, entities. The sum individual, he tells us, consisting of place p and time t (where p is a phenomenal visual field place not presented at t) 'misses being a place-time much as the scattered whole comprised of the body of one automobile and the chassis of another across the street misses being an automobile'.[10] As has already been argued, a mereological stance like this can provide us with a way of saving the concreteness of an object while recognizing its discontinuity. Let us keep on the mereological path for a while to see if a solution is genuinely in prospect. All that we have established at the moment is that the various Dumyat-stages can be summed to make a single scattered individual, just as any other scattering of items can be said to constitute a mereological whole. But this in no way assures us that the mereological whole in question is really a hill. Perhaps the whole misses being a hill in the way that Goodman's scattered car components miss being a car. So we need to establish just what considerations would lead us to count a scattered whole as constituting an object belonging to some natural, artefactual, or other, kind.

A comparison between the Dumyat case and a different form of discontinuity might help suggest an answer here. Figure 10 shows the history of a number of Dumyat-stages, whale-stages, and iceberg-stages, imagining this time that the stages are all of approximately the same length. I_1, I_2, and I_3 are extended iceberg-stages which, let us suppose, we would unhesitatingly allocate to the same iceberg if they showed spatio-temporal continuity; and likewise for the whale-stages W_1, W_2, and W_3. The gaps after t_1 and t_2 are meant to be very small, just as in the earlier case. So an observer watching location p_1 would seem to see Dumyat replaced instantaneously by a whale (at t_1) and the whale by an iceberg (at t_2). Those impressed by spatio-temporal continuity as a criterion for identity and unaware of the brief discontinuities in

---

[10] Goodman [1], p. 51.

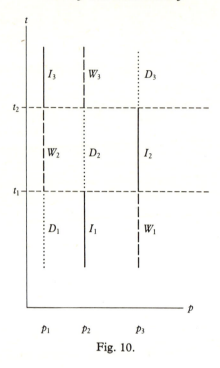

Fig. 10.

time between D_1, W_2, and I_3 might conclude that some one thing could begin its career as a hill, then change into a whale before becoming an iceberg. It might be easier to take such a view if one believes, with Quinton, that 'the temporal parts of an enduring thing would have been a perfectly good thing of that kind if they had existed on their own without the other phases which in fact preceded and followed them', and then the subsequent discovery of the discontinuities might be viewed with some relief.[11]

Now, in our latest case, D_1, D_2, and D_3 show spatial scatter as well as the sort of temporal discontinuity already displayed in Fig. 10. The problem is whether there is any way in which a mereologist could allocate these stages to one single item, that item being a hill. There is of course no problem about allocating the stages to an *individual*. Our problem concerns the kind or sort (if any) to which the individual belongs. We might think that whereas in our previous case Dumyat was 'hopping' on the spot in the new case it

[11] Quinton [2], p. 77.

'hops' from place to place. But what could underpin this allocation of separate stages to the one object in either case? Our three conditions will do the job. Firstly, the structure condition requires that each stage and its successor be similar in geometric structure. The similarity does not need to be exact, but there are limits of a fairly stringent sort to the degree of structural change we would allow in cases where the stages are separated by such brief gaps.

Our second condition requires similarity of *material* from one stage to the next, and again, although the requirement is not that there should be exact similarity, clearly we would not expect great changes to the material stuff of an object from moment to moment—not if we are going to count the object as persisting, anyway. Finally, the third condition requires that each stage—in Lewis's phrase—'causally depends for its character' on the stages immediately before it.[12] 'Character' here means no more than *structure* together with *matter*.

Applying the conditions gives us something like the desired result in both cases. Dumyat hops on the spot in the Fig. 10 case in that each stage seems to be causally dependent on the previous stage for its structure and matter, and the same relation between successive stages in the second case gives us grounds for allocating each of them, scattered as they are in space, to one and the same persisting object of a sort. The question of sortals will be discussed shortly. But that the persisting thing falls under the sortal 'hill' will, on my account, be a consequence of its manifesting appropriate structure and matter in each of its stages. We can further observe that the geometrical closeness in structure between stages explains the congruence, or near congruence, of the volumes of space coinciding with each stage.

4.5. CAUSATION AND THE HUMEAN

It might be objected that there can hardly be a *causal* connection between successive D_is for the simple reason that there is no means by which any causal mechanism could operate. For no D_i is contiguous in space and time with its neighbour, and even Hume, at

---

[12] Quoted from Lewis [3], although it should be noted that Lewis there is talking about what he wants in wanting his survival.

least in some places, requires such contiguity between a cause and its effect (see *Treatise* I. iii. 15). Now, it can hardly be replied to this point that Dumyat simply goes missing in the brief intervals: for if Dumyat has popped into a higher dimension, or gone off elsewhere for the vital fraction of a second, we have no puzzle. We would then have no interruption in its existence and so no episodic object. And it might, of course, be argued that in the kind of case described here, it is far more sensible to think of Dumyat as having gone elsewhere for these brief intervals rather than to imagine it has gone out of existence. Likewise, physicists are reluctant to count any of the forces of nature as acting at a distance, although I know of no evidence so far to suggest that, for example, there are *gravitons*. The case of gravity is indeed illuminating here. For although gravitons would provide appropriate quanta for mediating gravitational forces, we are still quite clear that bodies have gravitational effects on other bodies even while doubting that gravitons exist. Perhaps, if we were really sure that Dumyat goes out of existence every so many hours, we would look for new quanta to explain the replication of changes wrought upon one D_i in its succeeding neighbour. And if there were not at least prima facie evidence for each D_i being causally dependent on its predecessor—if variation between a given D_i and its neighbours could be as great as we please—then of course there would be no case for claiming survival from one D_i to the next.

Of course, as in Hume's famous discussion of the billiard balls (*Enquiry*, section IV), we are here speculating about things which threaten our underlying conceptions of physical reality. Principles of conservation of mass and energy, for example, are threatened by both kinds of case; if mountains did flash on and off, or if billiard balls ever remained at rest after colliding, then an overhaul of physics and mechanics would undoubtedly be required. This being so, it is natural to suggest that there really has to be more to the relation of cause and effect than is suggested by Hume's austere account, namely the *constant conjunction* of two kinds of event. The next step is to look for some mechanism which mediates the influence of one event on another. Anyone who is tempted to take such a step must then be doubtful that things like our hill episodes could exert genuine causal effects on each other, or—more precisely—be ingredients in events which are causally related. For what conceivable mechanism could bridge—as it were—the gap between the hill stages?

In thinking about this issue, we come face to face with a much bigger dilemma posed by the tension between our need to find explanations on the one hand, and our use of descriptive models in science on the other. The dilemma is not easily resolved. To get its full flavour, we can consider the distinction between *explanation* on the one side and *prediction* on the other. In a classic treatment, Carl Hempel argued that the two notions are symmetric. As he put it:

scientific explanation (of the deductive-nomological kind) differs from scientific prediction not in logical structure, but in certain pragmatic aspects. In one case, the event described in the conclusion is known to have occurred, and suitable statements of general law and particular fact are sought to account for it; in the other, the latter statements are given and the statement about the event in question is derived from them before the time of its presumptive occurrence.[13]

What Hempel means by 'deductive-nomological' explanation is one that satisfies the following pattern:

Covering Law(s)	The adiabatic lapse rate for dry air is 3 °C per thousand feet.
Statement(s) of initial conditions	The air sampled at point *A* is exactly one thousand feet higher than air sampled at *B*. Both samples are taken in the same non-humid air mass.
Conclusion	The temperature of the air sampled at point *A* is 3 °C lower than of that sampled at point *B*.

Here the covering law—or laws—will enable the conclusion to be deduced logically from the statement of particular events—the so-called 'initial conditions'. The conclusion itself deals with further particular observations. In its crudest terms, then, the formal pattern of such explanation is

Universal generalization:	$\forall x[Fx \supset Gx]$
Specific initial condition:	Fa
Conclusion (also specific):	Ga

Hempel's symmetry claim is that (with certain qualifications) the schema just given illuminates *both* the notions of explanation and prediction. Provided the covering generalization is a law—or, at

---

[13] Hempel [1], pp. 366–7.

least, lawlike—then it, together with the initial conditions, explains the conclusion.[14] Think of observing that the temperature of the air sampled at two points differs by 3 °C. If Hempel is right, we *explain* this observation by appeal to the generalization and specific initial conditions. Alternatively, given the initial conditions then—with the help of the covering law—we can *predict* that the samples will differ by the stated amount.

One difficulty with accepting the claimed symmetry is that we can apparently make sensible predictions even when ignorant of explanatory factors. Mendel, for example, was able to predict the outcome of cross-fertilization of different varieties of pea-plant while ignorant of what we would now take to be the explanatory causal mechanism—namely the genetic structure of the pea varieties in question. Likewise, epidemiological studies can give us the ability to make statistical predictions for disease rates in the presence of occupational or environmental hazards, even when we are at a loss to explain the mechanism underlying the disease, or are even ignorant of what the hazardous agent is. It is hardly a decent *explanation* of why a particular New Yorker has cancer of the lung to state that citizens of New York have high rates of lung cancer: indeed, it is not an explanation at all. What seems plausible, then, is that explanatory models will yield the ability to make predictions, but that predictive ability need not yield explanations.

Hempel, and his defenders, can reply to this that the covering generalizations must not only be general truths, but must have the status of being *lawlike*. Yet we must be wary of building into the notion of lawlikeness any claim that lawlike general statements are bound to be explanatory. One interest in Hempel's account is that the schema he gives itself provides an *analysis* of the concept of explanation: the analysis thus cannot without circularity use the

---

[14] Both Hempel and Goodman, among others, are aware of the problem involved in trying to specify just what makes a generalization a law or lawlike. It is intuitively clear, though, that not every general statement can do the job done by a law statement. If all the coins in my pocket have milled edges, for example, it certainly does not follow that a certain 20p piece which is not now in my pocket *would have* had milled edges *had it been* in my pocket. So the universal claim that all the coins in my pocket have milled edges is not lawlike. However, the statement that all acids turn blue litmus paper red is lawlike; for it does follow, given the truth of that sentence, that if a certain (non-acidic) sample of liquid *had been* acid it *would have* turned litmus paper red. Classic discussions of this problem can be found in Goodman [1] and Hempel [1].

concept itself. In the end, perhaps the fairest thing to say about Hempel's own concept of explanation is that it is a 'thin' one. Any account that insists on the symmetry he claims to hold between explanation and prediction will be an account of 'explanation' in only an attenuated sense of the word.

Hume's austere account of causation is itself a precursor of Hempel's work on explanation. For Hume, at least some of the time, gives us an account of causality which seems to rob that notion of any explanatory role. As he puts it in section VII of the *Enquiry*: 'we may define a cause to be *an object followed by another, and where all the objects similar to the first are followed by objects similar to the second. Or, in other words, where, if the first object had not been, the second never had existed.*' Ignoring the worry that Hume should really have been talking about *events* rather than objects, we can see that this account deprives appeal to causality of any rich explanatory force. In the place of an appeal to powers, forces, or causal mechanisms, we have simply a statement of general correlation. There is thus great similarity between Hume's schema and Hempel's:

Causal generalization:	All events of type A are followed by events of type B
Initial condition:	Event α is of type A
Conclusion:	Event α will be followed by an event of type B

It is hardly surprising, then, that this austere account of causation is just as unsatisfying as Hempel's model when our concern is with *explanation*.

One natural way of trying to enrich the Humean conception of cause is by appeal to fine structural considerations. Running diamond over glass with sufficient pressure will cause a scratch in the glass. Why? The explanation, we might think, lies not in the generalization that past encounters between diamonds and glass have had similar upshots, but that the fine structure of diamond is such that it is harder than glass. Likewise, we explain why sugar dissolves in water, or why adding chromium to steel makes the resulting material less liable to rust, by appeal to features of fine structure.

Here is an attractive move. Applied to Hempel's account, it suggests the analogous move of enriching his account of lawlike regularities by the addition of *models*. For Duhem such a move might be no more than evidence of shallow thinking.[15] But a suitable model for chemical reactions or for crystal structures will give us explanatory resources that generalizations alone cannot provide. This enriching move is not one to which I am at all hostile. On the contrary, we will shortly be looking at the relation between changes in things and alterations in their fine structure.

For the moment, we can perhaps note that the Humean has two replies to this latest move. One is to point out that retreating to details of crystal lattices or chemical structure explains nothing; for *at any level of structure* we are confronted again with the same old causal questions. Why does this atom of sodium occupy a particular position in a salt crystal? Hume's reply would be that all previously observed sodium atoms in such environments have taken up similar positions. Thus we have not reached any kind of ultimate explanation by appealing to the crystal structure in an account of the behaviour of salt.

A second reply is given by Hume himself. Suppose we say that diamond is hard because tetrahedral arrangements of carbon atoms are good at resisting pressure and deformation. But what justifies our confidence that the *next* diamond we pick up will have a similar fine structure? Only, apparently, a causal inference! As Hume says:

> The bread which I formerly ate nourished me; that is, a body of such sensible powers was, at that time, endued with such secret powers. But does it follow that other bread must also nourish me at another time, and that like sensible qualities must always be attended with like secret powers? The consequence seems nowise necessary. (*Enquiry*, section IV. ii)

Whereas the earlier Humean response threatened a regress of explaining constant conjunctions by underlying mechanisms which in turn display constant conjunctions explained by underlying mechanisms . . . and so on, the second reply suggests that every appeal to an underlying mechanism is simply question-begging.

These are undoubtedly powerful replies. And, like all the best forms of scepticism, it is hard to find convincing rebuttals. One consolation is that Hume's 'thin' notion of causality as constant

---

[15] Duhem follows Pascal in making somewhat astonishing claims about kinds of mind: 'The English mind is clearly characterised by the ample use it imaginatively makes of concrete collections and by the meagre way in which it makes abstractions and generalisations. This peculiar type of mind produces a peculiar type of physical theory; the laws of the same group of phenomena are not coordinated in a logical system, but are represented by a model.' (Duhem [1], p. 86.)

conjunction is ideally suited to our fantasy case. Once we are aware of the discontinuities afflicting hills, we can test to see if changes at one time leave their mark on later occasions. Sure enough, material quarried from one hill stage leaves its mark on later stages. As predicted by Hume, we will thus be led, having observed a change in one hill stage, to *expect* a comparable change in its successor. Of course, Hume would point out that no sound inference underlies this expectation. Hills that disobey the conservation principles are not logically impossible, and such things would not display this sort of regularity. One advantage of philosophical fantasy, however, is that we can control the plot, so long as we keep within the bounds of consistency. And in my story the hills obey conservation constraints of a sort: the stages do survive as their successors and we would, no doubt, in such situations find ourselves with suitably Humean expectations.

It may seem that even the Humean has to be committed to spatio-temporal continuity as a necessary condition of identity by dint of one last set of considerations. According to these, since identity is a causal notion, then persistence through time is bound to involve continuity from one stage to another. It may be anxiety on this very point which led Shoemaker to write, 'if material persistence requires spatiotemporal continuity, then this is because the relevant sorts of causality require it'.[16] Suppose, for example, it were argued

---

[16] The quotation is from Shoemaker [6], p. 242. It is interesting to note the similarities and differences between Shoemaker's account of unity as a causal relation, and my own. Many of his general remarks (e.g. about the inadequacy of the spatio-temporal continuity account of identity) are ones with which I have no quarrel. However, in his own account of how causation is involved with unity, there is a significant divergence from the position I argue here. Causation in my story is internal, so to speak, in the way it operates; it is a kind of binding force that ties the different components together into a long chain which constitutes the life history of 'he broad object. By contrast, Shoemaker gives an account in which causality has an xternal role to play. For him, a temporal part is a complex of property instantiations. A broad particular (like a saw) will thus have various causal powers in virtue of its temporal stages being co-instantiations of various properties. See his essays 'Causality and Properties' and 'Identity, Properties and Causality' in Shoemaker [6]. How can an account like this be relevant to cross-temporal unity? Shoemaker spells it out as follows: 'Since a specification of the essential nature of a property will involve a specification of the powers to which it has the potential for contributing, and since a specification of the powers will say what happens to their subject *over time* given certain conditions, the essential nature of a property incorporates the persistence conditions, that is the cross-temporal identity conditions, of the things to which it can belong.' (Shoemaker [6], p. 253.) As far as I can see, Shoemaker's account thus leaves to one side the kind of causal connection among stages that are so significant to the survival issue.

that if one event is the cause of a second event, then there is always some further event which is in causal relations to both. Likewise, if one stage is causally productive of some other stage, there would have to be some third stage which can be interpolated between the first two, and which stands in causal relations to both. The idea is that causation satisfies a kind of interpolation principle reminiscent of Craig's well-known lemma. A successful argument for such a causal principle would indeed show that the Dumyat case is not one where the various hill episodes can be causally related.

Nothing in the points made so far about explanation count against this argument. And if the argument could be established, even a Humean would have to admit that causal relatedness implies continuity. However, I can see no reason for taking the argument seriously as a point about causation. Think of the spatial correlate of the argument. It would involve maintaining that between any two causally related parts there will always be a third part causally related to the other two. The closer we look into the fine structure of objects, the less plausible such a claim looks. Likewise, turning our attention in quite the opposite direction, it is clear that distant objects exert gravitational effects on the earth. The theory of gravity, however, in no way requires that we be able to construct a chain of interpolated bodies between the earth and such distant bodies.

We thus come back to the case of gravity, which prompted the excursion into the theory of explanation in the first place. It now looks as if some ways of enriching the Humean account of cause would force us into denying that discrete and discontinuous stages are really in causal relations with each other. But we can also resist such enrichment by staying content with a 'thin' notion of cause (and with a correspondingly 'thin' notion of explanation). In doing philosophy of science, we sometimes fall prey to an all-or-nothing tendency, which I am eager to resist. The result of the present discussion should not encourage anyone to think that all cases of causal explanation will be equally thin. In some cases, we will be able to enrich the statement that there are Humean conjunctions with descriptions of mechanisms in terms of which we can understand the occurrence of the conjunctions. But there is no reason to believe this holds in all cases. We can state the principles governing gravity (for example, the inverse square law), associate gravity with a field, and still regard it as a force that acts at a distance. Our explanations of gravity may always remain 'thin', in my sense. Just so, if there turned out to be discontinuities of the sort imagined to afflict Dumyat, we would be able to give only 'thin' explanations of why changes in one stage bring about effects in later stages.

4.6. MINDS, RADIO SERIALS, AND DOORS

For the present I do not want to dwell at length on questions about matter, which will be clarified in the sixth chapter. We know that at the submicroscopic level what matter an item is made of is associated with the details of its fine *structure*. Our telemutation case in Chapter 3 has shown that things can survive a change of fine structure, hence a change of matter, so long as their macroscopic structure and overall dimensions remain fairly constant. Thus there would be circumstances where, if we managed to transmute the material of a certain object, while preserving its form, we would judge that the original object had, to some degree, survived *in*, or *as*, the new item. There are perfectly good reasons, given the nature of human perceptual mechanisms, just why we should make such judgements of survival.[17] It is hardly surprising, then, that the similarity of overall geometric structure between each D_i and its neighbours is an important component in underpinning our identification of the scattered whole consisting of the various stages with one thing of the sort *hill*. In terms of the notion of survival, the situation could be described in the following way. Each D_i survives as the subsequent D_{i+1} provided our three conditions are met. And the chain of survival relations among the stages is precisely what establishes the claim that the scattered whole in question constitutes one hill—a claim that can be made in either the Fig. 9 or the Fig. 10 case.

When we turn to the parallel psychological case in a later chapter, it might seem that at the level of functional description suggested by the use of terms like *intention, need, desire, memory,* and so on, a mental state is not to be taken as a concrete item. Nevertheless, it is possible to look for analogues for the three conditions. The contents of short- and long-term memory, material undergoing perceptual

---

[17] This is argued, among other things, by McCabe in McCabe [1].

processing, one's store of ambitions, intentions, and so on can call be regarded as in some sense psychological *matter*. This material is no doubt *structured* within devices (thus long-term memory has, among others, a semantic level of organization) which themselves have *structural* relations with each other. The recollecting from long-term memory of an experience entered some time before would be an example of how a structural change in one state is in part *causally* dependent on a material (and associated structural) change in an earlier state. We will follow up to implications of this analogy when we come to discuss the puzzles associated with amnesia and branching in Chapter 9.

To suggest a different application of the model proposed here, let us suppose that, as a kind of practical joke, the Stirling Philosophy Department records an entirely bogus episode of *The Archers*, and cunningly arranges for it to be broadcast in place of one of the regularly scheduled episodes. A soap opera is, of course, an episodic object whose scattered episodes are all allocated to the one item. Now it is immediately clear that our bogus episode of *The Archers* could pass for the real thing if we ensure that it satisfies the appropriate correlates of our three conditions. It might be objected that *matter, structure,* and *lawful causal relations* can only be talked about in a metaphorical way in connection with such an example. But if we achieve the dovetailing of our bogus episode with its neighbours, by means of reasonably stable characterization, good mimicry of the voices of the several characters, continuation of the action, adoption of the appropriate style, and so on, then we would have again satisfied at least metaphorical counterparts of our three conditions. One way of thinking about it is as follows. Let the fictional *matter* of an episode be the various characters, the village of Ambridge, its surrounding farms, and a number of happenings (which we can take to be event types). The *structure* of an episode is then given by the various relations exhibited in the episode among the characters, places, and happenings. On this view, structure changes throughout an episode. The supposed *causal* dependence of one episode on another may be revealed in the way the terminal structure of one episode induces a specific initial structure in its successor. More likely, perhaps, structural changes in earlier episodes map onto the structure of the current episode in an appropriate (though complex) way. Indeed, if we carried it off well enough, our episode might well have to be reckoned to the total of episodes that constitutes *The Archers*, and in this way our example threatens the view that the identity of the series depends on the authorized script in much the way that the identity of a musical work might be held to depend on the composer's score.[18]

We can further test the three conditions by considering what our response to various other cases might naturally be. Would we be inclined to count a stage of Mount Everest along with a subsequent stage of the Empire State Building as constituting one thing of a kind? Surely not, and the reason is that we have neither a structural, material, nor causal basis for such a claim. Now visualize a corridor with a number of similar doors facing on to it. We discover, let us suppose, that doors, too, are afflicted with Dumyat-like discontinuities. How would we decide whether a given door was hopping on the spot or changing places with others elsewhere on the corridor? Our conditions suggest, once again, the way to seek an answer. We make a scratch on one door-stage and then see if this slight structural modification reappears on the next door-stage to occupy the same doorway (assuming, of course, that we have settled the matter of the identity of the doorway). If it does, and the new door-stage is made of similar material to the original, then we have a fairly good case for concluding that we can allocate the new stage to the same door as we allocated the original. Our scratch test also provides prima facie evidence of the right sort of causal dependence between stages.

4.7. A NON-MEREOLOGICAL SOLUTION

All this looks like good news for those who are happy to accept a mereological stance. Since they are comfortable in the recognition of scattered objects as individuals in any case, mereologists would find the suggested conditions helpful in letting them identify, from among the vast range of individuals, those which are unitary, albeit discontinuous, objects of a kind. Would they need, in addition, a *sortal* condition to justify such assignments of stages to scattered wholes? We might at first think that it is the fact that each D_i falls under the same sortal which along with our other conditions clinches the question of Dumyat's identity. But here we must be

---

[18] See the discussion in Goodman [3].

wary; for it is not clear what *explanatory* force such a sortal condition would have. In the case of living things, what would lead us to class a number of objects as all falling under some same sortal? Domestic cats all display certain structural similarities to each other, have similar material constitution and depend causally for their structure and matter on the structure and matter of their parents. Indeed, as I have already argued, one natural way of thinking about survival is in terms of the way parents can be said to survive in their offspring, and where we have survival then we have some degree of structural similarity, lawful causal dependence, and—often—similarity of material constitution. So if—for the sake of the argument at least—we suppose that the sortal 'hill' can apply to any of our stages in the Dumyat case, our three conditions seem to explain why the same sortal applies to other stages. We add nothing to the conditions by attempting to impose a further requirement concerning sortals.

But does the sortal 'hill' apply to any of our stages? This is a matter over which we must be extremely careful. To count the various scattered Dumyat stages as stages of one hill is not to imply that any of the stages themselves is, properly, an item of the sort *hill*. Quinton's doctrine might come to mind here. No doubt there are things such that ten-second, ten-hour, or ten-day manifestations of them would be, in his words, 'perfectly good things of that kind'. But it is not clear that whales, icebergs, and hills are examples of such things. Suppose something looking like a mature whale puts in a ten-minute appearance in my garden. Naturally, I wonder where it came from and where it subsequently went. Now suppose that I find it had no previous or subsequent history: I saw the entire life of a ten-minute individual. Was it a whale, or a stage of a whale, that I saw? Either proposal seems doubtful, and the example suggests that Quinton's claim is not at all self-evident. To accept it is to deny that persisting things have histories—where this means more than a life of ten minutes—though of course this claim itself is not safe from scepticism.[19] There is, however, a truth which corresponds to Quinton's claim. This is that, roughly speaking, each stage allocated to an item of kind S should possess that structure in virtue of which a succession of such stages, connected according to our require-

---

[19] No claim, after all, is safe from scepticism and we can easily make sense of the last-minute creation puzzle. We do not *know* that the universe did not come into existence only five minutes ago, including us and all our apparent memories.

ments, would be an *S* rather than anything else. We will give this issue some more attention in the next chapter.

This, then, completes the description of one kind of solution to the puzzle we started with. To accept the solution requires in turn an acceptance of a mereological stance, and this is certainly not congenial to everyone. However, the mereologist has proved to be in a strong position for making sense of the bizarre state of affairs in which we find ourselves confronted with a world of discontinuous objects. What we must do now is shift metaphysical focus for a while and consider the prospects for a non-mereological solution. Such a solution is perfectly feasible, though leaving us with a rather more fragmented world than the mereologist's. For I want to suggest there is at least one way of coming to terms with the Dumyat puzzle which allows that in such an eventuality we would have to recognize that the world contains no broad objects. Whereas the mereologist saves the broad object at the cost of permitting it to be discontinuous, the alternative about to be mooted recognizes that each D_i is a new object and tries to preserve our use of the same name for each such object in the face of this recognition.

Let us agree that considerations about structure and so forth do indeed suggest that each D_i survives as its successor. Why not now use the name 'Dumyat' for any extended stage and use the argument from survival to justify using the name for any appropriately related stage? Of course, we are not now, literally, speaking of *stages* at all, for there is no broad object to which we are assigning the various things called 'Dumyat'. Rather, we are following the convention that we use a name to apply to an item or to any clear survivors or ancestors of that item. This is to depart from the orthodoxy that the *identity* of an object is what makes sense of the application to it of the same name at different times. But in a world lacking suitably broad objects, there may be little point in trying to persist with the orthodox view.

Strictly, then, any claim about Dumyat is really a claim about past, present, or future Dumyats. For any item called 'Dumyat' will—if our original case is recalled—last no more than 167 hours; and of course, we will not know in the normal run of things whether a new Dumyat has come on the scene even as we speak about the hill. Can we really make sense of this as an alternative to the mereological view just canvassed? I think we probably can, once we have managed to focus down onto a world where things have strictly limited persistence. Nor, incidentally, is it being suggested that in some way Dumyat supervenes on the various short-lived stages occupying a certain place. Rather, the present suggestion is that we drop the notion that there is some one persisting thing that is the aggegate of all the structurally and materially similar items that successively occupy one and the same place and that we do not retreat either to a conception of some supervenient item occupying that place. Instead, we believe that there is a sequence of Dumyat's, each one a different hill, and the survival of each hill in the sequence as its successor is what legitimizes the application of the same name to each succeeding item. We are in a position rather similar to that of the person who ostends various river-stages while uttering the same name; but instead of this procedure being used, as in Quine's example, to show that we are talking about one spatio-temporally extended object, we are to be taken as indicating that we are talking about a sequence of items, each of which is a survivor fo the item originally ostended.

One argument which is *not* being suggested here would be based on the theory that some underlying causal process is responsible for the appearance of each succeeding hill. We are thus not taking seriously the possibility that Dumyats come about as the result of a *production process*. Of course, it is open to us to suggest that there is some, perhaps divine, production-line involved in churning out each of the separate hills. But, as we saw in our discussion earlier, although each Dumyat might then replicate the others (plus or minus quarried stuff and forestry plantations) we would not be able to talk of one surviving in or as any of the others. We would have successive tokens of the type *hill*, indeed, but no survival.

That the production story is not what is being given here is quite easily seen, and since it is different it will require a different treatment. In telling our story, it was made clear that changes in one episode *showed up in the subsequent ones*. So the effects of today's quarrying, for example, will still show up next week and the week after that. This is typical of the situation in a *copying process*. Even if a divine being were producing each subsequent hill episode, the previous episode still has a causal role as the model from which the copy is made. So the theory of survival thus remains applicable, and our suggestion is that the survival of each short hill as its sucessor would legitimize our application of the same name to admittedly distinct objects.

Now although such a procedure seems possible in theory, would it not prove entirely unworkable in practice, due simply to the enormous difficulties involved in saying simple things like 'I mean to climb Dumyat tomorrow'? I suspect that, if we were to adopt this second solution, then, whatever our official metaphysical view, we would find ourselves speaking about Dumyat in much the way we currently do. This is not all that hard to explain. After all, we do use language in other contexts that seems natural even while we are aware that it is not quite exact. For example, the sentence 'The sun rose at 8 a.m. this morning' clearly needs to be paraphrased in terms of one mentioning the rotation of the earth before a truth can, strictly speaking, be expressed. A worse problem may seem to confront us if we recall the worries already expressed about Quinton's doctrine. Would not the claim 'Dumyat is a hill' now fall foul of the criticism that what we are doing is predicating '. . . is a hill' of some temporal phase of an object? This worry, though, is seen to be misplaced once we recognize that, on the view presently being canvassed, there is no *one* thing which each Dumyat is. Some objects may run for more than 167 hours. But in a world of impermanent things, perhaps 167 hours of a hill is all that we are going to get of it. The broad object, then, is the 167-hour hill; thus, while the mereological response to the puzzle was to wonder what features ensured that each D_i was a temporal part of the *same* hill, the present view takes these same features as explanatory of why we give the same name to each member of a sequence of distinct hills.

It does seem to me that this latest solution is considerably less attractive than the mereological one. Indeed, I have pursued it mainly to be able to contrast it with the mereological one, for this contrast reflects two different ways that science can have an impact on our thinking. According to our latest 'solution', we go on speaking as before while recognizing that our discovery has revealed a gap between our natural way of speaking and the way we have come to think—under the impact of science—things in fact are. The mereological solution, on the other hand, can be compared with the scientific discovery that the best microscopic description of seemingly solid and continuous objects requires us to recognize that they are composed of spatially discontinuous aggregates of tiny parts. The hardness of diamond, for example, can be explained by the structural relations among its discontinuous parts; likewise, the structural, and other, affinities between stages explains, on the mereological conception, how the scattered Dumyat-stages make one hill.

4.8. THE 'ONLY x AND y' PRINCIPLE

The three conditions appear to be sufficient rather than necessary for the survival of one stage as another. Given the plausibility of the mereological account, we might wonder if survival always underpins identity. One problem with taking such a line is that we can easily imagine a situation in which, after one of the gaps, two hills appear instead of just one. Indeed, these may be 'identical', and of course, this would mean that Dumyat was subject to fission. We have already looked at a case of fission, namely, the peculiar case of Theseus' ship (see Fig. 11). This time, we have changed the labels on the diagram, and have also acknowledged explicitly that we are thinking of three possible worlds, w_1, w_2, and w_3. Our symbols 'a', 'b', 'b'' and so on, this time are used, in Kripke's sense, as *rigid designators* for broad objects.[20] Each constant thus designates the same object in every world in which it designates anything at all. Now, a plausible view of the Theseus problem is that in w_1, b is a *continuer* of a in Nozick's sense, while in w_3, c is a continuer of a. As he puts it: 'To say that something is a continuer of x is not merely to say its properties are qualitatively the same as x's. . . . Rather, it is to

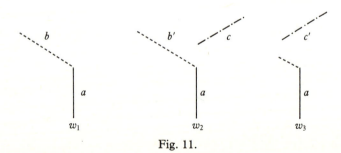

Fig. 11.

---

[20] See Kripke [2]. Notice that I am not here declaring myself for the necessity of identity, or for any associated doctrine of essentialism. Rather, I use the Kripkean mechanism simply to engage with those whose objections to the 'only x and y' principle start from Kripkean premisses. Essentialism and the necessity of origin are discussed further in Ch. 5.

say they grow out of x's properties, are causally produced by them, are to be explained by x's earlier having had its properties and so forth.'[21]

Using Nozick's terminology, the puzzle in w_2 is to determine which of b' and c is a's *closest continuer*, for in his view 'to be something later is to be its closest continuer'. An earlier proposal that we have already examined, due to Hirsch, is that we look for a spatio-temporally and qualitatively *continuous* succession of object stages that *minimizes change*. If we allow that there is continuity of material things in w_1, we can see that both the change-minimizing and the closest continuer proposals might seem to favour the verdict that a is one and the same as b', although neither Hirsch nor Nozick try to force this conclusion.

The theory of survival might seem to be usefully supplemented by these accounts. The theory allows that there is survival in each of w_1, w_2, and w_3 of a, allowing that in w_2, a survives as both b' and c. Why not, then, let change-minimizing or closest continuer-constraints determine our choice between the rivals in w_2 and thus settle the identity question? We could even introduce the notion of the *closest survivor* to apply to the item for which we would give our identity verdict. As we have seen, one virtue of thus speaking would be that we do not get distracted by considerations about spatio-temporal continuity.

Unfortunately, there is an objection to this way of proceeding. For the proposed way of dealing with identity in the w_2 case seems to leave us facing an uncomfortable dilemma. Either it turns out that what thing something is depends on the existence of other things, or the very existence of something depends on the existence or non-existence of other things. We can use an example from personal identity to illustrate the first horn of the dilemma. Suppose, as in Bernard Williams's example, I wake up one morning with all the memories of Guy Fawkes.[22] As we will see later, some theorists regard the presence of memories as a sufficient condition of personal identity. But if we agreed, even just for the argument's sake, that I am therefore Guy Fawkes, we get into trouble. For tomorrow, *you* may wake up with all Guy Fawkes's memories. By the memory criterion it follows that *you* are Guy Fawkes. But you and I are two

---

[21] Nozick [1], p. 35.
[22] The example is from Williams [1].

different persons. So either Guy Fawkes is two different persons, or neither of us is Guy Fawkes.

The problem this argument reveals is this. Surely, if I am Guy Fawkes, then the appearance of a rival cannot make any difference to this truth. So, in general, if x is one and the same as y, the truth of this cannot depend on facts about any other things. If we call this the 'only x and y' principle, then it seems to be incompatible with the approach just proposed—an approach that could be called a 'best candidate' theory. As Wiggins puts it, if we are willing to give our vote to a's closest survivor in w_2, 'we could walk up to the antiquarian's relic, seen as a candidate to be Theseus' ship, and say that, but for the existence of its rival . . . it would have veritably coincided as a ship with Theseus' original ship. But the idea that in *that* case it would have been Theseus' very ship seems to be absurd.'[23] What Wiggins is arguing here is that if we take 'c' and 'c'' as names of one and the same ship, then it cannot be the case that this ship has the same life history in both w_2 and in w_3. In w_3, if $c' = a$ then c' comes into existence at the very same time as a does. But this cannot be true of c in w_2. But those who believe in the necessity of self-identity will see the best-candidate theory as denying this principle, a principle enshrined in Butler's maxim that each thing is what it is and not another thing.[24] Wiggins adds: 'There is a temptation to add as a *step* to this argument: nothing might have been a different entity from the entity it actually is. But the temptation is to be resisted. We are discovering in this argument . . . the real intuitive grounds for doubting that anything might have been a numerically different thing from the one it actually is.'[25]

Recently, Harold Noonan has tried to strengthen Wiggins's argument here, thereby supplying the other horn of the dilemma. For, if each thing is *necessarily* what it is, then what it is cannot depend on the existence or non-existence of rivals. So, then, let us suppose that we avoid this particular horn of the dilemma by allowing that c is distinct from c'. The four-dimensionalist can take just such a line. But to do so is to risk being impaled on the other

---

[23] Wiggins [9], p. 95.

[24] This remark has become a philosophical commonplace since Moore used it as the epigraph for his *Principia Ethica*. However, despite the vast number of authors who cite it, the source of the remark in Butler is seldom given. After a vain search through some of Butler's works, I have decided to maintain this tradition.

[25] Wiggins, loc. cit.

horn: for it now seems that c' is not present at all in w_3. So what we are calling 'c'' in w_2 *would not have existed at all* but for the presence of its rival, b'. But this is just as absurd, Noonan claims, as our previous position.

Now what is this thing that would not have existed at all but for the existence of b'? Noonan speaks of it as 'the plank-hoarder's ship in situation 2', and perhaps the worry here could be expressed in the following way. In w_2 there are two ships, namely a (Theseus' original ship) which conventional wisdom identifies with b' (the continuously repaired ship), and also c (the plank-hoarder's reconstruction). But in w_3 there is just the one ship, a, which the best-candidate theory identifies with c', the plank-hoarder's one. The plank-hoarder's ship, c, is a ship in its own right in w_2, while in w_3 it is but a temporal part of a much broader entity. If we held the view that temporal parts of ships, or aggregates of such parts, are not themselves ships, then our present difficulty would seem to be intensified. For whereas c in w_2 is a ship in its own right, there is no such ship present in w_3 (for in that situation the plank-hoarder's ship is said by the best-candidate theory to be none other than Theseus' original ship).

Noonan, however, cannot claim this kind of support for his argument. For in another recent paper he explicitly maintains that 'it is reasonable to say that (some of) the temporal parts of an enduring object of sort S are themselves of sort S', and the qualification 'some of' here simply rules out those stages that are very short.[26] Let us suppose—for the sake of definiteness—that in w_2, the plank-hoarder's ship comes into existence at the moment the hull is complete. On Noonan's own view, then, an entity of the sort *ship* must also come into existence at that time in w_3. So some same ship is present in both w_2 and w_3, although only in w_2 is that ship a maximal aggregate of ship stages. So c is present both in w_2 and in w_3 (although in w_3 it is only part of the broader ship c'). This, however, undercuts Noonan's attempt to convict his opponents of absurdity. As he writes, the best candidate theorist '. . . must then acknowledge that the following is a possibility: we could walk up to the plank-hoarder's ship in situation 2 . . . and say (truly) that, but for

[26] In Noonan [7]. To be fair to Noonan, he does not give any support in the paper to the temporal-part metaphysic. Rather, he argues for the plausibility of the claim given *provided* we allow that objects have temporal parts.

the existence of its rival it would never have existed *at all*.'[27] So far from this being a claim to which the best-candidate theory is absurdly committed, it is one that—by Noonan's own lights—it would have to deny.

It is helpful at this point to consider what a mereologist would be able to say about our problem. Using the term *individual* in the mereologist's technical sense to apply to any object however scattered it may be in space-time, if a temporal part of a ship is an individual, so will a collection of such parts be. Further, the natural way for a mereologist to read the labels in Fig. 11 is as rigid designators for collections of temporal parts (Nozick, for example, does so in his discussion of related problems in the notes to his book). On this reading, of course, $b = b'$ and $c = c'$, quite uncontroversially. The best-candidate theorist who is also a mereologist can now make identifications as follows. In w_1 Theseus' ship is the individual consisting of the collection a together with the collection b (let us write '$a + b$' for short). In w_2 Theseus' ship is also $a + b$ (notice that $a + b = a + b'$) and in w_3 Theseus ship is $a + c$. Of course, the *individual* $a + c$ (which is none other than $a + c'$) is also present in w_2, but in that world, it is not a ship, let alone Theseus' ship.

Noonan is not out to get the mereologist. On the contrary, he explicitly allows best-candidate theorists to take the four-dimensionalist view if they so wish. But can he now convict me of absurdity in any of the things I have just said? Perhaps the point is that the *object* $a + c$ is just not present in w_2 at all. Since the stage a is, so to speak, already allocated, along with b to Theseus' ship, then there is nothing, namely $a + c$, which might have been a ship in other circumstances (say, those which prevail in w_3). But why deny the existence of the mereological individual in this way? One motive for doing so would be the belief that distinct objects cannot have temporal parts in common. Now, in the spatial case, there is no puzzle. The sides of my desk and the top of my neighbour's desk might, in other circumstances, have constituted one desk. Of course, they do not do so in this world. So the same parts can be parts of distinct objects. In the temporal case, we can think again of

[27] In Noonan [6]. The arguments attributed to him in the text are also presented in Noonan [5], [7], and [8].

Hirsch's example of the tree and its trunk.[28] A tree is not the same thing as its trunk. But one year, let us suppose, the tree is pollarded so that every branch is cut right back to the trunk. Until new shoots appear, the tree and the trunk coincide. Later, the tree recovers: it and the trunk continue to have different life histories, but these histories now share a common stage. Likewise, $a+b'$ and $a+c$, though distinct, share a common stage.

So it looks as though the best-candidate theorist who opts for the four-dimensional way can deal with the fission case without falling into absurdity after all. It does follow from this, certainly, that one and the same thing—Theseus' ship—is identified with different mereological individuals in different worlds, namely $a+b'$ and $a+c$ (remember that we are still using 'a', 'b', and so on, as rigid designators for collections of stages). This, though, is hardly surprising, given that principles of identity do not apply to cases of transworld identification without some modification. For alternative worlds are precisely those in which the possibly different histories of objects are realized. On what I have called the 'conventional' view, Theseus' ship is present in all three depicted worlds. It has the property of being $a+b'$ *in* w_2 and of being $a+c$ *in* w_3, and with this kind of world-indexing there is no problem about the necessity of such claims as 'Theseus' ship $=a+b'$'. Without world-indexing of properties—or some equivalent device—we would have problems, and not just problems about the necessity of identity. So we could now perhaps try to give a mereological gloss on Butler. Each *individual* is the individual it is and not another individual. But what *sort* of thing an individual is in one world (if any) depends on the existence or non-existence of other individuals in that world.

Salmon, as pointed out in the footnotes, has an argument rather similar to the one I give here, only his involves appeal to the *matter* out of which ship a is constituted. His account, like mine, preserves the necessity of identity. Thus it is *not* a contingent fact, for his account, that Theseus' ship is built originally out of certain planks and other bits. But it *is* a contingent matter thereafter just what matter we deem as constituting *that* particular ship. More will be

[28] Hirsch [2], ch. 2. Salmon does the same trick using matter that I perform here using stages. He notes that it is a *contingent* fact which matter constitutes a certain ship at a time later than its original construction. See Salmon [1], Appendix I.

said about problems of necessity of origin and identification of items across worlds in the next chapter.

4.9. BARE PARTICULARS

More will also be said in the following chapter about transtemporal and crossworld identification. It is already clear from my response to Noonan's arguments in the previous section, however, that the analogies between worlds and times are likely to be worth pursuing. Just as the same item has a number of different temporal parts, so the same item will be constituted of different stage collections in different worlds.

It is worth, however, noticing just what elements of my treatment of the best-candidate issue have involved *ad hominem* attacks on Noonan, and which have involved a real rejection of the 'only x and y' principle. Although Noonan's is the most sustained attack on best-candidate theories that I know of, it would be a breach of my own methodological norms to argue that my attack leaves it unnecessary to argue separately for the falsity of the 'only x and y' principle.

There are two claims which Noonan deems to be absurd but which, on my account, are sensible commitments of those willing to adopt the four-dimensional account. These are:

(a) events which constitute the origin of some entity of a certain sort in one situation may not constitute the origin of that, or any entity of the kind, in a second situation, even though all the events constituting the history of that entity in the first situation remain present in the second;

(b) two events may be part of the history of a single entity in some situation, but may fail to be part of the history of that, or any single entity of the kind, in a second situation in which both they, and all the events which were parts of the history of the entity in the first situation, remain present.[29]

Now Noonan does not take seriously the thought that the second and third situations depicted in Fig. 11 are likely to differ in ways consequent upon the premature destruction of the original ship in the third case. Of course, in any real situation where a plank-hoarder was at work, the history of the hoarder's reconstruction is

---

[29] Noonan [6], p. 81.

quite likely to be influenced by the early demise of the continuously functioning ship.

However, even if we stick with the artificial restriction that the two situations are alike in all respects except for the early destruction of the continuously functioning ship, we can see that there is nothing absurd about either (a) or (b). What removes any puzzlement we might at first feel in the face of these claims is the distinction between mereological individuals and objects belonging to natural or artefactual sorts or kinds. It is true that all the events constituting the origin of a certain individual in the second case are also present in the first or third situations. But the poblem, as the mereologist would see it, is to determine which of the individuals, or collections of individuals, in each case constitute ships, and indeed constitute Theseus' ship. It is a kind of lassooing problem. Here are these various individuals; our problem is to put a noose round the appropriate sum-individual constituting the ship we are after in each case.[30]

Thus (a) states a vital truth. Events which constitute the origin of an item of the sort ship in one case do not constitute the origin of an item of the sort ship in another. But in all cases, events which constitute the origin of a mereological individual constitute the origin of that same mereological individual. Likewise (b) states an important truth. There are events in one situation which are part of the history of a single object of the kind ship; in another situation, these same events are not part of the history of the same ship, nor of any ship at all! But in both situations, the same mereological individuals are present.

In thus distinguishing objects of sorts or kinds from mereological individuals we diagnose the sources of bewilderment in the face of (a) and (b) and give a plausible model for best-candidate theorists to use. Yet this does not show that best candidate theories are entirely satisfactory. As I will be arguing, in agreement with Parfit, there is a way in which acceptance of best-candidate theories leads to a trivializing of identity. If rivals do make a difference to identity or unity, and hence 'only *x* and *y*' principle is false, then it is almost an immediate inference to the conclusion that identity cannot be as important as is often thought. Unity, or identity, is important in

---

[30] I learned the vocabulary of 'lassooing' from Forbes [3], where it is applied to set theory rather than to the mereology.

normal situations simply because other important relations and characteristics are associated with it. The kind of fission case encountered in the literature on personal identity, like the fissioning of Theseus' ship, splits apart unity on the one hand from those other things that are of importance. As we saw in Chapter 3.4, the sea-going qualities of the original *Heraclitus* might, if they are preserved in the hoarder's reconstruction, make that ship an attractive purchase for someone for whom such qualities matter. Indeed, it is not hard to imagine a case like the second situation depicted in Fig. 11 where the continuously modified and refurbished ship turns out to give poorer and poorer handling qualities through time. Our identity or unity verdict, if it follows conventional wisdom, will through time become less and less well-aligned with our verdict on which ship gives the better performance.

It follows, then, that important relations and characteristics can be independent of identity. Without anticipating our later discussion too much, we can start to see even in cases like this that identity may not always be the important thing. So any support for the best-candidate theory is conditional on recognizing that it suits an account of identity where identity is not a very important thing. Indeed, identity or unity may depend on only fairly trivial things.

This said, we need to do justice to the intuition lying behind the 'only *x* and *y*' rule. The truth is that, where important relations between *x* and *y* are concerned, then whether such relations hold or fail to hold cannot depend on the existence of things other than *x* or *y*. Survival is one such important relation. Whether an item survives in or as another item does not depend, in the way identity does, on the existence or non-existence of other survivors. This conclusion will be argued at greater length in the treatment of personal identity and personal survival.

It remains to make sure that recourse to mereological individuals is not a recourse to anything metaphysically objectionable. It may seem that such individuals, while constitutive of things, are a kind of naked substratum out of which things as we know them are to be built. Further, how can a mereological individual fail to be something of a sort or kind? It will have, after all, identity conditions similar to those of sets: just as a set is something of the sort, *set*, so a mereological individual is something of the sort *individual*. This however, although true enough is not very interesting. To get clear on what is happening, let us consider for a moment why the philosophical nominalist is interested in individuals.

It is easy to see what is wrong with identifying collections of things with sets. Although we are often tempted to talk about a family as a set of people related in a certain way, of a species as a set of animals that can interbreed, and of the philosophical community as a set of thinkers, none of these descriptions can be taken very seriously. Sets, unlike species and communities, lack a geographical distribution; unlike families, they cannot make a joint decision. The reason for this is that sets are mathematical abstractions, incapable of causal commerce with things and lacking space-time coordinates. Sets therefore have an impact on ontology that is uncomfortable to the nominalist. Take *ZF* set theory with individuals (*ur-elements*) for example and consider how the iterative conception of set is employed. First, at the bottom of the hierarchy are all these objects which are clearly not sets—the individuals. At the next level of the hierarchy are objects which are the sets of individuals. Having constituted such sets, we move to the next level of the hierarchy, where we can lassoo objects from the previous two levels to make sets of this level, and so on.[31]

Now nominalists are disinclined to treat anything as other than an individual. But, as far as non-nominalists are concerned, once we have the individuals, the rest of the hierarchy of sets can be generated with a sudden and startling inevitability. The world is found to contain not just individuals and constructions from these of other individuals, but an infinity of sets, of sets of sets, and so on. The nominalist resists all this, accepting only the generation of individuals from other individuals. Thus take the individual consisting of the top of my desk and the legs of the table that is in the same office. This individual is not a desk or a table: even if I tried to unite these parts into an artefact it would be a strange-looking thing. However, unlike the set whose elements are the top of the desk and the legs of the table, the scattered individual has an extent in space-time and enters into causal transactions with other things. Thus, for example, its parts are supported by the floor—the legs directly, the desk top somewhat less directly.

---

[31] See Forbes [3] again for more detail on conceptions of sets. Ch. 6 of the same book distinguishes *intrinsic* from the *extrinsic* (that is, causally isolated) features of objects, a distinction that is useful in arguments concerning the 'only *x* and *y*' principle.

The individual, like the corresponding set, does have strict identity conditions. We can think of the essential characteristics of individuals in just the same way as we think of the essences of sets. Thus, destruction of one of the table-legs would be destruction of the individual just described, even though we might regard the table itself (and, obviously, the desk) as surviving such an occurrence. Just as sameness of members guarantees sameness of set, by the extensionality principle, so sameness of parts guarantees sameness of individual.[32] So I have been somewhat remiss in distinguishing things of sorts or kinds from individuals—but not seriously so. Individuals are in a sense things of a sort. But what I have been emphasizing, put more precisely, is that only some things of the sort *individual* are things that belong to genuine sorts as defined, for example, along the lines of note 1 to the first chapter. Like 'thing', 'individual' is not to be counted as a genuine sortal term.

How, then, can something be both an individual and something of a genuine sort—a table, a chair, a tree, or whatever? The worry behind the question might be the following. Since destroying a leg from the table destroys the individual that is the aggregate of table-parts, but not the table, then any identification of the table with the individual aggregate must be mistaken. But such a worry fails to take account of the difference between constitution and identity. The table-parts are constituents of the table, but, as I have already emphasized, tables are not to be identified with either their three-dimensional constituents (their spatial parts) or with their four-dimensional constituents (their temporal parts). What a table is—at the very least—is an aggregate of parts, together with a certain structure and causal relations among the parts. As soon as we introduce the notions of structure and causality, we transcend any reduction of the object (from whatever perspective we view it) to its parts.

In this section, I hope to have shown two things. First, that the defence of best-candidate theories, subject to qualms about the importance of identity, does not depend on purely *ad hominem* attacks on the opponent of such views. And, secondly, we have seen that individuals are not really bare particulars. On the contrary,

---

[32] Jonathan Lowe brought the implications of this fact forcefully to my attention. To deny that the terms 'individual' and 'set' are not genuine sortals does complicate the task of defining sortal terms.

they have some properties that are rather similar to the properties of things belonging to genuine sorts, as we would expect given the fact that particulars belonging to sorts are—on the nominalist account—composed of individuals.

4.10. DAFFODILS

This chapter has revealed the strengths of a theory built on survival as its foundation. Such a theory seems a better candidate for explaining unity than any theory of identity using continuity as its fundamental notion. In looking at the two ways of dealing with our discontinuous hill example, we noted that survival, moreover, had a role to play even if we took the three-dimensionalist's solution. Our latest consideration of best-candidate theories has at last revealed the truth in the 'only x and y' rule. This does not mean, however, that best-candidate theories are thus given a clean bill of health: rather, we are no longer faced with simple choices.

To conclude this chapter, we will look at objects significantly different from hills and artefacts. Identity theorists have paid little attention to the identity verdicts we pass on the billions of denizens of our planet whose volume, shape, and colour change dramatically and regularly. In the temperate regions, for example, plants go though massive seasonal cycles of reproduction, growth, decay, and dormancy. Daffodils are perhaps as good an example here as any.

Although the romantic poets took daffodils as symbols for early beauty and untimely death, an individual daffodil can in fact survive for a very long time. Of course, like other flowers, they are commonly described as 'dying' when their blooms start to fade; but we all know that what dies is just the bloom and the stem, and we expect the same daffodil to provide its same early display of colour the following year. In fact, absorption of some of the material present in the green parts above the ground is important for the survival of the bulb below the ground.

At first, it seems as if daffodils pose quite worrying unity problems. In the intuitive sense of the term, there is 'continuity', let us grant, between the bulb of early spring and the tall, graceful flowering plant of later spring. But during the plant's growth, overall structure displays rapid changes, as does coloration. The sudden fall from glory to the decay and reabsorption of the summer again goes on at a rapid pace. So here we face a real test for our conditions on survival. Do they make sense of the daffodil's early spring stages surviving as—or in—its later ones?

The problem of stage survival for daffodils, as we will see, is critical later in our discussion of personal identity. If a relation like survival is to be in some sense constitutive of identity, then its failure of transitivity would apparently show that identity is not transitive. But, on the contrary, identity is clearly transitive: if x is identical with y and y with z then x is identical with z. So if survival is not transitive, it seemingly cannot be constitutive of identity. Of course, the so-called *ancestral* of the survival relation will be transitive. This is the relation that x has to z if x survives as y and y survives as z (we could call this 'weak survival' if we liked). But weak survival is precisely what we have *not* been talking about when we have discussed the survival of one thing to some suitably high degree in, or as, another thing.

Here we see again proof of Locke's insight, or of what we learned from the Eusa problem. Different possbilities of change are associated with different sorts of things. The changes from early spring to midsummer are entirely natural for daffodils—although they would be bizarre if they happened to other things. In fact, given the matter and structure of a February daffodil-stage, the structure and matter of its May-stage are fixed (barring accident) within fairly determinate limits. Our problem is that our conditions seem to be flouted; for there may well have been large structural and material changes over the two months.

We do not, however, have to fall back either on notions of weak survival, or on continuity considerations. The weak survival account would emphasize that linking our February- and May-stages are other stages closer together showing appropriately high, neighbourly degrees of survival. The continuity account would emphasize that the changes have come about via a continuous process satisfying the intuitive ideal of continuity discussed earlier. But high-speed film might prove fatal to this latter story in just the way it might to our everyday beliefs about the continuity of hills. So let us stay with our survival conditions and see what appropriate modifications we need to make to them to ensure that our verdict is that a February daffodil-stage does survive—*to a very high* degree— in a May- or September-stage.

It has already been hinted that different kinds of components will play different roles in determining survival. In the case of the three-stage rocket, the final stage, although usually relatively small, seems to be the one whose continued existence and functioning is essential to the continued existence and functioning of the rocket. Likewise, theorists of personal identity have been more interested in the relation of brains to identity than of hands. An obvious reason for such interest, maybe, is that we can tolerate damage more easily to our hands than to our brains. Likewise, daffodils can tolerate damage to their flowers and leaves more readily than they can to their bulbs. By speaking of 'tolerating' damage, I mean they can go on existing, and doing the things daffodils typically do, despite such damage.

The notion that some components are of more importance than others is hardly surprising. In the case of the daffodil, the important point is that such components are largely hidden from our view. What we see each spring is not the most important part of the plant as far as its existence and reproduction are concerned. And if we now plot the relations between this vital, but largely hidden, matter and structure, then we find a high degree of survival of *it* in the later stage.

Not only do bulb- and root-stages count for more—as far as daffodils are concerned—than flower-stages, we should note that the appearance of new flowers each spring is yet another example of what we have called a *production process*. This time, the cause for the production of replicating blooms is hidden in the daffodil's DNA. But succeeding years' flowers, while replicating each other down to the finest details, are *not* examples of flowers, surviving from one year to the next. If anyone says that this year's flower survives as next year's, then this is evidence that the term 'flower' is being used to apply to the plant, not to the bloom. For last year's bloom no more survives as this year's than does the first jar from the production-line survive as the thousandth.

It might be objected that if I have not examined either bulb or roots, and have only a hazy recollection of just where a certain bulb is located, I can none the less reliably identify a particular daffodil by attending simply to structural features of the flower. Is this not a case of the allocation of successive spring flowers to the same broad but discontinuous flower, not unlike our allocation of the various Dumyat-stages to the same hill? But daffodils, unlike hills, are individual production processes: no two produce 'identical' flowers. So the reappearance of replicas each year assures us that the same production process is still going strong. What the examination of the bloom permits is our testing the claim that last year's daffodil is still around, still in the same place and so on. But to say all this is compatible with admitting that last year's bloom does not survive at all.

These two results involving daffodils are of great importance. Our survival theory has emerged, modified to account for the fact that some parts loom larger than others in determining survival. Moreover, we have seen that replication of certain components need not mean survival of the earlier versions of these components. We will find, perhaps surprisingly, that proper attention to these points about daffodils has the potential for unlocking some of the mysteries of personal identity and personal survival.

Finally, what are we to make of the objection that since survival is not transitive it fails to be constitutive of identity? The objection is far from fatal. It would have force only if survival and identity were to relate the same things. But survival is a relation between stages, and identity is a property of a unified particular, an item of one sort. The history of a daffodil will be typically part of the history of some spatio-temporally broader vegetable item. At some point, the heap of decaying matter before us no longer counts as a daffodil, even if its matter shows continuity with a previously existing daffodil. Hence there will be stages of vegetable matter before us now in which earlier daffodil stages fail to survive to that degree required for daffodil-unity. It is thus not a failure of survival theory that survival to some specified degree lacks transitivity. This is precisely what we expect from a relation the holding of which is constitutive of unity of things belonging to sorts.

5
Stages, Sortals, and Possible Worlds

We have at various points made use of possible worlds, without making our methodology regarding them very explicit. It is now time to come clean. One good reason for doing so is that some theorists have suggested analogies between possible worlds on the one hand and temporal parts on the other. Additionally, we have seen in the preceding chapter how easy it is to get confused when talking about identity across possible worlds. So it is worth spending some time getting the whole business of possible worlds straight.

The first question in this area is why modern philosophers have wanted to follow Leibniz in talking about possible worlds at all. The simple, intuitively appealing idea lying behind such modes of discourse is easily grasped. We all know that it makes sense to suggest that I might have woken, say, one hour earlier than I in fact did this morning. Moreover, I might have had something quite different for breakfast, washed my hair with quite a different shampoo, and cycled to the university by a different route. Had any of these 'mights' been realized, then my history would be different from the way it in fact is. Nor would it have been difficult to bring about such changes. The things just described were all within my power: it just happened that I did not do them.

The alternatives to my actual history that are possible, that is things that I might or could have done—or that could have happened to me—are so far things that lie within the bounds of physical and practical possibility. However, we could go further and speculate about things that might have been episodes in my history even though they are impractical, or contravene the laws of physics that we currently accept. Maybe I could have raised the level of the North Sea by one inch this morning, or perhaps have telecloned to Pluto! These may not seem such real possibilities as the ones mentioned earlier, but they do not in any way contravene the laws of logic: they involve no outright contradictions. However widely or narrowly we understand the notion of alternatives to my actual history, it seems plausible to maintain that at least some alternatives are real possibilities for me. And this gives us a route into the idea of a *possible world*. For such a world is simply one in which one of my various possible histories is realized. The *actual world* is thus one among many possible worlds; alternatives to the actual world are ones where the things that happen are things that did not happen in the actual world but *might* have happened in it.

The notion of a possible world, thus described, is not one with which we should be too comfortable. Clearly, we can be more or less bold in our construction of such worlds, and someone who has already engaged in thought experiments involving the teleclone and discontinuous hills can hardly take too lofty an attitude here. But we can still note that there are significant worries associated with the introduction of talk about possible worlds. A very immediate one is whether it could really be *I* who woke an hour earlier this morning in some world which is an alternative to the actual world. Suppose I try to imagine just what this other world is like. What did I do in it when I woke at that different hour? Did I get up and have a shower, thus rising earlier and showering at a different time? If so, the initial imagined difference is starting to have knock-on effects. Maybe all sorts of things in my day would have been different if I had woken that hour earlier. But the more of such alternative happenings we think about, the wider the gap between my history in the imagined world and my history in this—the real—world. And this raises the question of whether it is really *me* who is being described as doing these things in the other world. Maybe there are real and open possibilities about what I can do tomorrow. But are we really to take seriously the possibility that *I* could have been up and dressed before eight this morning?

This line of reasoning seems to be suggesting that the future is open in a way the past is not. In one way, this is true enough. For although I can do nothing *now* about what time I in fact got up this morning, I can take steps at least to try to get up at some different time tomorrow morning. This openness of the future, however, is a separate point from the one about possible worlds. For just as I can now take steps to ensure that I will likely wake at some set time tomorrow morning, I could have taken steps yesterday to try to ensure that I woke an hour earlier this morning. Whether or not I now take steps to ensure that I waken at some set hour tomorrow, it is possible that I may, and possible that I may not. But it was also possible last night for me to have taken—or not taken—such steps. All that is true in the actual world is that I in fact, from the possibilities available, took no steps to ensure that I would waken before eight today.

If I am right that past futures were just as open to me as the present future is, then it looks as though we can make sense of the idea that I might well have had an alternative history (indeed, very many are available). If we still hesitate over saying that it was *I* who woke at seven in some alternative world, then we do have an alternative way of putting this matter. We can say, instead, that some *counterpart* of me woke in that other world and did all these consequentially different things. The move has certain virtues. It seems to preserve, for example, our indiscernibility principle for x and y in the case where $x=y$. Recall that where $x=y$, then every property of x will also be a property of y. But if I rose at eight this morning, I can hardly also have had the property of waking at seven: that is a property of my counterpart.[1]

This consideration is by no means conclusive. For, as an alternative to talking about counterparts, we could quite easily talk instead about the properties I have in various worlds. If we like, we could index properties to worlds, in the way suggested in the last chapter when we were discussing Noonan's defence of the 'only x and y' principle. Thus I may have the property of waking at eight in w_a (where 'w_a is the actual world) but have the property of waking at seven in some other world, w_b. On this view, I do not, of course, have any incompatible properties. For the property of waking at eight in one world is not inconsistent with the property of waking at seven in some other.

[1] David Lewis gives a clear account of counterpart theory in Lewis [2], 1.9. See also Lewis [1], and [5], and Kaplan [1]. Some readers, wary of possible worlds, may argue that possible worlds are best thought of in terms of propositions. For them, to talk about a possible world is no more than a figurative way of talking about consistent sets of true propositions. I have no objection to this way of reconstruing my appeal to the possible. But, as Robert Stalnaker has argued, there may be something to be said for thinking of propositions as analysable in terms of possible worlds, rather than vice versa. For worlds are less structured than propositions, the latter having complex relations of entailment, contradiction, contrariety, and so on with each other. A sensible maxim of analysis (and of science in general) is to explain the more complex in terms of the less complex. See Stalnaker [1], ch. 3.

5.2. WORLDS AND TIMES

The case we have just discussed has an interesting parallel in the study of broad objects in one world. For, if we restrict our attention to the careers of items within a given world, we have to face a similar problem. This problem has led some folk to think that identity-through-time must be a very different beast from identity-at-a-time. Think of Theseus' ship again. Shortly after setting out on her voyages, her oaken tiller is broken, to be replaced by one fashioned of beech. But now our original ship has the property of having a tiller of oak, while the repaired ship has the property of having a tiller of beech. These are different properties; so how can our repaired ship be one and the same with the original one?

To take another case, Socrates, so we think, was bald in his maturity. But as a youth he no doubt had lots of hair on his head. So how can Socrates the youth be the same as Socrates the mature, since one has a property the other lacks? These problems do not really pose much difficulty for the indiscernibility principle, for it is easy to see how to deal with them. The properties of an item need to be indexed to times in just the way that in the transworld case, properties were indexed to worlds. Thus Socrates had the property of being bald in 425 BC, let us say, and the property of having a good head of hair in 455 BC. There is nothing very peculiar about that! Likewise the ship had a tiller of oak when it set out on its voyages, and had a tiller of beech some ten years later.

We do not have to take the step of indexing properties to times, just as we did not have to index them to worlds. Such indexing, however, is one convenient way of dealing with both problems. And the analogy between the two sorts of indexing suggests that it is fruitful to pursue further analogies between worlds and times. Alvin Plantinga, for example, has suggested that we can highlight some bad arguments for the theory of counterparts by pursuing the analogy. For instance, one way some counterpart theorists put their view goes like this. Suppose we imagine a possible world as being like an alien territory we view through a special sort of telescope (what Kaplan once called a 'Jules Verne-o-scope'). Now how can we go about identifying me in one of these other worlds? As we look through our Jules Verne-o-scope, we cannot keep our eye out for someone who has the same appearance, mode of dress, and physical characteristics as me. For these are all things that may be different in other worlds. Nor can we keep a look-out for someone who behaves like me, for this is also something that might be very different from the way it is in this world. So we can give no real help to the observers as they strain to see what is going on over there—we can give no principled means of *identifying* me over there at all.

If the counterpart theorist tries to infer from these difficulties that *I* do not in fact exist over there in the other world, but only a counterpart of me, then a big mistake is being made. For a precisely parallel move would, as Plantinga suggests, lead us to maintain that I did not exist in the 1950s.[2] Just think about the difficulties of trying to single me out then by looking for someone with either my appearance or behavioural characteristics. That would just not be on, for in those days, I was an unbearded child, painfully shy, and different in many drastic ways from the way I am now. Even someone who knows me very well indeed might be quite unable to pick me out from a picture-gallery of children of the time. It does not follow from any of this, however, that I did not exist in the 1950s.

More recently, George Schlesinger has taken the analogy a stage further. He suggests that we should think of particular things as having spatial, temporal, and *cosmic* parts.[3] If we take the sum total of all the spatial parts of an item at a time, then we have a spatially complete, momentary item. If we sum all the temporal parts of a broad object, then we obtain an item that is spatio-temporally complete. Finally, if we combine all the spatio-temporally complete chunks of an item in all the worlds containing it, then we obtain a cosmically (or conceptually) complete item.

Put another way, the suggestion is this. Unitary, broad objects are *five*-dimensional. For in addition to the four dimensions of space and time, we have to consider a fifth, conceptual dimension. We have already suggested that Theseus' ship might, in different worlds, be constituted of different temporal parts. But, if we want to give a conceptually complete account of what we are talking about when we talk about *Theseus' ship*, then we must include not only its history in the actual world, but its alternative histories in all the possible worlds containing it. After all, our concept of Theseus' ship surely allows that it might have had a different history. So what

---

[2] Plantinga [1], pp. 94–5.
[3] See Schlesinger [1].

we find in any world, under the name 'Theseus' ship' is only a part, a world stage, so to speak, of a conceptually broader individual. Let us suppose that Theseus' ship did once ply its trade in the Mediterranean. In another world, it never left the Aegean. Both items (Theseus' ship in each world) are themselves simply parts of a broader item which embraces all the world stages of Theseus' ship.

Schlesinger's view has many advantages. An obvious one is that it makes sense of the debate between counterpart theorists and their rivals. For, on this new account, both parties are right up to a point. The counterpart theorist is right to insist that different things are Socrates in different worlds. For each world, on Schlesinger's view, only contains a stage of Socrates. Think of identity through time again. Of course Socrates as a child was different from Socrates as an adult, in this world. For these are two temporal stages of one broader thing. Following this idea through, we can now think of an alternative to indexing properties to worlds. We can instead, distinguish stages of particular items in worlds. Thus $Socrates_a$ can be distinguished from $Socrates_b$ where the former is the Socrates we know in this world, and the latter is the crafty politician Socrates might have been in some other world. Each of $Socrates_a$, $Socrates_b$, ... and so on, is one cosmic part, or world stage, of Socrates. So counterpart theorists were on to an important point after all.

The theorist who maintains that the term 'Socrates' univocally designates just one item in all the worlds where it designates at all is also right. We can see this if we think of the temporal part analogy. Bertrand Russell was alive and working on the foundations of mathematics in the early years of this century. He was also alive and active in the peace movement in the 1960s. In Schlesinger's terms, Russell had a 'foothold' in both 1905, let us say, and in 1960. What we mean by this is that temporal slices of Russell were contained in both these years. So one person existed at both times. Likewise, it is just one Socrates who has a foothold in alternative worlds. In this sense, Socrates may be said to exist in many alternative worlds, just as Russell existed at many different times.

5.3. ONTOLOGY

It looks as if, in one way, it makes little difference whether we index properties or individuals to worlds and times. The important thing, after all, is not to say anything silly. We might even wonder if our earlier device is not simply equivalent to Schlesinger's. Compare, for example:

(1) Russell has brown-hair-at-t.
(2) Russell has white-hair-at-$t^\star$.
(3) Russell-at-t has brown hair.
(4) Russell-at-$t^\star$ has brown hair.

Are not (1) and (3), (2) and (4) equivalent? It looks as though, however we express the temporal indexing, we can use sentences like these to replace sentences like:

(5) Russell has brown hair.
(6) Russell has white hair.

We might say that (5) and (6) lack fixed truth values: rather, they are true *at* some times and false at others. Like Quine's eternal sentences, (1)–(4) have fixed truth values and can be included without embarrassment in our theoretical account of the world, giving objective information in a timeless way.[4]

This approach will not do. Although (1)–(4) are timelessly true, they achieve this in very different ways. Sentences (1) and (2) introduce dated properties, by incorporating time reference into predicates. But (3) and (4) refer to dated individuals by associating the time reference with a proper name. Whereas we can introduce dated properties without making any new existential claims, we cannot say the same for the introduction of dated individuals. To talk about the item 'Russell-at-t' is to talk about a *new* entity which is not the same thing at all as Russell himself.

The issue here is one of ontology. In a Quinean spirit, I am suggesting that the introduction of new names designating individuals is more ontologically significant than the introduction of new predicates.[5] Now, many aspects of our discourse on things and their properties is obscure. And it is open to anyone to claim that a theory of things is best constructed by taking properties as fundamental. This is perhaps not the right place for an argument about ontological preferences, but it is worth refraining from

---

[4] Quine writes 'The relation of eternal sentences to our logic is like that of silver dollars to our economy, mostly we do not see them, but we reckon in terms of them.' (Quine [2], § 47.)

[5] See, for example, the essay 'The Scope and Language of Science' in Quine [5].

dogmatism. For on the conception of philosophy as theory, it is necessary that we be prepared to shift our preferences if so required by a good theory. So let us simply assume, for the purposes of the present inquiry, that Quine was right in holding that ontology is more under control than ideology, without this assumption committing us to any long-term metaphysical claims about the dubiousness of properties. But if we accept the Quinean point, then the form of words in (3) and (4) needs extra justification.

Luckily, it is quite an easy matter to supply this justification keeping within the spirit of the enterprise so far. We live, so we think, in a world of persisting items, themselves of various sorts or kinds. Socrates, Russell, Bradley's dog, my desk, and Mount Everest are all examples of such things. Since we have already assigned the term 'individual' a mereological sense, we need a new piece of vocabulary for such things. In keeping with our previous practice let us call them *particulars*, where 'particular' is our term for what Wiggins calls a 'continuant'. Of course, our persisting things need not trace a continuous path through space-time: thus we count a discontinuous hill as an enduring particular even though it is not, in any literal sense, a *continuant*. We then take it that, given our current ontological preferences, particulars are the basic furniture of the world. From this position, we can start to build theories.

Our problem here—put in its most general way—is to explain the unity or identity of a particular. Why is it that out of the mass of mereological individuals around, us, only certain ones are particulars? So far, the theory we have been mooting states that the unity of a particular is the consequence of certain relations among other things: these other things are the temporal parts or stages of particulars. The account seems, on the face of it, to be parallel to the physicist's. Here are all these diamonds, notably hard. This hardness is explained by appeal to the tetrahedral arrangement of carbon atoms in the crystal structure. Here is a fluid that resists compression. Again, the relations among its particles explains its incompressibility.

Now we can obviously identify, use, and trade in diamonds and various fluids without knowing any of the chemistry or physics relevant to explaining their properties. Likewise, we can use, identify, and handle the particulars in our environment without having any philosophical theory of their unity or identity. So temporal parts no more enter into our everyday descriptions of what is going on in the world around us than does the fine description of crystal structure. Rather, temporal parts are *theoretical entities*, with a role relative to specific theories of the unity of particulars. So we are admitting that our recourse to such items is ontologically significant, but we are at the same time giving a justification for this important move. The justification parallels the one we might give for the introduction of other theoretical terms and concepts. The existence of genes as particulate determinants of heritable characteristics was required by a decent theory of inheritance. Or, to take a more philosophical example, Frege's use of the notion of *sense* in his semantics is an argument for the introduction of such a notion into the theory of language.

Theoretical entities are not to be lightly introduced. We could modify Ockham's maxim to suggest that they be not introduced without utmost necessity. But we must also appreciate that the most interesting question about a proposed theoretical entity is not whether it exists but whether it contributes usefully to an illuminating theory. We have so far seen that there is a role for *stages* in two different theories of the unity of things. On one, the continuity theory, stages form parts of a continuous path through space-time supposedly traced by enduring particulars. This theory has not fared so well as its rival. The rival is the theory of stage survival. Let those stages that display a high enough degree of survival from one to another be said to be S-related. Then the alternative theory of particular unity is that a particular is no more than a maximal, non-branching S-related sequence of stages. By 'maximal' here we mean that no stage which is S-related to some member of the sequence has been left out of it. For simplicity's sake, let us leave aside the issue of what to say in a world in which branching, or fission, of large particulars is commonplace.

One important strand of empiricist thinking is at odds with both survival and continuity theories. Hume insists, famously, in the *Treatise* that all our distinct perceptions are distinct existences and that the mind never perceives any *real* connection between distinct existences (i. iv. 6). Quine's old notion that bodies are postulated in order to unify our divergent experiences may be thought to be about the best an empiricist could do by way of development of Hume.[6]

---

[6] See n. 8, ch. 2.

Taking all this seriously, we could have begun with the conception that temporal parts are themselves the real primitives. They would be the real-world correlates of Hume's distinct experiences. Then the problem facing us would have been how to get enduring things—particulars—in on the act. Their role as theoretical entities would have been to unify into appropriate chains those stages that are *S*-related.

In this way we would have ended up at a position close to Quine's. Broad particulars would themselves be no more than posits, objects of theory. As has already been pointed out, Quine's account can hardly claim much support from common sense. By contract, it looks like a virtue of my alternative mode of theorizing that it keeps the enduring particulars of common sense as the basic items of the world, introducing stages as new theoretical entites. There is a limit to how far we can press this supposed advantage, however. As Kant points out, in reviewing Hume's treatment at the hands of the Scottish common-sense philosophers, good sense and a critical intellect are of more importance to a philosopher than simple common sense.[7] In the end, those who are strongly wedded to common sense are liable to cavil at our penchant for explaining the unity of particulars at all. For, to them, as we have already noted, such unity is immediately obvious to common sense in the first place!

So, to identify enduring particulars as basic items is to break with the tradition represented by Hume and Quine. Notice that in so doing, we are not necessarily taking all identifications of particulars as final. Rather, we should think of such identification as provisional. Our final theory will very likely justify the vast majority of our normal identifications, but it is also likely to legislate for some areas where our provisional identifiations will need to be revised. There is no reason why we should resist this impingement of theory on everyday practice—unless, of course, we think the theory is worthless! Perhaps more worrying is the thought that there may well be areas where theory cannot legislate at all, that not every

---

[7] 'I should have thought that Hume had as good a claim to sound sense as Beattie, and on top of this to something that Beattie certainly did not possess, namely a critical reason, which keeps common sense within limits, so that it does not soar into speculation and lose itself, or if speculations alone are at issue, does not try to decide anything, not knowing how to justify itself concerning its own principles; for only thus will it remain sound sense.' (Kant [2], pp. 8–9.)

problem case has a solution. But we should be no more worried by this (though no *less* worried) than by the fact that there are physical problems, and physical observations, about which physical theory is baffled.

5.4. THE PROPERTIES OF STAGES

With this account of our project in mind, we can look more closely into the nature of these theoretical entities we have introduced. One way of getting to grips with stages is to tackle the irritating question of whether the stages of an *F*-thing are themselves *F*-things. Although we have already encountered this question, and laid the foundations for answering it, we must be wary of thinking it an easy one. It is hard to retreat from some initial opinion here, and get away from thinking that it is just obvious that a desk-slice, for example, is (or is not) a desk. The right answer has already been hinted at rather broadly. This is that a *proper* desk-slice in one world is not a desk in that world, but some desk-slices—if carved carefully enough—could have been desks, that is they are desks in some other possible worlds.

A number of authors, including Lewis, Noonan, Quinton, and—perhaps—Schlesinger, do seem to think it plausible to count a proper temporal part of an *F*-thing as itself an *F*-thing. By a 'proper' temporal part I mean a temporal part that is less extensive than the whole to which it belongs. The real problem is whether we are to count such proper stages as, let us say, two hours of a television set, a tree, or a whale as themselves television sets, trees, or whales.

We can adapt from George Schlesinger one argument for the claim that proper parts of *F*-things are *F*-things. It will not do. He points out that if Fred came to dinner with him from 6.30 to 8.30 yesterday evening, then we can take it that all of Fred's spatial parts were present in the Schlesinger house, although only a two-hour temporal part was.[8] But suppose that Fred was someone who had just *come into existence* a few moments before 6.30 and who vanished into thin air immediately after 8.30. Schlesinger writes that in this case 'our experiences with him during the two hours of his visit

---

[8] Schlesinger [1].

would be absolutely indiscernible from what they would be if we had visiting us but a very small temporal part of a person with a life span of ninety-five years'. Such an argument, however, no more shows that a two-hour-long Fred is a person, than an experience caused by a cardboard model of a car shows that cardboard models are cars.

As we have already noticed, experience is non-specific. What is qualitatively the same experience may be produced by different objects. We can see this most easily by reflecting on replicas. My experience produced by staring at one metal model of the Eiffel Tower may be indistinguishable from the experience brought about by staring at another, exactly similar, model. But the models are different. As Alan Millar has put it, our normal decriptions of experiential content are *overdetermining*.[9] So, a skilful cardboard replica of a car could, in certain circumstances, produce in us experiences that would be indistinguishable from experiences brought about by our seeing a real car. We could therefore say that it is possible for us to have a visual experience of a car (in the presence of the cardboard model) even though we are not really *seeing* a car. And if Fred's twin brother came to dinner with the Schlesingers, they might have the same experiences that they would have had in the presence of Fred, even though it was not Fred who was causing those experiences at all.

This overdetermination of experiential content means that it is unsafe for us to draw conclusions about things on the basis of our experiences alone. I can have an experience of a person, to take an extreme case, when what is causing this experience is not a person at all. Readers who do not like Millar's terminology can always interpret the phrase 'experience of a . . .' as 'experience *as* of a . . .'. However we express it, though, the point seems incontestable: the Schlesingers' experiences may have been experiences (as) of a person, while this item, Fred, turns out not to be a person at all.

We can tell stories that will let the visitation by the two-hour Fred count as a visitation by a person. One of these, for example, is that the two-hour Fred was produced by teleclone at just before 6.30 and sent off, again by teleclone, just after 8.30. Provided we believe that telecloning is not destructive of personal identity (something we should be very cautious about!) then we could make sense of the

---

[9] The point is carefully argued in Millar [1].

idea that the two-hour Fred was a slice of some broader, enduring thing.

Alternatively, we can think of the bizarre world of short objects discussed in the previous chapter. If we count discontinuous items themselves as short particulars, then perhaps Fred is simply one of them. Two-hour Fred may then be a survivor of some previous Fred and go on to be survived by some following Fred. Our referential practice might again be justified on the grounds that we use the same name to apply to close enough survivors of some item. Although we previously argued that this sort of account of discontinuous objects was less attractive than the mereological story, it is not so unattractive as to be senseless. So again we have a way of making sense of the idea of a two-hour Fred.

However, neither of these stories, or anything like them, seems to be involved in the Schlesinger examples. If the two-hour Fred is the *entire* life of a particular which is unrelated by survival relations to any other particulars, then it is hard to see why the Schlesingers think they have a *person* as their dinner guest at all. Of course, as we have seen, their experiences were just like those they would have had in the presence of a person, but we need more than experiential evidence.

One reason for not counting anything so short as Fred as a person is that we have certain fundamental ideas about persons. They are morally responsible agents, exercizers of concepts, sophisticated users of language, and so on. In order to deploy concepts, acquire moral principles, and learn language, persons need to be in certain relationships with their environment. These relationships include being in it long enough to engage in learning processes, for example. The two-hour Fred just doesn't seem to be around long enough to get started on any of the tasks that are needed to enable him to grow into a person.[10]

It might be objected to this that a miracle, or a freak of nature, may have been responsible for letting Fred acquire all the

---

[10] I mean, of course, 'to grow into a person viewed four-dimensionally.' It might seem that there is a disanalogy between the spatial and temporal segmenting of particulars. George Schlesinger has suggested that whereas when we slice a television in half spatially we obtain two half-televisions, when we slice a television temporally we obtain things which at least *look* and work like televisions. His suggestion only holds good up to a point. If we take a one-hour slice of a person, then that slice lacks many characteristics of typical persons (the ability to watch a feature film from beginning to end, to read a book, and so on).

characteristics of a person instantaneously. This sort of appeal to the bizarre, however, starts to weaken the case for the obviousness of Fred's being a person, being one of us. It is now starting to seem as if he cannot be one of us without something rather special being introduced to explain this. But maybe we should go back to the central issue. Armed with the interesting information that it is at least not obvious that Fred is a person, we can consider again the general claim that a two-hour slice of an F-thing is itself an F-thing. We will look at a common objection to the claim, and try to find what truth lurks in the objection by considering two replies that might seem to scupper the objection itself.

So let us consider the objection that if a stage is part of a larger whole, then it just cannot be a thing of the same sort as the whole. A spatial part of an F-thing, the objector continues, is not an F-thing, and so why expect temporal parts to behave differently? So put, the objection itself seems open to attack. The first attack on it is that spatial and temporal parts combine into wholes according to quite different principles. If we chop the front third off a car, we probably do not have a car remaining. But if we chop three years off the life of a television set, we still have a television set—simply one with a shorter life-span than the original.

This reply to the objection, however, is not a clear winner. Suppose we think of my television less three years of its history. Where is this other, shorter television? It is not here in the actual world, apparently, for my television set is in its tenth year and still going strong. So maybe there is a possible world in which my television set blew up last year. In that world, the stages constituting my television set for its first nine years undoubtedly constitute a television set. But none of this shows that such a television set is here in the actual world. Rather, in terms of our previous account of possibilities, we seem at best to be describing a case in which my television set would have had a shorter life.[11]

---

[11] There are two different cases to be considered here. First, there are those worlds which, relative to some suitable standard of similarity, are like enough the actual world to contain my television (enjoying some history which is an alternative to the one it in fact has). A quite different case occurs when some alternative world contains world-stages of television sets whose temporal stages are stages of my set in the actual world even though my television (or its counterpart) does not exist in that world. If it were to turn out that references to my desk or to Socrates were normally references to what I have called the *world-stages* of particular things, rather than to the five-dimensional object, then the haecceitism I am inclined to defend would have to be given up.

If this response to the original objection is not clearly a winner, maybe the second response will fare better. According to it, spatial parts of *F*-things are themselves *sometimes F*-things. Thus the spatial analogy used by the original objection breaks down. Noonan, like Wiggins, points out that the Pope's triple crown has parts which are crowns, and Schlesinger states that to have been immersed in part of the Dead Sea is to have been immersed in *the* Dead Sea, for its spatial parts simply replicate each other.[12] Schlesinger's point does not seem convincing, for it looks more like a point about immersion than about parts of the Dead Sea. In the case of the Pope's crown, as in other cases (like triple rings, multi-strand necklaces, and so on), we have to take care about how we section the objects in question. It is true that if we divide certain *F*-things judiciously we will get from them parts that are *F*-things. Looked at the other way round, starting from a number of *F*-things, we can combine them into a larger *F*-thing (like linking up two trains, or convoys, to make larger ones). Is there, then, a temporal analogue to this, where we are able to link up *F*-things in time so as to make new, larger *F*-things?

Once we get the hang of it, the trick is easy. Consider something like an *utterance*, where we take utterances as being meaningful stretches of speech. If I am careful, I can prolong an initial utterance by adding a further utterance, and so on. Utterances are not the only things that are prolongable. A soap opera, conceived as a series of episodes, can be extended into a larger soap opera by the addition of further series of episodes. In other words, we can find a range of temporal cases that are analogous to the spatial cases where inheritance of *F*-ness by a whole from its parts is possible. Notice that not all sections are equally good. An utterance-stage may be an utterance, but many utterance-stages are not utterances at all (for they fail to be meaningful). Some cuts in series of episodes leave us with series of episodes, but some do not. This parallels the spatial case, of course. Some divisions of a long train make a shorter train, but not every spatial division of a train is a train.

So we have found ways of defending the second response to the original objection. But how can a winning reply of this sort bring out the truth in the original objection? What we have to observe is

---

[12] In Schlesinger, loc. cit. Wiggins originally discussed the case of the Pope's triple crown in terms of its relevance to what he called the *counting thesis* in his [2].

that we have the same degree of difficulty in finding appropriate examples in both spatial and temporal cases where portions of *F*-things are themselves *F*-things. And this suggests that we should take the analogy between the spatial and the temporal cases most seriously. What we have found is that in neither case is there any *general* rule that parts are of the same sorts as the wholes from which they are sectioned.

It does now look plausible, though, that we should accept some of the things said by those who would maintain that temporal parts of *F*-things are themselves *F*-things. Spatial parts, after all, have many properties in common with the things they are parts of. Likewise, temporal parts will have structure, shape, colour, and components in common with the items they are parts of. But in neither case are we forced to the conclusion that parts have *all* the properties of the containing particulars. Moreover, if we can explain some of the characteristics of a whole object by reference to properties of its spatial parts, then we could hardly expect such parts to have every property that the whole object has. For then there would be no room for explanation at all.

Likewise, if we seek to explain some of the properties of temporal wholes by appeal to temporal stages, we cannot again expect wholesale sharing of properties. For instance, some changes in objects over time must be, in the linguist's phrase, 'suprasegmental' properties of broad things. What constitutes the changes in these cases will be shown by differences in properties of the stages. By contrast, the property of surviving as its successor will be a property, in normal cases, of a stage rather than of a broad object. Incidentally, telecloning thus counts as an *unusual* case, for it is one in which one broad object survives to a very high degree as another broad object.

What was wrong with the original objection, then, was its insistence on a disanalogy between spatial and temporal parts. But pursuing this analogy has helped us see that there are difficulties with the doctrine that in general a temporal part of an *F*-thing is itself an *F*-thing. For we now see that such a view would have, as its spatial correlate, a doctrine we would not want to hold, even while admitting many commonalties between properties of parts and properties of wholes.

In discussing the example of the television set, it was suggested that to say that a nine-year stage of my television is a perfectly good television in its own right really amounts to saying no more than that my television might only have existed for nine years. In other words, there is a possible world in which the nine-year stage of my television constitutes a perfectly good thing of the sort *television set*. Even if that stage is *my television* in that world, it does not follow that it is my set—or any other set—in this.

This strategy was already deployed in our attacks on Noonan's defence of the 'only *x* and *y*' rule. For we suggested that the individual consisting of $a + c$ does not constitute a ship, let alone Theseus' ship, in the world where there is a rival to the plank-hoarder's ship. Yet in another world that individual is a ship, and may indeed be Theseus' ship. But even as we make this point, we have to take care. For we are coming nowhere near suggesting that any old stage or sequence of stages of an actual particular will always be a thing of some sort in some possible world. It is easy to imagine a world in which my television set blew up after nine years. But it is not nearly so easy to imagine one in which its yesterday-stage just comes into being, like Schlesinger's dinner guest. For its yesterday-stage in fact carries a lot of history in it—the history of these preceding stages that have left their mark on it.

I am not trying to rule out all fantasies of last-minute creation. Robust scepticism is a serious challenge to any philosophical theory. Yet the very generality of its challenge makes it potentially less damaging to the position being advanced here. For any identity or survival theorist can be got at by the sceptic. So we can admit that there is at least a logical possibility that the world came into existence only five minutes ago. It is logically possible that all its particulars came into existence carrying traces of phoney history, just as the Schlesingers' dinner-guest passed as a plausible person. But this sceptical worry cannot itself be the real ground for our adopting the Quinton doctrine. Or if it is, then defenders of the doctrine ought to make clear that it is this kind of scepticism which underpins their decision to count stages of *F*-things as themselves *F*-things.

The safest conclusion, then, is that—failing outright scepticism—some of the stages of an actual particular of sort *F could* have themselves constituted a particular of sort *F*. Let us now take, for example, a stage of my television set, running from yesterday dawn until noon today. That extended stage might have been a particular in a world of discontinuous things—where thirty hours of television set is as much continuity as we are likely to get. But in this, the actual, world, that stage is not a television set, and hence, in this respect, not something of the same sort as the larger chain in which it is a link. None the less, the stage has very many of the properties we expect television sets to display. It occupies a volume of space, has components (temporal parts of which coincide with the stage), shows pictures, emits high-pitched whistles when switched on, and so on. Because we are here dealing with an extended stage, it also shows changes, whereas an instantaneous stage would not. So the error (if it is one) of thinking that a stage of a television set is a television set is a perfectly natural one. It is not unlike the error (if it is one) of thinking that my entire television set rather than just a minute temporal part of it is now in the sitting room.

5.5. SORTALS AND RECOGNITION

Although epistemology is not officially our concern until Chapter 7, we can look briefly here at an epistemological problem faced by those who maintain that stages of *F*-things are themselves *F*-things. This problem is critical for those who envisage us latching on to facts about particulars by latching on to features of stages. If the direction of explanation is to go from stages to the wholes of which they are stages we have to answer the following puzzle: How do we know to which sort a given stage is to be allocated?

We can think of relations among stages as being of two kinds— diachronic and synchronic. Consider the situation in Fig. 12.

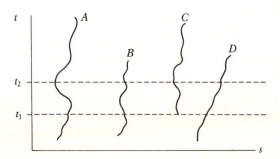

Fig. 12.

Suppose that A, B C, and D are all particulars, that is, maximal, non-branching, unified stage-collections. A temporal part of A, at t_1, say, stands in both horizontal and vertical relations with other slices, both slices of A and slices of the other particulars. The slice of A at t_1 thus stands in horizontal, synchronic relations with the slices of B, C, and D at that time. But it also stands in the important vertical, or diachronic, relation with later and earlier slices of A— slices that are all stages of one and the same particular.

Now suppose further that A and C are both particulars of the same sort. Perhaps the sort in question is a living natural kind, and so we can expect changes in such particulars between their juvenile stages and their mature stages. As we know from the Eusa problem, there is no general rule about the nature of such changes: they will be the changes that are *appropriate* to the kind in question. If the slices from A at t_1 and from C at the same time fall under the same sortals as A and C do, they may do so while exhibiting few superficial resemblances. C at t_1 may be a seedling while A and t_1 is a mature plant. The problem for the theorist who insists that stages of F-things are F-things is to explain how we *recognize* that both these slices fall under the same natural-kind sortal.

Of course, science may be called on to help us here. The individual gene complement of each member of a biological species will be closer to that of other members of the same species than it is to members of other species. On Putnam's deictic-nomological view of natural kinds, natural kinds will display 'horizontal' similarities with each other. Thanks to the fact that fine structure is correlated with features of superficial structure, we are able—for the most part—to latch on to these 'horizontal' similarities. The superficial features of water correlate nicely with the features which, on Putnam's view, define its *essential* nature: that is, H_2O. Science thus reveals the real nature of things.[13]

But the normal observer can have none of this help. We latched on to the existence of natural kinds long before we had the sophistication to probe much into the fine details of biological

---

[13] For a statement of the deictic-nomological view, see Putnam [3]. The addition of the theory of structure to Putnam's account looks very attractive, provided we can cope with the problem of growth and change. Certainly for natural kinds like iron, water, gold, and diamond, there seem to be decent 'horizontal' similarities among different specimens which can be described in terms of common macroscopic structures. And there seems also to be a stable relationship between macroscopic and microscopic structure.

structure. So the problem remains: if A at t_1 and C at t_1 are both to be recognized as falling under a common sortal, we may have to do this despite their divergence in superficial structural features. It may be very hard to think of any suitable similarity standard by which one is readily counted as similar to the other.

The obvious answer to our problem is that we do recognize immature members of biological kinds by virtue of our knowledge of what is the typical range of changes for items of the kind in question. We know what variation a particular belonging to the kind is likely to show during its natural life. Of course we sometimes get this wrong. Even experienced mushroomers occasionally pick members of poisonous species, mistaking them for fungi that can be safely eaten. But without our knowledge of how particulars belonging to a kind develop, grow, and mature, we would be unable to make synchronic judgements about which slices belong to which kinds.

It follows, then, that we cannot explain our recognition of a broad object as being of sort F by saying we recognize it as a sequence of stages, themselves of sort F. For any such explanation would be circular. My main concern in this chapter, of course, is ontological. And my argument has been that a broad particular of sort F is itself a maximal sequence of stages which are themselves usually *not* of sort F. The argument in this section, however, suggests that to *recognize* a slice of an F-thing as a slice of that kind of thing requires us to know something about broader things than slices. Of course, once we have the notion of an F-thing, there is a perfectly trivial way in which we can identify particular F-things as sequences of stages which show sortal-covered persistence. In just such a way do we identify particular bicycles, for example, as structured collections of *bicycle parts*.

5.6. REAL POSSIBILITIES

There is one more way with possible worlds about which we need to say something. As we have seen, we can get somewhat carried away by the notion that any old logical possibility can have a place in some possible world or other. Maybe this morning I could have breakfasted on Cyclops' eyes, or gone to sea in a boat of gossamer. As an antidote to this kind of extravagance, we might perhaps follow

Quine and Goodman by trying to anchor other possible worlds more securely in the real world.[14] To do this, we need only make a simple decision about what the basic *components* of the actual world are. Perhaps we could choose the elementary particles. Then the real world is constituted by one distribution of such particles, and alternative possible worlds are no more than alternative possible distributions of the same particles. Maybe we need not go so far as this. If we accept the trees, rivers, and minerals of this world as the basic components, we could simply content ourselves with new permutations of them and material obtained from them.

The question we now must face is whether this austere way with possibilities threatens our earlier conclusions. Take, for example, the notion that my desk-top together with sides of some other desk might easily have constituted one desk. Perhaps, for example, the tops were stacked at one place in the factory, the sides elsewhere, and it was partly a matter of chance which sides got matched up with which tops. In thus understanding real possibilities, we are thinking of individuals that are already present *in the actual world.* Here is my desk, and over there another. The individual consisting of the top of my desk and the sides of the other is thus here as well, albeit missing being a desk.

In the temporal case, we can think likewise of removing the last three years of my desk's history. That means subtracting stages amounting to three years from one end of a chain, leaving us with a collection of stages that constitutes one individual—an individual that is very much present in this world. That individual constitutes a desk in some other world. What this example makes clear is that our new austere way with worlds does not in the least threaten our conclusions. Instead, it starts to clarify the nature of the confusion that has perhaps afflicted some defenders of the Quinton doctrine. For they perhaps have not distinguished carefully enough between two questions:

(1) Is this individual present in world α?
(2) Is this individual in world α a particular?

My desk-top and the sides of the other desk miss being a particular.

---

[14] Goodman does this in the way already described in Ch. 2, n. 1. Quine sometimes writes of possible worlds as alternative distributions of elementary particles. See the essay 'Propositional Objects' in Quine [7]. David Lewis discusses Quine's proposal in Lewis [2], 4.1.

So long as our interest is in particulars, we will be unimpressed by the existence of all these other individuals in our world, even though we agree that, in other circumstances, many of them might have been particulars themselves.

This consideration might suggest that we can give an account of the degree of similarity between different possible worlds by noting, among other things, facts about temporal parts of items. On current essentialist wisdom, the spatial parts of an item are extremely important in determining the answer to this question. Can my desk—this very desk at which I am now writing—have been made of different components from those of which it was originally made? As far as Kripke and other essentialists are concerned, it is not possible that this very desk could have been made of quite different matter, or of quite different *spatial* components. It might seem that our earlier examples of telemutation and survival after telecloning militate against taking this doctrine of the essentiality of origin at all seriously. But in a moment, we will find that there is, surprisingly, good reason, given the theory of survival, to take the points about necessity of origin quite seriously indeed. For the time being, though, let us follow up the implications of the idea that temporal parts are *parts*.

Of course, temporal parts of objects seem to aggregate together into whole objects according to quite different principles of organization from those applying to spatial parts. It is not easy to say, however, in the case of either sort of part, just what a *part* really is. We can give unhelpful accounts in both cases that let too much in. For example, consider a particular as being spatially complete at a time. We can carve out indefinitely many spatial parts of the particular, only some of which will be the separable, unitary items that we normally mean to refer to when we speak of a thing's 'parts' or 'components'. It will not do to take Mellor's line and argue that parts in our narrower sense are precisely those things changes in which are temporal and spatial parts of the changes in the containing thing.[15] For although this is no doubt true, we need a prior understanding of which parts are things in order to recognize

---

[15] Mellor writes: 'What makes one thing part of another is that some of its changes are spatial or temporal parts of the other's changes. Thus the musical activities of the players are the causal mechanism, the parts, spatial and temporal, of the orchestral events which constitute a Halle concert.' Mellor [2], p. 137.

the truth in what Mellor says. So Mellor's account does not define what parts in the narrow sense are.

By contrast, Mellor's account of the temporal parts of events will, I think, help us give some account of the temporal parts of spatio-temporally broad particulars. Thus do our enemies help us, for Mellor is no friend of my brand of four-dimensionalism, since he is concerned to maintain that only *events* have temporal parts. On his account, events aggregate together into larger events according to the operation of cause and effect. If we accept his very thin account of causality, then the components of a broad event—say the firing of a gun—are further events which are causally linked to each other in that the occurrence of any one makes the occurrence of its succeeding event more probable than that event would otherwise have been. Thus squeezing the trigger causes the falling of the hammer which in turn causes the explosion of the gunpowder in the cartridge which in turn causes the propulsion of the bullet along the barrel and so on. Not all broad events fit this pattern, but many do.

Events which fail to fit this pattern of sequential causation can best be thought of in terms of our notion of *production processes*. Thus, another example of Mellor's concerns the event of *walking to the door*. Of this broad action he writes, 'the action's parts are the sucessive steps *en route*. They are the deliberate causal mechanism of the action as a whole, i.e. each step is itself an action which is a causal precursor of the step that follows it.'[16] This, however, is surely implausible, even given his weak notion of *cause*. For, other things being equal, the fact that someone has taken a number of steps in a certain direction does not make a further step in that direction any more likely. Rather, in this case, we have an underlying cause—my intention to go the the door—which is productive of each step in the sequence. In just the same way, the row of stitches produced by a sewing machine involves an underlying production process rather than any causal dependence of each stitch on its precursor.

Events, albeit fascinating and fundamental, have not been my concern in this work, and I do not propose to start investigating them now from the point of view of the theory of survival. If Mellor is right, however, my treatment of particulars as broad, four-dimensional items means that I am in effect treating them rather like

16 Mellor [2], p. 132.

events of a sort, and many four-dimensionalists would be happy with such a description. But, in the light of what I have just argued, we should be wary of associating the four-dimensional view of particulars with the account of things like human actions. For these, as we have just seen, are best thought of as sequences of events linked by some common producing cause. Most particulars, however, are—on my account at least—not to be thought of in this way at all. They are sequences of episodes linked by causal dependency, but not produced by some underlying cause. By contrast, the traditional notion that some divine being conserves the world from moment to moment would fit far more happily with a view that assimilated particulars to actions.

This leaves us, then, with just one way of thinking about particulars, namely, as broad items whose temporal parts enter into causal relations with each other. What kind of causal relations can these be? In the case of something that persists in a relatively unchanging way, we can think of such relations as being pretty minimal. There is some causal dependence of features of an item at one time on features of that item at an immediately preceding time, and so on back to its origin. Indeed, one thing that makes us suspicious of stories, like Schlesinger's, in which a particular just comes into existence is that we can think of no *causal* explanation for this. Mountains, at least those outside of books like this one, do not just appear and disappear in the world as we know it. If someone turns up at my door at 7.00 one evening then that slice of the person depends for its characteristics on the existence of some preceding slice. Mellor's thin notion of causality seems appropriate in such cases.

In the case of an object which changes, the causal relations between stages become much more complex. Our causal condition on survival requires that changes that happen to one stage show up—other things being equal—in later stages. Moreover, living things that grow to maturity and then fade into death show changes of a determinate and lawful kind throughout their lives. Again, the changes in their temporal parts, together with the causal dependency from stage to stage, means that their histories have a recognizable pattern. None of this means that I am trying to define the notion of *event* in terms of changes that take place from one momentary stage to the next.

An apparent objection to these claims about causal dependency might run as follows. There is nothing to be explained in the persistence of a particular. All that can be legitimately explained is the coming to be and passing away of particulars. For example, the objection goes on, think of the scratch my desk acquired yesterday. The desk bears the same scratch today. The persistence of the desk explains why the scratch is still there. But it would be monstrous to try to explain the persistence of the desk as caused by the relations among stages with scratches. Thus the scratch is evidence of the persistence of the desk because its reappearance in successive stages depends on the persistence of the desk itself.

This may look like a powerful defence of the primitiveness of persistence. Persistence, on this account, is rather like inertia. A body's change from its state of rest or uniform motion needs to be explained by reference to forces acting upon it: but rest, or uniform motion along a straight line, is a natural state of things. So persistence is just a natural state of things.

This is not, however, something I wish to deny. The objection, in fact, takes me as engaged in an explanatory exercise with which I am not really involved at all. Admittedly, part of the survival story is that stages are in causal relations with each other—for the structure and matter of one stage is itself causally dependent on the structure and matter of another. Thus the manifestation by one desk-stage of a scratch, is causally dependent on the acquisition of a scratch by another stage.

However, these causal claims are compatible with two different accounts of persistence. They are compatible, first, with the claim that persistence is itself primitive. In this case, persistence underlies the causal relations among stages. Properties of one stage are communicated to other stages via the persisting thing in just the way that a vibration in one part of an aircraft is transmitted through the airframe to other parts. Alternatively, we could try to give an account of the history of a particular in persistence-free language, just as we could try to describe the spatial extent of a bridge by listing its components and their relations. On this latter account, we could talk about a persisting thing as being no more than a succession (not necessarily continuous) of momentary, or short, stages. Of course, we would still have causal relations among stages even though this time there would be no appeal to the persisting thing as the medium for transmitting such relations. The spatial analogue would be the attempt to explain the transmission of vibration through the airframe without appeal to the properties of the airframe itself: rather, we would refer to transmission of the vibration from one component to the next, and so on.[17]

Neither of these ways of interpreting causal claims about relations among stages involves us in explaining persistence itself, and so the objection is thus misconceived. However, if the features of one stage of an object are causally responsible for features of another stage of the same (or a different) object, then there is a kind of minimal causal dependency that might appear to be explanatory of persistence. We can put it like this. The existence of the stage which figures in the description of the cause is itself necessary for the occurrence of the effect. Thus, the desk-stage which originally acquired the scratch had to exist in order for (the event of) its being scratched to be causally responsible for a later stage's displaying the scratch. The existence of that earlier stage, then, is part of the causal story linking events involving it and the later stage. It follows that, in a minimal way, stages play some role in the existence of other stages.

Now there is an entirely natural way we speak about items as being responsible for the effects that they are causally involved with in this rather remote way. Think of Hume's billiard balls. The motion of one ball is transmitted to the other by their collision. We quite commonly speak of this phenomenon in terms of one ball making the other one move. Strictly speaking, of course, it is the existence of the one ball that is necessary for the occurrence of the event whose effect is the motion of the second ball. Likewise, then, we can talk about one stage being responsible for a feature of some other stage. Yet even in making this point, it should be clear that we are not giving any explanation of persistence—otherwise we could be accused of giving an account of persistence in the case of the two billiard balls. There is, of course, preservation of things like scratches, dents, and other features of desks, from one desk-stage to another. But none of these considerations suggest that the account

---

[17] Do we explain persistence by stating in what persistence consists? In the text, I assume that the notion of explanation is so rich that in addition to knowing in what persistence consists, someone looking for an explanation of persistence would also want to know *why* the particular in question persists. Whether or not we think wholes are more than the sum of their parts, explaining the persistence of a whole (a sum of parts) is likely to involve more than appeal to relations among its parts, assuming that persistence is explainable at all.

of unity given here—which involves unity being a causal notion—amounts to an attempt to explain persistence.

What we have, then, are the preservation of changes affecting one temporal part in features of later parts. Earlier stages play a causal role in the production of later stages; and so the sort of survival that takes place from stage to stage of a broad object can be assimilated—as we have assumed all along—to the other kinds of survival we have looked at (the survival of one broad thing as or in some other broad thing). This being so, is there any special weight we should give to those stages or slices that embrace the origin of a particular? After all, given a suitable sequence of causal impingements and changes over time, the structure and matter of any particular is likely to be very different from its original. So why should an item, or its counterpart, not start off in some other world with a slice that is structurally similar to, but materially different from, that one from which (so to speak) it starts in this world? Moreover, if spatial parts do matter to transworld similarity or identity, why should temporal parts not be equally important?

So far, I have tried not to take any stance on issues like the necessity of identity or of origin.[18] It is not hard to keep my treatment compatible with certain varieties of essentialism while not endorsing or supporting such a metaphysical position. However, an interesting feature will now emerge. We will find that the theories on identity and survival mooted so far do support a version of the thesis of essentiality of origin. If Salmon is correct in maintaining that this thesis does not follow simply from Kripke's theories of reference, then some essentialists will no doubt appreciate the support their position receives from the arguments I am about to give.

Let us begin, then, by considering what it would be like to take seriously the notion that an object's identity is at least in part defined by its *temporal* parts. Think, for example, of the number of half-hour slices that constituted Napoleon, or his escritoire. If temporal slices are significant for the identity issue, then perhaps Napoleon *could not* have had very many slices more or less than he in fact had. The same goes for his escritoire which, we can suppose,

---

[18] There is an extensive literature on this topic and on Kripke's apparent attempt to derive the point from his thesis on reference. See Noonan [4], and ch. 7 of Salmon [1], both of which contain references to further reading.

lasted rather longer than he did. A particular that is very like Napoleon, or his escritoire, but differs significantly in the number of its half-hour slices from these particulars in the real world just would not be (or be counterparts of) these particulars.[19]

Common sense, however, seems to rebel at this. Surely Napoleon might have died as a child, or his escritoire been destroyed in a fire some years before it came into his possession. These seem to be real possibilities, and the claim that Napoleon *could* not have differed by more than a few dozen half-hour slices from the history he in fact had seems extraordinarily restrictive. Now maybe this point of view is the one that will prevail in the end. And I certainly have no argument to offer against it. However, it does not seem to be terribly silly to maintain that temporal parts might matter in the way suggested. Suppose, for example, that we distinguish the way the world in fact *is* from the way it *might have been*. Maybe, given how the world in fact is, Napoleon and his escritoire could *not* have consisted of only a minute fraction of the temporal parts they in fact had. But maybe this world *might have been* so constituted that Napoleon *could* have consisted of just one half-hour slice. So, when contrasting worlds containing Napoleon, we have to take care about relative possibility and similarity. A world containing a brief Napoleon may not be possible relative to this world, although possible relative to some other world possible relative to this world. On this account, the relative similarity of worlds, which determines

---

[19] Of course, there is a paradox in the offing here. For consider that an item may be just the same, even if consisting of slightly different temporal parts from those it in fact has. We now devise a chain of worlds, each containing items that differ only slightly in this way. But, at the extremes of the chain, we find items that differ almost entirely in their temporal parts. For a discussion of the spatial version of this paradox, due originally to Chisholm, see the not entirely satisfactory attempt to resolve it in Appendix I to Salmon [1]. Salmon develops a variant of Chisholm's paradox, which he calls *The Four Worlds Paradox*. Suppose, for the sake of the argument, that we allow that up to 5% of an item's original matter could have been different. Then ship *a*, in one world, might have been constructed in some other world from a collection of planks that differs by precisely 5%. In a third world, another ship, *b*, is constructed from a collection of planks that differs by 8% from *a*'s original constitution. Now imagine that in a fourth world, *b*'s structure is the same as *a*'s structure, its planks are the same as *a*'s and it differs by no more than 5% from its constitution in the third world! If we suppose that the second and fourth worlds just described are entirely alike in other respects, then it is odd (to say the least) that we have to recognize them as containing different ships. Counterpart theorists can construct their own paradox by appropriate modifications of the above argument. My own attempt to resolve the temporal analogue of this puzzle is given in the next section.

their relative possibility, depends on the existence of temporal parts. For one way of measuring similarity would involve counting the number of temporal parts of specified duration common to particulars in different worlds.[20]

This proposal, which differentiates *real possibilities* from *possible possibilities*, might be made clearer if we take a spatial analogy. Think of all the components that constitute my (actual) garden shed. Although it is already fairly small, as sheds go, it might have been constituted from a slightly different collection of planks, struts, panes of glass, hinges, and so on. But let us imagine a shed constructed from less than a quarter of the spatial parts of my shed's original components. Would we count this diminished structure as being my shed, or a counterpart of it? The world we are imagining is not one that, as it happens, lacks a shed in my garden.[21] On the contrary, it seems to contain a different shed *in place of* the shed that is actually in my garden. Notice that, of course, the components of my shed could also have been arranged into something that was not a shed—but that is a different problem.

This thought-experiment inclines us to maintain two things:

(1) there are possible worlds in which there are sheds, albeit not *my* shed, consisting of less than a quarter of my shed's components; but this, the actual, world does not contain any shed consisting of less than a quarter of my shed's components.

(2) it is not a *real possibility* that my shed might have consisted of less than a quarter of its original spatial components.

These parallel our claims about temporal parts. Given the way the world is, it is not a real possibility that my television might have consisted of less than a quarter of the half-hour slices it has. Nor

[20] As David Lewis points out, similarity is a vague notion, and talk of interworld comparison is also vague. There will be worlds similar to this one which fail to contain particulars present in this one. In talking, however, of counterfactual possibilities for Napoleon, or my television, we are restricting our attention to worlds containing Napoleon, my television, or their counterparts.

[21] The phrase 'my shed' is ambiguous. For, of course, the description 'the shed in the corner of my garden' can be true of more than one shed and thus need not be a Kripkean rigid designator. In my usage in the present section, I am taking the phrase *not* as a description but, like a proper name, as designating the very same object (or counterpart thereof) in all worlds where it designates anything at all. See the discussion in Kripke [2].

does the *individual* in this world which consists of less than a quarter of my television's half-hour slices constitute a television at all. However, there are possible worlds in which there are televisions with histories minute compared to the history of mine. All we deny, as in the shed case, is that such worlds are similar enough to ours to be accessible from it.[22]

Relative to the similarity standards we seek when looking for worlds containing counterparts of items in this world, temporal parts may be counted as significant to interworld comparisons. This claim is controversial, of course, but not to be dismissed on this account. After all, we are not very good at distinguishing fantasy from possibility at the best of times. It is not my purpose to insist that fantasy never makes sense, or that we restrict our imaginings simply to real possibilities. Rather, I am suggesting a way in which those committed to possible-worlds analysis might count temporal parts as important to similarites among worlds. Our normal attitude, of taking the spatial parts of a particular at origin as being definitive of it, while its temporal history is indefinitely variable, may simply reflect our own *timebound* perspective. We know, after all, much more about the spatial extent of particulars than we do about their temporal extent. And maybe our ignorance of the temporal extent of ourselves, and the things around us, leads us to confuse real with merely possible possibilities.

5.7. ESSENCE AND VAGUENESS

So far, three central claims have been argued for in this chapter. First, the notion of stage, or temporal part, has been shown to be a theoretical notion, akin to the theoretical concepts deployed in the sciences. Second, it has been argued that there is no general rule to the effect that stages of *F*-things are always themselves *F*-things. Since stages are parts, it is sensible to regard the issue of applying sortals to stages as of one piece with the issue of applying sortals to parts. As we have seen, there are occasions where parts of *F*-things are *F*-things, but such occasions are the exceptions rather than the rule.

---

[22] The qualification again required here is that we are trying to access worlds close enough to the actual world *in respect of* containing my television set.

It could be argued that the conception of stages as parts is also responsible for the position adopted in the last section. This third, and no doubt contentious, claim has suggested that the temporal constitution of an item is part of its essence. Now it is commonly argued by essentialist philosophers that the spatial components of an item are themselves essential to it—certainly, those components which constitute it at its origin are so. In the next section, I will be supporting the doctrine of the necessity of original constitution in a some what novel way. But it is worth getting clear on some of the issues faced by anyone who is inclined to support the third claim (although I do not expect may readers to give this specific doctrine immediate support).

The whole issue of individual essence (those features which are essential for a particular's being the particular it is) is notoriously complicated, and prone to problems. Yet the move of identifying material constitution with at least part of something's essence gets away from some more dubious account of the haecceity or 'thisness' of a particular. If a bicycle could stay the same while changing all, or nearly all, of its parts, if it could be as big or as small as you like, then the very particularity, the 'thisness', of the bicycle would seem to be something mysterious, bare, residing in some secret individual substance that underlies all its properties. Of course, like those philosophers sceptical of possible worlds in general, and essences in particular, we could simply scrap all such talk. But I want to maintain essentialist modes of thinking for the present, and explore what Forbes calls 'tolerant haecceitism' for a while.[23]

In the last section, I made some suggestions about temporal parts along the lines that haecceitists make about the spatial parts of particulars. On the generous conception of talk about particulars being ambiguous among three-, four-, and five-dimensional readings, there is a limit to how much sense can be made of the notion that individuals are absolutely identical in different worlds. Indeed, on one extreme version of the view, the recognition of the existence of cosmic parts puts paid to any haecceitist notions.

---

[23] The doctrine is explored in ch. 7 of Forbes [3]. It is useful to contrast Kripke's haecceitism with the kinds of objections to the doctrine given in Lewis [5]. My search here is for a version of haecceitism that reconciles what I think is right in theories of rigid designation with what seems right in counterpart theory. In discussing essence, it should be observed that the present chapter deals with *individual* essence, while what might be called *sortal* essence is dealt with in Ch. 6.

However, on my version of the theory, there is some sense to be made of the claim. For, taking particulars as three-dimensional wholes, the tolerant haecceitist maintains that my desk might have had a slightly different original constitution from its actual original constitution—say 10 per cent of its components might have been different. And, of course, through time, it is possible for the constitution of the desk to change some more.

The haecceitist's motive here is straightforward. When constructing possible worlds, we are concerned with the alternative histories open to this very item, my desk. Yet such construction has got to start from a sensible point. One such is the notion that this very thing, my desk, is a collection of parts here in the actual world. Any alternative histories for it have got to be open possibilities for the very collection of parts constitutive of it.

Further support for the doctrine comes from the necessity of identity. If my desk is one thing it is necessarily that thing. Even if I give my desk two different names—names that I just think up on the spot—these names must name just one thing. It is a contingent fact that I have just thought of the names 'Ferdinand' and 'Jessica' to give to my desk: yet it is necessarily true that Ferdinand and Jessica are the same desk.[24] If we are at all impressed by these considerations, then we may find a motive for taking a similar line with regard to the temporal constitution of particulars when they are regarded as four-dimensional wholes. For again, if we want our construction of possible worlds to be anchored in the actual world, we need to consider things in their actual four-dimensional extent before pronouncing on what possibilities are open to them.

One problem we have in dealing with temporal parts is that although we can engage in relatively comprehensive spatial surveys of some particulars, our own limited access to the spatio-temporal trajectories of most things means that we just do not know the extent of their life histories. However, let us try to adopt a timeless perspective. On such a perspective, items in the actual world do (tenselessly) have a certain extent. My television does persist for a number of years (though I do not know what this number is). I

---

[24] It is a theorem of the modal system S5 that if $a = b$ then it is necessarily the case that $a = b$. It is easy to demonstrate this result informally. Suppose that each thing is necessarily self-identical and that $a = b$. b thus has the property of being necessarily identical with itself (that is, b), and since by hypothesis a is b, then a has that property, i.e., a is necessarily identical with b, QED.

persist, like any other living thing, for a number of years also, although again I do not know what this number is—nor am I sure that I would want to know it. It is relative to this world, with particulars having the histories they have in it, that other possible worlds are constructed.

In technical terms, a world that is possible relative to a given world is said to be *accessible* from that world. Although we are interested in speculating about possibilities, we know that certain constraints on this speculation distinguish real possibilities from pure fantasy. Given, the training and muscular development required, a career as a gymnast or acrobat for example, is not a real possibility for me. Nor, for that matter, is a career as a concert pianist, although given my musical aptitude, a career as a concert pianist might have been a possibility for me when I was younger. But what is meant by this last claim? It presumably means that at some suitable point in my life I could have taken steps and made decisions which would have produced a long-term effect: namely that the succeeding sequence of person-stages constituting me would have been stages of a musician and not of a philosopher. But if this is what the claim means, then it does not mean that my life would have been constituted by significantly different stages, although these stages would show the changes appropriate to stages of a musician.

So the suggestion about constitutive temporal parts being part of a particular's essence does not rule out alternative life possibilities for the particulars in question. Indeed, it is compatible with there being a great many worlds accessible to any given particular. What the speculations do rule out is the thought that the life of the particular in question could have been composed of a great many more—or a great many less—of the stages than those which do in fact constitute it. As far as artefact and other non-living particulars are concerned, the claim, as I have suggested, is hardly more than a temporal variant of the claim about necessity of origin. Any world with a world-stage of my desk in it, when thought of four-dimensionally, must contain an item which has very much the same aggregate of time-slices in it as my desk has in the actual world. It is therefore not a real possibility that my desk might have been destroyed two minutes after having been built.

Although it is hard to imagine a case of it, we must be wary of a counter-argument here which suggests that a large artefact could be continuously changed into a small version of itself by gradual erosion of its components. After all, an accumulation of tiny changes may lead in the end to a great change—as we have already seen in the case of Theseus' ship, where plank by plank the material of the original is lost and replaced by new material. In the background there is the worrying paradox of *sorites* here: a couple of grains of sand subtracted from a heap will not diminish the heap to any significant extent. But after enough subtractions we will be left with something that is patently not a heap.

It may be that sorites-thinking underlies resistance we might have to the temporal version of the constitution claim. After all, my television set might have blown up last year and been destroyed. Likewise, it could have been destroyed the year before that, and so on. Although my television set has, in fact, so far been around for about ten years, we are led to think it possible that it might only have existed for six hours. I remember, very clearly, that once, as a child, I sat down, tired, on what I thought was a disused railway line, one hot summer day. The sound of a whistle, and the sight of a uniformed official running towards me waving a flag woke me from my day-dreams. Coming round a bend just behind me was a steam locomotive pulling a small passenger train. Of course, I jumped up and ran away, frightened and embarrassed. But for that official's watchfulness, that might have been the end of me: and so I might only have existed for seven years. But is it anything more than sorites-thinking that makes this claim look plausible?

Let us think, then, of a world in which there is an object which, in terms of half-hour stages, constitutes a chain strikingly similar to my first seven years. But in that world, the chain ends there—no station master came to the rescue. Is that object in that world me? This is, I think, a very difficult question, and in part it is a difficulty about personal identity, rather than a difficulty about stipulating whether an object or its counterpart are present in a world. To help us in tackling it, let us think of a different case that still poses a problem for the haecceitist. One that we can couch in three-dimensional terms goes this. Suppose that we imagine a world in which there is a desk made from 50 per cent of the components of my desk here. In this world, there is another desk which also contains 50 per cent of my actual desk's components. Is my desk, or a counterpart of it, in that world?

If we stick with counterpart theory for a moment, then there clearly seems to be a problem about maintaining that either one of the two desks, but not the other, is a counterpart of my desk. For any claim that one has, in terms of material constitution, the other has as well. Why not say, then, that in this imagined world both desks are counterparts of my desk in this world, although neither is similar to my desk to a very high degree. But this amounts to a denial of the necessity of identity. For, in terms of counterpart theory, the necessity of identity claim reads: if c is a counterpart of a in any world, and c' is a counterpart of a in the same world, then c is identical with c'.[25] But this claim will not hold in the example given, where both desks appear to be counterparts—to some degree—of my desk.

The way to deal with this problem, Forbes suggests, is to accept that essences are fuzzy. The counterpart relation is not a matter of absolute hit or miss, but is also fuzzy—it can hold to greater or lesser degrees. The fuzzy logic which Forbes uses requires us to accept degrees of truth (and the associated theory of fuzzy sets requires us to accept that set membership is not an all-or-nothing affair either). However, if once we can accept these strange notions, we can start to get away from the traps set by sorites premisses. It is not the case that it is wholly true that an object with a slightly different original constitution in some other world is the counterpart of my desk. Rather, that claim is slightly less than wholly true, but not nearly so close to being wholly untrue that we ought to reject it. However, we cannot expect to keep finding counterparts of that object in some further world, and counterparts of those in other worlds, and so on, without coming some time or other to an item which is certainly not a counterpart of the one from which we started. Looked at another way, the conditional 'if x (in world u) differs only slightly from y (in world v) then x is a counterpart of y' is not entirely true. Thus

---

[25] Since on counterpart theory items are bound to one world, we have to formulate all Kripkean claims in terms that reflect this. On the Kripkean understanding of the reference of constants or proper names, a name of a necessarily existing thing will name something in every possible world. But if 'a' names a contingently existing thing, then there will be worlds where that name fails to name at all—namely those worlds where, as it happens, a just does not exist. If counterpart theory is to make this distinction among existents, there will be worlds where a contingently existing thing does have a counterpart, and some where it does not. Suppose 'a' is the name of a contingent object in a given world. We then let 'a' denote a's counterpart in those worlds where a fails to exist—thus ensuring that nothing is named by the constant in those very worlds. A useful account of counterpart theory and its troubles is found in ch. 3 of Forbes [3].

accessibility will not be transitive, and we will not be able to construct a chain of worlds accessible from the actual world such that the last element in the chain contains a counterpart to my desk that has no components in common with it at all.[26]

Of course, it is just as well we cannot do this, and that we can find some way of resisting sorites moves. Otherwise, the very thisness of my desk would be something entirely mysterious and puzzling—for it would be present despite the entire replacement of my desk's material stuff. The notion that counterparthood is a vague relation thus seems to save the day in the face of sorites problems. That it is such a vague notion may be part of the explanation of our difficulty in the face of the question which triggered this particular detour into counterpart theory—namely whether that seven-year-old child killed by the train was me, or at least a counterpart of me. If we follow Forbes we may come to the conclusion that the answer to this question can only be given to a degree. Yes, to some extent that item over in the other world is me despite its short duration; but to some extent it is not me as well. Our problem—as with all problems of vagueness—is knowing where to make the cut-off point.

Has our detour into counterpart theory not lost the point of haecceity? If all we are looking for, so to speak, in other worlds are counterparts of objects in the actual world, then what sense was there in maintaining that this very object, me, or my desk, could have had a different history? The answer to this question strikes us when we realize that the thisness the haecceitist is after is simply the grounding of possibilities in the actual world. If we are going to

---

[26] Background to this puzzle is given in n. 19. The solution to sorites problems by resort to fuzzy logic and degrees of truth looks promising: promising enough indeed, to persuade many people to give up their suspicion of a notion of truth that is so far removed from the traditional all-or-nothing concept. However, in a recent article, Charles Travis tries to dissolve such paradoxes in a different way. In the same article (Travis [1]), he discusses Michael Dummett's and Crispin Wright's theories on vague predicates, learnability, and observationality. Whatever solution we give to puzzles about transworld identification, that they can be solved might perhaps go some way towards reassuring a sceptic like Quine. For he is well aware of the analogy between worlds and times, but dismisses the sort of development I engage in here because 'you can change anything to anything by easy stages through some connecting series of possible worlds' ('Worlds Away', Quine [10], p. 127). As a good extensionalist, Quine is also troubled by the fact that since there are myriad ways of stacking up temporal parts to make broad objects, then 'any two physical objects in different worlds are shared as realisations not by just one intermundane but by countless ones' (ibid. p. 126). For those of us no longer under the spell of the extensionalist myth, however, no such additional problem looms (see ch. 7).

make decision on real possibilities, we will want to draw a line around a certain class of possible worlds and declare that accessibility from the actual world goes no further than them. Even if it is true to a degree that a world containing a desk constituted from 50 per cent of the parts of my desk here does contain a counterpart to my desk, that does not show that such a world should be regarded as accessible from this, the actual, one. We can thus restrict accessibility by adopting various standards of variation in material constitution.

Just so, when considering the class of worlds to which we can have direct access, we can make restrictions in terms of temporal constitution. Clearly, such restrictions may well vary from one kind of thing to another. Just as there is no determinate answer to the question of how much material variation an item can withstand while remaining the very same particular, so there is no general and determinate answer to the corresponding question about temporal parts. But anyone who is enough of a haecceitist to want to restrict the range of real possibilities open to an item will have to consider the permissible degree of variation in both spatial and temporal constitution. Incidentally, it would be at best a careless way of putting my suggestions to say that the (spatial or temporal) *size* of a particular is to be counted as part of its essence. My point is better put in terms of numbers of each kind of part.[27]

On one view of the cosmic-part theory, there is no truth in haecceitism at all. This is what I have already called the 'extreme' version of the position. According to it, since world-stages are distinct things allocated to the same cosmic particular, there could be no sense in talking of the very same particular being present in different worlds.[28] This is not my position, however. For, according

---

[27] The overwhelming objection to putting the matter in terms of *size* is that we can apparently envisage cases where things can grow or shrink while not changing the number (or arrangement) of their parts. Cases in fantasy and children's literature are numerous (think of Alice in Wonderland, or Mrs Pepperpot). The temporal version of this fantasy would be entirely parallel to these spatial cases. Thus, in the case of the shed, I did not envisage my shed shrinking to a quarter of its size: I explicitly described the small shed as having been built from less than a quarter of the original components. See also the remarks about size in n. 13 to Ch. 1.

[28] See also n. 11. Schlesinger takes the cosmic-part theory as establishing that all items are worldbound. Thus, for example, the S5 proof of the necessity of identity (n. 24) is often taken to pose problems for counterpart theory. Yet, as Schlesinger has argued in correspondence, there is no merit in the claim that where $a = b$ the reference of a will be the same as the reference of b at every world; for 'a exists at most

to me, the particular taken in all its five-dimensional glory, is present in all the worlds in which it has world-stages. What the haecceitist is after, on my account, is a conception of world-stages that ties them quite strictly to the constitution of one particular world-stage—the one in the actual world. To say that the very same particular is present in a number of worlds accessible from this one, then, is to maintain that we will only count worlds as accessible from this one when the world-stages of the particular under consideration vary, in terms of their original material, and their temporal parts, only within certain strict limits. Of course, however strict the limits, we can find routes from those other worlds to further worlds, where items that are counterparts of the counterparts are bound to figure. But, as already suggested in the last section, this takes us from cases of real possibility to cases of only possible possibility.[29]

5.8. TEMPORAL PARTS AND THE NECESSITY OF ORIGIN

We can now turn to the vexed issue of the necessity of origin. Although it seems the merest common sense to maintain that no particular really *could* have consisted of quite different original components, the position stands in need of some justification. Strawson gives the following apparent counter-example:

If someone said: 'The *QEII*, you know, might have been built of quite a different lot of steel from that which it was actually built of'—and gave his reasons—would it not be absurd to reply: 'In that case it wouldn't have been the *QEII* at all—the *QEII* wouldn't have existed—it would have been a different ship of that name'?[30]

in a single world. In any other world, we can have neither *a* nor a counterpart of *a*, but at most something wholly distinct from *a* which is related to it by virtue of being a co-part of some larger entity.' My view is not so extreme as this. Of course, a world-stage of *a* is at one world and no other; but particulars can be at lots of worlds just as they can exist at lots of times. The important thing is not to confuse claims about world-stages with claims about particulars in their five-dimensional glory.

[29] My comments on possible possibilities should be compared with Salmon's in Salmon [1], pp. 238–40. Although he considers only the three-dimensional version of our problem, my extension of the treatment to temporal parts is no more (although, equally, no *less*) conservative in its implications than his.

[30] Strawson [6], p. 235. The passage is also quoted by Salmon in Salmon [1], ch. 7.

Strawson's argument, as noted by Salmon, is meant here epistemically, rather than metaphysically, But we can consider it in its full metaphysical ramifications if we like. Think of the special kitchen unit that rather neatly fits into that awkward corner in the kitchen. Could we not maintain that the corner could have contained *that very same unit* even had it not been built of the same components?

But switching the case, from a one-off artefact like an ocean liner, to a mass-produced item (as many kitchen units are) gives the game away. For we are back to our old problem of *types* and *tokens*, and the vagueness inherent in what I have called our *opportunistic* referential practices. By 'same unit' or 'same ship', we often mean 'unit (or ship) produced by the same *production process*'. My specially designed corner unit may have lots of replicas filling awkward corners in many kitchens. None of these replicas, however, are copied from my unit, and if it were destroyed it would not survive as any of them. The features it shares with them are a result of them all having been produced by the same production process.

In the type sense, then, the same ship, or kitchen unit, could have been made from different components, provided these were similar enough to the components actually used and organized into the same structures. Had the ship (type) which we call 'the *QEII*' been made of a different lot of steel, it would not have resulted in a ship of a new type, but simply in a different token. We will later see that there are special difficulties about distinguishing persons as types from persons as tokens. But even in their case we can make a point about necessity of origin, while being unclear—ultimately—about the status persons are to have.

Suppose, for a moment, that telecloning were to occur, that a chain of telecloned items showed appropriate relations of survival and that therefore we maintain that particulars can be *one and the same* despite having been telecloned. Imagine that my desk has just been shipped from Stirling to Antananarivo. of course, it might have been telecloned (if I could have afforded the bill). And so, once we admit that telecloning is possible, there is a world in which this very desk might have had a different material constitution from the one it in fact has. Does this mean that we should abandon any doctrine of necessity of origin?

Perhaps surprisingly, the very things that would incline us to maintain that the same desk persists through telecloning also force us to accept the necessity of origin. For surely, anyone who maintains the identity of something through telecloning will make this depend on the fact that it *survives* telecloning, and the survival is due to the fact that telecloning involves a *copying process*. Now any copying process requires an *original* for it to work on. My desk thus participates as the original, being involved in a *causal* process which ultimately produces its replica. The matter and structure of the original is thus of great significance: the copying process requires it and the success of the teleclone depends on its replicating the matter by similar matter and the structure by similar structure.

Persons, and other animals, may be thought of as structured collections of cells. But—on this thin conception of what a living organism is—we recognize the importance of their origins to the identity question. The fusion of any specific pair of sex cells is—in the natural course of events—extremely unlikely. So most organisms are the product of individually improbable happenings. Unrelated members of the same species are, given the variability across species, unlikely to match each other in fine structure, and hence in details of their components. (More will be said in the next chapter about matter, material, and components.) So, imagining that identity is always determinate, what would make one badger or human being the same cell collection through growth and maturity—and even through telecloning—is the operation of high-quality copying processes. But again we note that copying requires an original. Each event of copying thus leads us in a chain back to the first original—the creature as it was at origin (whenever *that* is!). The necessity of *origin* is thus no more than a special case of the necessity for a copying process to have an *original*.

These claims are not meant to suggest that our previous worries about identity and survival are not to be taken seriously. Rather, I have been showing how survival theory as so far developed can be applied to a metaphysically interesting area to yield results that are congenial to theorists of a certain temper. Even if a reader, then, fails to agee with my own qualms about the issues discussed in previous chapters, or about the nature of persons, there may still be a point in considering the benefits of the theoretical framework yielded by survival theory. The basic insight that a chain of items linked by survival may all be allocated to the same broad item has proved to have unexpected applications in these metaphysically treacherous areas.

It is now time to turn away from this particular range of problems. In the next chapter, the focus will be change in the real world. By the end of it, a theory of identity and survival will have been sketched out that is ready for application to the really puzzling sort of case we find in the literature on personal identity. Before turning, however, to these fascinating cases, space is made for some speculation about this world of particulars in which we find ourselves. The question of how the world manages to afford us our idea of unified particulars is put, and answered. That answer is given in the next chapter but one.

6
Structure and Stuff

Just as the issue of *individual essence* was discussed in the last chapter, this one can be thought of as clarifying, in part, the nature of *general* or *sortal essence*. The notions of replication, structure, and stuff are applied to a number of cases, illustrating how a relative atomism about the nature of things is possible. Since structures are nested within other structures, the survival conditions can apply to structured items at various levels. However, the components of artefacts have their role and location within artefacts determined, as we shall see, according to quite different principles from those applying to the components of natural objects.

One very simple view of inanimate objects is that they are, in Locke's words, 'mere masses of matter'. Such matter has a certain complexity, and a natural idea is that we can perhaps explain the properties of, and some of the changes affecting, such 'masses' in terms of facts about their component parts. Ever since the fifth century BC when Democritus and Leucippus first championed atomism, the notion that we can account for the features of objects in terms of the number and configuration of their unchanging, smallest components has been a powerful spur to philosophical and scientific thought about the nature of things. Dalton's chemical atomism, and the resulting development of atomic theory and quantum mechanics, are clear modern descendants of this ancient idea. In philosophy, one of the great works of the twentieth century, Wittgenstein's *Tractatus*, presents an atomism which is both an heir to the theories of Democritus, yet far removed from the empirical concerns of physical science. Wittgenstein's notion that the world contains 'simples' seems to depend, ultimately, on his view that the sense of words is something determinate. But without the configurations of such atomic simples there would be, in his view, no facts.[1]

---

[1] This is the burden of the propositions 2–2.0272. Hence he writes at 2.0272: 'A configuration of objects forms an atomic fact.'

Not only is the notion that there are atoms, or simples, a useful one to use when we are concerned to describe the merely material world, it is also a handy one to deploy when we turn to the description of living things, whatever their degree of complexity. I am not thinking here of the perhaps metaphorical deployment of the notion of items being structured out of atomic components, in the sense in which a Humean complex idea is constituted out of simpler ideas. Rather, for an example drawn from the present century, think of Bertrand Russell's neutral monism, which led him to the claim that brains differed from rocks not by virtue of being made, ultimately, of different *stuff*, but rather because brains are of a much higher degree of complexity than are rocks.

It might be thought that atomistic theories of matter must now be under the gravest suspicion, thanks to the development of physical theory in the twentieth century. Obviously, we now believe that atoms are not the qualitatively unchanging simples of Democritus and Wittgenstein, but rather complex, highly differentiated items composed in turn of particles that are themselves far from ultimate. However, not every atomist has claimed that atoms must be indivisible. Even some of the earliest atomists held a kind of 'relative' atomism in which what we take to be atomic relative to one standard may itself be complex relative to another.[2] Wittgenstein also, having declared the 'objects' of the *Tractatus* to be unalterable and simple, goes on to hint at a version of relative atomism when he remarks: 'Even if the world is infinitely complex, so that every fact consists of infinitely many atomic facts and every atomic fact is composed of infinitely many objects, there would still have to be objects and atomic facts' (4.2211). On reflection, some kind of relative atomism seems to be straightforward common sense. Relative to a hedgerow, the plants of which it is composed can perhaps be thought of as its atoms; but a holly bush is itself a complex thing relative to its stem, leaves, roots, and berries; the latter, in turn, are themselves complex relative to a finer level of description, and so on.

---

[2] Andrew van Melsen argues in his article on Atomism in *The Encyclopedia of Philosophy* ed. P. Edwards (London: Collier-Macmillan, 1967) that any doctrine allowing the divisibility of atoms is not genuinely atomistic. None the less, he reports that Alexander of Aphrodisias, and other Aristotelians, were relative atomists, allowing the divisibility of atoms. I understand that a similar doctrine is also found in Epicurus, although he maintains that atoms are only *finitely* divisible.

The main concerns of this book are questions of survival, identity, and related questions regarding our allocation of various objects to sorts, or kinds. The view for which I have been arguing so far might be thought to be compatible with relative atomism of the kind just sketched. One of the insights, common to all atomistic theories, is that it is in terms of its parts and their configuration that it is best to approach the description of the properties of an object and the changes affecting it. Another, much subtler, insight, deriving from the relativism just mentioned, is that different kinds of components make different contributions to the nature of an object. Both insights have already been the subject of discussion, and form a significant part of the defence of the views I am urging here.

Let us think, then, of simple cases in which an object has components which are configured, or structured, in a determinate way. A simple example is a diamond ring consisting—let us imagine—of a single diamond set in a gold mounting on a gold ring. We can at the outset distinguish in a fairly crude way between what we might call *local* and *global* structure. At the global level—the one accessible to us at the macroscopic level—let us think of the ring as consisting of just three parts: the stone, the mounting in which the stone is set, and the band. At the same level, though perhaps with the aid of a jeweller's glass, we can note the facets of the diamond and a small scratch on the band. Microscopically, or submicroscopically, we would note quite different facts about the ring. The stone is composed of carbon atoms in regular arrangement: their tetrahedral structure is distinctive of diamond and accounts for its strength. The gold parts are also arranged in a regular crystalline structure distinctive of gold. Close inspection would also show an arrangement of gold atoms that leaves numerous electrons free to move about in the material. In virtue of these free electrons, we can identify gold as a metal which conducts electricity.

In what way is structure, either at the local or at the global level, relevant to questions of the ring's identity? The answer to this question is very easy once we consider, for example, how we would go about *replicating* this particular ring. The best kind of replica, of course, is one that is indistinguishable from the original. To do this in the case of the ring, we should have to construct a new ring from exactly the same materials (having, therefore, all the same *local structures*) and, shaping exact replicas of the components, we would have to locate these replicas in just the same configuration as is shown by the original. Suppose, though, that for cheapness, we decide to use glass instead of diamond, and a shiny yellow alloy instead of gold in our replica. The difference between the original and the replica is now that although we may be able to preserve the same global structure—that is, components of the appropriate shape and size in the right configuration—the new replica has quite different local structures. By contrast, suppose we try to keep the local structures the same, but interfere with the overall structure of the ring. We melt the gold band and mount and enclose the diamond inside it. This time we have not interfered with local structure at all: the diamond still displays its ordered arrangement of atoms, the gold is still a lump of metal. But we no longer have a replica of the ring at all. We have replaced the ring by a gold-encased diamond.

These two very different cases are only the start. We have seen how to have better and poorer replicas of our ring, and also how to change it into something that would not be a ring at all. What if someone—an apprentice in the workshop—tries to make a copy of our original ring, but botches the job? the best ingredients have been used—pure gold and a real diamond. So the local structures are all replicated, but the overall structure leaves something to be desired. The band, suppose, is of a different width from the original and the mount is only the crudest of copies. Here we have an incomplete, or simplified replica: and for some purposes (though probably not in this case!) such a replica does perfectly well. Simplified, or crude, replicas are still replicas.

A greater departure from this standard of replication takes us to cases of scale-, and not-so-scale-, models. In what way does a small model aircraft replicate its original, or a three-times-life statue? In each case we have preservation of a great deal of overall structure (more accurately, of overall, *external* structure) together with maintenance of proportions despite changes in dimensions. The statue, then, keeps the leg and trunk in proportion, and in the same configuration relative to each other, while changing the dimensions of each. The scale model of the Boeing preserves relative configuration, but likewise keeps things in proportion. In neither case is there any attempt to preserve local structure: we don't expect scale models or statues to be of the same stuff as the original. An interesting feature of models, statues, and so forth is their loss of some important features of overall structure. For example lots of components are hinted at in a statue, but replicas of them are not present at all. A statue may have bronze arms and legs, but it will not have bronze bones, a bronze heart, or any other of thousands of vital parts—at least not outside fairy-tales. Likewise, our scale model may seem to have engines, and wings, but it really lacks the internal components that are so essential to engines and wings carrying out their functions. Even so, it is amazing how much we can learn from a good model. Wind-tunnel tests on a model will reveal an enormous amount about the flying characteristics of a proposed aircraft.

This loss of component detail typical of statues and models is continued in those 'replicas', if we can now call them such, where there is no attempt to preserve anything but the overall shape and rough dimensions of some original. A child's plasticine model of bus, for example, may lack counterparts for virtually every component we can think of, yet still be recognizable as a bus. Clearly, there will be a large area of unclear cases here, where we will not be sure what counts as a replica of what. Yet it is fairly clear that our appeal to the two levels of structure so far identified gives us a way of describing such cases: and that is an important first step in getting clear on what matters in any argument about replication.

By making this classification of cases, we have been able to distinguish many different kinds of *copying process*. If we think about different kinds of causal process that can be applied to an original, telecloning—rather like dismantling and rebuilding—is one which preserves the same local and the same overall structures. Pseudomorphism and telemutation (see Chapter 3.7) involve preservation of overall structure but *new* local ones. Reduction in overall structure and in local structure to an appropriate degree gives us the case of simplified replicas, scale models, and statues. By contrast, a process that preserves local structures but thoroughly replaces overall structures yields a new object. Notice that in this last case, the new object may be either of the same, or of a different, sort from the original. So a statue melted down and cast in a new mould makes a new item of the sort *statue*, but in the example of wrapping the diamond in gold we did not have a new ring. Again, change in both local and overall structures will yield a new object which may, or may not, be of the same sort as the original. Our relative atomism with regard to structure can prove extremely useful, then, in describing very many cases of change and survival.

In earlier chapters, the term 'survival' has been used to apply simply to the relation that exists between an original and some other item when the latter preserves in an appropriate way some feature, or features, of the former. It follows, as we have seen, that *survival* in my sense can come in degrees, and where the features preserved are very slight, it may even seem a bit odd to talk about survival at all. Our gold ring does not survive the transformation of its material into a diamond encased in gold. But a replica of the ring preserves certain features of its original and—were the original lost—then a nostalgic owner might be grateful that the original survives to some degree in the replica. To the extent, then, that a statue or a model preserves structural features of an original, that original can be said to survive in the statue or model.

It is clear, then, that survival involves questions of degree. A rather good example of this is found if we look at the mechanism of inheritance. A given child receives half of her gene complement from one parent and half from the other, so we believe. Genes, or at least combinations of genes, are responsible for features of overall structure—like facial features, length and shape of leg, and so on. In some cases, it is rather obvious that a child has preserved some features that are specific to one parent. To this extent, it makes sense in my usage to say that the parent survives in the child. Now, of course, it may be that the parent, in turn, inherited a feature, or set of features, from one of the child's grandparents. There is no guarantee that the quarter of its gene complement that a child acquires from a specific grandparent will result in obvious preservation of structural features: it all depends on what takes place during meiosis.[3] But there will be some cases in which we will be able to say that a child has inherited a number of features from one grandparent. In such cases the grandparent survives, to a certain extent, in the child. Of course, the extent of survival that we are talking about here may be pretty minor indeed. And to talk

---

[3] Different gene combinations get produced due to the shuffling that goes on in sexual reproduction. Dawkins assures us that 'it would be theoretically possible for an individual to endow one of his sperms with chromosomes which came, say, entirely from his mother. . . . In this unlikely event, a child conceived by the sperm would inherit half her genes from her paternal grandmother, and none from her paternal grandfather.' (Dawkins [1], p. 28.) This would be a case where the grandfather did not survive, genetically speaking, in the grandchild at all. My remark in the text is therefore based on what is statistically more probable—that most children get around a quarter of their genes from each grandparent.

about survival in this way is to make no large metaphysical claims. Indeed, it will only be when we have very high degrees of survival that anything of much consequence will be established. None the less, these simple cases at least make clear just what kind of thing survival is.

Once we have seen that different things can be related by the survival relation, we can start to consider just what sorts of structures are relevant to judgements of survival, and to think about the related question of how to decide which of various candidates is an item's closest survivor. Clearly, in dealing with items taken three-dimensionally, our notion of structure is tied to the notion of the *geometrical* arangement of the components identified. A one-twentieth scale model of bicycle preserves, in this sense, certain structural invariances. This is related to the kind of structural invariance that psychologists have noted as explaining our ability to recognize others despite ageing, disguise, make-up, and so on. McCabe suggests that our ability to discriminate such structural invariants amounts to a kind of direct perception of universals.[4] Yet epistemology is not my concern in this chapter, related though it is to the issues under discussion. Of course, to specify what a person or a diamond ring is is to specify, among other things, how much of the universe consists of this person or that diamond ring, and what parts of it do not. And such specification, in the end, could not take place without our having certain cognitive capacities, including certain perceptual, and recognitional abilities, as well as the universe offering certain features for these. to operate on.

However important structure and structural invariants may seem to be, there are surely—so it might be urged—a large class of things which have little or no macroscopic structure to speak of. A lump of rock, a cake-mix, or a dollop of mortar are everyday things which seem to have shape, or to be capable of taking up various shapes, while having no specifiable components relative to which we can talk about structure at all. Of course, at some suitably fine level of analysis, these things do have local structures depending on just what the ingredients of the cake-mix, and the proportion of sand in the mortar, are. If a child, however, makes a model of a lump of rock in plasticine, then we are satisfied if the model is accurate in shape,

----

[4] See McCabe [1]. Andy Clark first drew my attention to the relevance of McCabe's paper to survival theory.

of approximately the right volume and—perhaps—replicates the colour of the original. Is this an example where an appeal to structure is now seen to be redundant? Not at all. Rather, it is a case which shows that *shape* is itself a degenerate case of structure. For an object to have a structure, it must at least have a shape, and occupy a certain spatial volume. Now, in the case of a typically structured item, its shape is the result of relative location of its components. But in the case of something which is amorphous and therefore lacks clearly differentiated and separably discernible components, what has been said so far about structure translates simply into claims about shape. Whereas a good replica of a ring preserves structure (and hence automatically preserves shape) a good replica of a ball of dough is another ball of dough similar in shape and colour. Perhaps less good is a ball of some other material which preserves shape and colour; and less good still—though perfectly appropriate for many purposes—is a ball of some material which is roughly the right shape even though different in colour and overall dimensions.

All this talk of good and less good replication might foster the notion that there is some absolute standard of replication relative to which we can always settle a survival question. Yet it would be vain to search for any such standard. I have taken it as relatively uncontroversial that if we wish to replicate one thing in another thing, then for the second thing to be the best possible replica it must share local and global structure and overall dimensions with the thing it replicates. Thus the best replica for a ball of dough is another ball of dough that would be indistinguishable at all levels of structure from the first. Talk of other levels of replication being 'less good' than this ideal should, I think, be taken with the appropriate pinch of salt. A photograph may preserve some features of an object in the way that a sculpture in bronze does not; and vice versa. Yet, with this caveat, we can still make sense of the spectrum of cases encountered so far.

I think that enough has been said in this section to indicate one kind of view we can take about material particulars thought of as three-dimensional. Such things are made of matter, and take up space. The matter they are made of is, however, closely related to the structures they display: and these structures are, at various levels, explored by physical and chemical theory. The volume of space they occupy is associated with shape, which, for many objects is itself the result of structural relations holding among discernible macroscopic components. For other, amorphous things, the kind of shape they have may be to some extent determined by the kind of matter they are made from (but even here, the kind of matter they consist of is not independent of structure at some finer level). All objects will display nestings of structures, whereby items which are basic components modulo one level of description become themselves structured wholes modulo some finer level.

6.2. COMPONENTS

In the last section, we simplified matters in our examples by taking global or overall structure to be for the most part macroscopic, and local to be microscopic. But, if structures are nested within structures, that will be only one way of making the local/overall distinction. Moreover, we have not yet followed up the implications of taking the concept of component in the way suggested by what I have called 'relative' atomism. For just as what is local differs from what is global, relative to some agreed metric, so what is a component, in the designer's sense, is very different—as we shall see—from what is a component understood in some other way.

The combination of these points leads to a more complex story about the metric of change than is commonly attempted. Think, for example, of the refurbishment of Theseus' ship. Suppose a windlass breaks and is repaired in such a radical way that the original windlass fails to survive the process to any significant degree. This means that, relative to a specification of local and overall structures appropriate to the study of windlasses, the old windlass has been replaced rather than *just* repaired. The new windlass will therefore show significant structural differences from the old one. But if we now change our frame of reference and consider the ship as a whole, itself an item with overall structure, then the windlass features, from this perspective, as one rather insignificant element of *local* structure. So its replacement by the radical repairs in no way threatens the survival of the ship. In saying this, I am assuming that we can—in the end—develop some theory of artefact survival and artefact identity. Before we get too excited about such a prospect, however, we will have to consider the prospects in general for such a theory. As we will see, it is very doubtful if an entirely satisfactory theory of such matters can ever be produced.

At this point, one possible form of criticism should be anticipated. It might be thought that our distinction between local and global structure leads us into a kind of *disappearance theory* of matter. For are we not, in effect, suggesting that what matter an item is made from depends, ultimately, on the kind of fine structure present within the item? At first sight, the move seems attractive. For we do tend to classify *materials*, in many cases, by distinguishing different structures the same elemental stuff can take up. Thus, textbooks typically show diamond and graphite differing as shown in Fig. 13.[5] On the left is represented the unit-cell of the diamond crystal structure, showing the powerful co-valent three-dimensional bond which creates a tetrahedron of nearest neighbouring atoms. On the right is a representation of the more naturally abundant form of carbon, where this time the co-valent bonding takes place in a planar, rather than three-dimensional form. The carbon atoms here form 'planes' as it were, these planes being bound together by relatively weak bonds (known as van der Waals bonds). Since the planes can move easily with respect to each other, this form of carbon has extremely good lubricating properties.

The important thing to notice here is that both our materials are composed simply of carbon. The different crystal structures in which the carbon atoms participate account for the noticeable differences between diamond and graphite. But even in giving this much explanation, we realize that we have not done away with

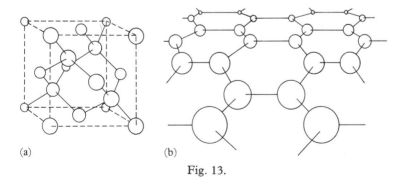

(a)   (b)

Fig. 13.

[5] Reproduced from Ian Wilson [1] pp. 42, 52.

matter: for the matter, in the sense of the *elements* which constitute diamond or graphite, has itself an important role to play in our story about structures. So, in our earlier cases of survival, should we have talked about preserving *material* rather than *matter*?

Unfortunately, the terminological issues here are not at all clear. If we are distinguishing matter, as occupier of space, from the form or structure that matter may exhibit, then matter includes material. On the other hand, it will not do for a relative atomist to rest happy with the elements as clear examples of matter and call everything else *material*; for what distinguishes carbon from hydrogen, say, is the difference in number of nuclear particles and electrons in the atom—a distinction which surely deserves to be recognized as including both matter and structure. For most of the cases we are likely to care about, the matter of which an item is constituted will be further structured. Thus a car—to take a complex artefact—will have some highly-structured components (engine, gearbox, seats) as well as components that have less by way of structure. But even in a plastic construction set where the bricks clip into each other, the 'simple' components—the bricks—will be structured (for otherwise they would not clip into each other at all).

Thus when we apply our three conditions on survival, we can take the matter-condition as holding of structures which are local relative to the item in question taken as a global whole. But we could, if we wished, give an account of atoms in which, relative to them as global wholes, protons, neutrons, and electrons are unstructured components. Then we could decide that atom A survives as atom B under these conditions: (1) B has the same number of electrons, protons, and neutrons as A (sameness of matter); (2) they are arranged in B in just the same way as in A (sameness of structure); and (3) the matter and structure of these items in B depends, in an appropriate causal way, on the structure and matter of A. If we were able to devise a teleclone machine that worked on atoms, satisfaction of our conditions would give us grounds for believing that atoms can survive telecloning.

Although the telecloning of atoms is rather fanciful, one sort of replication or survival problem is a regular worry in daily life. If I have sent my car, or my camera, for frequent enough repairs, I may not know *how many* cameras or cars I have owned over the last few years. Hirsch, who is attracted by compositionalist solutions to this kind of problem, rather arbitrarily suggests that we need not worry about the loss of up to one-third of an artefact's components at any one time. For so long as that third is replaced by similar components in similar arrangements, we still have—he thinks—the same artefact.

By constrast, Wiggins is very doubtful about any addition or subtraction of matter whatever.[6] Suppose we have two stages, separated in time, which show no change either by addition or subtraction. We seem to have a quite unquestionable case for assigning them both to the same particular. As soon as we depart from this situation, it becomes enormously difficult to supply any kind of identity conditions for artefacts. The only case so far in which identity claims have been defended was in connection with episodic natural objects. There, it was argued that an assignment of the discontinuous stages to one broad particular could be defended by appeal to a chain of survival relations. Why, we might wonder, can we not do the same in the case of artefacts?

I share Wiggins's doubts and, moreover, I think it is possible to give some clear reasons why the question of artefact identity is so tricky. Let us start by thinking some more about what are—relative to the whole artefact—*local* structures or components. In both artefacts and natural objects, we can identify components as *functional* parts within a larger item. Living things, whose continued existence depends on repair, nutrition, and homeostasis, are themselves intrinsically functionless, in my view, but with components (organs, glands, veins, nerves) which have a functional role in securing the continued existence of the whole item. Thus the human temperature-control mechanism is a functional device just as much as the thermostat in an engine is. Of course, someone designed the engine and its thermostat, and no one, according to my beliefs, designed human beings or any other living thing. This is not to deny that we could take what Dennett calls the 'design stance' in describing, for example, the roles of plants and animals in ecosystems. But such a move is purely a heuristic device—it does not mean we have to take voles, humans, or spiders as being the products of anyone's, or anything's, design.[7]

---

[6] 'What supports the ontology of artefacts, and what has made it possible in the first instance to treat artefacts as continuants, is the availability of an indubitably sufficient condition of artefact identity . . . it excludes all addition or subtraction of matter whatever.' (Wiggins [9], p. 97.)

[7] This is a tricky matter, the more so because different theorists of function have different views about just what are cases exemplifying function. I discuss these matters in a paper on the moral standing of natural objects, in *Environmental Ethics* 6 (1984), where I refer to some of the literature on function.

In non-living natural objects, we have greater difficulty in identifying functional components. Let us decide that the grass cover, forest, scrub, and even the soil on a mountain is no part of it. This will work well enough for those mountains which are largely rocks, or aggregates of rock. Now it is hard to see what could be meant by identifying some portions of rock, or even microscopic structures within it, as having a function. So let us suppose that rocks, hills, lumps of ice, glaciers, and clouds lack functional components altogether.

If we stay with the non-living natural objects for a moment longer, we can notice that what (non-functional) components they do have are there as a result of natural happenings. Of course, some such happenings are adventitious or random. But once a volcano erupts, or a movement takes place along a fault, the subsequent cooling and crystallization of minerals, or chemical changes induced by pressure, are themselves well-ordered and lawful. The same is true of living things. Whether a body is invaded by a virus or struck by a missile may be unpredictable; but the consequent occurrences again take place according to fairly well-understood physical, biological, and chemical principles. Likewise, although nature displays great variability, the growing plant or animal develops according to well-known regularities, and the positioning of organs and other components displays a quite uniform pattern within determinate limits. Without this degree of uniformity— within which the majority of natural variation occurs—taxonomy based on the study of plant and animal structures would never get anywhere.

By contrast, components of artefacts get into place according to *quite different* principles. There are no natural laws governing where carburettors and alternators should be placed in a car engine. Of course, the designer has to take account of natural laws in all sorts of ways. There is no point in using a ductile material for the teeth of gears, or placing the fuel tank where gravity would have to be overcome in filling it. But these constraints leave designers significant amounts of freedom. This elbow-room can make it hard for us to identify components in an unfamiliar engine, or find our way around in a strange control room.

What does then, constrain the designer's choice, and location, of components? The answer would seem to be that these are chosen according to the function of the artefact being designed. For artefacts unlike natural objects do have *intrinsic functions*, and it is the designer's task to come up with a set of components, sutably arranged, that will fulfil these functions efficiently. Even then there will still be lots of elbow-room. Over the years, designers will play, as it were, with the positioning of components—like alternators and carburettors—where their exact positioning is of no obvious consequence to the efficiency of the whole artefact.

6.3. STRUCTURE AND FUNCTION

We seem to have discovered an important distinction between components, in the designer's sense, and *natural components*, as we might term them. This distinction crudely amounts to a distinction between components for which there are no fixed specifications as to size, location, and so forth and those for which there are fairly precise, lawfully determined specifications. Further, we have suggested that this distinction is itself a consequence of a fairly obvious difference between those items—artefacts—which have an intrinsic function or set of functions and those other natural objects which are intrinsically functionless. Of course, natural objects often have roles to play within artefacts—like the shrubs in a garden, or the lead ballast in the keel of a boat. Our pruning of the shrub to give it the desired shape can be likened to our hardening of the steel for a knife-blade. In each case, the skill of the gardener or steel-worker is to work on the natural material so that law-governed changes occur within it in order to suit the ends for which the larger artefact is designed.

Now these apparently simple points about components and functions are extremely relevant to our queries on artefact identity. It turns out, indeed, that artefacts display two kinds of peculiarity with respect to the unity question. First, fairly slight changes in components can turn an artefact of one sort into an artefact of quite a different sort—bad news for theorists who are looking for simple accounts of sortal-covered continuity. Second, there are also cases where massive component changes in an artefact will in no way inhibit us from claiming that it continues the same. Both kinds of case are to be explained by the features of functionality and design peculiar to artefacts. For although structure supports function, artefacts—being function-specific—display both of the peculiarities cited. The existence of such cases will make it extremely difficult for us to develop any plausible account of artefact identity.

Let us start by looking at a case of the first sort: an apparently minor set of changes that turn one artefact into a new one. My desk-lamp is one of those which swivels on a weighted base, and is jointed and sprung in such a way as to allow a wide range of angles for its deployment. Struck by its similarity to a robot-arm, I decide to make it just that. A small motor is wired to the base using some of its existing cable. The rest of the cable is used for wiring up a second motor, and a simple grab device, while the shade and bulb-holder are removed. Finally, a system of wires and pulleys link the two motors to critical points in the assembly, and the last of the lamp's cable is used to wire it into a set of control switches. Using them I can get it to dip, swivel, and pick up some objects.

This case brings to our attention some of the difficulties in dealing with the metric of change. Many authors on identity have a strange predilection for trying to measure change in terms of volume, number of components, and so on. Now this is something of which we must be wary—as the lamp example shows. We can easily imagine arranging this transformation without coming close to Hirsch's magic proportion of replacing more than a third of the lamp's parts. In fact, the weight and volume of the lamp are neither of them, let us suppose, greatly increased by our modifications. And, for continuity theorists, there is the embarrassing continuity of the majority of the lamp through a process that results in its replacement!

What has changed most dramatically is the *function* of the artefact. What had been an item for shedding light has been transformed into an item for picking up and moving objects. It is this radical change in function that leads us to classify the arm as a different *sort* of thing from the lamp. Notice, incidentally, that the destruction of the lamp depended on removing certain *critical components*. Without a bulb-holder, our artefact cannot be a lamp of any sort. By contrast, retaining the bulb-holder, removing the shade, and installing the grab just next to the bulb might have given me a dual-purpose artefact—something that remained a lamp, but had acquired the ability to function also as a robot-arm.

If the lamp example shows how slight changes may have large repercussions, then the next case will show the converse. Suppose a custom car enthusiast buys a perfectly ordinary saloon car and then proceeds to hot it up in various ways. A new engine is fitted; parts of the floor are cut out and stronger sections welded in their place; the suspension is radically modified; new wider wheels are fitted, and the brakes uprated; to finish off, various fancy bits are added—perhaps spoilers, aerodynamic skirts, new fleece and leather bucket seats, diminutive steering wheel, and so on. Not only is this a perfectly familiar case, but the owners of such monstrosities seem quite untroubled by identity qualms. Of course it's the same car. It just shows you what can be done with a clapped-out old saloon. *It's* worth far more now than I bought *it* for, and if I sold *it* now, I'd get back more than I've put into *it*! The catalogue of changes here are all put down to *modifications*—a term that can embrace almost anything.

How can we explain this amazing retention of identity? Quite simply by remembering the points about function and components. The changes have not altered the vehicle's basic functions—it still transports people, makes loud noises, and attracts the odd glance. Indeed, the proud owner would maintain that it fulfils these functions far more effectively now. Any car manufacturer has choices about which carburettors, shock absorbers, wheels, and so on to use in building a car. Our enthusiast has simply changed lots of these earlier choices by changing the nature of the components and, quite probably, their location as well. Of course, all this is not to deny that this sort of meddling can produce new—or different—cars.

The compositional and continuity theorists, of course, again face a problem, this time because the changes are so large. Little of our original vehicle has survived the enthusiast's attentions, and its structural arrangements are significantly different. This time, however, the survival theorist is also in a spot of bother. As far as the lamp case was concerned, there was no difficulty for that view. For the lamp can survive in the arm while not being identical with it—that is a commonplace of the survival view. But in this new example, there seems to be little help for the survivalist: structure and matter have both changed significantly, although we can no doubt tell a decent causal story about how the character of successive stages depends to some extent on the character of earlier stages.

We can now start to see why it is impossible to produce an account of artefact identity by using any, or combinations, of the following conditions:

(a) spatio-temporal continuity of enough material;
(b) preservation of enough components;
(c) survival, that is replication by appropriate causal means of structure and, possibly, matter as well.

A tempting proposal, then, is to try supplementing some or all of the above by reference to sortals. Perhaps what we should say is that in the case of artefact-stages *A* and *B*, we cannot decide identity (that is, whether they belong to some same artefact) without first knowing if *A* and *B* fall under the same, or different, sortals. If we took this course, then the examples considered so far would suggest that sortal-covered survival was perhaps the best candidate for yielding plausible results. Of course, this suggestion has an immediate drawback. As we suggested in the last chapter but one, there are no convincing reasons for taking proper stages of real-world particulars as themselves falling under sortals at all.

There is less objection, however, to allowing proper stages some functional properties. So perhaps we could get something like the proposed suggestion off the ground by maintaining that what we need, for stages *A* and *B* to be assigned to the same artefact, is that they both fulfil some same function or set of functions. Then it would be a matter, perhaps, of seeking to adapt our survival conditions. But this means that we could take survival to a fairly low degree together with preservation of function as the conditions under which the stages are to be assigned to the same artefact. This might, in the end, be the best we could do in constructing an account of artefact identity. But, if so, it simply leaves us facing the following new version of the Theseus' ship puzzle.

Suppose this time that our continuously functioning ship is modified by an ancient enthusiast. Each time gear fails or comes up for repair, it is likely to have gear of a new design put in its place, and over time the original ship starts to look different, handle differently, and so on. Obviously, we can imagine quite drastic changes along these lines. The plank-hoarder this time manages to produce a ship-stage that is much more *like* the original in terms of structure and components. Its claim to be Theseus' ship is ruled out because, in the intervening times, while waiting for the plank collection to build up, there has been a sequence of ship-stages with survival of one in/as the next and preservation of functions. And that sequence, by the proposed conditions, should be allocated to one and the same ship. But once the antiquarian's ship-stage appears on the scene, we have to admit not only preservation of function on its part, but preservation of the original functions, together with far closer replication of matter and structure. And shouldn't *it* win hands down this time against the rival? The plank-hoarder's stage is surely the closer function-preserving survivor of the original stage (so long as it is moderately seaworthy).

Now a supporter of the *only x and y* rule would maintain that we should not be influenced by the availability, or otherwise, of rivals in this situation. But someone supporting such a view has no obvious way of maintaining one identity rather than the other. The changing ship is like the modified car—so long as it goes on functioning *as* a ship—we can hardly say that Theseus' original has ceased to exist. Yet the antiquarian's version has authenticity on its side. The survivalist might say that here we have a clear case where identity cannot be decided, but survival has occurred *twice over*. Survival theorists would win the argument hands down, were it not for certain complicating factors. One is the *sorites*-like step which goes: a slight modification to an *F*-thing results in an *F*-thing. Since we can readily imagine changing a boat to a caravan by a number of individually small modifications, it is clear that the step cannot be applied recursively. And, as we saw earlier, the survivalist can hardly make appeal to sortals: for even if we change our boat into a caravan, the boat may survive in (or as) the caravan. So even if artefact identity were sortal-relative, artefact survival would not be. The prospects, then, for any theory of artefact identity are bleak, and the theory of artefact survival seems to fare not much better.

6.4. ARTEFACT IDENTITY

It is ironic, perhaps, that the things we make ourselves—artefacts—give us some of the biggest headaches about identity. We have already seen, though, that the maxim 'no entity without identity' needs to be taken less than seriously. For I may not know how many different objects I have produced while modifying some original artefact, yet still be sure that my original artefact still survives to some extent the latest changes. In this case, I may be willing to concede to the identity-theorist that the Mark-20 version of my car is definitely not the same car as the original I bought. The changes have gone too far for identity to have been retained. But I still have a car, and it was a car I bought. So what I don't know is how many entities of the sort *car* my tamperings have produced. Of course, this is perhaps not what Quine's maxim is intended to rule out. And we can surely agree that the Mark-20 version is one car, that is, one item of the sort *car*.

But how do we know this? What is it that marks an item as belonging to the *sort* in question? For Locke, a sort was no more than a collection of objects associated with an abstract idea (*Essay* III. 3. § xv). Thus to every concept, the modern Lockean might say, there corresponds a sort. The terms true of such sorts are supposed—as we saw originally—to provide us with principles of counting the things in the sort. One epistemological reading of the fancy phrase 'provides principles of counting for A's' is simply that anyone who understands the term in question has the ability (in some situations at least) to establish how many A's are in a certain location. Without rehearsing our earlier qualms, let us just turn to the question of how we can do this for classes of artefacts.

One answer refers us back to the issue of function. Artefacts have intrinsic functions, or sets of them. So to be able to count the number of cars in my street our sortal possessor must be able to recognize those things that function as cars, distinguishing them from items functioning as bicycles, lampposts, and so on. But how do we recognize something as functioning one way rather than another? In Gibson's phrase, cars *afford* transport, seating, exhilaration, and so on.[8] The problem is to know how we are able to recognize the existence of such *affordances*. My answer to this question is that we do so because cars have certain structures and we are able to recognize them as possessing such structures. For instance, the relative disposition of doors, seats, and steering-wheel is significant in our recognizing an object as affording transport.

The notion that such structural arrangements really are, in some way, in the world and available to us perceptually, runs up against philosophical resistance based on a certain picture of the environment. According to this picture there are no structural weightings of the sort just described as far as a truly objective account of the world is concerned. Of course, we can maintain that car doors co-

---

[8] 'All these offerings of nature, these possibilities or opportunities, these *affordances* as I call them . . .' (Gibson [1], p. 18). An affordance is a kind of invitation to action.

occur with car seats and steering-wheels in a way they do not co-occur with bicycle-spokes. But this claim, the objectors will argue, can only be made relative to a prior identification of such things as car doors, steering-wheels, and bicycle-spokes. These prior identifications depend on the concepts we bring to experience, the objection continue, rather than on real similarities and differences in the world. The objection here is a powerful one, based on what I call *the extensionalist myth*. Its full treatment must wait till the following chapter. But, for the moment, let us simply suppose that the myth is false. Suppose we do live in a highly structured and organized world, and many of our concepts thus reflect, rather than impose, the patterning of the world.

No such supposition involves us in the belief that *function* can always be read off from structure. N. R. Hanson was led, notoriously, to the view that perception was, for skilled eyes, a matter of *seeing as* precisely because he noted this point. I can examine a transistor, or a sonic scalpel, at great length and still remain bemused as to its function. But, of course, structure also supports function. We give artefacts a certain structure to enable them to fulfil their functions. So, the obvious conclusion is that through experience we learn to recognize things as having a certain function by virtue of recognizing their structure. This does not, however, mean that I and the Eskimo see different things when we look at snow, although we can make some sense of the claim that we see the snow as different things. For I may see as treacherous footing what the Eskimo sees as good snow-shoeing material.

In Gibson's terms the Eskimo and I differ with respect to our ability to recognize the *affordances* of snow, cars, and seals. But, of course, what we see when we look at snow, cars, and seals must in some basic way be the same. Indeed, the similarity of our visual experiences is required if I and the Eskimo are to learn interesting things about each other's environment. It we focus specifically on artefacts, then we need only reflect on our own experiences of visiting ancient buildings or museums to realize that although structure supports function, we cannot always infer the function of an artefact simply by seeing its structure.

Artefacts, then, on my account are highly structured, function-specific things. But although we can recognize the structures artefacts possess, we cannot always infer function from this. Thus, someone unacquainted with lamps, robot-arms and other technological paraphernalia would be able to watch me transform my lamp into a robot-arm yet be unaware whether I had changed one thing of a sort into a different thing (of the same or a different sort). Nor would the same person be able to pronounce on whether the series of car modifications some enthusiast has just done has left us looking at the same or a different car. In this latter case, as we have seen, it could be that the untutored eye is no worse off than the knowing eye.

In order to recognize function when confronted with structure, we have to have acquired certain cognitive skills. These skills do not just involve knowing what the functions of various things are. Unacquainted as I am with the finer points of mountaineering, I may nevertheless know the functions of crampons. Yet, facing a set of crampons, I am unable to say what they are. The skills involved in recognizing functional things, then, must involve familiarity with the structures designers regularly use to fulfil these functions. And in these days of rapid technological change we have to keep this information up to date.

Identity and survival thus come apart to some extent. The untutored eye can discern structural changes and invariances that are relevant to survival. But only the person up to date with contemporary robotics and electric lighting will be aware that I have changed my desk-lamp into a new item. In saying these things, of course, we have still failed to give a decent theory of artefact identity. But by now it should be clear that we are unlikely ever to come up with one.

6.5. PETRIFIED FORESTS

The problem of structure and function, raised by looking at the status of components in artefacts and in natural objects, led us naturally into considering the question of artefact identity. Whereas appropriate chains of survival-related parts constitute the history of natural objects, a survival-related chain of stages can be allocated to more than one artefact. Moreover, chains in which the survival relation is not evident to a very high degree may none the less count as the history of one artefact. These two findings make the prospect of any regimented theory of artefact identity somewhat remote.

Even if the essence of artefacts is going to be a permanent puzzle to us, we can make some sense of an essentialist account of the nature of natural things. However, there are one or two problems associated with petrified forests, the case of Lot's wife, and with the life histories of insects and amphibians that need attention and these will be dealt with in this and the following sections.

It is worth noting in advance that one response to some of these cases would be to take identity and survival as coming apart in a more drastic way than that envisaged at the end of the preceding section: survival would no longer have any role to play in the account of unity for natural things. Better than this, I will argue, is the common-sense option that survival does have a role in the unity story, and that even in apparently extreme cases—like the metamorphoses of insects—we still have survival of significant structures from one phase to the next. Indeed, nature works with surprisingly limited transformations. However, the question of whether a certain larval phase survives as some future larval phase is a technical, empirical one, not to be resolved by the philosopher.

Although our conclusions on artefact identity have not been terribly helpful, we have now discovered enough about structures and stuff to say something about some well-known current problems in the theory of identity. As was indicated in the first chapter, continuity under a sortal is often thought to be distinctive of unified, numerically identical things. We have seen many reasons since then for doubting that *continuity* in space and time is really all that important. But now let us reflect for a moment on the points about sortals.

For a theorist like Wiggins, one reason for an interest in sortals is that by using them we are able to give fundamental answers to the all-important question 'what is *that*?' (where we imagine pointing to something or other as we ask the question). We previously noted that sortal nouns are precisely those which, unlike mass nouns, provide principles of counting for the particulars to which they apply. Now, of course, it is easy to imagine that associated with each sortal noun is a sortal *concept*, grasp of which enables us to identify sorts and use sortal nouns. Although I say this is easily imagined, it does not follow that such a move is justified.[9] We can speculate, for

---

[9] It may be thought pedantic or conservative, but I think it is simply *prudent* to pause before assuming that every noun has some concept associated with it. Now, even if in some way words have their attached concepts, is it safe to assume that we know what these concepts are? Logicians have long been prone to assume, for

example, about whether there might be sortal concepts which fail to match, in any neat way, the sortal nouns of English. But let us reason as if no such problems exist.

Having sortal concepts under which items fall still does not, according to Wiggins, provide us with the right answer to the 'what is x?' question. For suppose the thesis of *relativity of identity* were true. On this account, it is possible for x to be the same F as y, but not the same G, even where both F and G are proper sortal concepts. Think, for example, of languages and dialects. I speak the same language (English) as a Norfolk farmer, but not the same dialect. So x may be the same language as y, while x is not the same dialect as y.

Earlier I used the phrase 'relative identity' as a synonym for 'qualitative identity' or 'similarity'. It is important not to confuse the existence of similarity with this doctrine that identity itself is relative. The two things are related, however. For what the theory of relative identity says might be glossed as follows: some cases of identity are really are really just cases of similarity; for x can be identical with y *under one sortal*, but be distinct from y under some other sortal.

This kind of sortal-relative theory need not, of course, deny that sometimes we have clear cases of what we might call *absolute* identity (namely where $x = y$ and x remains identical with y no matter what sortals they fall under).[10] Wiggins's own view is interestingly neither a relativist nor an absolutist one. For he insists that to say '$x = y$' is simply to say something which entails that x is the *same something* as y. This may look like a move towards the relativity of identity, but Wiggins goes on to insist further that no two sortals that apply to x throughout its career will diverge in the identities they license. So suppose $x = y$, and x is a *ship* throughout its entire history, and is also a *vessel* throughout its entire history. Then x is the same ship as y and x also is the same vessel as y.[11]

example, that the concepts of negation, conjunction, and the conditional associated with classical logic are just the same as those associated with 'not', 'and', and 'if' in English. Fortunately, this belief, once so widely held, is seen these days as requiring justification—not to say modification.

[10] This position is held, for instance, by Griffin in Griffin [2].

[11] Wiggins's defence of his position is comprehensively laid out in ch. 2 of Wiggins [9]. He calls his thesis D (the thesis of the sortal dependency of identity). Wiggins' view must thus be carefully distinguished from relativism in the style of Geach, who writes: 'When one says "x is identical with y", this, I hold, is an incomplete expression; it is short for "x is the same A as y" where "A" represents some

Wiggins thinks that sortal concepts which present-tensedly apply to a particular (he would say a *continuant*) at every moment throughout its existence are rather special. He calls them *substance-concepts*, crediting them with giving the privileged and most fundamental answer to the question 'What is x?' We can see what Wiggins is getting at if we contrast these concepts with a different kind, namely sortals which apply only to stretches of a particular's existence. Such *phased sortals* include nouns like 'girl', 'tadpole', 'youth', 'sapling', and so on. If we believe that particulars have a *nature* or essence, in virtue of which they are what they are, then substance concepts will be what describe, in a general and fundamental way, the natures of things.

There is already an adequate literature dealing with the thesis of the relativity of identity and Wiggins's thesis that identity statements need to be sortal-dependent.[12] It should be clear, however, that the approach to identity and survival suggested in this book promises to take us further than Wiggins's one. For, as has already been claimed, our ability to grasp sortal concepts and apply them depends on a prior ability to recognize structures and be aware of the degree of structural change that various sorts of things can tolerate. If Wiggins is right in claiming identity is sortal-dependent and that, as he puts it, what 'a man who says that a is b commits himself to is that a and b are the same something', then identity will have to be *structure*-dependent.[13] Again, Wiggins's claim that the elucidation of $a = b$ depends on the kind of thing a is, can be put in our terms as the claim that the elucidation of a's identity depends on the sorts of structure it possesses.

We encountered earlier the sad case of Rover, whose trip to Mars had such disastrous consequences for his macroscopic and microscopic structures. To recap, we named the amorphous blob, into which Rover turned, 'Clover', and we noted that continuity theorists might maintain identity between Rover and Clover. Now,

---

count noun understood from the context of utterance—or else it is just a vague expression of a half-formed thought.' (Geach [3], p. 238.) He also writes: 'On my own view of identity, I could not object in principle to different A's being one and the same B' (Geach [1], p. 157). Although the latter quotation clearly commits Geach to relativism, the former represents a view that is distinct from Wiggins's one, and considerably stronger.

[12] The eager reader can follow up references in Griffin [2] and in Wiggins [9].
[13] The remark is quoted from Wiggins [9], p. 46.

although Wiggins is interested in elucidating identity by appeal to both sortals and continuity, he is able to avoid the identification of Rover and Clover. There is, after all, no genuine substance-concept under which they both fall. Indeed, if Rover were to count as one and the same as Clover, this would be a clear counter-example to one of Wiggins's main claims—namely that for any particular at all, there is some genuine sortal which is true of it at all the times at which it exists.

Like the Rover–Clover case, the Biblical story of Lot's wife also threatens Wiggins's principle. When Lot's wife looked back at the ruins of Sodom and Gomorrah, she was transformed into a pillar of salt. Wiggins spends some time trying to convince us that no one thing can be both a woman (at one time in its history) and a pillar of salt (at some other time). In his terms, this means that *woman* and *pillar of salt* are *not* phased sortals which restrict some underlying substance-concept (the way *sapling*, for instance, restricts *tree*). If true, this is clearly an important point. For it shows yet again that mere spatio-temporal continuity is not sufficient for particular identity. We have seen already that such continuity is not even necessary for identity, by thinking about the discontinuous hill.

Wiggins, however, has to argue against the possibility that one and the same thing may be first a woman and then a pillar of salt without being able to make the appeal we can make to survival. For, on my account, the question of whether this pillar of salt on the Jebel Usdum was once Lot's wife can be approached via the question: does Lot's wife survive as or in this pillar of salt? If survival is the more primitive relation, underpinning identity, we should always tackle the survival question when in doubt over the identity one. Once we put the survival question, however, we see ways of being able to answer it.

Suppose first that the pillar into which Lot's wife turned was a pretty uniform forty-foot affair, with apparently no external features of structure to make it look at all like his wife. In other words, we are *not* imagining a pillar that looks like Lot's wife in the way a statue in salt might. In such a case, there is no structural or material support for a survival claim. And, accordingly, we take it that Lot's wife has ceased to exist by this divine act, and does not survive in or as the pillar of salt. Such a result rules out the identity claim as well.

By contrast, it is much harder to know what to say if we think of the case as akin to pseudomorphism (see Chapter 3.7). Suppose God has been able to bring about a kind of fossilization of Lot's wife in the way that whole forests have been fossilized over time while yet the minute structures of the trees are preserved. Helen Morris Cartwright, in her review of Wiggins, writes of the Lot's wife example: 'The case is in one way no worse than that of a tree in the Petrified Forest which stands where there was once an oak. We can suppose that the oak has *turned into* a petrified one, but *it* is not now a petrified tree.'[14] Clearly, a survival theorist would not share Cartwright's intuitions here. For if Lot's wife's organ-structures, the disposition of her limbs and even her facial features, are captured in the sodium chloride, the conditions on survival make the survival claim plausible. Would we fail to understand what Lot was saying if, in subsequently returning to the fatal spot, he pointed out the salt-pillar as being his wife?

The referential situation in this example does not seem a lot different from other cases involving pictures, models, and statues. The murderous duke in Browning's poem says, speaking of his last duchess:

> . . . Fra Pandolf's hands
> Worked busily a day, and there she stands.
> Won't please you sit and look at her?

but he is, of course, looking only at a painting. It was precisely the existence of this sort of referential practice that supported initially the claim that one thing could survive in another—the parent in the child, the author in the book, or even the duchess in the picture.

A Quinean objection to this might be that the model, the painting, and so on are cases simply of *deferred ostension*. On this view, we can say 'That's a horse' while pointing to something that is quite definitely not a horse.[15] The statue, model, or whatever we are pointing at, depicts, or represents, some horse at which we are pointing—so to speak—at one remove. Applied to the last duchess, the duke is, on this account, speaking about *her* while gesturing, let us suppose, towards Fra Pandolf's painting. If we take this objection seriously, then there can be no real prospects of someone surviving in a painting or a statue. For the move, in effect, denies

---

14 Cartwright [3], p. 599.
15 See Quine [2], p. 108, Quine [7], pp. 39–42.

that there really are the right kinds of causal and structural relations between the original and the representation.

To see what is wrong with this objection, we need to wait till the next chapter. For the moment, however, notice that there are statues and statues. Some rusty iron bars and nails may purport to be a representation of the sculptor's friend, yet leave us completely in the dark as to the sex, age, size, and species of the friend. In such a case, Rex, or whatever, would not be said by me to survive even to a low degree in the sculpture. By contrast, a bronze of a racehorse that is accurate to the finest detail—as if we were looking at a miniaturized fossil of the horse—will be one in which the horse survives to some degree. With the Quinean objection shelved for the moment, we can begin to make sense of why the case of the petrified forest is so tricky. The petrified tree-trunk that I inspect does not contain the same matter as the original tree-trunk. But its structure is astonishingly similar. So, has the trunk survived? Yes, it has, just as well as the fluorite crystal survived the same process of pseudomorphism. Is the survival of a high enough degree to constitute identity? This is a ticklish question. Unless we engage in some urgent conceptual development, we will not get an answer to this question. But, at the same time, it is unclear whether we should even bother to try.

We are drawn two ways in a case like this. On one side, we are sure that the original tree-trunk has been destroyed, for the petrified trunk is not alive, does not conduct water and nutrients, and so on. On the other side, we naturally refer to the fossil as being the trunk of a tree which grew in this valley so many millions of years ago. Our recognition of the survival of the trunk, albeit with altered matter, is perhaps what prompts our referential practice. If so, then survival, not identity, is what underlies some of our demonstrative conventions and our use of anaphoric pronouns (as suggested by our second solution to the problem of the episodic hill in Chapter 4.6). At the same time, perhaps destruction of the trunk's matter counts against us identifying the original with the fossil. The plausibility of this result can be shown by looking at a further case of radical replacement.

We are all familiar with the variegated stages of development shown by many insects and amphibians. That a tadpole will one day be a frog, a nymph living under water a dragon-fly, or a caterpillar a butterfly are all things of wonder and amazement to us. It took a great deal of empirical study to discover the sequence and nature of such changes. Having made such a discovery, though, we are liable to think that one same thing is first a nymph, and later a dragon-fly, or that one same thing is first a tadpole and later a frog. If we recall the Eusa insight that identity is suited to the nature of the thing, we will look for kinds of structural features in these cases different from those in the cases of trees, stones, and hills. Yet, if our conditions on survival are to be at all plausible, they need to legislate for these new cases as well.

That the conditions are plausible is clear if we accept one controversial point. This is that it is an *open question* whether the very same thing is first a tadpole and then a frog, or first a caterpillar, then a butterfly. A less controversial point we must also accept is that our referential practices are not always underpinned either by the existence of identity or by the presence of survival. To see that this is so, think of poor old Clover—the amorphous blob who fails to share even Rover's DNA. Pointing to Clover, I say '*This* was once Rover' and you know what I mean even though what I am pointing to is not a dog, is not identical with Rover, and is not something Rover survives in. So pointing to a butterfly, for example, and saying that *it* once was a caterpillar will, in this case, not count for very much at all—and certainly does not constitute, on its own, evidence of either identity or survival. To this extent, Cartwright's verdict, quoted above, is reasonable.

So now let us consider the developmental phases of advanced insects. Such creatures hatch from eggs into a larval phase. Development through this phase is associated with moulting—a kind of less radical metamorphosis than pupating. Our caterpillar, if we take this as an example, will, after several moults, enter its pupal phase where many of its tissues are rearranged. Emerging after this dramatic metamorphosis, *it* is no longer a caterpillar but a butterfly. Of course, the caterpillar does not survive to a very high degree in the butterfly, and we will certainly want to deny that a caterpillar is the same thing as a butterfly. What is important to the identity question is whether it is *one same thing* which is first a caterpillar and then a butterfly.

The reason that it is important to treat this as an open question is that empirical investigation is required in order to provide an answer. Different answers will be given according to what the investigation finds. As far as superficial structure is concerned, we can observe that some notable external features of the caterpillar survive in the butterfly. For instance, the caterpillar's front set of legs apparently grow during the pupal phase into the butterfly's legs, while other legs are apparently changed. Now let us imagine different structural possibilities within the organism. Suppose that in the pupal phase absolutely every structure in the caterpillar's nervous, circulatory, and endocrine systems is changed; its organs are rebuilt, and located in new places. In this case only the DNA and the front legs, let us suppose, survive in the butterfly.

By contrast, suppose (what I understand to be closer to the truth) that during the pupal phase certain of these physiological structures are simply modified and new ones (for instance, reproductive organs) are added. Pupation then looks like something familiar in the history of all living things, namely *growth*. What is interesting is that the growth takes place in a sudden spurt hidden from prying eyes. Such a phenomenon is, however, no more specially puzzling than the development in mammals from fertilized ovum through embryo to foetus. In both kinds of case, the developmental phases are characterized by a change from the rudimentary and undifferentiated to the sophisticated and differentiated.

The two cases just imagined are thus very different. If only the DNA survives, and very little else, then our caterpillar has turned into a butterfly, but survives in the butterfly to only a very slight degree. By contrast, if many structures remain in the butterfly, only nested in richer structures, then our caterpillar has survived the metamorphosis to a significantly greater degree than in the first case. Notice how we can make these points about survival without worrying about the identity question. For we have not yet determined, in cases like these, the sufficient degree of survival of one phase in another which will permit us to assign both phases to one and the same thing.

So let us now venture a radical suggestion on identity. Suppose that we find insects who change dramatically in the pupal phase, or that we discover that in certain species of frog there is no survival of tadpole structures in later frog structures. These, of course, are logical rather than physical possibilities, given what we know about animal anatomy. Never mind this, however. We suppose, therefore, that in these cases, chains of stages show high degrees of survival from one stage to the next, but little or no survival from an early stage to some very much later stage. So the lawful principles of development of the creatures in question are structure-transforming rather than structure-preserving. In such a case, I suppose we might come to hold that we could have identity without survival: as long as life continues, there would be identity, but some earlier phases of the creature would not survive in later ones.

6.6. IDENTITY AND SURVIVAL

If we were to take the line just suggested we would start to see just why survival is, in Parfit's phrase, 'What matters'. By seeing that identity is not what matters, we begin to see the possibility of the irrelevance of our radical decision on identity to other concerns— concerns that are normally thought to be associated with identity. For example, in the case of the creatures just mentioned, the history of earlier phases might well *not* show up in later phases; damage sustained, let us suppose, during some larval stage might make no difference to the structures produced in pupation.

Thinking of our survival relation in terms of later to earlier, we observe that it is an information relation of a sort (in fact, it is a highly restricted concept of information). For when *a* survives as *b* we can read off information about *a*'s structure, and, often, *a*'s material, from the inspection of *b*. Up to the end of the last section, it has been assumed that where an identity claim is appropriate, this will be associated with evidence of suitably high degrees of survival. Of course, it is not *a*'s identity with *b* about which we would be speaking; the unity or identity claim would concern some same thing of which *a* and *b* are both stages. We have also recognized survival in the absence of unity—for example in the double survival of Theseus' ship.

So we can have survival without identity—as when one thing survives in quite a different thing (think of the lamp and the robot-arm, or one mountain-stage surviving in another). We can also have a case of survival where the issue of identity is indeterminate (Theseus' ship again). It has been a great virtue of the survival relation that it applied in these cases, yielding a way of talking about important connections between things. Our subsequent strategy— encouraged by the four-dimensional account of the episodic hill case—has been to see survival as the more basic relation, the one that matters, and the one that is in some way constitutive of identity. It now looks, however, as if our radical suggestion about imaginary insects throws doubt on the utility of survival in giving any account of identity.

The suggestion that there can be identity without survival would not be inconsistent with our earlier finding that if each thing survives as itself then identity must involve survival. For all we need do is admit that our latest examples show that some things—our imaginary insects—do not survive as themselves. This would mean that there would be nothing trivial (perhaps contrary to appearances) in the claim that something *survives as itself*. But this new notion of *same creature*, embracing such structurally diverse stages, is a very peculiar one. Let us go back to our old case of Rover and Clover. Now Clover, being a relatively amorphous blob, failed to be a *dog*. Yet suppose Clover, in some strange way, is alive. It would seem to follow—by parity with our argument on insects—that some same creature can begin its career as a dog and then continue, after exposure to Martian radiation, as a blob. This is as much a natural change, after all, as the transformation of our caterpillar. Pupation turns caterpillars into butterflies, and Martian radiation turns dogs into blobs.

There does seem to be something very wrong with all this. It is as if we have mistaken the continuation of life, no matter what the circumstances, for the persistence of one and the same living thing. Our imagined insects, like our dog–blob, do not seem to present us with the persistence of any one creature, animal, or whatever. The very failure of survival makes the identity claim seem odd. But the hesitancy in reaching a firm verdict here is important. For some theorists might well go along the road of saying that we can have identity without survival. Such a route leads, at least, to a possible development of the concept of identity.

So what is the right thing to say here? I think we probably end up in a position not far removed from Wiggins's, though supported in a somewhat different fashion. The real reason why tadpoles and frogs, nymphs and dragon-flies, caterpillars and butterflies are all just phases in larger lives is that the earlier structures do in fact survive in the later ones. Moreover, it is an open, and scientifically proper, question what to say about these cases in advance of making the discoveries abut structures. A world very like this one in superficial details might be one in which we would not allocate caterpillar and butterfly to one larger, unified entity. The 'radical' suggestion simply confused the actual case—where there is survival—with a superficially similar case where there is not.

Moreover, if we think back to the daffodil case, we recall that some structures seem to be privileged, or more vital, than others.

This insight is invaluable here. The geometry of various physiological systems and the retention of genetic structure will be from the scientist's viewpoint of more significance than changes in superficial features. In this way we can entrust to the specialist the job of specifying the nature of the creature or creatures we are examining. Of course, like Wiggins, I could resist extending this view to items falling under sortals other than *natural kind* terms. For there is no counterpart in artefacts to the law-governed development, and retention, of structure that we find in natural objects. None the less, it is interesting, almost surprising, that the natural world displays such limitations on structure-transformation as it does, a feature connected, no doubt, to the general application of physical and chemical laws. From inspection of the information-theoretic character of our survival relation, it is clearly possible that a might survive as b and b as c while a fails to survive as c. Yet, if what has just been said is correct, nymphs do survive, to some degree, in dragon-flies, and even day-old embryos survive in chickens.

Thus a plausible case can be made for rejecting the radical suggestion, and for maintaining that survival *to some degree* of one stage in a later stage is a necessary condition for assigning both stages to one and the same unified thing. However, we cannot expect, in general, to be able to say to *what* degree the survival must occur. We are indeed in no better a position here than Wiggins, or Locke, for whom identity is suited to the idea for, in Wiggins's words,

Starting off with the idea of a sortal predicate whose sense is such as to involve its extension . . . we are led to speculate what holds together the extension. So soon as we find that, we also find lawlike norms of starting to exist, existing and ceasing to exist by reference to which questions of the identity and persistence of individual specimens falling under a definition can be arbitrated. Such norms will be supervenient on basic laws of nature . . .[16]

So if the question of appropriate degree of survival for a particular of a certain sort troubles you, look up the appropriate textbook—but don't expect a general rule to be forthcoming to cover all species. As the Kafka story reminds us, what is normal for an insect—namely metamorphosis—would be perfectly extraordinary for a human.

[16] Wiggins [9], pp. 85–6.

The issues of which sortal concepts are natural-kind concepts and of how much commitment to essentialism we are involved in when recognizing some sorts as forming a natural kind by virtue of a shared *nature* are topics that are well explored in other treatments of identity and essentialism and to which I do not wish to add here.[17] However, if (anticipating some results from the next chapter) it is at all plausible to maintain that items of the kind *cat*, let us say, all share certain structural features which set them apart from other kinds and, incidentally, enable us to identify them as cats, then we must be wary of a new kind of identity problem. For the possibility arises that we could take an item of a certain kind, apply various changes and deformations to it so that, intuitively, we would have destroyed it, yet produce at the end of this process a further item recognizably of the same kind. This would be easier to bring about if, perhaps, the kind in question allowed large amounts of superficial structural variation among its members.

The theoretical (and possibly *merely theoretical*) point that is made by this latest speculation is simply that we may have to allow that *a* can be transformed into *b* in such a way that *b* replicates *a* to a high enough degree to be of the same kind (hence of the same sort) as *a*. But *a* does not survive as *b*, nor are *a* and *b* stages in the life of one thing of the kind (though they may be stages in the history of some other sort, e.g., 'aggregate of organic molecules'). It is easier and less fanciful to illustrate the case by means of an example involving artefact-kinds. Suppose we press some plastic material— wax or clay—into a mould. Now we take the product, a bowl perhaps, and, after admiring it a while, we deform it into a lump of clay before pressing it back into the mould to form a bowl again. What we have before us is the same clay, but not the same bowl. Why not? The answer is that our original bowl, although a token of the same type as our new bowl, hence instance of the same design, does not survive in or as the new bowl. In effect, we have used the same *production process* to produce the two bowls.

Here we have a case, then, where the original bowl has been transformed into a new bowl, yet the original does not survive, nor are we confronted with two phases in the history of one bowl, even though both are bowls. Likewise, if we could engage in some

[17] Wiggins has perhaps the subtlest account of identity and its connections with essentialism in Wiggins [9]. However, Putnam's account of natural kind terms is strikingly interesting, in Putnam [3]. See also the discussion in Salmon [1], ch. 4, 5.

topological surgery on a cow's heart and change the numbers of its valves and chambers so as to transform it into a recognizable and fully functional dolphin's heart, all this without waste of organic material, we should still have produced a new heart rather than a new phase in the life of the old one. Again, our topological surgery is more like a production process (for producing dolphin hearts) than a copying process.

This example suggests one last way of trying to deal with metamorphosis. Imagine a creature which changes so radically through pupation that only the DNA survives. We suggested before that in such a case we might support both survival and identity claims by maintaining the importance of this genetic structure. (After all, it is present in every cell of the creature: it just happens to be hidden from direct inspection). The DNA itself, however, functions as the controlling factor in what we might now regard as a production process: pupation. Every member of a species varies from every other; the secret of this variation lies in the DNA. When we claim, then, that something survives the metamorphosis, we do not just mean some creature or other of this species is still around. It is more as if we mean *the design* or the *recipe* for producing that individual survives (and that recipe differs from individual to individual). Think again of the clay pot. The pot did not survive remodelling into the next pot; but the *design* did. But now what survives is not so much the insect as it was before pupation, taken concretely, but something much more abstract (recall the cautions in Chapter 2 about this vocabulary). No more need be said just now, but this issue will recur in our treatment of personal identity. Notice, though, that talk of survival of this kind is no longer talk of 'survival' in our preferred sense of the term. The survival of recipes and designs does not involve the relation of structure, matter, and cause in the way stage survival does.

Interestingly, this other sort of survival will be something that we have to focus on again. In the case of persons, there is also the possibility of two kinds of survival, namely survival in the special sense defined by our three conditions and survival of the sort designs and recipes can enjoy. It may seem strange that some of the puzzles about insects and other creatures emerge again in the treatment of personal identity. However, if this is not evidence of continuities in nature, it is at least evidence of the continuity of puzzlement.

6.7. COLOUR, CAMOUFLAGE, AND OTHER DISTRACTIONS

Is colour an ingredient or aspect of structure? As we will see in the next chapter, the unrestricted conception of structure as *information* would force us to count colour as structure. But my earlier specification of structure as being *geometric* was most certainly meant to rule this out. Compared with the information-theoretic notion of structure, my concept is highly restricted and would be less able to do the explanatory work required of it were it not so. This is not to deny, however, that we can borrow some of the benefits of the more general concept and claim them for our own—but more on that later.

There are lots of biological speculations about why we are receptive to colour and what the evolutionary advantages of such a capacity are. And our ability to sense colour depends on the presence of appropriately structured objects—that is, objects whose surface structure transmits wavelengths of light in selective ways. But none of these considerations force us to count colour itself as a further structural feature.

The case of some sorts of camouflage shows how colour can in fact interfere with our perception of an item's geometric structure. The coloured stripes of a tiger, for example, make it hard for us to perceive the continuous outline of the tiger unless we are remarkably skilled observers.[18] This attempt, so to speak, to hide structure confirms the importance of structure to the identification of things as being of a certain sort. Colour seems at best to be a helpful adjunct to such identification rather than an essential ingredient in the story of what a thing, fundamentally, is.

We can draw on two related sources for support in being thus cavalier with colour. One is the empiricist tradition which distinguishes primary and secondary qualities. For colour to be a secondary quality, indeed, is not for there to be no corresponding primary qualities. On the contrary, as just observed, an item's being coloured in various ways that depend on ambient lighting is

---

[18] 'I had covered thirty yards, hoping fervently that if the tiger charged he would come from in front (for in no other direction could I have fired), when I caught sight of something red on which the sun, drifting through the upper leaves, was shining; it might only be a bunch of dead leaves; on the other hand, it might be the tiger.' Jim Corbett, 'The Bachelor of Powalgarh' in *Man Eaters of Kumaon* (Oxford: Oxford University Press, 1960). Other stories reveal that Corbett was indeed a skilled observer: but even he had his difficult moments—as the above passage shows.

grounded in structural features, usually of its surface. To the extent that we are accurate in identifying the colours of objects we are, then, gaining by that route information about surface structure. The second argument derives from physical science. From the specially privileged perspective of physics and chemistry, colour has no role to play in our best account of what the world is like. This does not mean that physics, especially optics, and chemistry have nothing to say about colour. But what they have to say concerns those structural features that determine selective reflection of light and the workings of eyes. Admittedly, biology and ecology have things to say about colour. This time, though, we can point out that, unlike other aspects of their theories, those involving colour are reducible to physics and chemistry in a limited way. The limitation is this. Suppose a certain display of colours is important in the courtship activities of some species. Then I am not claiming that the account of courtship is reducible to some story involving chemical signals and game theory. All I would maintain is that any reference to colours in such accounts can be paraphrased in terms of light reflection, fine structures of various surfaces, and the physiology of the perceiving animal. With this limited reductionism I would hope there would be no quarrel.

For those who would want to count colour as part of the structure of an item there is thus the following prospect of describing structure, provided they grant me the claim that such talk can ultimately be cashed in terms of colourless geometric structural features. We can both agree that a certain creature has an orange triangular patch on its forehead bounded by a white line, but agree also that at a suitably fine level of description the colour words drop out in favour of a description of the geometry of the skin or fur cells on the creature's forehead.

Of course, colour is epistemologically important—hence its central role in many phenomenalist accounts of our knowledge of the world. Given the realism implicit in the arguments of this book, it is clear that I would have little sympathy for phenomenalism in general, or even for those forms of it which respect the difference between what is fundamental in metaphysical theories and what is epistemologically basic. However, the realms of epistemology and metaphysics are not totally disconnected. Even if we stay neutral on the issue of whether conditions of identity in some way organize our tests for judging identity, we can still ask if our judgements of sameness and difference correspond to sameness and difference 'out there' in the world. An attempt to link the objective and subjective domains in this way is liable to raise the hackles of many empiricists. Since the following chapter attempts to make just such a link, I begin it by diagnosing a view which underlies a great deal of empiricist thinking. This may not be any way to placate an empiricist, but at least it may prevent my speculations being rejected for the wrong reason.

7
Similarity and Affordance

7.1. THE EXTENSIONALIST MYTH

The reader who is suspicious of speculative ventures into psychology and metaphysics may skip this chapter without losing sight of the main thrust of survival theory. But the chapter is important for the project of the book, for here we will confront some rather difficult questions about what the world is like and—in particular—whether those structural relationships that matter so much to the survival question are available in the world or imposed on it by us. Such a query has a distinctly epistemological flavour and any good empiricist in the tradition of Hume and Quine would therefore look to psychology for clues to its solution. Before so doing, we will survey an influential picture of how the world 'really' or 'objectively' is—a picture which provides us with a datum line for further theorizing. This picture is generated by a powerful quasi-religious doctrine which I have chosen to call the extensionalist myth. But do not let this use of the term 'myth' suggest that the picture is false. It may well be true. Its truth, however, is not something for which its adherents usually argue; rather it is taken as the foundation on which other arguments are built, supporting them like the deeply held convictions of a religion.

One way into the myth is by reflecting on the notion of 'individual' which has already been deployed mereologically. Recall that any old collection of matter can, on this view, constitute an individual. Moreover, as we saw, any old collection of object-stages, however scattered, also constitute an individual. Thus, on this conception, there is an individual consisting of the yesterday stage of my telephone, today's stage of my tennis shoes, and my desk in all its four-dimensional extent. So viewed, there are indefinitely many individuals in the universe—indeed there will be uncountably many. We can show the latter result by constructing an appropriate counterpart to Cantor's diagonal argument establishing the uncountability of the real numbers.[1] Since our names for particulars will be at most countably infinite, it follows that we could not possibly have names for all these individuals.

Looked at in this way, one question about human recognitional skills immediately arises. For although we can make sense of the world as constituting uncountably many individuals, our natural way of describing the world we experience is as a world of particulars, these particulars standing out, as it were, from other particulars. We might thus wonder how it is that we pick out from all the individuals available 'out there' just a certain number as being *the* particulars—a particular being a nameable, unified thing of a certain sort. Of course, as soon as we suggest that *this* is what a particular is, we see the connection between the question of particulars and the question of qualities or properties. For if a particular is of sort S, say, then one of its persisting, properties will be that it has S-ness, S-hood or S-ity, or however we designate the property. So my desk is a particular and throughout its life it exhibits the property of desk-hood. Socrates, being human, exemplified humanity through his life, and so on. We do not need to talk with the three-dimensionalist to make this point. On the chain theory, particular things are maximal aggregates of stages, related by whatever the appropriate unity relation is. And, put in these

---

[1] If I show briefly how to do the trick for real numbers, the reader will be able to do the same for individuals. Let us suppose *per impossibile* that there is an infinite listing of real numbers, beginning thus:

$r1$ 0.0010120 . . . .
$r2$ 0.0102324 . . . .
$r3$ 0.0202453 . . . .
$r4$ 0.1235234 . . . .

We have supposed that each real number in the interval will occur on the list as an infinite decimal, and each such decimal is arbitrarily assigned to one of the positive integers (thus we have just listed real numbers one to four). Now, a countably infinite set may be defined simply as one whose elements can be put into one–one correspondence with elements of the set of natural numbers. To show the uncountability of the reals, Cantor's method is simply to construct a real number which is bound to be missed out by the listing process. Consider the real which is represented by the decimal 0.0105 . . ., that is, the diagonal on the above table. For each digit in this diagonal decimal we do either of two things: (i) if it is between '0' and '8' inclusive, we replace it with the digit which is one larger than it, (ii) if it is the digit '9' we replace it with '0'. The resulting decimal is bound to differ from the first number on the table in the first place after the point, from the second in the second place, and from the ith in the ith place: thus it *cannot* be on the table. Hence there are more reals than can occur in a countably infinite list.

terms, our suggestion so far has been that the unity relation in question is that of *survival* in the sense explored in earlier chapters.

On either view, then, particulars are possessors of properties, and stages of particulars are also possessors of properties. And maybe, then, an investigation of properties will clarify the question that is worrying us. Before getting optimistic over this route, we need to reflect on what a property is. However, reflection on this simply plunges us back into the extensionalist myth again.

If we think of how we can define ordinary properties, like the property of being a desk, a rabbit, having two legs, being red, and so on, we note that there are two dimensions along which such definitions can develop. On the one side, there is our *understanding* of what expressions like 'is a desk' or 'is red' *mean*. On the other is the question of what things are desks, and what things are red. On some accounts of meaning, indeed, it is possible to unite the two— for example, by connecting meanings of whole sentences with the conditions under which these sentences are true. But let us think, for a moment, in terms of two separate things here: meaning on the one side, and things that are desks, red, or whatever, on the other.

Following Carnap, we can distinguish the meaning, or *intension* of an expression from the class of things of which that expression is true. Let us call the class of which the expression is true, the *extension* of the expression. So 'is a desk' has an intension, or meaning (whatever that is); and it also has an extension, namely the members of the class of desks (for desks, and nothing other than desks, are what 'is a desk' is true of). Since it is true of the thing at which I am presently seated that it is a desk, it belongs to the extension of the expression 'is a desk'. We need not commit ourselves to the view that to say an expression has the members of a certain class as its extension is to say that it *refers* to that class. On Frege's view, the reference of a predicate expression like '. . . is a table' is in fact a concept (a 'first-level *function* of one argument' in his technical terminology).[2] There is much to be said in favour of

_____

[2] The notion of *concept*, like that of *sense*, is part of Frege's technical apparatus. If we take a simple sentence like 'Jeff has floppy ears', the proper name refers to an *object* (something complete, or saturated), while the remainder refers to a *function* (something incomplete, or unsaturated). On the basis of these simple proposals, Frege built a powerful and persuasive semantics, one of the modern legacies of which is categorial grammar. The characteristics of objects and functions match those of expressions designating them. Thus 'Jeff', like the whole sentence given as an example, is a complete expression, while '. . . has floppy ears' only becomes

distinguishing concepts as what certain kinds of expression refer to, from the extension of the term or concept in question. Think of it like this. A predicate expression has an extension because the concept to which it refers has an extension: that is, there are things which fall under the concept in question. If the concept is a sortal concept, then the items constituting the extension of the concept all belong to one *sort*. Here, although we are following Frege's doctrine on concepts, we are not following his account of *extension*: his notion of the extension of a concept was rather more cumbersome. Those, however, who are happy to take predicate expressions as designating their extensions may continue to adopt this reading. Nothing of substance depends on it.

Our question, to recap, was whether the investigation of properties might shed some light on the nature of particulars and hence on the question of how we divide the world up into items of well-defined sorts. But now we see that a property can be defined in two ways. And neither way affords us a great deal of help. We could, taking the easier case, try identifying the property of being a desk with the set of things of which the expression '. . . is a desk' is true, or which fall under the concept, *desk*. But this route takes us no closer to a solution. For how are we to explain why this class of things—desks—is singled out for special treatment, as a sort, while the class consisting of all the desks together with all the world's railway-cars does not constitute a sort.

The difficulty here is in fact parallel to our problem with individuals. Just as any aggregate of individuals constitutes an individual, so any collection of items constitutes a set or class. So the collection of all the items belonging to two different sets also constitutes a set. And, of course, we can choose to make up sets in much more haphazard ways, if we so wish. Now suppose it is pointed out that desks are much more similar to each other than any are to railway-cars or propellers. This is to impose differences where there are really no distinctions, our extensionalist would retort. For, in an objective description of the real world (if such could be imagined) each item we choose belongs to just as many sets

---

complete, or saturated, upon completion by an appropriate expression. This incomplete expression, however, could be fed in to a second-level function expression (e.g., 'something . . .') in order to produce the complete sentence 'something has floppy ears.' For a clear initiation into the Frege semantics, see Montgomery Furth's introduction to Frege [3].

as any other item. So, viewed in this 'objective' way, each thing is similar to everything else and to just the same degree as well! If this move by the extensionalist seems too fast, then we can flesh out the argument as follows. We have already seen how to distinguish a technical notion of *individual* from our more natural notion of a unified *particular*. Likewise, we can now introduce a technical notion of property★ such that to every set there corresponds a property★. Just as the set of desks was proposed for identification with the property of being a desk, so the set consisting of desks together with railway-cars can be identified with the property★ of being a *deskar*, let us say. Of course, the word 'deskar' has just been coined for the property★ in question, since English provides us with no word for it. Rather, our property-terms in English apply to just a tiny proportion of all the properties★ there are. But now we can note that railway-cars and desks are similar in a way we have not previously taken account of: for any desk will be a deskar just as any railway-car is. But this is only a start. There are uncountably many properties★, and hence uncountably many similarities out there in the world. So, if the extensionalist is right, it looks as though the world itself can furnish us with no weighting of properties to account for our allocation of particulars to sorts.[3]

---

[3] To be fair to the extensionalist, it should be observed that the theory of projectible predicates in Goodman [1] could be applied to the current problem. More recently, George Schlesinger has suggested two criteria for singling out genuine from spurious disjunctive properties. Neither will work, however, if we take the extreme extensional line. His first criterion is that '$P \vee P'$' applies to a genuine property, provided the component properties common to both P things and P' things are not common to things of other sorts. Alternatively, '$P \vee P'$' applies to a genuine property where the presence of the disjunctive property can be established without establishing whether P or P' is present (see Schlesinger [2], pp. 15–16).
To see how these are meant to work, think of 'man or woman' as applying to a genuine property (that of being an adult human being). Then, by the first criterion, properties common to both men and women are not shared with any other things; by the second criterion, the presence of humanness can be established without establishing whether it is a man or a woman that is present. Schlesinger is undoubtedly on to something here. For the psychological results cited in the present chapter show that it is plausible to regard the world as containing items with a high degree of *correlational structure* (see 7.5). But Schlesinger's criteria clearly involve properties rather than properties★ and cannot therefore satisfy the extreme extensionalist. In terms of properties★, women have just as many properties★ in common with trees or planets as with men. Only after agreeing to modify the extensionalist myth—perhaps as a result of the arguments in the present chapter— would it be possible to try getting the required results using Schlesinger's criteria.

7.2. SIMILARITY

Since similarity (or relative identity) involves possession of some common property, the extensionalist myth assures us that the world is far different from how we naturally think about it. We can borrow some helpful terminology from Hume, and extend it to the question we are discussing here (at least as far as relations are concerned). We can take similarity, in Hume's terms, either as a *natural* or as a *philosophical* relation (he himself took it as sometimes one and sometimes the other), and spell out the differences thus.[4] If we choose arbitrary objects *a*, *b*, and *c*, then according to the extensionalist myth *a* is bound to be just as similar to *b* as to *c*. This is to take similarity in the *philosophical* way. But, according to our *natural* ideas about these matters, *a* is likely to differ in its degree of similarity to *b* and to *c*. The reason for this, after all, is that in terms of properties (but *not* in terms of *properties**) we are likely to find *a* having rather more properties in common with one of the other two than it has with the other.

So we can immediately extend our notions of *natural* and *philosophical* to properties and individuals. The extensionalist has given us a philosophical notion of each (namely properties* and mereological individuals), while our natural ideas of a property and of a particular are far more restricted than these. Likewise, in Chapter 5.6 we could have distinguished between (spatial and temporal) parts, and parts*, of particulars. What extensionalists, like Quine, owe us, then, is an account of how, finding ourselves in a world of philosophical individuals and properties, we come to describe it, and indeed seem to see it, as a world of natural individuals and properties.

The extensionalist answers here are fairly limited. Trying to avoid the sceptical ones, we can perhaps classify the answers as

[4] Hume's theory of the association of ideas is under the gravest suspicion from those who, like Goodman, have doubts about similarity (what Hume calls *resemblance*). According to *Treatise* I. i. 5, the mind naturally associates together the ideas of objects which are similar, close in place and time, or related by cause and effect. The resemblance or similarity in question must be in properties, not in properties*. However, Hume does want to allow that we can compare apparently unrelated things—as when we observe that one item is closer to a second than it is to a third. Hume may have thought that some resemblances give rise to association of ideas, while others do not; in which case, resemblance is *sometimes* a philosophical relation. Even though Hume never writes in terms of properties*, I think the extension of his vocabulary, as suggested in the text, is natural.

making appeal to three things. First, we may have specific innate abilities—for example, we may be born with the ability to discriminate natural individuals and natural properties. This appeal to specific innate abilities looks rather like the old-fashioned appeal to innate ideas; and it is of little pleasure to the empiricist to be driven to this resort. Even if we make the innateness claim respectable by dressing it up as a point about genetically-determined hard-wiring, the empiricist remains uncomfortable, and rightly so, for this move reduces the interest of the core-empiricist doctrine that all knowledge is a product of experience. Assuming that our extensionalist is also an empiricist (a safe assumption) then this first answer is low in its appeal.

A second answer still makes reference to innate skills, but makes these far less specific than on the first story. Suppose we accept that natural selection is bound to have left its mark on us. We are adapted to our environment and are born with instincts, skills, and abilities already wired in, or at least with something wired in which allows such skills to be triggered by appropriate environmental stimuli. On Quine's account, one such innate endowment is not so much an innate idea but a propensity to weight equal differences unequally. We come equipped with a 'quality space' that immediately inclines us to count some pairs of items as showing more similarities than others.[5] As psychologists have often observed, children seem adept at generating classes of similar things—and, from our adult perspective, we can both spot the mistakes they make, and appreciate the similarity they have noted. Thus it is perfectly understandable if a child, green in speech, describes boots, socks, and slippers as all being 'shoes'. The similarities are real and natural; we have simply, in our mature sophistication, become interested in differentiating among the admittedly similar.[6]

[5] 'If the child is to be amenable to such training, however, what he must have is a prior tendency to weight qualitative differences unequally. He must, so to speak, sense more resemblance between some stimulations than between others . . . In effect therefore we must credit the child with a sort of pre-linguistic quality space.' (Quine [2], § 17.) 'Might we say that a thing is more similar to one than another if it shares more properties with the one than with the other? But what counts as a property? Classes, certainly show no favourites; a thing shares no more class-membership with anyone thing than with any other . . . Our innate standards of perceptual similarity show a gratifying tendency to run with the grain of nature. This concurrence is accountable, surely, to natural selection.' (Quine [9], § 5.)

[6] For psychological reflections on the mechanism of differentiation, see Rosch *et al.* [1], Kemler [1], and Aschkenasy and Odom [1].

The quality-space theory is much friendlier to tough-minded empiricism. It leaves plenty of scope for learning from experience, while accounting for the child's speed at latching on to language and to adult concepts. And of course, it leaves the extensionalist myth untouched. The world 'out there' is uniform in its similarity distributions. It is we who come equipped with the propensity for bias (a useful propensity, indeed). Quine has managed to combine this second answer to our question with the third. For, notice that the quality-space hypothesis, on its own will go some way towards explaining our natural idea of *property*, but leaves us no clearer on the distinction between individuals and unified particulars. Our quality space will let us identify the ball in the garden today as distinct from the grass, the trees, and the house. But it will surely not let us identify the ball today as the *same* as the ball yesterday.

Of course, we could introduce an individualist parallel to the idea of a quality space. We could call it a 'particularity space', which might manifest its operation by a tendency on our part to count similar things as numerically the same. Hirsch, for one, has suggested that we do indeed have an innate 'sense of unity' as he calls it, but I take this as amounting to something more than a particularity space.[7] Hirsch is right, however, to worry about the question of how we could *infer* from our experience the sameness, or unity, of a particular. As Hume pointed out, distinct perceptions are distinct existences. Yet—barring fancies about episodic hills and the like—we generally are pretty sure that many of our distinct perceptions are of the same persisting thing.

Quine's initial answer to this problem was not to postulate a particularity space or sense of unity. Rather, he suggested that persisting things are themselves posits, theoretical entities, whose role in unifying experience was spotted a long time ago in human history.[8] After the initial shock of this third response to our

---

[7] 'We explain people's focusing and tracking behaviour by reference to their experience of unity. Put in these terms, my point about infants is this: A seemingly plausible (indeed, a seemingly compelling) explanation of the infant's focusing and tracking behaviour, and the similarity of that behaviour to our own, is that the infant experiences the world as broken up into units in essentially the way that we do.' (Hirsch [2], p. 262.)

[8] 'Considered relative to our surface irritations ... the molecules and their extraordinary ilk are thus on a par with the most ordinary physical object. The positing of these extraordinary things is just a vivid analogue of the positing or acknowledging of ordinary things: vivid in that the physicist audibly posits them for recognized reasons, whereas the hypothesis of ordinary things is shrouded in prehistory.' (Quine [2], § 6.)

quandary, we can see the benefits of Quine's proposal. Hume's point about distinct existences being granted, it is clear that the existence of persisting things could never be a deduction from our experience. Quine's proposal thus avoids the absurdity of trying to deduce the indeducible. Also, it avoids the tendency to idealism which creeps up on these who try to identify particulars with constructions out of experience—the *phenomenalist* strategy.

However, like all interesting forms of empiricism, Quine's theory of particulars seems highly sensitive to attack from our old friend the sceptic. Is the theory of persisting things unique to humans and others of equal conceptual sophistication? For if it is, then other animals presumably lack this theory, yet behave remarkably consistently with the theory that they take the world to consist of persisting particulars. Of course, we can only make guesses at what it is like to be a monkey, a cat, or a salmon. Yet the behaviour of all these, and many other creatures, is quite remarkably like our behaviour in respect of persisting things. Maybe all this shows, however, is that we are speaking about low-level theorizing. And such theorizing can be done by cats as well as kings.

The sceptic, however, need not rest here. This, after all, is scepticism about the theory that leaves us with the persisting objects, and simply queries the peculiar status assigned to them by Quine. But a more serious form of scepticism asks the following difficult question: why adopt the theory of particulars? If our answer is: 'it works!' then the sceptic need only respond by pointing to all the other theories that worked, until they were replaced by better ones. The question of theory superiority is not so much a question about *true* versus *false* theories (though such vocabulary is tempting). Rather many rather poor theories have been retained over the years simply for lack of anything better. If persisting objects are posits then it is by no means patronizing towards them to wonder if some better posit might not one day do a better job in our theory of the world.

Having seen the possibility of a parallel between similarity spaces and what we have called 'particularity spaces', we might wonder conversely why Quine opts for similarity spaces in the explanation of property classification, but for postulates of theory in explaining our belief in persisting objects. Why not use theory in both cases? It might seem that our classification of items by property is itself highly theoretical: we posit that the world is populated by trees, tables, trapezes, and termites because by so doing we get the smoothest account of our sensations coupled with reasonable conceptual economy. But a moment's reflection shows why this attempt to dispense with quality spaces would not do for the Quinean. For the uncountable infinity of properties* in the world gives us too much raw data to approach with theory. Quality spaces sort, weigh, and segregate this data into manageable chunks, so to speak, which correspond pretty directly to properties. Indeed, the thrust of Quine's thought, over the years, has been to move towards particularity spaces and 'body mindedness' rather than become too theoretical about properties.[9]

The resort to quality spaces and particularity spaces thus leaves us with a compromised empiricism. In order to have scope for learning from experience, we need to come equipped with mechanisms that structure and sort that experience in the first place. For the world out there—of Kantian things-in-themselves—provides too many similarities and too little differentiation. Of course, the compromise is not too extreme. We still have a doctrine that is recognizable as empiricism. Our innate mechanisms are a prerequisite for our learning from subsequent experience and for our theorizing about the nature of the world. One nagging worry, certainly, is that these mechanisms may themselves limit our ability to construct decent theories of the world. Lorenz has drawn attention to the discrepancy between the skills of the water shrew and the sewer rat. The shrew shuffles and gropes its way to food along devious paths, often involving circuitous and looping routes. Its principle of operation is to follow a route which has previously led to food, but it seems to lack the ability to conduct spatial surveys of its environment and find short cuts. The smarter, sewer rat will search for food over equally circuitous routes but will, when once having identified a food supply, return to it by the shortest available route.[10] To the human observer, the water shrew's capacities seem limited, though no doubt adequate. The rat seems more like us, more accurate in its ability to sort out its environment.

---

[9] 'The well-known Gestalt effect is basic: the readiness to recognise a simple and unified figure, ignoring interruptions of outline . . . Man is a body-minded animal among body-minded animals. Man and other animlas are body-minded by natural selection; for body-mindedness has evident survival value in town and jungle.' (Quine [9], p. 54.)

[10] The example is from Konrad Lorenz's paper, 'Kant's Lehre vom Apriorischen im Lichte gegenwartiger Biologie', a translation of which appears in Bertalanffy and Rapoport [1].

But wait a moment. The sobering thought that the example may suggest is that, compared to some as yet unevolved creature, we are as limited in our capacities as the shrew is compared to the rat. Our quality and particularity spaces are, after all, no more than our evolved response to the environment. But there is no inference from the *success* of such a response to its *accuracy*. Some smarter creature than us, equipped with better innate mechanisms, might come up with much cleverer, more successful theories of the world. So it would be superior to us, although—of course—coming no closer to acquiring a true, or correct, or accurate picture of the world. For, if the extensionalist myth were true, an accurate picture of the world would be one that recognizes it as possessing uncountable similarities among uncountable individuals. And such a picture is so alien to our normal response that we have difficulty grasping what it would be like to see the world in that sort of way. Perhaps, indeed, the true extensionalist can make no sense of the idea of *accuracy* in our image of the world—simply noting that some images provide conditions for more sophistication of response than do others.

Adherence to the extensionalist myth can thus drive us into quite remarkable positions. And philosophers are renowned for their ability to stay with a position however contrary to common sense its implications. Indeed, some philosophers, like Quine, take it as a merit of their own epistemological position that it is a common-sense one—for science is simply an extension of common sense, and epistemology is part of science (of psychology, say). The reflections in this section, however, are meant to have shown that one thing adherents of the myth cannot claim is that common sense is on their side. Common sense, indeed, holds that the sewer rat has very likely a more *accurate* (and thus more efficient) image of the world than the water shrew. And we, on the same view, are very likely possessors of a more accurate image than the rat. Moreover, it seems monstrous to common sense to suggest that trees are just as similar to monkeys as they are to other trees. None of this, of course, is to establish the falsity or the absurdity of the extensionalist myth. And it would take a great deal more than the reflections indulged in here to shake that myth from its special place in the heart of empiricists. But the problems encountered here do suggest that some alternative strategy for dealing with the similarity question is in order, and to this we now turn.

7.3. CRITICAL REALISM

The title of this section does not indicate any engagement on my part with currently fashionable debates about realism and anti-realism. Rather, the terminology is used by the psychologist W. R. Garner, whose theories on structure and information, though compatible with the extensionalist myth, are capable of yielding a different account of our knowledge. Like other recent work in the psychology of perception, Garner's is concerned to make points both about holism and about features of pattern recognition discussed by *Gestalt* theorists (for example 'goodness' of patterns, and the distinction between 'figure' and 'ground').[11]

It was, however, Garner's concern with *structure* that first drew my attention to his work. Like J. J. Gibson, he takes structure, or information, as a feature of a stimulus that contrasts with its energy: 'Stimulus energy', he writes, 'provides activation of the sense-organ, but it is stimulus information or structure that provides meaning and is pertinent to what I would call perception.'[12] More specifically, the intrinsic structure of a stimulus (as opposed to any extrinsic representing or signifying structure it may possess) is processed by the perceiver along various *dimensions*.[13] For example, Fig. 14 displays two dimensions, form and shading. Each dimension itself has two *levels*, for the forms are either circular or triangular, while the shading is light or heavy.

As well as the dimensional structure each of the figures displays, there is also the possibility of some such structures being *correlated*. Imagine, for example, a chart containing figures where all the

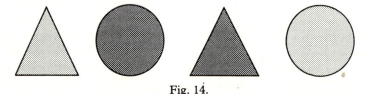

Fig. 14.

[11] See, for example, Koffka [1].

[12] Garner [2], Lecture 1.

[13] I follow Garner and other psychologists here in using the term of art. 'Dimension' is a useful term, being wider in import than our natural understanding of the term 'property'. In its current sense, the term differs little from its meaning when first introduced by Titchener to apply to any attribute of sensation.

triangles are heavily shaded and all the circles are lightly shaded. In such a case we have *redundancy* of information. Garner points out that, in general, as we select fewer and fewer stimuli from a set the greater the correlation of dimensions. For the moment, let us ignore correlational structure, and think simply about dimensional structure.

One question we might raise is whether there is some fixed number of dimensions along which any given set of stimuli can be differentiated. After all, when faced with an isolated stimulus—say a card containing just one figure—we do not know what to say about its properties. Consider Fig. 15, for example, where we are to imagine each rectangle as representing the psychologist's card. What do we say about Card A, when presented with it alone? Obviously we are being shown a triangle. Is it a big, or a small, triangle? Well, we don't know this until we are given some more cards to look at. Suppose, then, that we are shown a further card, Card B, and asked to say something more about Card A by comparing both. We are likely to maintain that the triangle on Card A is *large* and *central*. So now we have introduced two new dimensions of classifying the stimulus which we originally described purely in terms of the dimension of shape.

Of course, we can now go on to introduce further cards to the series. Imagine our description of Card A in the light of the addition of card C. We now observe that the triangle on Card A is a *single* triangle without a central spot: in other words, two further dimensions of classification have been added. As Garner puts it: 'The single stimulus has no meaning except in a context of alternatives ... Each descriptive term used defines what the alternatives are by defining what the stimulus is not. Thus the organism infers sets of stimulus alternatives, and, without these inferred sets, no-one can describe the single stimulus.'[14]

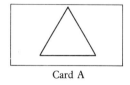 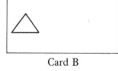 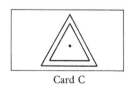

Card A   Card B   Card C

Fig. 15.

[14] Garner [2], p. 185.

Notice that all the dimensional structure we are able to assign our first stimulus was, in a sense, there all along. Card A did present a central, single triangle without a central spot, though of course our initial description was not along these lines at all. The dimensional structure, then, in terms of which we discriminate perceptual stimuli is, in Garner's view, already there. The perceiver's contribution is not to impose structure on an unstructured world. Rather, it is to *select* structure from the enormous amount available in the world. Thus Garner comes to defend critical realism, which combines a realistic attitude to the existence of structure with a critical account of perceptual processes and principles. The hope is, indeed, that the principles by which we select dimensional structure from the mass available in the world are straightforward.

Garner's work on temporal pattern recognition perhaps suggests that such principles are exceedingly simple. Using door-buzzers purchased from the local dime store, Garner and his associates studied combinations of two element patterns. For example, representing the two different buzzers' sounds as X and O, respectively, we could play this pattern to someone:

OXXXOOXOOXXXOOXOOXXXOOXOOXXXOO . . . etc.

The question arises: since the same sequence of eight noises occurs over and over again here, will different people come up with different patterns (there will be eight different structures to be chosen, after all), or are we more likely to fasten on one sequence as being *the* pattern that is repeated here? By ingenious experiment Garner was able to isolate the kinds of principles that lead us to select one pattern out of all the possible ones here.[15] In fact it seems that a repeated pattern of two elements is perceived as being like a composite of two one-element patterns. If we mark gaps by ' ', then the pattern above is a composite of

'XXX''X''XXX' . . . etc.

and

O'''OO'OO'''O . . . etc.

Of these two 'gappy' patterns one is selected as *figure*, the other as

[15] For full details, consult Garner [2], especially Lecture 3 and the refs. mentioned there.

ground. Although Garner had hoped that the 'goodness' (in the Gestalt theorists' sense of simplicity and regularity) of the one-element patterns would determine which was selected as figure and which as the ground, this idea was not vindicated experimentally. Instead, it turned out that other factors determined this choice. However, for one-element patterns, the following organizational principles emerged in respect of favoured patterns:

(1) start with the longest run
(2) end with the longest gaps

It can also be observed that

(3) principle (2) is more powerful, on the whole, then principle (1).

For the extensionalist with a tolerance for innate principles, here is a pleasant result. The principles of organization are simple, and widespread enough to represent either an innate mechanism, or the operation of a device dependent in part on innate mechanisms. In the buzzer experiment, for example, there are eight possible starts to the repeated pattern: so of the eight patterns available, choice of only one by us must involve the operation of something like quality spaces, or pattern spaces, on our part. So far, then, Garner's critical realism seems to take on board the extensionalist myth rather than provide an alternative to it.

7.4. CITY BLOCKS AND CORRELATIONS

Garner's work suggests something that looks pretty plausible a priori. This is that what properties we assign to objects is dependent on those similarities and differences occurring among the objects around us. If all convex surfaces were red and all the red items were convex surfaces, we might not discriminate redness from convexity. More important, though, is the fact, given extensionalism, that there will be lots of structures for which we could have more dimensions: the needs for partitioning the world into understandable chunks only require a certain degree of differentiation. To differentiate beyond that degree would not be cost-effective as a perceptual or cognitive strategy.

The idea that we go in for a strategy of maximum differentiation compatible with the lightest cognitive load prompts a further idea. Could it be the case that there are dimensions of discrimination to which we are sensitive but of which we are not consciously aware? The observation that saturation and brightness of colours are dimensions of which most adults are unaware, while yet they make a difference to subjects' responses, raises some fascinating problems. A discussion of many of these would not only take us far from the concerns of this chapter but would also firmly disallow its claim to be a chapter of philosophy. But the issue of the subject's awareness of dimensions is related to one of our own central concerns. For it raises the question of how we are to judge *similarity* and how similarity is to be measured.

A not unhelpful way of thinking about similarity responses is to engage in developmental speculation. Imagine normal children growing up in a richly structured environment, surrounded by artefacts and natural objects of various sorts. In order to latch on to the language spoken around them, children presumably must have some mechanism for spotting similarities and differences in the objects around them. Otherwise, adult utterances of 'apple' or 'shoe' in the presence of distinct objects have little chance of triggering an appropriate capacity for response in the children. One simple picture is that young children pick out one or two salient perceptual *features* of objects and, building on these core components, gradually add more and more of the features associated with the meaning of the word.[16] At first, therefore, children would tend to overextend their early vocabulary—applying it to items that share similarities over only a few dimensions. Although experimental data does not appear to confirm this picture, we can see that built into it is the ability of the child early on to pick up similarities along a few dimensions.

It is suggested by Kemler, for one, that existing data on child-language use and acquisition is much closer to a rather different hypothesis. On this one, children learn words for highly salient specimen *objects* ('mama', 'store', 'chair', 'tree', etc.) and their overextensions are to other objects that are highly similar overall to the examples (other women for 'mama', slippers for 'shoes', and so on). Again, on this second view, the child has the ability to latch on to similarities—this time overall similarities among objects rather

[16] See E. V. Clark [1].

than similarities along dimensions (that is, similarities among properties).

These divergent theories on child language coincide with two different kinds of similarity discussed by Garner, and seem to coincide, indeed, with two different geometries of similarity. We can illustrate this quite simply by imagining three objects, A, B, and C, such that A and C are similar along one dimension, but different relative to a second; while A and B are similar along this second dimension but different along the first (Fig. 16). In the diagram we have taken the two dimensions as Y and X. If we think of the degree of difference or dissimilarity between A and C as a *distance* along the Y dimension, then we can call this d_y. Of course A and B are at the same place along the Y dimension, that is, they are the same with respect to it, but they have distance d_x from each other along the X dimension. Given these differences, we might wonder if there is any general way of answering the question: what is the similarity between B and C (or, equivalently, what is the difference between B and C)? There are two obvious ways of trying to measure the required distance (call it 'd_{xy}').

First, d_{xy} might just be the *Euclidean* distance, that is

$$d_{xy} = (d_x^2 + d_y^2)^{\frac{1}{2}}$$

Just such a Euclidean metric seems to work for experiments involving the dimensions of brightness and saturation. However, Garner notes that experiments using the pairs of dimension brightness and size, and brightness and form, give quite different results. The distance formula for these dimensions is

$$d_{xy} = d_x + d_y$$

This second measure of distance can be called the *city-block* metric

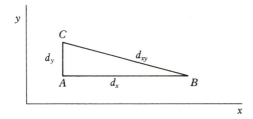

Fig. 16.

(for it gives the measure of distance between places diagonally located in a city laid out in regular blocks). Other sets of dimensions give results that lie between the Euclidean metric and the city-block metric.

Garner uses these different features of different dimensions to define two distinct properties of dimensions. *Integral* dimensions are those which provide a Euclidean metric, while *separable* dimensions provide a city-block metric.[17] Interestingly, he proposes a further pair of distinctions associated with these:

(1) Integral dimensions are those occurring where there is a true similarity structure (differences among objects or stimuli are greater or less); but, from the subject's point of view, such dimensions are not perceived *as dimensions* at all.

(2) Separability is dimension-based, so that the subject is aware of the dimensions in question; but now there is no question of measuring the closeness or distance between stimuli, that is, similarity structures beome unimportant.

Finally Garner proposes a third constraint. This is that—despite their apparent unawareness of integral dimensions (lack of 'psychological reality')—subjects *can* differentiate integral dimensions (for they can respond to changes in them).

Garner's proposal forces us to avoid simple theories of similarity. If separable dimensions are taken to be something like properties, then the implication is that conscious classification of items by property makes us blind to at least some real similarities and differences among the items. Conversely, we can note relative similarities and dissimilarities among sets of items, and even arrange these in some quantitative way, while being unaware, consciously, of just what features are responsible for such overall similarities. The similarity-blindness induced by separable dimensions is, although surprising, more readily accepted if we look at one of Garner's examples. In one test, subjects were given nine plastic chips—three circular, three square, and three triangular. Each circular chip was a different colour—one blue, one red, and one yellow—and likewise for the square and triangular chips. Thus the nine chips were the result of combining three levels of the one dimension, colour, with three of the other, shape.

[17] See Garner [2], Lecture 5.

A typical experimental task was as follows.[18] A subject was given a new chip—let us say a red triangle, with an instruction like: 'Select the identical chip from your own set and add any others you like to the original one.' Given this instruction, 69 per cent of Garner's subjects did one of the following:

(a) selected their red triangle and laid out the other two red chips,
(b) selected their red triangle and laid out the other two triangular chips.

Again, if given, let us say, a blue circle and a yellow traingle and told to select their matching chips and then add any others they liked, 61 per cent of his subjects would either

(a) lay out the matching chips along with all their other blue and yellow chips; or
(b) lay out the matching chips along with all their other circular and triangular chips.

What seems to matter, then, in this kind of matching task is representing the total set along one dimension at least. But in so doing, the subjects were bound to group together things that *differed entirely* along the other dimension. Thus they were acting as if blind to the other dimensional difference.

A sceptic might object at this point that the integrality–separability distinction is none other than a close relative to the distinction between scalar properties—those admitting of degree—and non-scalar ones. Things cannot be more or less triangular, but they can be more or less bright. So we can make sensible judgements about whether a certain red light is more like a bright blue light or a dull green one, but we cannot judge sensibly whether a certain blue triangle is more like a green square than it is like a red circle. Perhaps the sceptic is right here, and we have stumbled upon one more case of psychologists dressing up in technical talk distinctions that are pretty obvious in the first place. But the sceptic would have to come up with more convincing examples to win our support (things *can* be more or less triangular, triangles *can* be judged more similar to squares than to circles), and even if the sceptic is correct,

---

[18] I here simplify and condense the experimental results which are given in more detail in Garner, loc. cit.

we can still reflect on the earlier developmental question using either our everyday vocabulary or the psychologist's.

That question was concerned with two different theses about the child's entry into language. On the one, the child starts with separable dimensions, identifying commonalities between particulars using these. As the child matures, its language use reflects increasing sophistication at acquiring further discriminations along separable dimensions. The view, by contrast, that children spot overall similarities btween certain objects (mother and other women, shoes and boots, slippers and socks) suggests that they may be sensitive to similarities and differences without being aware of specific dimensions. In this case, then, the child's view of the world involves a similarity structure, propely called, and classification by Garner's integral dimensions.

On the latter view, maturation on the child's part may be accompanied by a move away from integrality in perception towards a more properly dimension-based, separable, classification. This would suggest that the child gains an understanding of non-scalar properties during development. Of course, other accounts are possible. Maybe development involves not so much discovery of *new* dimensional differences as increasing sophistication within the integral mode. Or perhaps the move is simply from unawareness of dimensions to awareness of dimensions.[19] To read this latter account back into Garner's work, we would have to describe our adult subjects in the last experiment mentioned not as being similarity-blind, but rather as being aware of all the dimensions available for classification and consciously *choosing* to classify by one rather than another.

These latest speculations advance our thinking on similarity somewhat. For they suggest that objective similarities and differ-

---

[19] These options are reviewed in Kemler [1]. Referring to Clark [1], she writes: 'Clark proposes that the child first attends to one or a few salient perceptual features as the basis for meaning and gradually adds more and more criterial features to the definition, as language learning progresses. Such a hypothesis predicts overextensions of early words to referents that have a very small number of properties in common. It also predicts that early in language acquisition, overextensions will be frequent since correct (adult) usage depends on taking account of a very large number of partially relevant properties. These predictions do not fare very well in the light of the data. What the existing data suggests is much more in line with the hypothesis that young children, learning language, are primarily attuned to overall similarity relations among object wholes, as the integrality–separability hypothesis predicts.' (Kemler [1], pp. 315–6.)

ences are available to the child thanks to the presence of structure in the world (Garner's critical realism) and that the child quite possibly starts its entry into language, and into the adult's perceptual sophistication, by detecting overall similarities among objects. But how—if the extensionalist myth is correct—could we apply Garner's programme here? For, of course, the world is full of structure and—unless we opt for innate quality spaces or the like—we are still liable to be puzzled about the child's initial success. One last step, consistent with the Garner programme, does the trick: we recall Garner's own point about correlational structure.

We already noted Garner's observation that selection of a subset from a total set of stimuli always involves redundancy—that is the correlation of more than one element of structure. In the case of the nine plastic chips used in the experiment described above, suppose we select the subset consisting of a red triangle, green circle, and blue square. That we would still have a three-element subset if we changed the red triangle to a blue one, or the green circle to a red one, is obvious. More complicated situations arise when the correlated structure does not involve any pairing of dimensions. More generally, natural structures must also show redundancy and correlation of this sort. We recognize a bird against the sun, in the shade of the woods, and against a stony background. Perhaps its colour gives it away in the last case, its shape in the first, and in the woods we rely on a glimpse of something which makes the right sounds. So form, colour, and song are all correlated, and in ideal circumstances we are faced with masses of redundant information.

Likewise, trees show impressive co-occurrences of leaves, branches, trunks, and roots of a quite distinctive kind. And fur and wings do not co-occur nearly so regularly as fur and feathers. What this suggests is that the world is not structurally, nor informationally, uniform. And indeed, Garner's own examples we have considered so far involve non-uniform structures. Our repeated buzzers allowed at most eight patterns to be recognized; the plastic chips represented the combinations of three levels of only two dimensions. If the world were the way the holders of the extensionalist myth think it is, then it would not be differentiated and 'chunky' to even the degree of Garner's experimental set-ups. For, remember, the world according to the extensionalist is thoroughly uniform in respect of similarities and differences among things.

Eleanor Rosch and her associates have gone rather further than this.[20] They have done experiments which seem to show that in our deployment of common nouns in English we use certain of them to signify basic objects, which have four features:

(1) a high number of attributes in common
(2) have motor programs similar to one another
(3) have similar shapes
(4) can be identified from averaged shapes of members of the class in question.

Thus, among artefacts, the terms 'furniture', 'seating', and so on do *not* refer to basic objects, while terms like 'table', 'lamp', 'chair', and so on *do*. 'Bird' does not refer to a basic object, but 'eagle', 'crow', and 'sparrow' do.

Here I am not wanting to commit myself to anything as extreme as Rosch's thesis. We can admit that the world is structured and that such structure is unevenly distributed, while leaving open the question of whether some objects are basic, relative to others. And once we acknowledge linguistic and cultural influence on our classification of items around us, we note that the story of what is a basic object, and what are the characteristics of such objects, is bound to be complicated. Rosch herself notes this, proposing that we operate in our cognitive classifications with *prototypes* which suggest that distinctions among items are simpler and more structured than they are in reality.

7.5. SIMILARITY CIRCLES

Once we recognize correlational structure as a real feature of our world, and notice that properties are unevenly grouped around us, then it becomes hard to see why we were ever attracted by the extensionalist myth in the first place. The existence of correlated structures seems so entirely obvious that extensionalist denials of it start to seem perverse. Moreover, some of Garner's studies make a further move plausible. In Fig. 17 is a simple set of figures which are formed from combining the following two-level dimensions— circle or square, vertical or horizontal centre-line, wavy or straight

[20] As described extensively in Rosch *et al.* [1].

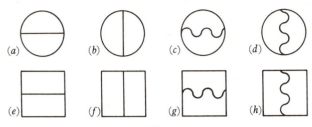

Fig. 17.

centre line. Clearly, there are all sorts of natural ways we might group these figures into similar sets. But let us think, instead, of the *discrimination* problem. On Garner's account, the total set of stimuli provides a dimensional structure for the classification of each individual stimulus (indeed, we ensured that the figures were precisely the result of reproducing all combinations of our three dimensions).

So let us now try to select certain subsets from the above total set. Consider, for instance, just the two figures (*f*) and (*d*). These show a simple correlational structure. For the straight vertical line is correlated with the square and the wavy line with the circle. So now we have redundancy of information. We could still discriminate two items here either without the centre line, or without the shapes. Again, if we examine figures (*g*) and (*h*) we will note that the waviness of the line and the shapes are redundant given the orientation of the lines. The ultimate in redundancy, of course, comes with the selection of just one item, say (*c*). Here, any two of our dimensions are redundant, for we would have no difficulty in discriminating the circle alone, a horizontal alone, or a wavy something alone.

But, like a good extensionalist, Garner notes that any subset of discriminable items is bound to have redundancy and correlational structure. Take, for instance, the set (*b*), (*g*), and (*f*). This, time, there is no simple correlation of structures (as in the previous cases). Instead we have only partial redundancy. The centre line's orientation and waviness are redundant for discriminating the circle from the squares, and waviness is redundant for discriminating the squares from each other. Garner calls this kind of partial correlation *complex* correlational structure.

As is fairly obvious, we are able to spot simple correlational structure far more readily than we can spot complex correlational structure. Indeed, it is only Garner's commitment to an information-theoretic concept of *structure* that leads him, I suspect, to describe this latter case as involving correlational structure at all. Bearing this in mind, let us now return to the similarity question, thinking about our ability to detect overall similarities among presented items. Here I cite one set of experiments by Whitman and Garner.[21] Let us consider the nine figures in Fig. 18. In the light of what has just been said, it is clear that these figures have a high degree of *simple* correlational structure: the triangles have their gap on the right, the squares have it on the left, and the circles have no gaps. Circles have no lines, triangles one line, and squares two lines. Whole dimensions are thus correlated—form with both gap position and line number. The experiment involved presenting the figures one at a time, in random order, to subjects. After examining all nine, subjects had to reproduce them all by drawing. The median number of such trials required for learning all nine figures turned out to be *two*, with no subject requiring more than seven.

By contrast, quite different results were obtained from running exactly the same procedure in regard to the figures in Fig. 19. This time the *minimum* number of trials for learning the set was seven, the median twelve, and some subjects took as many as nineteen

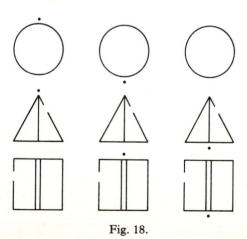

Fig. 18.

---

[21] These are described in Lecture 4 of Garner [2].

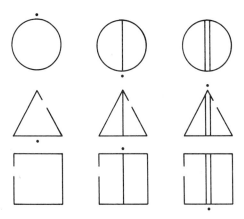

Fig. 19.

trials to get it right. Observant readers may have noted that the same figures occur on the diagonal in both sets. Yet Garner points out that these figures were as hard to learn as the set within which they were nested. This, incidentally, suggests that subjects learn sets as a whole rather than the individual items. We have to consider, now, what features distinguish these two sets of figures. As we have seen, the first set showed a high degree of simple correlational structure. The second set, however, shows no such redundancy. The only simple redundancy this time is between form and position of the gap. Of course, as good extensionalists will hasten to point out, the set shows more complex redundancy, but, as noted already, such redundancy is very hard to spot. The present experiment gives good confirmation of this. For the presence of complex correlational structure in the second set did not seem to help with learning. Indeed, this and other experiments by Garner and his associates suggest strongly that ease of recall is aided by the presence only of simple correlational structure.

It would be tempting to continue the exploration of this topic. As Garner has demonstrated for some items, like patterns of dots, simple correlational structure seems to be associated with the *Gestalt* property of pattern 'goodness'. The *Gestalt* theorists were intrigued by our sensory preference for seeing things in terms of regular, stable, simple, symmetrical shapes even when the stimuli presented were themselves none of these things. Such regular patterns were described as 'good', and structural redundancy seems at least sometimes to be correlated with goodness in this sense.[22]

Of course it is bold to try to generalize on the basis of a few experiments involving lines and curves. And it is not my intention to argue that we have now encountered plausible grounds for outright rejection of the extensionalist myth. But I hope that an alternative to that myth is now beginning to seem at least defensible. For we can suggest that what Garner calls *simple correlational structure* is in fact a significant factor in our ability to latch on to similarities and differences in the objects around us. Our understanding of properties is dependent on our possession of mechanisms that make us sensitive to the dimensionalization, in psychologists' vernacular, of our experience. But this dimensionalization need not—as we have already observed—involve conscious awareness on our part of just what all these dimensions are. Children, very likely, are able to spot similarities and differences among items long before grasping anything so fancy as the concept of a property.

Our ability to structure our experience along the dimensions we do is itself dependent on the world's affording us suitably structured items. To adapt a remark of George Schlesinger's to this purpose, we can say we live in a user-friendly universe. The total set of structured items yield the natural dimensions along which we classify things. And simple redundancies of the sort mentioned already—leaves co-occurring, for example, with bark, twigs, branches, and trunks—enable us to sort the items around us into sets of similar things. Further, a set of items matched by these dimensional preferences will be, typically, elements sharing a *property* in the natural sense. The property of being a tree, then, will be a property of a set of items sharing structure on several dimensions such that, given the total range of objects around us (and the dimensions thus provided), each item will show a high degree of simple correlational structure. Thus, living in the world we do, it is hardly surprising that we classify items as trees, clouds, and cows. For this is but a further development of a skill that would

---

[22] Garner is not alone among psychologists in taking the suggestions of *Gestalt* theorists seriously. Many philosophers have also regarded *Gestalt* theory as having relevance to the theory of identity: see, for instance, the number of references to Koffka and Köhler in Hirsch [2].

lead us naturally to classify all the circles in Fig. 18 separate from the triangles and the squares.

Of course, the sets in Fig. 18 can also be classified into other natural groups—for instance, those with spots above them. But the taxonomic problem here is hardly like the problem of distinguishing trees from bears, or desks from motor cars. The co-occurrence of structural features among motor cars is massive compared to commonalities between cars and desks. Indeed, our triangles, squares, and circles pose a taxonomic problem closer to the one posed by the classification of flowers, reptiles, or even mammals. In such cases, relative weight along certain dimensions may be of some significance and, as already indicated, attention to one dimension can induce a kind of blindness to others. However, the discussion of taxonomic strategies and family resemblances can safely be left to those who specialize in such topics. For our purposes here it is only important to emphasize the overall plausibility of the general strategy.

The alternative to the extensionalist myth is thus not a radical one. In fact, there are ways of reconciling the suggestions here with a fairly tough extensionalist line. None of us want to quarrel much over terminology, after all. So whether complex correlational structure should be *called* 'correlational structure' is not itself a very interesting question. Let us give the extensionalist the point that the world provides structure aplenty—including both simple and complex correlational structure. My suggestion, then, is that it is the existence of simple correlational structure as a real feature of the world which makes it friendly to users, which permits us to identify real similarities among objects. I do not deny the existence of far more information, hence far more similarity, than we in fact use. It is just that similarity, like information, comes, as it were, in different forms.

The extreme extensionalist who is wary of reconciling the two doctrines has one last opportunity for disagreement. For our examples, after all, have started with elements in them which are clearly defined objects with clearly defined properties. Our figures have lines in them with properties such as straightness or waviness. Our examples from natural and artefactual objects have likewise taken objects—like branches and leaves—which undoubtedly themselves have properties—like texture and shape. So, then, we have apparently presumed the very thing we were supposed to be establishing, namely the existence of well-differentiated objects and properties independent of our cognitive organization.

There is a limit, though, to how far the extensionalist can press this point. Consider, for example, a simple pairing task. There are, let us suppose, two green leaves and two red pencils on my desk. Of the six possible unordered pairings of these four items, two seem natural—the leaves with each other and the pencils with each other. Such pairings would unite the items by similarity. Now the extensionalist's point about similarity can be made in this way. Since pairing one pencil with one leaf forms a set just as pairing the pencil with the other pencil does, the pencil is—by this criterion—as similar to one of the leaves as it is to the other pencil. Now I understand what the extensionalist is saying here, and I have outlined in this chapter a reply to it. For the dimensional structure provided by our set of four objects allocates simple correlations of structure to the leaves (say colour, texture, form, and lack of rigidity) and a distinct correlated structure to the pencils (rigidity, colour, form, and texture). The objection cannot now be made that I am presupposing a clear distinction between pencils and leaves in order to make this point. For the extensionalist too has to identify these items in our normal way simply in order to discuss the unusual similarity pairings allowed by the myth. These pairings are simply ruled out in my view because any redundancy of structure they involve is not of the simple kind already discussed. The account given here thus does not seem to be circular in the objectionable way suggested.

A final, somewhat ironic, observation can now be made. In looking for similarities among sets of objects we are engaged in an enterprise reminiscent of Carnap's celebrated construction of property classes from so-called 'elementary experiences'. In his *Aufbau*, Carnap sought to show, in effect, how partial similarity detection could lead to the constrution of *similarity circles*, these circles containing all the items possessing some common property. A sympathetic account of Carnap's ingenious work is given by Goodman who points out, however, that the programme, as described by Carnap, faces two serious difficulties.[23]

***

[23] The one not discussed here is what Goodman calls the problem of 'imperfect community'. Carnap's programme, together with the problems, can be found described in ch. 5 of Goodman [2].

One of these difficulties, the *companionship* problem, arises because, given a set of items exemplifying the properties p, q, r, and s, let us say, Carnap's method will not enable us to construct the appropriate similarity circles where the properties occur in the following clusters:

a: pq b: rsq c: pqr d: r e: s

If $p, q, \ldots$ etc. are all taken to be colour properties, then we could imagine listing all the pairs of our five items which have colour similarity to each other. Thus the pair $\{b, d\}$ are colour-similar as are, of course, b and e. Carnap's method was to try to construct colour-classes given *only* the information as to which pairs of items were colour-akin. The construction seems rather easy: if we list on a table all the pairs of colour-akin items then we just try to construct maximal classes every pair of members of which is listed on our table. The pairs here are unordered. For much of the time this works well. But for the example given, it does not. Consider the table of all the colour-akin pairs:

a:a   b:b   c:c   d:d   e:e
a:b   b:c   c:d
a:c   b:d
        b:e

Now let us try to build maximal classes, each pair of members of which is listed on the table. Clearly $\{d, e\}$ is *not* such a class, for the pair $\{d, e\}$ does not occur on the table, although the other two pairs in the set do occur. And this is good news for items d and e differ in colour. What, then, about $\{b, c, d\}$? All the pairs of this class do occur in our table (namely $\{b, b\}, \{b, c\}, \{c, c\}, \{c, d\}, \{d, d\}, \{b, d\}$). Next, we have to ascertain if it is maximal, that is, see if the table pairs either a or e with all the elements in our class. But $\{a, d\}$ is not on the table, nor is $\{e, c\}$, for example. Thus $\{b, c, d\}$ is maximal, and corresponds to the colour property r.

The good news does not last long, however. For we can see that there is going to be a problem about isolating the colour class for property p. Looking at our clusters of properties, we note that p occurs in both a and c. So $\{a, c\}$ ought to be a colour class. But it isn't! For b is paired on our table both with a and with c, so in order to build a maximal class we have to extend $\{a, c\}$ to the superset $\{a, b, c\}$. Inspection of our clusters shows us that this is the class for property q. And the problem with property p, as we can now see, is that it occurs always in companionship with q. So Carnap's technique cannot isolate it.

This result is a sad irony. For, of course, in our terms, this kind of companionship is a case of simple correlational structure. If our speculations in this chapter have been correct, then it is the fact that various features in the world are regular companions to each other that enables us to make the classifications we do. Without companionship along many dimensions the child would never be able to master the language of everyday objects, let alone get into the more sophisticated classification and differentiation typical of normal adults. Carnap was a good extensionalist. And it is the very extensionalism to which he was committed that makes a problem out of nature's way of helping us cope with the universe—the uneven, companionly distribution of information.

8
Memories, Bodies, and Survival

We have so far tried to explore the prospects for a theory of identity based on the concept of survival. This exploration has met with mixed success, recorded in our narrative of it. The attractive side of the proposal is that it gives us a means of understanding the unity of persisting things without commitment to spatio-temporal continuity. We can also see how the survival relation, being one that admits of degrees, captures subtleties to which an all-or-nothing notion of identity was indifferent.

A further attraction of the theory of identity given so far is that it copes with a number of outstanding difficulties. For example, since survival even to a high degree is not transitive, but identity is, it seemed that survival to a high degree could not be straightforwardly constitutive of identity. Suppose that what is constitutive of identity for anything is a chain of survival relations among its stages where closely neighbouring stages are survivors of their predecessors in the strong sense, but only the *ancestral* of the survival relation holds between stages widely separated in time. Weak survival of this sort obviously lets in too much. We have seen how continuity theories face this same problem in the case of the dog that turns into an amorphous blob. Either continuity or weak survival, without any other conditions, would force us to count the dog as the same as the blob while yet our pre-theoretic intuitions suggest that this would be silly.

Further, the degree of survival manifested by the stages of persisting things differs from one sort of thing to another. Changes that are perfectly normal for a bluebottle would be extraordinary, and destructive of identity, for a cow. The response to these cases is typically to announce that identity is sortal-relative. But we have already seen that such a claim is highly dubious for a number of reasons. In the end we have accepted a new version of the thesis of sortal relativity, namely that living in a world of structured particulars, we have learned to allocate our sortals according to the nature of the particulars around us. We recognize, in other words, that there are different principles of change for different sorts of things: but they do not change according to the sortals we use to describe them; rather, we allocate sortals in a way that reflects differences among things.

The failure of appeal to sortals in helping us out of the difficulty common to survival and continuity theories forced us back to considering whether some strong kind of survival underpins identity. If we do turn to this form of solution, then we once more have to face the problems associated with the formal nature of the relations in question. One attractive way out did suggest itself here. What we need to do is recognize that the unity or identity of a broad object requires survival to some high enough degree of certain of its structural features. This will mean, of course, that there will be occasions on which it is hard to tell if a number of stages show high enough patterns of survival for us to count them as all belonging to one unified thing. Thus there will be difficult cases, and possibilities of fuzziness. Yet, having once found a maximal set of stages constituting a unified particular, the question of its identity is no longer a matter of degree or argument. Identity, or unity, having been established, that item—whatever it is—obeys the classical laws of identity. In this form, the unity of particulars other than artefacts and persons can be plausibly described in terms of survival.

In turning now to the problems concerned with the nature of persons and the issues of personal identity we will finally discover the limits of survival theory. We will discover, in fact, that not all issues concerning the survival of person-stages can be satisfactorily resolved. And failure to resolve these has serious consequences. For our theories of morality and responsibility require that we can operate with appropriate notions of personal identity and personal survival. In this chapter, I introduce some of the central themes in the personal identity debate. The assessment of one distinctive recent contribution to this debate, by Parfit, is carried out in the following two chapters.

The structure of the following three sections is meant to give a natural introduction to the topic of personal identity. After an initial review of some of the things we say and think about persons, it is noted that there is some difficulty in deciding whether the term 'person' is a natural kind term. It seems we do have the capacity, given what we currently think, to develop the concept of a person as a natural kind concept; but such development is not in any way mandatory. The memory criterion of personal identity is then discussed, followed by an account of what is meant by talking of 'criteria' in such cases. Two simple accounts of the idea of a criterion are given, on the stronger of which a criterion of identity is that which is constitutive of identity.

8.2. PERSONS AND NATURAL KINDS

The interest that we feel concerning persons no doubt reflects to some extent our own self-interest. All of us are persons, and we are—at least in our own eyes—beings of some importance. Moreover, many of the important things in our lives are at stake when we consider personal identity and personal survival. Consider the question of whether I should now feel regret for behaviour I engaged in as a child. Is it rational for me to care about this? And is it rational for me to care about the way I behaved last week? One salient difference between my childhood and last week is that the latter seems much more closely related to me as I am now than the former. In many ways, I have changed greatly since I was a child. In some respects, these changes are for the better. There are thus things that I did then which I would not consider doing now. For I would now think of these as being wrong, although I did not then so consider them.

Think of the following example. I still remember the time when I experimented with some paraffin I had discovered in a bottle somewhere in the house. It smelt terrible, and so I wondered what would happen if I poured it on some food. Getting a chair (for I was then fairly small), I gained access to a shelf in the larder on which stood a plate of cakes ready to be served at tea. Very carefully, I poured small amounts of the paraffin over each of the cakes. Later, having finished tea before the rest of the family—taking care to eat none of the treated cakes—I listened outside the door while the others ate their cakes, and commented on their peculiar flavour.

Now although I can remember the incident just described with great clarity, I wonder if I should still feel troubled by guilt over it. Indeed, the guilt was a long time coming, for at the time, and for a considerable period after it, I felt rather proud of what I had done.

If I am now a very different person from the person I was as a child, then perhaps it is silly for me now to be troubled by guilt over what I then did. For it is like being troubled by guilt over what *someone else* has done. By contrast, if I said something tactless or hurtful to one of my friends last week—something I should have known better than to do—then I might quite properly feel troubled about this. For I now, and myself last week, are psychologically and physically close enough, so it seems, to be undoubtedly one and the same person.

Of course, there are cases, even here, where circumstances might incline me to distance myself from what I have recently done. Perhaps I was in a transport of rage, and said things that I later regretted. In such a case, I may think of the occasion, however recent, as one in which I was *not quite myself*. Losing one's temper, like drinking too much, may provide an occasion for acting *out of character* and behaving like someone who is *not my normal self*. As the italicized locutions reveal, we have perfectly ordinary ways of speaking about personal identity in these kinds of cases, ways that seem to capture a notion of what a person is, and what it is to be the same person, that is of some moral significance.

Also of some importance to us, mortal as we are, is the issue of death. Many people frankly confess that their religious faith gives them something without which their lives would seem meaningless. And—in part—what they may have in mind is the prospect of survival after the death of their bodies. Although we cannot investigate here the issue of whether, in fact, people can survive bodily death, we can ask whether the notion that they do makes sense. Such a notion involves the further ideas either of disembodied existence, or of the reconstitution of the body after its destruction (its resurrection). Both of these ideas are worthy of further study in their own right.[1] The problem with reconstitution of the body long after death is that we have to ask whether the reconstituted body is the same as the original, or simply a replica of it. If it is the same, then the argument for this would have to be based on compositional theories of identity which, as we have seen, allow us to disassemble and reassemble the same thing. The disassembly and the reassembly, in this case, is rather more

---

[1] For a start on this study, see Penelhum [2]. The issue concerning disembodied existence is also touched on in Shoemaker and Swinburne [1]. For problems about the reconstitution of people after their death see Parfit [2] and Parfit [4].

dramatic, and the problem of reassembly may be made difficult by such expedients as cremation, or burial in densely populated areas.[2] Since religions like Christianity involve belief in a being with quite supernatural powers, then these problems are perhaps not problems of principle for the doctrine of resurrection. On the other hand, the issue of disembodied existence seems much easier to resolve. Nothing in what follows will suggest that persons can exist without any form of embodiment. Indeed, the existence of a disembodied *anything* is a notion of which I can make little sense. Notice, that this is not the same as the question about the existence of *abstract* things (however we understand that term). Numbers, for instance, are abstract, but not disembodied: it makes no more sense to say of numbers that they are disembodied than to say they are embodied.

However, there is a way in which our interest in persons can properly be described as an interest in the *supernatural*. For notions like those of *value*, and of *self-consciousness*, strike us some of the time as being quite different from other concepts with which we operate. It is as if we recognize that we might give a complete description of the universe while leaving out any explicit mention of either of these things. Yet they are of overwhelming importance to us. Values, and self-consciousness, thus become two of the great mysteries of our lives. We can search physics and psychology textbooks in vain for illumination on them. And so we can come to think of the *natural* as somehow different from the domain associated with human consciousness and human values. It is as if we stand apart from the rest of nature by virtue of our possession of, and interest in, these very features.

At the same time, we recognize all sorts of connections between ourselves and other living things. We can hardly be entirely separate from the rest of nature, for the simple reason that, as the natural sciences inform us, these is a remarkable closeness between our DNA and that of the primates, and we have apparently evolved as a species in just the same way the other species on the planet have done so. It is likely then that apes and dogs, and perhaps even squirrels and snails, have consciousness (even if not our form of self-consciousness) and live lives in which value plays a part (even if

---

[2] See Parfit [4], § 77.

not value in the rich form in which we theorize about this notion).[3] In the end, then, it is not silly to wonder if there could be animal but non-human persons—a topic that thinkers in this area have rather surprisingly neglected. Not equally neglected, however, is the issue of whether there could be computer, or robot, persons.

This issue of our place in nature is connected with the problem of whether to treat the term 'person' as a natural kind term. Recall that natural kinds are supposed to be a subdivision of sorts, and so natural-kind terms are a subclass of sortal terms. We have already seen that it is arguable that the non-uniformity of information in nature underlies our ability to distinguish the particulars around us as falling into sorts. And we have seen that on the Putnam, deictic-nomological view of natural kinds, interpreted according to the theory of structure, members of a natural kind have to show appropriate structural relations to each other along what we called the 'horizontal' dimension.[4] Viewed in this way, it is hard to see what would justify a decision that persons are a natural kind. Of course, all the persons of which we have knowledge happen to be human, and humans constitute a natural kind. But if we encountered a rational parrot, or indeed, a rational artefact of the right kind, it would seem perverse to deny it the status of personhood on merely biological grounds.

However, we need to tread carefully here. As Wiggins has argued, a naturalistic conception of persons may force us to rule out the possibility of ever encountering artefactual persons.[5] On this naturalistic conception, the sortal *person* is a restriction, as Wiggins

---

[3] This point may seem controversial for those who take the distinction between human and other animals as being absolute and one of kind, not of degree. Contemporary Marxists often put the point in terms of subjectivity versus objectivity: humans, as subjects, act on and transform the world; animals, as objects, are acted on, and respond to their environment. In fact, we simply do not know enough about either humans or animals, or have sharply enough defined concepts, to get very far in resolving this sort of issue.

[4] See the discussion in Ch. 5.5 and footnote refs. to Putnam. Shoemaker uses the vocabulary of synchronic and diachronic identity, but points out that C. D. Broad used terminology not unlike my 'horizontal' and 'vertical'. In Broad's case the terms are 'transverse' and 'longitudinal' (see Shoemaker [6], p. 251). For more on the two unities see sect. 7.

[5] '. . . artefacts [like robots and automata] are not identified and invididuated under concepts that are extension-involving . . . nomologically grounded, or vital activity-determining; whereas extreme difficulty proves to attach to the project of diminishing the degree of extension-involvingness, *animal*-dependence, and even *man*-dependence, of the concept of a person' (Wiggins [9], p..175).

puts it, of the very general natural kind, *animal*. Such a view allows enormous leeway to us. It could turn out that we are wrong in thinking that dolphins and whales are not persons; and while any animal we discover on a remote planet is a candidate for personhood, the Wiggins view simply prevents us from looking at artefacts and bits of rock with expectations of finding any of them to be persons.

What we seem to be facing again here is the problem of analysis versus development. It is clear that a case could be made out along Wiggins's lines for taking 'person' as a restriction of a natural kind term. But we have already developed concepts of the person in, for example, the law, that make Wiggins's account seem unduly restrictive. Corporations, universities, and the like are legal persons, and not long ago, the proposal that mountains and valleys should enjoy the status of persons in law was only narrowly rejected by the US Supreme Court.[6] What these legal cases show is that we already have the potential for developing the concept of a person in ways that violate the idea that persons are simply kinds of animals. As I will argue in the final chapter, the situation with our concepts is more extreme still. There is nothing that we can call our 'concept of a person'. Our talk about persons, rather, is hospitable to all kinds of conceptual development, and may itself fail to be consistent under analysis.

This being so, Wiggins's naturalistic concept of a person is a perfectly proper development of some aspects of our person-talk. If we stay, for a moment, with this particular development, we can gain some further insight into a case mentioned already. Think again of the issue of parents surviving in their children. If we think of this in terms of Wiggins's naturalistic view, then we can see two very different ways in which to talk about the production of persons.

---

[6] See the material in Christopher D. Stone's *Should Trees Have Standing?* (Los Angeles: Kaufmann, 1974). While preparing the final version of the manuscript, I received his latest paper on the standing of trees, published in *Southern California Law Review* 59 (1985). In it he writes: 'In some instances, Unorthodox Entities were fitted into the CNPP (Contemporary Normal Proximate Persons) framework by overlooking distinctions that might have been drawn. Under this approach, by denominating the Unorthodox Entity a "person", it was thereby treated indistinctly from a CNPP ... Some of these efforts were abandoned, and now appear anachronistic, such as the occasional criminal trial of an animal during the middle ages.' Of course, we can talk about *merely* legal persons, but we would have to be very sure that the 'merely' is not simply question-begging.

On one of these accounts, we take the gene pool as ultimately the producer of persons. Mammalian mating, in general, is in fact just a process for producing more animals of the given kind. On the genetic determinist's view, the genes we possess are themselves what influence (at least to some noticeable extent) our mating behaviour. But if we take this view, then our talk of parents surviving in their children is just as inappropriate as saying that one car from a production line survives in a later car from the same line. On the genetic determinist's view, the ultimate survivor is the gene pool.[7] What I am passing on to my childen is not so much something of me but some of the recipe which produced my behavioural characteristics among lots of others. What lives on is the recipe, and not the particulars exemplifying it.

By contrast, we can think of genes and reproduction in a quite different way. Parents are supplied, thanks to nature, with amazing copying devices over which they have little control as far as the finer details go, but which ensure that they pass on certain of their own structures to their offspring. Being responsible for the upbringing of my children I can also add to, or subtract from, the effects of this inherited structure. The kind of conditioning of their children in which many parents engage is another process of bringing it about that certain of their characteristics continue in their children. The parent who is successful in this way, can be said to survive in the child. Some parents, influenced by a concern for their children's autonomy, may try to ensure that they do not condition their children in the way just described. They may even be anxious to bring it about that the child is not someone in whom they survive at all.

According to this second point of view, we can make real sense of what the Master is up to in the novel mentioned in Chapter 1. If conditioning of the children is carried on intensively enough, and if genetic determinism is false, then, no matter what the genetically-coded characteristics of the children he has kidnapped, the Master can ensure that he does indeed survive in them. He will not wholly die to the extent he can control their mental and emotional development. So to the horror of kidnap, the Master is adding the horror of indoctrination and corruption. To the extent that he is an

---

[7] I take it that this is what is being said by 'selfish gene' theorists like Dawkins. See Dawkins [1].

evil person, his success in altering the children's personalities will be success in making it the case that people who are evil in just the way he is continue in existence after his death.

Now I suspect that both of the positions just described figure in our thinking about parental survival. In talking about the case of the Master, we may not be too scrupulous over distinguishing between whether he is trying to survive in the children (second view) or whether he is himself simply a part of some larger process whereby evil schemes survive (first view). Nor is this the right place for me to say what is wrong with genetic determinism. What is important is that the distinction between production and copying processes can throw some light on this issue and on the two different conceptions of what the relation of parents to children might be. Certainly, to the extent that we are troubled by the thought that our choice of a mate and our subsequent decision to have children may itself be simply part of some much larger production process over which we have little individual control—to that extent, we can seriously doubt that we survive in our offspring. The disanalogy identified here will return to plague us later. For it will transpire that we have two quite different ways of thinking about persons and their characteristics—ways that are apparently incapable of being merged into a single account of what persons are.

8.3. MEMORY AND IDENTITY

It is very hard for us to overcome a kind of Cartesianism that is implicit in much of our thinking about ourselves. We naturally think of a person as some kind of amalgam of mind and body—a union that is very close despite the different natures of the two kinds of things. Associated with this distinction between the mental and the physical are two different sorts of tests or criteria for personal identity—psychological and physical. The topic of criteria will be examined in the next section. Even, however, if we take the term 'criterion' as a synonym for the term 'evidence', we can note the possibility of these two sorts of evidence. Jones may be judged to be the same person as Smith due to a notable psychological resemblance, or simply because Jones has undoubtedly the same body as Smith. In most discussions, the physical criterion for personal identity is *bodily continuity*, and the psychological one is *memory*, or—more generally—*co-consciousness*.

Bodily continuity, of course, can only be used as evidence of identity if we are sure that animal bodies generally trace out continuous paths in space and time. Anyone who was not sure of this, however, might well modify the body-continuity account along the lines suggested in our earlier discussion of discontinuous objects. In this case, what we would look for as evidence of personal identity would be an appropriate non-branching chain of survival relations among body stages. However, even with this modification, appeal to a body condition for personal identity has seemed unsatisfactory to many thinkers. Locke can be credited with giving perhaps the most sustained defence of the alternative, psychological view of personhood.

For Locke, a person is a

> thinking intelligent Being, that has reason and reflection, and can consider itself as itself, the same thinking thing in different times and places; which it does only by that consciousness, which is inseparable from thinking and as it seems to me essential to it: It being impossible for anyone to perceive without perceiving that he does perceive.[8]

The last remark suggests that 'that consciousness' is some kind of self-consciousness, although Locke's discussion of this in the subsequent pages turns out to be obscure as well as fascinating. Staying with Locke's general conception for the moment, we might wonder why *memory* has a special role in this sort of account of the nature of persons. Locke puts it like this: 'For as far as any intelligent Being can repeat the *Idea* of any past action with the same consciousness it had of it at first, and with the same consciousness of any present action; so far is it the same *personal self*.' Here we have an interesting and high-level conception of what a person is. For Locke, we as adults have already lost touch with much of our earlier life, for we are no longer capable of co-consciousness with how we were then. There are countless actions that I have forgotten about. But then I cannot be the same person as the one that did these things. Locke apparently thinks that I may be the same human being as did those things even though I am not the same *personal self*. As well as this, he also thinks that it is possible for one and the

---

[8] This, and the following two quotations are from the discussion in Locke [1], II. 27.

same person to be two separate human beings: 'For should the Soul of a Prince, carrying with it the consciousness of the Prince's past Life, enter and inform the Body of a Cobbler as soon as deserted by his own Soul, everyone sees, he would be the same Person with the Prince, accountable only for the Prince's Actions: But who would say it was the same Man?'

Now, it is part of my project here to argue that several different developments of the concept of person are possible, although this will not include defending Locke's relativism. Locke's view represents one such interesting development. There is a way in which we can very clearly make sense of his view that I have lost some of my past selves due to the feebleness of my memories. Look at it like this. Viewed from the inside my past life does not seem to have any discontinuities at all. I seem to be able to look back on an uninterrupted career. Yet I know full well that sleep, day-dreaming, and absorption in various tasks have already produced gaps in my memory of the last twenty-four hours. I cannot now account for everything I have done in these hours.

An immediate objection to this co-consciousness view is that surely we can distinguish memories we have readily available to us and those that can be brought back by various forms of jogging and association. Indeed, in an extreme case we can even think of hypnosis or other psychological tricks to get us to recall what had seemed to be lost. But even if we extend the Lockean conception to allow for potential, as well as readily available memory, we notice that there will still be impressive blanks in my inner account of my career. Sleep, or complete concentration on a task, are things in which we 'lose ourselves', in which we lose that consciousness of perception which looms so large in Locke's view.

The inside view of our own lives, then, does not itself make allowances for gaps in our memories of the past: for our access to our own past is through the memories we now have. Just as memories are backward-looking, so too there are forward-looking psychological states. Ambitions and intentions, for example, are states or experiences we have now in respect of future activities. Just as a memory I have at one time can be lost at another, so an intention formulated some long time ago may not have been fulfilled, but no longer is active in my repertoire of psychological states.

The way memories, intentions, longings, and the like bridge my psychological states at different times makes it natural to use Parfit's phrase 'psychological connectedness' when talking about this variety of co-consciousness. My states at one time will typically be psychologically *connected* to a greater or lesser degree with my states at other times. Memory is one particularly impressive variety of psychological connection, and it too shows this feature of holding to greater or lesser degrees.

We seem to keep track of our memories and intentions in a way that we do not update other aspects of our mental lives. This may be partly due to the phenomenology of memory compared to that of other mental states and occurrences. A large class of memories—*experience memories* we might call them—present themselves as records of actual past experiences. So an experience memory is indexed, by its very mode of presentation, to the event it commemorates. By contrast, the skills I have acquired in various areas—though no doubt ingredients of my total psychological repertoire—are not indexed in this way to the occasions of acquisition or to occasions of exercise. Of course, I may recollect an occasion on which I exercised a particular skill, or remember a perhaps painful learning experience: but this is a feature of experience memory again.

We might argue that the distinction just mooted is made fairly evident by our modes of referring to memories and skills. To state the nature, or content, of an experience memory is to state *of what* particular experience it is a memory: but to state the nature of a skill it is usually only necessary to give some general description. Thus the memory of saying goodbye to Linda in June (specific) contrasts with the ability to ride a (that is, *some*) bicycle. Indeed, a further feature of skills is non-transparent. Not all my skills can be specified in respect of those situations in which they may be successfully exercised. Yesterdays's success at steering the required heading during a severe squall was not doubt the result of my having previously acquired the necessary skills. But I would not have felt confident about predicting in advance that I would in fact have displayed the necessary skill.

We could, then, coin a phrase, and talk about the *deictic transparency* of memories, intentions, and the like. This feature might well account for why some writers weight memory more heavily than procedural skills, habits, sense of humour, and so on when discussing personal identity. Locke certainly writes as if the co-consciousness exemplified by memory is of enormous significance. Now maybe he is right—and I will certainly be arguing that one consistent development of the concept of a person can take place along Lockean lines. Parfit also tends to discuss psychological connectedness in the context of dealing with memories, intentions, and ambitions. Yet our non-theoretical assessment of sameness and difference of person lays no special weight on these particular psychological states.

Thus if someone loses their sense of humour, or can no longer navigate with the accuracy and flair previously displayed, we tend to think that they have undergone a fairly drastic change. And this change is certainly as drastic as having lost memories of many past experiences. In fact, some people are notoriously vague when it comes to experience memory, yet this seems not to occasion us much anxiety over their identity. Nor are we surprised when elderly people appear to enjoy vivid memories of their remote pasts: what makes them no longer the people we once knew (still speaking informally) is the deterioration in their skills and abilities, the loss of certain habitual responses, their failure to appreciate jokes they would once have enjoyed, and so on. The Lockean can certainly make sense of one way in which we do frequently speak of the senile. The notion that they are 'returning to childhood' is supported by the apparent co-consciousness, via memory, between their senescent and juvenile selves.

But even to make this admission is to be aware at the same time that many other features of their juvenile selves are no longer present. It is only in a highly artificial way that they can be identified with their younger selves. For the relatives and friends of someone who was once a person of action and resource, quick intelligence and sparkling humour, the retreat into childhood of later life will be a matter of deep regret. Senility is in no genuine way a return to some former self: it neither continues the person's mature self, nor genuinely supplants this with some earlier self.

An example like this shows clearly both the strengths and weaknesses of memory or co-consciousness as a criterion of identity. The memory criterion seems undoubtedly to support some of our claims about personal identity. At the same time, memory alone, or even connectedness among a number of equally high-level conscious states, seems hardly enough to support a very full-blooded conception of personhood. Notice, in conclusion, that both memories and skills are acquired via causal processes.

Although memories, as already pointed out, present themselves as records of actual past experiences, not all such presentations would count as actual memories. Thus I might seem to remember doing something simply because, some time ago, the event in question was described to me in vivid terms. So vivid was the description that, through time, I have come to believe (quite falsely) that I did the thing in question. To be genuine memories, then, apparent memories must depend causally in an appropriate way on the rememberer's own past experience.[9] This condition will have to be weakened when we come to consider some conceptual variants of this form of memory. The thing to note just now, however, is that skills, habits, modes of response, and so on are also acquired by a

---

[9] The standard argument for introducing a causal condition into the account of memory is in Martin and Deutscher [1]. I have avoided mention in the main text of the classic objection to the memory criterion, namely Butler's objection that memory presupposes, rather than constitutes, personal identity (see Butler [1]). There are two reasons why I take this avoiding action. One is that the kind of circularity identified by the Butler objection is liable to arise for any criterion of personhood— even the body one. The second is that it is rather difficult to move from the informal notion that memory is a condition of personal unity to a more precise statement of the criterion itself. However, let us try to give some kind of precise statement of the memory condition. Memory discloses, in the usual case, my own past to me in a specially direct way. No doubt this is because memories are causal records of our actual past experiences: I thus cannot have a memory of seeing the Queen when she visited my school unless it was I who then had that experience. But other people at school with me no doubt also have memories of seeing the Queen on that very occasion. So the experience recorded in my memory is of a type that might well be common to me and others. There must, then, be some restriction on content so that the experience I now recall could not have—as a matter of fact—been had by anyone other than me. What I recall, then, is an experience such that given its nature, and where I was at the time, it could not have been the experience of anyone other than myself. Thus, if I now have a certain memory, it must—as a matter of fact—be the case that I really had the experience disclosed by that memory. In reflecting on this, we begin to see the force of the notion that memory discloses, and is to some extent constitutive of, identity. Notice, however, that I have only dealt with the usual case. It would be straightforward to formulate the claims just made in such a way that puzzles can arise. Suppose that someone, A, has a certain experience that could not have been had by anyone else, given how things were at the time. We, of course, have to allow that any experience-type is capable of being had by more than one person. Now B later recalls this very experience in memory, as does C some time later still. Does it follow that B and C are one and the same with A? Not necessarily, for it may be that B is only assured by the presence of the memory of having had that original experience, as is C. But this does not necessitate that B and C are one and the same person. Now suppose that experiences rather like memory experiences are commonplace. These experiences are like memory as I have described it except that the recalled experiences may not be those of the person now doing the recalling. This variation in the story gives us quasi-memory, which is discussed in sect. 6.

causal process. This time we cannot make the distinction between genuine and apparent skills depend entirely on the existence of some appropriate causal process (presumably a learning process). Some people, for instance, have prodigious musical talents which are not easily explained by the amount of pratice they have undertaken, and others can train for as long as they like and still acquire little of the skills. But even for skills we can, in many cases, make the distinction between the genuine and the apparent (or faked) depend on the causal process. On the basis of limited training, I may succeed in faking possession of a skill to a higher degree than I in fact possess. This time, as in the case of memory, my skill is more apparent than real simply because I have not been through the appropriate (that is, long enough) causal process of learning.

Whether dealing with memories, or with things like skills, we have to notice that persons are items with *histories*. Viewed in purely psychological terms, the ingredients of our mental states and episodes not only record our present awareness but also celebrate our pasts by way of the habits, skills, capacities, and memories laid down over a lifetime. The same is true of the initiation of action based on previously formulated intentions, or in accordance with our overall ambitions.

8.4. CRITERIA OF IDENTITY

Memory as a criterion of identity has both its strengths and its weaknesses. More of both will be encountered shortly, but let us decide just now what to say on the vexed issue of criteria. Any enterprise like mine has to face this problem.

Attempts at analysis try to do at least one of two things. Either, there is an attempt to say in what the phenomenon under analysis consists, or—more modestly—there is some specification of what sorts of thing count as evidence for the obtaining of the phenomenon in question. So, an analysis of what it is to have measles might maintain that having measles consists in being infected by a certain virus, which infection is symptomized by a typical rash, a temperature, and some cold-like symptoms. A weaker, or more modest, analysis might maintain only that having a certain sort of rash, along with other symptoms, is *evidence* that measles is present, although recognizing that having measles amounts to more than merely this.

When Wiggins maintains that the concept of identity is primitive and unanalysable, he is suggesting that we can give no ultimate account of that *in which identity consists*. But when he says that the concept is capable of discursive elucidation in collateral terms, he is *not* suggesting that we can only state what counts as evidence for the holding of identity.[10] Wiggins's position is not unlike mine. He is interested not so much in tests or evidence for the holding of specific identities. Rather, he is seeking an account of what it is that organizes tests or evidence, while not denying the primitiveness of identity.

We can now further complicate the story. It may be evidence, for those who know someone rather well, that a certain person is lying if, while speaking, that person touches his or her ear in a certain way. But, however reliable this indicator, we have in no way elucidated the concept of *lying*, or even the concept of Smith's lying, by citing it. However, we do go some way towards elucidating the concept of measles by indicating that measles is typically character-ized by a certain sort of rash. The existence of this typical symptom does tell us something about the disease.

For a philosopher who is prepared to make the distinction between those truths that depend on matters of fact on one side and, on the other, those that are conceptually or necessarily true, there is a simple way of dealing with these points about analysis. Analysis in our strong sense tells us in what a phenomenon consists as a matter of *conceptual necessity*. It is necessarily, or analytically, true that someone who has measles is infected with a certain virus. The more modest sort of analysis tells us what *necessarily counts as evidence* for someone having measles. If certain symptoms are present it follows analytically that the person in question is likely to have measles.

We can readily translate talk about phenomena into talk about

---

[10] Wiggins's position is not terribly clear. To the extent that he and I are after the same thing in searching for criteria of identity, then my search seems to take us further than does his. He writes: 'The Aristotelian *what is it* question does both less and more than provide what counts as evidence for or against on identity. It does less because it may not suggest any immediate tests at all. It does more because it provides that which *organises* the tests or evidence . . .' (Wiggins [9], p. 53). He also refers us to Frege's remarks in Frege [1], § 62: 'If we are to use the symbol *a* to signify an object, we must have a criterion for deciding in all cases whether *b* is the same as *a*, even if it is not always in our power to apply this criterion.'

concepts. So if we are worried about flitting from one sort of talk to the other, we can be easily reassured. Suppose an analysis of personal identity is meant to tell us in what such identity consists. In terms of *concepts* rather than phenomena this analysis will tell us in what the correct application of the concept of personal identity consists. Our example about the disease of measles could just as readily have been treated as an example dealing with the correct application of the concept of *measles* (or the concept of *having measles*). No more than this was involved in the use of the convenient term 'phenomenon'.

The notion that analysis reveals conceptual or analytic entailments between the existence of certain kinds of evidence for a concept's holding and the reasonable applicability of that concept is one associated with the later philosophy of Wittgenstein. In this way he was a kind of behaviourist about pains and other 'inner' states. As he put it: 'An "inner process" stands in need of outward criteria.'[11] That the existence of certain kinds of typical pain-behaviour entails that someone is probably in pain is an important result, if correct. For instance, it would follow that the concept of pain is applicable and learnable in certain public situations while yet it applies to interior, and in some sense *private*, happenings.

Those of a severely empiricist turn may well be unable to make much sense of all this talk of conceptual truths and analytic entailments, however well it seems to fit with some of the things we do in philosophy. For them, however, there is no need for worry. Our distinction between two kinds of criterion remains, albeit made only in the terms initially used. In the sense in which criteria are evidence of the presence of some phenomenon, we can now not distinguish merely accidental symptoms (like touching one's ear when lying) from non-accidental symptoms (like Wittgenstein's

[11] Wittgenstein [3], I. § 580. An even stronger notion of criterion reverses the direction of entailment given in the text. The symptoms of measles may be criteria for the presence of the disease in the sense that if someone has measles then it follows (analytically) that they are likely to manifest at least some of the symptoms. This strong idea of criterion is easily confused with the one given in the text, but without some fairly tough restrictions it would be of little help to us in exploring questions of personal unity. As it stands, this new notion of criterion would force us to hold that when people are in pain (to take the usual example) they are likely to be manifesting symptoms of pain. The notion of criterion given in the text simply suggests that since pain usually does manifest itself in certain typical ones, anyone displaying these symptoms is likely to be in pain. In other words, what is analytic is the claim that pain behaviour is evidence for the presence of pain.

notion of typical pain-behaviour). But for my purposes this will not greatly matter. The important distinction, after all, is between criteria understood as evidence and criteria as being what a phenomenon consists in.

If we think back to the case of the discontinuous hill in Chapter 4, we can ask whether non-branching survival of earlier episodes as later ones is a *criterion* of the hill's identity in any of the senses distinguished here. Perhaps the most plausible way for the survival theorist to reply to this question is to maintain that we do have a criterion in our strong sense; for non-branching survival of the various stages is precisely that in which the hill's identity consists.[12] In this way, the survival theorist can give an account of the identity or unity of a broad particular in terms of the survival of shorter items (its episodes). But remember that although on this account survival is thus more primitive than identity, this is not a truth about survival *in general* and identity *in general*.

A modern Lockean could try to make this very same point about memory, and other conscious episodes. Personal identity consists— on this account—in co-consciousness, or at least in the existence of overlapping chains of co-conscious episodes. But a different, less Lockean, memory theory can also be imagined. On this theory, memory, or indeed co-consciousness in general, is a criterion of identity in only the modest sense. This could be because personal identity is ultimately unanalysable, or simply because memory is just a symptom of personal identity which is itself something over and above the presence of co-consciousness. In this case, co-consciousness is no more than good evidence of the existence of this further thing—personal identity—but is in no way constitutive of that identity.

Having now introduced the notion of memory as a condition of identity for persons, we can start to get to grips with the conception of the self urged on us by a modern kind of Lockean—namely Parfit.

---

[12] This claim requires immediate qualification. As will be clear in what follows, there are prospects for giving an account of unity for cases where there is equal branching among fissioning particulars (see Ch. 10.1). More importantly, as is argued in this chapter, the reductionist tendency in my remark has to be taken in the context of the previous claims that particulars are distinct from their life histories or trajectories and in the context also of my later claims that person are not ontological parasites. The fact that persons and other particulars are not ontological parasites does not, however, mean that they are simple, or non-complex. And for any complex particular, its unity will involve relations among its parts.

However, I start by looking at two specific claims that Parfit wishes to defend. The first concerns the difference between reductionist and non-reductionist accounts of identity, and this is discussed in the following section, noting some difficulties raised recently by Shoemaker. Although I will give grounds for supporting Parfit's reductionist stance, Shoemaker is right, I will argue, to maintain that the decision to accept reductionist or non-reductionist accounts of the person is not one that we would make solely on empirical grounds.

In the light of our earlier discussion of the 'only x and y' principle, it is now possible to suggest what the defenders of the rule have got right. This is the second Parfit thesis that I want to defend in this chapter. According to it, whether one thing survives as another does not depend on the existence or non-existence of anything else, and never depends on any merely trivial circumstance. It should not be thought that my defence of these components of Parfit's view means that I am also in the business of defending his conception of the self. On the contrary, I will be arguing that the most plausible development of the concept of the person is one that merges both psychological and physical considerations. However, I also want to show that Parfit's development of the concept of the person is a perfectly possible one. In the end, all conceptual development in this area will be stymied, according to me, by a thoroughgoing, and irresolvable, duality in our thinking about persons. That this is so will be argued in the last two chapters.

8.5. DUALISM AND REDUCTIONISM

Following Parfit, it is helpful to distinguish two very different accounts of identity.[13] In the case of persons, nations, armies, university departments, and so forth, we can take either a reductionist or a non-reductionist view of identity. One easy way of explaining the difference intended here is to consider the question of *how much* information is necessary for telling us all that matters in an identity problem. In crude terms, the reductionist is content, at some point, to declare that enough information is available to let us

---

[13] See, e.g., Parfit [3].

know all that matters in a certain situation, *even if* we are still puzzled about what to say about identity in that situation. The non-reductionist will, at the *same* point, maintain that there is still some further fact to be ascertained—namely, the fact of identity.

Let us, for example, consider the question of whether it was *one and the same department* of economics that gave Amanda a degree in 1972 and gave Beatrice a degree in 1982. In the interval between these two dates, members of staff have come and gone (let us imagine that we know all the details), the head has changed three times, the syllabus has changed, and so on. If we know all these details, it need not necessarily make it easy to say whether the department is the same or different. In fact, the more we dwell on such changes, the more puzzled we are likely to become on this identity question.

Many people would say in a case like this that *if* we have to make a decision on identity, we can only do so by stipulation. For if we know all the facts about staff changes, syllabus changes, and so on, then we know *everything that matters*. Those who take this view are reductionists on the identity issue. By contrast, those who maintain that, despite this wealth of information, there is still an important question remaining undecided (the identity question), are non-reductionists. Of course, as long as we do not declare our answer or stipulation in such a case, there is a question that remains unanswered. But the non-reductionist persists in maintaining that a matter of substance is still unresolved, even in the face of this information. So the non-reductionist is unwilling to make a stipulation on the identity question.

Certainly, non-reductionism about the issue just mentioned— the identity of our economics department—looks just silly. But in other cases, the position does not strike us as silly at all. Although there may not be deep, further facts about the identity of economics departments, we tend to think that, even though we have lots of information about a case of personal identity, there *is* some deep, further fact to be decided in that case. Suppose we have a great deal of information, for example, about a set of mental episodes, and their relations to one another. If we are still puzzled, in the face of this information, about the identity issue, then it does not seem so strange to maintain that there is some fact of personal identity about which we are properly puzzled. On my view, there is a simple explanation for this feeling. Because our concept of the person is indeterminate, and we thus have no clear conditions for personal identity, we think our bafflement reflects some profound matter that is somehow escaping us. Our recognition of conceptual indeterminacy is slow in coming. For Shoemaker, Parfit, and the other reductionists, however, the non-reductionist's conviction that there is some deep, further fact of personal identity does not reflect conceptual indeterminacy at all. Rather, it is just as silly as the response the non-reductionist is forced to make to the problem of the economics department. Stipulation may be just as sensible in the one case as in the other.

There is yet a further response to puzzles about personal identity. For dualists, like Swinburne, the fact that no amount of obtainable information about mental episodes, body stages, and their relations settles the identity question shows that this question concerns the existence of some non-physical, immaterial entity. A dualist need not be driven into holding very strange views, for example the view that persons are capable of disembodied existence. A *functionalist* account of mind, after all, is surely compatible both with dualism and with materialism. Contemporary functionalists, admittedly, are usually sympathetic to materialism. But the core of functionalism is a set of three ingredients. First, a *state of mind* can be given a functional characterization in terms of its roles in relation to other states of mind (some of these being perceptual states). These roles will themselves be *causal* roles—thus my belief that the ice on one part of the lake is thin is causally connected with my desire to avoid going on that area. Secondly, there will be critical causal links between states of mind on the one hand and behaviour on the other. Thus my behaviour in leaping aside from the path of an oncoming vehicle is causally connected with my beliefs, desires, and habits, which are themselves in turn causally linked, in a complex aetiological network, to other pieces of behaviour. Third, mental states can be realized in—and causally associated with—very different sorts of physical structures and events.[14] Thus two people who are in similar states of mind need not, on that account, share similar brain or central nervous system states.

None of these core doctrines involves a rejection of dualism by the functionalist. To get from functionalism to materialism, then,

---

[14] My account of functionalism here is very close to that given by Shoemaker in Shoemaker and Swinburne [1].

we need to add to the above doctrine. We have to insist that a mental state is nothing other than some complex physical state (while observing that many different physical states may implement very similar states of mind). On this view, minds are a kind of hardware—and differently configured hardware can produced functionally equivalent states.

By contrast, the Cartesian dualist might maintain a functionalist account and simply deny that minds are no more than appropriately configured pieces of hardware. Descartes himself maintains in his sixth *Meditation* that 'I am not only lodged in my body as a pilot in a vessel, but . . . am very closely united to it, and so to speak so intermingled with it that I seem to compose with it one whole.'[15] On one way of understanding this view, I may be a separate thing from my body, yet I can only act through a body and many of my states are causally associated with, and realized in, bodily states. Such a dualist can simply maintain a one–one correspondence between mind and body. To each normal, living human body there corresponds a mind, and vice versa.

This modified dualism is an attractive option if we take seriously puzzle-cases like Locke's example of the Prince and the Cobbler. The soul or mind of the Prince needs to the capable of 'entering and informing' the body of the Cobbler, but it need *not* be capable of disembodied existence. The modified version of dualism also makes minds separate from, and independent of, particular bodies. On this account, the mind is really rather like a program running on the body as its computer. To change bodies successfully is to manage to transfer the program to a different machine. So long as there are no big compatibility problems, the software should run well enough on the different hardware.

This qualified version of dualism has not been introduced in order to recommend its claims over materialism. Our thought about persons, in fact, involves both materialistic and non-materialistic elements. The only point being made at the moment is that a sophisticated dualist can also be a reductionist. When faced with the tale of the Prince and the Cobbler, such a dualist need not insist that there is bound to be some deep, further fact—the fact of identity—about which the story has left us up in the air.[16] The reductionist

---

[15] Descartes [1], i. 192.

[16] There is a lingering suspicion that what the non-reductionist may be after is recognition that there is always a deep, further fact about identity that may be in

tells us that in cases like this, there is no further significant evidence that we are lacking. All the important facts are already before us: we know everything that matters. Just as the materialist can agree with this suggestion, so can the sort of dualist that has just been described. And even those who believe with me that our concepts are neither so clear-cut, nor well defined, as is commonly supposed can agree that what is puzzling about this situation is not that there is some further fact about which we are lacking information. Reductionism, therefore, commends itself to a wide variety of theorists, and will be taken as the most sensible option to pursue in what follows.

We have to take care, however, not to confuse the reductionist claim with a trivial and uninteresting one. As Shoemaker points out in a recent study, it is not clear just what distinction Parfit has in mind.[17] Parfit takes the non-reductionist as committed to the claim that persons are in some way separately existing entities, quite distinct from their experiences, and at the same time, he regards the issue between the reductionist and the non-reductionist as hinging on matters of fact.

One confusion that it is easy to fall into here is to take the non-reductionist as simply disagreeing with the reductionist about which facts are important for survival and identity. But this cannot be the issue at all. If, after getting all the information about our imagined economics department, you insist that there is still some further fact about the identity issue which I have ignored, you do not thereby reveal yourself as a non-reductionist. Rather, you are simply in disagreement with me as to what kind of information is relevant, and thus ultimately in disagreement about what matters. If this is all that Parfit's distinction involved, it would be highly uninteresting: 'non-reductionist' would simply be a question-begging label to attach to anyone disagreeing with me about what is constitutive of unity or identity.

If, however, there is more to the issue than this, it looks as if the

---

some way verification transcendent: this is the fact of the existence of some incorporeal soul. If this is all that the reductionism issue involves, then I am wrong to argue, as I do later in the section, that the decision for or against reductionism depends on more than factual considerations. But, equally, we do not need to introduce the vocabulary of 'reductionism' in order to discuss this kind of possibility.

[17] See Shoemaker [7].

disagreement between the reductionist and the non-reductionist can hardly focus simply on matters of fact. In the study already mentioned, Shoemaker has difficulty specifying just what non-reductionism might be. However, the non-reductionist position can be characterized in either of two ways. In one form, non-reductionism is the claim that there is always more to identity or unity than can be captured by facts about those things that are, as a matter of fact, constitutive of a particular, whether we consider that particular as three-, four-, or five-dimensional. In another form, and with specific reference to persons, non-reductionism is the doctrine defended by Chisholm and others to the effect that persons are not ontological parasites but are primitive or basic entities. In this latter form, the doctrine is often contrasted with Hume's phenomenalism about persons, the theory that persons are constructions out of perceptions. Accordingly, I will discuss Chisholm's claims in a later section, after dealing further with Hume's view.

However, we can use one of Chisholm's examples to illustrate he first form of non-reductionism. Suppose that a table is scrutinized on three separate occasions. On each occasion, it is constituted by a collection of parts, but these part collections are different each time. Thus, on the first occasion, the table consists of collections A and B, on the second, of collection B and C, and on the third, of collections C and D. Forgetting our earlier qualms about the theory of artefact identity, let us suppose that despite these differences of constitution the table before us, on these three occasions, was always one and the same. On Chisholm's account, the table is not an ontologically basic thing, it is a construction out of the part collections. In terms that derive loosely from Butler, we might say that the table is only the same table in a *loose and popular* sense of 'same', while the collection $A + B$ is, in the *strict and philosophical* sense of 'same', not the same collection of parts as $B + C$.[18] Although not endorsing Chisholm's

---

[18] In his example of constitution in ch. 3 of Chisholm [5], Chisholm in fact identifies the table as consisting of three extended temporal parts, one being $A + B$, the second $B + C$, and the third $C + D$. Although he argues that the table is a 'successive thing' made of different things at different times, he is—surprisingly—hostile to the idea that the introduction of temporal parts is useful to discussions of identity through time. In trying to show that any solution to the problem of identity through time presupposes the concept of persisting thing, Chisholm fails to consider the sort of account given in the present work. Of the five ways he envisages question-begging attempts to explain the unity of rivers in terms of their stages, not one comes

distinction between the two senses of 'same', nor his claims about what is or is not ontologically basic, I am able to make sense of his claim that the table is a construction out of the part collections. Each part collection constitutes a stage of the table at a given time, and the table itself is a suitably linked chain of such stages.

In allowing that the table is a construction in this sense out of its various part collections, I am being reductionist. The non-reductionist would argue here that there is more to the table than this string of part collections. Now, as has already been shown in Chapter 5, there is some merit in this claim if it means that tables can be thought of as five-dimensional items as well as four-dimensional. I have argued that there is more to a given table, indeed, than a four-dimensional chain of table-parts linked according to the three conditions on survival. But this claim alone does not make me a non-reductionist. For I am willing to specify what more there is to the table in question by going on to describe the set of worlds containing world-stages of the table, and these will be constitutive of the table viewed in all its five-dimensional richness. The non-reductionist, however, would still maintain, even at this level, that there is more to the table, some further deep unity, over and above this collection of world-stages.

It should now be clear why non-reductionism is a peculiar doctrine. What more could there be to the table viewed three-dimensionally than a certain sum of spatial parts? What more could there be to it four-dimensionally than a sum of temporal parts? Non-reductionist answers to this question are likely to be given in terms of the traditional notion of substance, and—like Hume—I am

close to the theory of survival suggested here. (Chisholm [5], ch. 3, pp. 138–144). Chisholm incidentally provides a means of trying to convince anyone sceptical about the existence of temporal parts. If the table described is allowed to change its components over time, then we can simply identify the stages of the table with each separate component collection for as long as it endures. Thus for as long as $A + B$ endures, it is a stage of the table, as is $B + C$, and so on. But now, to deny that $A + B$-for-Monday-morning is also a stage of the table is like accepting that a drawer is part of my desk while denying that a section cut from the drawer is part of the desk. It is possible to make a distinction between functional components and parts in some wider sense. In a recent paper, one author distinguishes *parts* as structured, non-arbitrary components, from *pieces*, which are arbitrary sections of a whole (see Krecz [1]). Any theorizing along these lines needs, in my view, to be done in terms of cause, matter, and structure, and must also take account of the distinction between functional, designed items, and natural, functionless particulars which have, of course, functional parts.

anxious to work if possible without such a notion. But if this really is what non-reductionism amounts to, then Parfit is wrong to regard the truth of reductionism as merely a matter of fact. Indeed, to present the issue as a factual one is simply to run the risk of being taken to make the uninteresting claim already dismissed. None of this yet shows that reductionism about persons is the only plausible option. Thus I agree with Parfit that we might be persuaded to accept a non-reductionist account of personal identity, although I share Shoemaker's conviction that the decision to accept such an account would not depend simply on empirical or factual considerations.

We will find in the next section that the importance of identity is often defended by appeal to two apparently plausible principles, principles that are apparently violated by reductionist accounts of what is important in the puzzle cases. But what has just been argued suggests that, in general, identity need not be the thing that matters, the thing that concerns us in the face of these puzzles. For identity can either be settled by stipulation or be left unresolved. But *what matters* can hardly be something that could be treated in this way. This proposal receives additional support if we agree with Parfit that issues of identity will sometimes depend on what is happening to things other than those whose identity we are studying, and further that identity will sometimes depend only on the most trivial facts. The case of fission, as we will see, provides just such results.

8.6. FISSION

Parfit has an interesting argument to show that no criterion of identity can meet two plausible requirements. Let us understand 'criterion' to mean that in which identity consists (our strong sense). Whether we are dualists or not, we will find Parfit's argument a compelling defence of the reductionist (or 'complex') view of identity.

The two plausible requirements are due to Bernard Williams.[19] First is our familiar 'only x and y' principle:

> Whether x is identical with y cannot depend on what happens to any things apart from x and y.

[19] See Williams [1]. The Charles and Robert case is described in this article.

Next is a point about what matters:

> Since identity is sometimes of great importance (for example in cases of personal identity) whether identity holds or not cannot depend on a trivial circumstance.

It is worth being sure, to begin with, that these requirements really are plausible. After all, we have already seen reasons to be suspicious of arguments in defence of the 'only *x* and *y*' rule.

We can try to establish the reasonableness of the first condition by rehearsing Williams's own case of Charles and Robert. Charles wakes up one morning, let us imagine, with what appears to be lots of Guy Fawkes's memories. After a great deal of research, we become convinced that his memory claims are to be trusted (for example, we find that by using them we can consistently and plausibly fill in gaps in the known historical record). So, after a time we come to regard Charles as really having Guy Fawkes's memories.

Now for a theorist in the Lockean mould, this is a strong case for going on to maintain that Charles really *is* Guy Fawkes. After all, here is the very sort of co-consciousness that Locke regarded as being so important. Suppose, however, we were to resist the Lockean move for a moment. Does this mean that we would have to deny that Charles really did have Guy Fawkes's memories? We would not need to deny this if we were to develop the concept of memory in the right way. For experience memories could still be records of actual past witnessings—only now the witnessing might originally have been done by someone other than the person now doing the recalling. What of the causal condition on memory, though? If, as materialists, we imagine that memories are normally held by some kind of 'trace' or other configuration in the brain, then we would expect my ability to remember another's experiences to be causally dependent on states of both my own and that other person's brain. Science-fiction machinery can easily be imagined— machinery that copies structures and patterns from one brain and 'writes' this into another. Although Williams's story contains no such machinery, we can imagine that some such appropriate cause is at work, even though we have no idea what it actually is.

Not only can the concept of memory be developed in this way, but so too can concepts applying to other mental states and events. Normally, I act on my own, rather than upon others', intentions.

But, again given suitable machinery, there seems no reason why I should not now form an intention that a certain act be performed next week even though it is not I who is to perform it. I can intend that you so act next week if, for example, the brain-scanning and writing device can do the same trick for intentions that it does for memories.

While we could take these newly developed notions of *intention* and *memory* to be the notions of intention and memory we would want to work with (our everyday notions being indeterminate enough to let us so do) theorists have often distinguished them by referring to *quasi*-memories, *quasi*-intentions, and the like.[20] Parfit shortens this to *q-remembering*, *q-intending*, and so forth. If all our memories were q-memories, we should have to be most careful about making memory claims. For we would have to be careful to distinguish those cases where we were recalling events from our *own* pasts from cases where we were recalling events from the pasts of others. There are also other difficulties concerning q-memory which will be considered later.

We can now return to the Charles and Robert case, armed with these distinctions. Even if Charles is distinct from Guy Fawkes, he may well be able to q-remember his experiences. The co-consciousness theorist who lays great weight on memory might be inclined to count Charles as being one and the same as Guy Fawkes. In response to this move, however, Williams is able to deploy a cunning strategy. If we admit it is logically possible for Charles to waken with these radical additions to his psychological structures and matter, then surely it is equally possible that someone else should do so too—say his brother Robert. If the memory criterion, however, were to determine that Charles is Guy Fawkes, the same criterion would force us to count Robert as being Guy Fawkes as well. But this would be absurd. For Charles and Robert are two, and hence distinct. So they cannot both be identical with Guy Fawkes. This argument, then, shows that the Lockean identification of Charles with Guy Fawkes is mistaken.

If Williams's argument here is convincing, then it is so because of its appeal to the two conditions already mentioned. First, we think that the issue of Charles' identity (or non-identity) with Guy Fawkes cannot depend on what happens to his brother (the 'only *x*

---

[20] Thus Shoemaker in Shoemaker [1]. cf. Parfit in Parfit [1], as well as in his book.

and *y*' rule). And, if we are thinking about Charles himself, then anything that happens to his brother cannot be significant (second requirement). Parfit takes this point further. No reasonable criterion of identity can possibly meet both requirments. For identity will sometimes depend either upon what happens to other things or upon merely trivial things (where the alternatives are not exclusive).

Parfit's claim acquires further confirmation if we allow ourselves the possibility of fission. Studies of person fission will, indeed, confirm our earlier results obtained when discussing the 'only *x* and *y*' rule. In no case of fission can any reasonable criterion of identity be found which satisfies the two requirements, and so we have to give up the normal conviction that identity is the thing that matters. If the conditions are plausible conditions on what matters, then this cannot be identity.

Let us consider a case which makes appeal to both physical and psychological considerations. We suppose that there is available the technology to transplant brains. Now imagine that we can also bring the two hemispheres of someone's brain into the same cognitive, informational, and intentional states. Surgery is performed on a person so treated and one of the hemispheres of his or her brain is removed. This hemisphere is transplanted into the skull of another person whose brain has been irreparably damaged in an accident. After surgery, two people wake up claiming to remember the past of the one original person.

If both resulting people agree in terms of their memories (or *q*-memories), intentions, styles of response to situations, and so forth, then our original person has—so it seems—split into two. Of course, only one of the resulting persons has the same body as the original person. For the other, just one hemisphere of the original person's brain constitutes the only physical link between them. For those to whom identity is very much a matter of physical persistence, one hemisphere may not be *enough stuff* to establish identity.

We will shortly look in more detail at the physical criteria for personal identity. For the moment, though, let us take it that any physical criterion of identity is likely to concern itself more with the brain than with any other part of the body. Even so, one hemisphere may hardly be enough to constitute identity. The physical facts suggest that the original person survives to a greater degree as the person who has the body and rest of the nervous system than as the person with the transplanted hemisphere. Even, then, if we were to suggest that the original person survived the surgery as *both* resulting persons we might still want to allocate identity to the item which shows the higher degree of survival. So, with our attention on the brain, we might give our identity vote for the person who has *more than half* of the brain of the original person, remembering that removal of one hemisphere leaves the other hemisphere, mid-brain, and lower brain intact.

In this case, the high-level psychological relations between the original person and the survivors of the surgery are on a par. Someone who gives weight to physical differences in determining identity would want to identify one of the survivors, but not the other, with the original person. And such a theorist might well choose the one who has retained more than half of the original brain. Does the theorist who argues in this way satisfy the first of the two plausible requirements mentioned at the start of this section? It looks as if this is so. For as long as the determining factor in such a case is *possession of more than half* of the original brain, then our verdict on identity of one survivor will make no reference to what happens to the other. Indeed, suppose that through some misfortune the surgery has fatal consequences for the person who has had one hemisphere removed. The only survivor is the combination consisting of the new body and the transplanted hemisphere. Our imagined theorist might consistently declare that although our original person has to some extent survived as the person with the transplanted hemisphere, there is not enough persistence of physical stuff to justify an identity claim.

But a physical criterion of the sort just described would not satisfy the second of the plausible conditions. After all, we can readily envisage a case where a future person has slightly more than half of my brain, and compare it with another one in which a future person has slightly less than half of my brain. If we now imagine that in both cases the future person's psychological relatedness to me is not affected by these slight differences, then identity is going to depend on only a trivial difference. The consistent theorist has to maintain that I am identical with the person who has slightly more than half of my brain material, and not identical with the one who has slightly less than half, even though I survive—psychologically speaking—to the same degree in each!

As we saw to start with, there are two morals we might draw from such a case. On the one hand, we could give up the requirements, while on the other we could give up the belief that identity is the important thing. Indeed, Parfit's suggestion is that we do both of these things.[21] We give up the requirements on identity, thus allowing decisions on identity to depend on trivial differences and facts involving other things. But then we have to give up the idea that identity is what matters in such situations. Just as we can settle the question of the identity of clubs, departments, and the like by stipulation in some cases, so we can either leave the question of personal identity unresolved (for it may be indeterminate) or we can settle it too by stipulation. But then we have not settled *what matters* by stipulation.

Parfit argues that correlates of Williams's two conditions do in fact apply to what matters. If we follow Parfit's earlier pratice of calling the relation that matters *survival*, we can maintain that survival satisfies the two conditions. Thus, first of all, whether *a* survives as *b* does not depend on the existence, or non-existence, of any other item. And whether *a* survives as *b* never depends on any trivial circumstance (like the possession of some exact number of brain cells).

Returning to our fission case, we thus maintain that the original person survives as both products of surgery. Moreover, in the modified example, where one person dies, we can maintain that the original person survives as either of the products of surgery independently of what happens to the other. Again, I can survive as the person who has more than half my brain or as the person with less than half my brain. What matters in each case is not the exact number of brain cells but my degree of psychological relatedness to these future persons. Following Parfit, then, we are at last able to reconcile what looked like plausible requirements on identity with the fact that identity seems frequently to be indeterminate or determinable merely by stipulation. Of course, it does *not* follow from any of this that Parfit is right in thinking that what matters in puzzle situations regarding persons is 'psychological continuity and connectedness'. We will return to the assessment of Parfit's theory in the following chapter.

In the next section, we will look further at the relation between persons and their bodies. A concluding thought for this one,

---

[21] At least this is how I mean to interpret the discussion in Parfit [4] § 91.

however, concerns the importance of identity. If we follow Parfit's line we will come to think that we have been cruelly deceived in the past. A whole literature has sprung up on the topic of personal identity because we thought that such identity was a matter of consequence. Yet, as we have just seen, identity has only been regarded in this light through a kind of confusion. In normal cases, the things that matter on Parfit's account—psychological relations of various kinds—are associated with identity. In the puzzle cases, and in some of the non-normal cases of daily life, these things have become separated. So why identity has seemed to us to matter is simply that it was associated with these other important things— even though it need not have been. When we turn to the study of amnesia in the next chapter, we will have further corroboration of Parfit's claim. For there we will find it possible to separate identity judgements from judgements about what matters to the unity of life experienced by normal persons.

8.7. BODIES

Hume was never satisfied with his treatment of personal identity. His frustration with the topic is clear: 'For my part, when I enter most intimately into what I call *myself*, I always stumble on some particular perception or other, of heat or cold, light or shade, love or hatred, pain or pleasure. I never can catch *myself* at any time without a perception, and never can observe anything but the perception.'[22] His diagnosis of our plight as being the result of the confusion of identity with relation (that is, similarity) is at the same time insightful and unhelpful. It is insightful because it draws our attention to the issue we have earlier confronted—namely that any account of *unity* has to distinguish the *distinct* stages of a unified object from each other. So when we say that this boat before us now is the same as the one we saw yesterday, we are not identifying one boat-stage with another. Rather, we are allocating both stages to one and the same boat. But Hume's own account of personal identity is unhelpful precisely because he sets too high a standard on identity in the first place, urging, for instance, that any impression of self would have to be constant and unchanging throughout one's life.

---

[22] Hume [1], I. iv. 6.

The problem of how a *bundle* of Humean perceptions—feelings, sensings, emotions, rememberings—is tied together into the experience of one person is an extremely difficult unity problem. We can call it a *synchronic unity* problem, for it arises even when we take brief cross-sections of our experience. Here I am sitting at a desk, writing, thinking, occasionally looking at the furniture in my room or the trees outside my window, feeling slightly disgruntled, aware of a desire for a cup of tea, and so on. All these things are part of my psychologial experience here and now, and so they are one and all *mine*. But what gives this bundle of disparate items its unity?

By contrast, there is the *diachronic unity* problem. This current bundle of Humean 'perceptions' has multiple relationships with past such bundles. So not only have we the problem of explaining what makes all my current psychological states mine, but we need to come up with some account of how these past bundles—in some cases very different ones—have been mine as well. And some past bundles which were very like this present bundle have not been mine at all.

As we will see in the next chapter, the theory of matter, structure and cause can go some way towards solving both problems. My current psychological bundle has a certain structure among its elements, even though I am not consciously aware of all the ingredients that participate in this structure. Thus my processing mechanisms, and many aspects of my cognitive equipment, function in a way that is quite hidden from conscious inspection. Likewise, successive bundles that are mine stand in the survival relation to each other. Again, it should not come as a surprise that some of these items related by survival are not themselves available to self-consciousness. This, however, does not diminish their importance in the account of what constitutes a unified life.

Historically, the most sophisticated response to Hume came from Kant, who attempted to answer both unity problems. My ability to fuse memory, present sensory awareness, and central conceptual processing—an ability essential to my recognition of my desk and my application to it of the appropriate concepts—shows that one knowing mechanism, one centre of consciousness, is constituted by these various strands in the bundle. Moreover, my recognition of objects as persisting over time is itself a simultaneous celebration of the persistence through time of this one processing bundle, namely me. Notice how clever Kant's move is. For bodies, indeed bodies *other* than my own, have been brought in on the act in order to solve both the synchronic and the diachronic problems.[23]

Kant's appeal to the objects around me as themselves grounding my own identity is not just a solution to Hume's problem: it is, in fact, a solution which to some extent accepts Hume's own constraints on a solution. Without the existence of other bodies, there would be no grounding for my own identity, and without it there would be no chance of my recognizing the world around me as containing objects at all. This account avoids any appeal to privileged perceptions of the self. However, it gains this benefit only at the expense of making the issue of self-identity 'transcendental' in Kant's terms—the unity of the self is thus not so much something we can grasp through experience but is itself a *precondition* of the kind of knowledge and experience we have.

An account of self-identity that is transcendental in this way is not the only one we can give. We can admit that, viewed from the lofty transcendental perspective, there is a reciprocal dependence between the self and the objects (particulars) around it. The argument establishes something about the relation between knowledge and existence. For it tells us that the existence of one sort of thing is necessary as a precondition for our knowledge of another sort of thing. We can come back to this point in a moment, but, looking at Kant's argument in this general way, we can notice that it goes no way towards specifying just what the unity of self consists in. Nor does it say very much about what constitutes evidence for the existence of a unified self. Kantians, when faced with this issue, are able to retreat to a less grand, 'empirical' perspective, from which to tackle the unity question. But labelling is not an important issue here. The point is that the sort of transcendental argument given by Kant seeks to establish certain roles played by objects and by selves, while not saying very much about what either of these things are.

One extremely down-to-earth way of trying to say more about what a unified self might be comes from the body theorist. On this account, both diachronic and synchronic unity of the bundle arise

---

[23] Although giving what I take to be a rough, but historically accurate, statement of some of Kant's views, I am not concerned here to defend any particular line of Kantian interpretation. The arguments on 'apperception' in Kant [1] are both fundamental and obscure. Useful commentaries include Bennett [1] and Strawson [3].

from its association with a particular body. Any theory of unity by asociation has certain strengths. We are familiar with the obvious unity of perception, thought, and action displayed by persons. Surely a being equipped with just one body, two legs, one mouth, and so on will be one with just such a unified point of view on the world, no matter how many diverse processing operations are going on within it. No doubt it is like something to be me, and one of the things it is like is to have my body with its various capacities and limitations, and to experience the world from my (or its?) point of view.

We can go further than this, though. Our response to other people is to some extent a response to their bodies as much as to their psychological features. We have our own characteristic features, stances, modes of walking, smiles, and so on. Friends and enemies signal their presence to us long before we can recognize their faces, simply by displaying their characteristic gaits or stoops. If bodies are bound up in this way with recognition, then they are not surprisingly bound up with our likes and dislikes, our loves and our hates. As Williams writes:

While in the present situation of things to love a person is not exactly the same as to love a body, perhaps to say that they are basically the same is more grotesquely misleading than it is a deep metaphysical error; and if it does not sound very high-minded, the alternatives that grow out of suspending the present situation do not sound too spiritual either.[24]

It is useful to consider these two responses to Hume in close proximity. The body theorist has made a rather different appeal to bodies from the one made by the Kantian. If we were to elaborate the body theory more fully, we might get some clear idea of how that theory answers the question: In what does identity consist? Perhaps, for example, the existence of the brain and nervous system is more vital to the unity of self than the persistence of other parts of the body. But instead of dwelling on this matter here, let me draw a moral from these two rather different replies to Hume.

---

[24] Williams [5], p. 81. As becomes clear in what follows, I have a great deal of sympathy for Williams's position on our body-based situation. Irritatingly, this situation is important enough to make various conceptual legislations seem unattractive. Neither psychologically-based or brain-based theories of the person can yield an ultimately satisfying account of what a person is: for neither seems to do justice to the importance of bodies to our conception of *who* someone is and *why* we feel and think about others in the way we do.

The Kantian response clearly has an epistemological dimension, linking existence and knowledge. A unified self (where we mean 'transcendental' unity) is a precondition of knowledge or awareness of other particulars, and existence of other things is in turn a precondition of our knowledge or awareness of self. There are thus two ways in which knowledge would not get going. First, if we failed to remember past witnessings, or failed to build up a repertoire of concepts applicable to our experience, then such experience would be chaotic and ununified. Failures in the bundle of this kind would be enough to stop the knowing enterprise getting underway.

By contrast, a point that Kant himself emphasizes, if we found ourselves in a shifting universe where there was neither colour nor shape, nor general structural constancy around us, then again our processing activities would grind out neither awareness of self nor awareness of other particulars.[25] We have already noted that Garner's empirical work makes it plausible to start from the assumption that the world is not informationally uniform. But it is not informationally chaotic either. Our cognitive capacities, as Kant perhaps realized, work best on an informationally lumpy, coherent world.

Now the epistemological dimension of all this can be rendered more clear by thinking about consciousness in distinction from *self*-consciousness. Locke himself builds self-consciousness into the very concept of a person which 'can think of itself as itself, the same thinking thing, at different times and places'. Awareness of self, the Kantian argument goes, is not just the result of our having various

---

[25] The previous and the present paragraphs represent only crude attempts at Kantian exegesis. However, the claim that existence of other things is a precondition of empirical self-consciousness is stated clearly in his notorious 'Refutation of Idealism': 'I am conscious of my own existence as determined in time. All determination of time presupposes something *permanent* in perception. This permanent cannot, however, be something in me, since it is only through this permanent that my existence in time can itself be determined. . . . the consciousness of my existence is at the same time an immediate consciousness of the existence of other things outside me' (Kant [1] B275–6. cf. also his remarks at B291–4.) He deals with the question of the shifting universe in the following passage: 'If cinnabar were sometimes red, sometimes black, sometimes light, sometimes heavy, if a man changed sometimes into this and sometimes into that animal form . . . my empirical imagination would never find opportunity when representing red colour to bring to mind heavy cinnabar' (Kant [1], A100–1). It has to be noted, of course, that Kant is unable to draw any conclusions from such an observation concerning the world of things in themselves: rather these are facts about the world *as it appears to us*.

processing, perceiving, and remembering strands in our mental bundles. For such awareness depends on the cognitive bundle being located in the right sort of world, a world with suitable informational characteristics, including stability of suitable structures over time. The world around us, then, has to be a certain way in order for us to have the very awareness of self which poses the problem of self-identity in the first place.

By contrast, let us suppose that a cognitive bundle of some sort could bring its own distinctive mode of processing to the world, be associated throughout its functional life with one body, and yet fail to have any awareness of 'self as self'. For all we know, this may be the case with very many animals other than ourselves. In a non-chaotic world, we (if no one else) can still make sense of the idea of such a creature having an identity, of it persisting through various changes, and of being, in some sense, one and the same conscious being. We can even make headway in imagining what it would be like to be such a creature. For we all of us have times in our lives when we lose our awareness of self, and yet have our usual modes of response to the situations around us. Although a conscious creature which lacked self-consciousness would not be able to pose to itself the problem of its own identity its ability to function in a coherent and cognitively organized way may well depend on the world around it being non-chaotic in the way we have just described.

The Kantian thus seems to be on to an important point, and this is more than a merely epistemological one. The point applies to conscious and self-conscious beings alike. To the extent that the unity of a processing organism depends on its *maintaining* certain habits, styles of response to its environment, and so on, then the existence of an environment that is stable and structured in certain ways is necessary to that organism's unity. Even so, the transcendental argument still fails to tell us just in what such unity consists.

If Kant's arguments are more about the question of how unity of consciousness is possible, rather than about what such unity is, then they have nothing to tell us about inside knowledge, so to speak, of our own unity. It may be that there is, in fact, very little to be said about this. There may be more to be said about such unity from an external perspective. But one thing seems certain, whichever point of view we take. This is that there is more to be said than that such unity is possible only given certain pre-conditions.

There is a large problem about the issue of our 'inside'

knowledge, as I have called it, and this is as good a place as any to make a note of it. This problem does not just arise for theorists of personal identity, but also for those who want to talk about any other psychological experiences—longing, hoping, intending, remembering, and so on. Take, for example, experience memory, already discussed. The account we have given analyses such memory as involving a present memory claim which is connected in a causally appropriate way with some actual past experience. But the 'inside' view of experience memory involves none of this. I do not notice that I am now claiming to have been frightened by the bull in the field yesterday and then observe that this claim is causally associated with yesterday's experience. On the contrary, remembering yesterday's experience involves to some extent re-living, or rehearsing the same sights, sounds and feelings I experienced then. Moreover, in some mysterious way it is clear to me that what I am now experiencing is memory rather than a piece of imagination or a day-dream. Our analysis of memory, then, has been thin, or shallow, to the extent that it has omitted this phenomenologically significant aspect of memory as we actually experience it. Put another way, our account of memory is very much an *outsider's* account, an account that goes no way towards telling us *what it is like* to remember an experience. Nor is it clear that we could ever adequately put into words just what having a memory is really like.

The defender of the body account of personal identity can build on this observation. Of course, to say that to be the same person is to have the same body, or to have kept the same essential bodily components, gives us no very great insight into *what it is like* to be one unified person. But what it is like to be a unified person, and what it is like to be aware of being a unified person, our body theorist points out, may be something that forever defies our descriptive powers. None the less, we can at least try to give an outside account of the unity of a person, and this is precisely what the body theorist is trying to do. Whenever we have before us the same living human body, then, according to the body theory, we almost certainly have before us the same person. If we object that the body theory gives us a thin account of the matter, then the obvious retort on behalf of the theory is that standard accounts of memory and other psychological experiences are just as thin.

Where do these considerations leave us? We are certainly not yet in a position to claim that the body theory has a great deal going for it. For we would first of all have to look at its rivals in order to assess its strengths and weaknesses. However, the comparison of the body theorist with the Kantian has enabled us to separate out a number of distinct issues. The Kantian can give us an interesting story linking epistemology and ontology: we are told what conditions must in general be satisfied in order for there to be unity of self and awareness of such unity. The body theorist claims to give us an account, albeit a thin one, of what the unity of self consists in. We have noted that the memory theorist of personal identity can give us an account of personal unity too. And this last account, as we have just seen, will be thin in the way the body theorist's is. For it will use an account of memory that does little justice to the experiential content of our acts of remembering.

Although, as I have already indicated, the most plausible prospect for a theory of personal identity or personal survival seems to be one which links the psychological with the physical, we have now seen how two problems about mental unity—synchronic and diachronic—might seem best overcome by the association of mental states with a body. The body theorist, additionally, has positive things to say in urging adoption of a body criterion of personal identity. As Williams has argued, we find ourselves in a deeply body-based situation. From Kant, however, we have also learned that our situation may be body-based in more than one way. The very possibility of experience as we know it may depend on the existence of other bodies with stable and structured features. In presenting these views, I have tried to show some of the things that any account of personal identity must take on board. If I were in the business of constructing such an account, then I would take the points from Williams and from Kant, as I have given them, as putting significant constraints on it. However, it has to be kept in mind that at least part of my intention in these chapters is negative. I am hoping to make clear that there is ultimately no one concept of the person the core of which can be unmasked by analysis.

A classic problem for any philosophy of mind is the worry about the ownership of mental experiences. Parfit's recent defence of a no-ownership theory leaves a large question mark hanging over his account, for it is not clear that any kind of bundle theory can be defended against obvious objections to it. These are matters to which I turn in the following sections. In defence of bundle theories, even if not of Parfit, I point out that some apparently powerful counter-arguments are epistemological, rather than ontological in force. It is clear that if anything like my survival conditions are to operate at all in the psychological realm, then minds must be bundles of some sort, displaying vertical and horizontal unity.

The discussion of these problems leads into the study of related problems about the existence of what Chisholm calls 'ontological parasites'. Discussing this point allows a distinction to be made between two very different approaches to identity, foundationalist and non-foundationalist. At this point we are able to conclude the introduction to the general problems associated with personal identity.

8.8. OWNERSHIP

The combination of a neo-Humean bundle theory and the outsider's body theory looks attractive. If there is a problem about specifying just in what the unity—either synchronic or diachronic—of my psychological bundle consists, then this might be solved by noting that the bundle is tied to just one body. If one part of the body—the brain—is more important for identity than any other part, then there is no problem about tying the unity of my bundle to my brain. Were we to try, however, to keep the two accounts separate, treating it as only an accident that my experiences, desires, needs, cares, intentions, beliefs, and so on are all tied to *this* body and this brain, we would find ourselves faced with the problem of *ownership*.

The worry about ownership arises for any account that is *phenomenalist* about persons. It is important to realize that the account of identity urged in this book is not a phenomenalist one, nor is the version of the bundle theory currently under consideration. As I understand them, the traditional doctrines of phenomenalism are attempts to explain what objects are in terms of sensations, sense-data, or other essentially private, or subjective, items. If objects are 'constructions' out of such private items, then they are not separate from, and independent of, perceivers in the way that we pre-theoretically imagine. This, of course, is not an objection to phenomenalist theories. The conclusion that objects are in some way observer-dependent is an exciting one, but not one that I am in the business of defending here. On the contrary, if phenomenalism were true, the realist claims in the present work would require massive reinterpretation in the appropriate idiom. If we were to be phenomenalists about personal identity, then the bodies of persons would be constructions out of sense experiences and the psychological unity of a self would likewise be a construction out of psychological experiences. But which experiences? Just as we find it awkward to think of redness, hardness, and sphericity as sensory properties which we somehow fuse together as characteristics of the child's toy now before me, we find it strange to think of memories, intentions, beliefs, and other psychological states waiting, as it were, to be fused into a self constructed out of them. Just as the owner of the redness, hardness, and so on is the toy, so the person, or conscious subject, is the owner of the psychological states. Just as there is no unowned redness in the universe, we might argue, so there are no unowned beliefs, desires, or thoughts. Any decent phenomenalist theory has to face these problems about ownership, giving an account that settles our intuitive doubts.

However, there is still a problem about ownership for the non-phenomenalist bundle theory which is up for assessment at present. The problem can best be illustrated by considering ways in which items can be constructions out of other items, when no phenomenalist claim is involved. One clear way in which this can come about is in the study of the metaphysics or ontology of particulars. On such a theory, one category of item might be taken to be more basic than some other category. The less basic items are then constructions in a non-phenomenalist sense out of the more basic ones. The kind of construction involved is the sort that is bound to occur in any kind of reductionist explanation, including a reductionist account of identity. We have already met one such reductionist account in the present chapter, namely Chisholm's account of tables as ontological parasites. Clearly, an account of persons as items that are constructed out of psychological states—Hume's 'perceptions'—could be just as non-phenomenalist as Chisholm's, while still treating persons as less basic than the items constitutive of them.

It has to be recognized, however, that such a reductionist, non-phenomenalist account of persons stll encounters the ownership problem. If we resist the idea that psychological states are owned by the body or brain that has them, then what prospect is there for a theory like Parfit's which tries to account for the unity of a person in terms of the psychological relations between bundles of perceptions at different times? We might object that there surely are not lots of free-floating bundles all over the place, with it being an open question which ones are mine and which are yours. Instead, different bundles are allocated to me because they are all mine. The identification of the bundle is determined by the identity of the person, and not vice versa.

The synchronic issue raises a similar problem. Suppose I see a tree, you hear some Bach, and simultaneously someone miles away from either of us is aware of having an itchy back. In the normal case, we would associate the three experiences here with three different people. But why? If there really is a serious problem of synchronic unity, then we need to find some account of that relation in virtue of which all my current experiences are mine and yours yours. This move once again has the appearance of getting things the wrong way round.

As so often, A. J. Ayer writes with sensitivity to the problem facing us:

I find myself here in the sort of dilemma that frequently occurs in philosophy. On the one hand, I am inclined to hold that personal identity can be constituted by the presence of a certain factual relation between experiences. On the other hand, I doubt if it is meaningful to talk of experiences except as the experiences of a person; or at least of an animate creature of some sort.[26]

Ayer's own solution to the dilemma is to suggest that although there are no unowned experiences, it is by no means necessary that experiences should be preceded and followed by the experiences which as a matter of fact precede and follow them. This suggestion, however, is considerably weaker than what is needed if we wish to develop Parfit's conception of the person. For on the latter version of the bundle theory, experiences belong in a system of experiences and it is a matter of empirical discovery to ascertain just which bundles of experiences do constitute unified systems and which do not.

Are problems about ownership going to be too much for this

---

[26] Ayer [2], p. 197. For a famous statement of objections to the no-ownership view, and a defence of the primitiveness of the concept of a person, see ch. 3 of Strawson [1].

modified bundle theory? One thing we have to be sure of is that problems about ownership are not simply due to our having a special point of view on psychological phenomena. For of course I am not just something that remembers, imagines, feels, thinks, and doubts. On the contrary, I have an inside view of my own experiences and, as already noted, a kind of criterionless access to them. We must not be led by this feature of our *knowledge* of our own states to the denial that these states, and the entity which is their subject, can have their identity explored and described in interesting ways. To illustrate this point, two epistemic arguments which fail to show anything fundamentally wrong with the bundle theory can be briefly considered.

The first, due again to Chisholm, points out that persons are items with certain *self-presenting* states.[27] For example, if I feel happy, then, according to Chisholm's account, I am certain I feel happy and moreover the proposition I know to be true in such a case makes essential reference to me. Put in other terms, it is not the case that, in order to know I am happy, I have to find some means of identifying happiness, and then go on to judge that I have it. Following Shoemaker, we could put much the same point by observing that predicates attributing experiences are essentially adjectival. Happiness, like sightings of trees and other experiencings, does not just float about with the question of whose experience is in question being left open. Rather, to be aware of being happy is to be aware of myself, at least in part, for it is I who am happy. Moreover, such awareness is by no means indirect.

A more recent argument from Evans makes a related point. According to Evans, we have to recognize some judgements as being what he calls 'identification-free'.[28] In the case of such

---

[27] Chisholm's definition is: '*h* is such that it is self-presenting to S at *t* = $_{df}h$ occurs at *t* and is necesarily such that, whenever it occurs, then it is certain for *S*' (Chisholm [5], p. 25).

[28] See Evans [4], p. 180: 'When knowledge of the truth of a singular proposition, [*a* is F], can be seen as knowledge of the truth of a pair of propositions, [*b* is F] (for some distinct Idea *b*) and [*a* = *b*], I shall say the knowledge is *identification-dependent* . . .' cf. this with the following passage from Chisholm: 'Consider the sentence "I feel depressed". It does not imply that there is a relation between me and some other entity; it simply tells one how I feel. The adjective "depressed" in other words does not describe the *object* of my feeling.' (Chisholm [5], p. 48.) Clearly, these are two very different accounts of what might be odd in one analysis of first-person experience reports. However, both Chisholm and Evans seem to agree that there is something wrong with any straightforwardly relational account of such reports; their difference is one of locating the mistake in such an account.

judgements, knowledge of their truth is not dependent on any identification component. So, to take a case of particular interest to us, let us try to analyse the judgement 'I remember the last royal wedding.' On Evans's account, it would be quite wrong to analyse this as:

(i)   the last royal wedding is an actual past event
(ii) someone witnessed that event
(iii) their witnessing stands in the appropriate causal relation to my current memory experience
(iv) the person who witnessed the event was I

The mistake here lies in clauses (ii) and (iv). They suggest that a memory judgement involves both a component about a past witnessing and also a component that identifies the subject of the witnessing as myself.

What it is right to say about the case of memory is as follows: 'Memory is not a way of possessing knowledge about an object of a kind which leaves open the question of the identity of that object. If a subject has, in virtue of the operation of his memory, knowledge of the past states of a subject, then that subject is himself.'[29] Note,

---

[29] Evans [4], p. 245. There are two distinguishable ways of thinking about q-memory. If we take memory experiences as reliable indicators of past experience, then it seems legitimate to extend the notion of memory to cover the case where I have q-memories of some other persons's experiences. In the standard case, of course, my memories are reliable indicators of my own past experience; in the case of q-memory, memory experiences are reliable indicators of someone's past experience, not necessarily my own. However, closer to Evans' conception, perhaps, and worthy of some consideration, is a rather different form of q-memory. Think for a moment of remote experience, conceding the possibility of feeling sensations that originate in bodies other than our own. If I now find myself feeling pains, itches, and cramps originating in the arm of some other person, then it is still plausible to identify these experiences as experiences of mine (and, likewise, those acts which I bring about by movements of the other arms are my acts). Thus another way of thinking about q-memory is that it is a faculty by which I record past experiences of my own, even though these experiences were associated with a different body from what is usually counted as mine. As Alan Millar has pointed out to me, the situation would be rather like one of having senses located in another body. See, in connection with that idea, the discussion in Strawson [1], pp. 90 ff. George Schlesinger has argued in correspondence that accepting the notion of remote experience destroys any prospects for a causal account of personal unity. For an extreme case of remote experience is one in which all my experiences become associated with an alien body (say the body of a mouse), while becoming at the same time dissociated from my present body. But then, he argues, I would have become a mouse. My own view is that we can make sense of my becoming a mouse, but only in terms of the causal story I give: my present and past experiences and mental states have appropriate future

incidentally, that memory is thus a different kind of beast from q-memory. If *q*-memory were commonplace, then our analysis of memory judgements along the lines discussed above would be entirely sensible for the case where we were sure that the remembered event had been witnessed by me (in q-memory terms, I would be q-remembering an event from my own past). But since q-memory is not commonplace, then Evans is surely right to object to the proposed analysis.

In the normal case, then, memory discloses the subject to the subject, just as a self-presenting state does. But if memory judgements thus involve no identification component, then a normal memory claim will, as Shoemaker has put it, be immune to error through misidentification.[30] For anyone, like Shoemaker, Parfit, or myself, who takes the possibility of q-memory seriously, this immunity will be merely circumstantial. Nevertheless, we have to admit that in the normal case, memory discloses my past to me pretty directly; indeed, it does so in an apparently fundamental way.

Recognition of this truth does not, however, throw doubt on the prospects for developing a bundle theory of the self. Both the Evans

---

successors in the states and experiences of the mouse, and its future states show appropriate causal relations to my previous states. If Schlesinger were to deny the existence of such causal connections, then it seems to me that there would be little sense to be made of the claim that I had turned into a mouse.

[30] See the essay 'Self Reference and Self Awareness' in Shoemaker [6]. The terminology in the following sentence is also Shoemaker's. As he puts it: 'A statement like "I am facing a table" does not have this sort of immunity, for we can imagine circumstances in which someone might make this statement on the basis of having misidentified someone else (e.g. the person he sees in a mirror) as himself. But there will be no possibility of such a misidentification if one makes this statement on the basis of seeing a table in front of one in the ordinary way (without the aid of mirrors, etc.); let us say that when made in this way, the statement has "circumstantial immunity" to error through misidentification relative to "I".' (Shoemaker [6], p. 8.) Interestingly, Evans argues that if we had q-memories in ignorance of their aetiology, we would probably get ourselves into a muddle. In other words, q-memory could only be a source of knowledge about the past if subjects were aware of the situation (and thus knew, for example, that someone else's memories were available to them). See Evans [4], ch. 7.5. The issue does not seem quite so clear to me. If I wake tomorrow with lots of apparent memories which fail to fit my actual history, then I might get into a muddle. Instead, sure that I have access to someone's past, I may search for the person whose past I am now recalling. If q-memory were commonplace, we might trust it to the same extent we now trust memory, even when ignorant of just whose experiences we are reliving.

and the Chisholm points are essentially epistemological. In memory, and in other states, the subject is aware of the subject's past or present experience and thus of the subject. But to agree with this is not to cast doubt on the claim that what it is to be a subject of experience is to be a suitably unified bundle of experiences. Although my awareness of myself here and now, like my awareness of my past, is primitive and fundamental, this does not establish that I myself am a fundamental entity of any kind, or that my unity is incapable of further elucidation or analysis.

8.9. STRICT AND PHILOSOPHICAL IDENTITY

Even if the epistemological points just considered leave the bundle theory of the self as a live metaphysical option, they may still be thought to motivate the gravest suspicion of it. Perhaps it can be argued that although it makes sense to deny that tables have, 'strictly and philosophically', a unity in themselves, none the less persons do have a sort of primitive unity that we cannot analyse further. Writing about Humean bundles, Chisholm asks us to consider 'What is the nature of the bundle and what is the nature of the bundled . . . the items within the bundle are nothing but states of the self or person. And . . . what ties these items together is the fact that the same self or person apprehends them all.'[31] Although this states the opposing view, the passage goes no way towards establishing it. Let us agree that we have direct awareness of ourselves: indeed, in being aware of any experience, we could add, we are thereby aware of ourselves as experiencers. It still does not follow that our own unity is in any way primitive. There seems to be no reason why we should not enjoy direct awareness of things whose identity is itself complex and dependent upon relations among its parts.

In order to find an argument for Chisholm's view, we need to return to the notion that some things may be regarded as ontological parasites relative to other things—relative, in fact, to those things which constitute them. In Chisholm's vocabulary, we could then deny the claim that the ontologically parasitic things are unitary in any 'strict and philosophical' sense. For in making any claims about

---

[31] Chisholm [5], p. 52.

these parasites, we could always retreat to the philosophically stricter, and more austere, way of talking which involves reference to their constituents alone. Thus, if the table, constituted of components *A* and *B* on Monday, is said to be red, what we can say is that the collection $A + B$ is red. In this, and other descriptions of the universe, references to the table can be systematically replaced by reference to the parts which happen to constitute it at a given time.

Chisholm would argue that persons are quite definitely different from tables. Whereas reference to things other than the table can stand in for reference to the table in any description of the state of the universe, no stand-in for reference to me—or any other person—can be envisaged. Thus, he argues,

> There is no reason whatever for supposing that *I* hope for rain only in virtue of the fact that some *other* thing hopes for rain—some stand-in that, strictly and philosophically, is not identical with me but happens to be doing duty for me at this particular moment.
>
> If there are two things that now hope for rain, the one doing it on its own and the other such that its hoping is done for it by the thing that now happens to constitute it, then I am the former thing and not the latter thing.[32]

Even if we agree that no part collection is, 'strictly and philosophically', the same thing as a table, for a table can persist despite changes in its parts, we need not agree that there is a disanalogy between the cases of tables and persons. To agree about the claim regarding tables is to accept a *theory* about tables. If the theory is true, part collections and tables will share certain of their properties. But likewise, if I am constituted by different bundles of experiences at different times, then I will share certain of my properties with the bundle constituting me at a given time. Hoping for rain might well be such a property. We might even venture to suggest that in a complete description of the universe, *I* need not be mentioned, so long as it is mentioned that the bundle currently constituting me hopes for rain.

Putting matters in this way raises the question of reductionism again. For it may turn out that, although some items are ontologically parasitic, it none the less happens that a description of the universe that failed to mention them would be incomplete in a

[32] Ibid., p. 104.

fairly serious way. Think of my car, for a moment. It is a collection of car parts. Yet many collections of car parts lack the kind of unity my car has—for they are scattered collections, while it is unitary, with the parts physically connected and causally interdependent in such a way that the whole item functions (more or less) in the way cars ought to function. An ontological reductionist could claim primitiveness for the car components, maintain that the car is thus an ontological parasite, and yet maintain that a description of the world that made no mention of the car is incomplete. For the aggregation of the components into my car is a matter of some significance, even if cars are not ontologically basic in any way. To say that my car is in the car-park just now, is to say no more than that one structured, causally interconnected collection of car parts is in the car-park; but having the concept of a car enables us to identify and individuate such part collections.

We can think of matters another way. It may be that there is no more to a person than mental states in appropriate structural relations. A person is a unified, causally integrated bundle at a time; through time, a person is a causally connected sequence of such bundles. Now one reductionist move here might be to deny that persons are anything over and above mental events and states. But this would be wrong. For just as statues are more than clay—they are at least clay *with a structure*—so too prsons are more than collections of mental states: they are at least causally integrated, structured collections of such states. Now I will happily concede to the parsimonious ontologist that structure is not another ingredient in the world, alongside car components and mental events and states. However, it does not follow from this that a description in terms of bundles will give us everything we need in a description of the world. Rather, the sense in which my bundle hopes, fears, denies, and believes at a certain time is—on my understanding of the bundle theory—one in which a suitably structured bundle (that is, a person) does these things. These considerations do not give Chisholm what he wants, that is, they fail to admit the basicness or primitiveness of persons, but they qualify my opposition to his position in an important way.

This objection to Chisholm does not, of course, go any way towards establishing the plausibility of the bundle theory. Nor should we dismiss the puzzling nature of the criterionless insight we enjoy in respect of our own states. Our concern here, though is not to explore the question of what it is *like* to be one person; we can give an account of what it *is* to be one person, while letting the phenomenology of self-awareness go.

In the end, it seems to me that the issue of the primitiveness of persons leads us to a problem that is as much one of philosophical temper as one that can be resolved by argument. There is a well-known debate in epistemology between those who are foundationalist about knowledge and those who are not. It is possible to distinguish a similar difference in identity theory, between those whom we might call *foundationalist* about identity and those who are not. Here is how a foundationalist argument might go. Suppose that the identity of x and y is always grounded in relations among things that are distinct from x and y. Then we can ask what the identity of these other things is grounded in. By the principle just given, it will be grounded in relations among different things. Thus if we claim that each temporally extended thing has its identity grounded in relations among its temporal parts, we will have to be prepared to maintain that the identity of each temporal part is grounded in relations among yet other things, and so on.

If the regress is not to be infinite, the foundationalist argues, there must be some identities which are themselves primitive and not grounded in anything else. I fully accept that for those attracted to this line of argument, the identity of persons is a sensible foundation from which to construct the identity of other things. Yet, although I have used examples from Chisholm which might seem to suggest otherwise, I find myself out of sympathy with this whole position. Indeed, my use of Chisholm's cases only involved me taking him as presenting one possible theory about the nature of things such as tables, rather than allowing that ultimately table parts are more primitive, or fundamental, than tables themselves.

Are there any reasons why we should be generally suspicious of foundationalist programmes? Focusing simply on metaphysical issues, I would suggest two reasons for suspicion. First, there seems to be a general difficulty about making sense of the notion of what is 'primitive' or 'basic' when this is intended in an absolute sense. It is relatively clear what Chisholm is after if we think of him giving a theory about items such as tables: relative to this theory, we take table parts as more primitive, and tables as constructions out of them. This is not to say, however, that in any final or absolute sense, parts are 'really' primitive and tables are 'really' non-primitive.

There can only be foundations where there is a superstructure, or at least the intention to build further. So the notion of what is primitive is bound to be tied to a conception of non-primitives whose features will be explained, reductively, by reference to the primitives. But once we note the theory-relativity of the notion of the primitive, it is an immediate consequence that what is primitive for the purposes of one theory may be taken as non-primitive for the purposes of another.

Thus I have taken the unity of temporal parts as primitive, for the most part, in giving a reductionist account of the unity of broad particulars. Noting, however, the dimensional ambiguity in our conception of particulars, I have suggested that a temporal part can be thought of, quite properly, as having a spatial unity (as indeed, can a particular viewed four-dimensionally). So I have not taken stages as being absolutely primitive; indeed, I would not be sure what was meant by the unrelativized claim that they, or anything else, are basic entities. This consideration shows what is peculiar about the second form of non-reductionism isolated in 8.5 above.

There is a further reason for suspicion of the foundationalist claim, connected to the one just given. If philosophical theorizing has anything in common with scientific theorizing it will be its provisional nature. Philosophy, like physics, chemistry, and the other sciences, is revisable, and therefore secure only to a degree. It seems highly unlikely (to put it mildly) that we will ever be in a position to declare one branch of theoretical science finished, complete, immune from further revision. But only if we were in possession of the complete, finished account of nature could we be secure in identifying any category of entities as fundamental, *at least for the purposes of that account.* Of course, I may be wrong about this, and so only the first ground for suspicion could be defended; but I think there are good grounds for thinking that there is no first philosophy and so no special security for philosophy over and above what can be claimed for the various sciences.

The denial of foundationalism in the form just given is not a denial of the interest of certain foundational programmes. Descartes's attempt to build our knowledge of the world on the foundation of the *cogito* is interesting, on my account, as an attempt at one particular sort of epistemological theory. Perfectly proper would be a theory that built in quite the opposite direction, and the next issue, after developing such a theory, would be to test its strengths against the Cartesian one. Even if we then decided to favour Descartes's theory over the rival one, nothing would follow about the primitiveness of the *cogito* in any absolute or final sense. It is precisely this attitude that should be encouraged towards the present version of the bundle theory. It has been shown that the theory is not phenomenalist in the way Hume's original version of it seems to have been, and it makes no absolute or final claims about the primitiveness of experiences. Indeed, it recognizes, that as far as our own insider view is concerned, we do have direct awareness of ourselves, even though denying that the phenomenology of such awareness establishes the primitiveness of the self.

The view that persons are basic particulars is not one that can be rebutted simply by a general denial of foundationalism. And since many people are attracted to the notion that persons are in some way primitive, let me end this section by making a brief conciliatory remark. It seems to me that sometimes the status of what is primitive is not always clear. Thus, it is not part of my programme to deny that the concept of a person is primitive in the sense argued originally by Strawson. His arguments are connected, indeed, to some of the Kantian considerations touched on earlier in the chapters, the satisfaction of which I accept as a desideratum in any theorizing about persons.

Is it possible, however, to think of persons as bundles while accepting the primitiveness of the concept of a person? I think so, and for the following reason. To have a concept of the person is to be equipped with the capacity to recognize and pick out those things that are persons from those things that are not. As Strawson has shown, the exercise of such a capacity involves the recognition of things other than myself as persons, and such recognition involves attributing to other subjects of experience both predicates of a psychological sort, and predicates of a physical sort. As I understand him, the primitiveness of the concept of a person comes about as follows: 'a necessary condition of states of consciousness being ascribed at all is that they should be ascribed to *the very same* thing as certain corporeal characteristics . . . That is to say, states of consciousness could not be ascribed at all *unless* they were ascribed to persons.'[33] But now what is being denied is that we have any

[33] Here is Strawson's remark in context: 'What we have to acknowledge . . . is the primitiveness of the concept of a person. What I mean by the concept of a person is the concept of a type of entity such that *both* predicates ascribing states of

concept or idea of a primitive sort of a pure subject of experience, of a pure Cartesian ego (in the popular, rather than the scholarly, sense of that notion).

These points about concepts, it seems to me, leave plenty of scope for rival theories about the nature of things falling under the concept in question. From the fact that a certain recognitional capacity is primitive and that certain items are basic in our scheme of recognition, it does not follow that there is nothing to be said about the identity of the recognized things. So what sense, then, can be made of no-ownership theories? Just this, that whatever the situation in regard to our recognitional capacities, the following questions are open and worthy of consideration. First, how much unity do I possess at this moment? Reconstrued in terms of my bundle, this question asks to what extent my various mental states and dispositions are co-personal, that is correctly attributed to one and only one subject of experience. That there is a question over the existence of such synchronic unity is shown by the fact that in cases of multiple personality, for example, there is no guarantee that we would not wish to develop an account which permits more than one person to be associated with a particular body at a given time.

The second question which is also open, and not settled by the considerations given by Strawson, concerns the degree to which I remain one person over the various vicissitudes of my history. Of course, the pedantic claim here is that the question is not open, for the reference to 'my history' already reveals the answer. But it is apparently sensible to wonder whether certain changes in someone's character are enough to yield a new person. Encouraged by these reflections, some—like Parfit—do not balk at writing of their former and their future selves. If it is agreed that there are open questions here, then it has to be conceded that there is something in the no-ownership theory after all. For in each case, the interesting question has concerned the number of owners of a set of mental experiences.

consciousness *and* predicates ascribing corporeal characteristics, a physical situation etc., are equally applicable to a single individual of that single type . . . a necessary condition of states of consciousness being ascribed at all is that they should be ascribed to the *very same things* as certain corporeal characteristics, a certain physical situation, etc. That is to say, states of consciousness could not be ascribed at all, *unless* they were ascribed to persons, in the sense I have claimed for this word.' (Strawson [1], pp. 101–2.)

To talk in terms of bundles, however, is not to adopt the view that persons are ontological parasites in Chisholm's sense. As we have already seen, the ontology of particulars is complicated by the fact that the very same particular can be considered relative to various dimensions. This consideration itself shows that simple reductionism with respect to any particular is not plausible. The very same thing is present in a certain volume of space, at a number of different times, and in a number of different worlds. None the less, the spatial unity of a particular consists in a certain sum of causally interdependent parts, its spatio-temporal unity consists in survival relations of the appropriate kind among its stages, and its cosmic unity consists, according to the theory of real possibility, in the similarity among the sums of its temporal parts in different worlds. Anyone accepting this kind of view about particulars is going to accept the same account applied to persons, and acceptance of it is incompatible with straightforward reductionism.

8.10. CONCEPTS OF THE PERSON

This quick sketch of some central issues concerning persons and personal identity gives a background against which I can now put forward my central suggestion. There is, I suggest, no well-defined concept of a person which can be analysed and put forward as *the concept* with which we all operate. Nor is it clear, in my view, that talk about persons, consciousness, self-consciousness, and the identity of animals is even consistent. In some circumstances, I would conjecture, we are likely to be body-minded, as when we discuss the identity of amnesics. More will be said about amnesia in the following chapter. By contrast, we are able to switch to psychological accounts of personal unity in order to discuss (even sceptically) Lockean soul migration and the like. Our everyday modes of thinking about persons, that is, are hospitable to both body-based and memory-based accounts of identity. An intermediate strategy, which perhaps commends itself to us strongly in these days of materialist and functionalist theories of the mind, is that persons are to be individuated by a brain-based theory of identity. This strategy seems to hold together both physical and psychological criteria of identity, and we will study it further in the following chapters.

As we have also seen, Parfit has a very interesting argument to show that personal identity is not what matters. If he is right, then there is a particular difficulty we have to face in talking about our concept of the person. We cannot put the problem of my survival in terms of my identity with some future person; nor can we even use the possessive 'my' with any assurance in talking about 'my survival'. It must be borne in mind therefore that to talk about Parfit's concept of the person is already to describe his position in a misleading way. But—given our current linguistic resources—it is convenient to continue talking in this way. For it is important to recognize that he has made a distinctive contribution to the debate on the nature of persons.

If my overall approach is along the right lines, then we will have scope for developing a range of accounts of personhood, including Parfit's. The indeterminacy in our everyday ways of thinking, speaking, and worrying about persons shows up most clearly in our ability to sympathize with, and feel attracted to, very different accounts of personhood. The puzzle cases confirm, as it seems to me, the fact that we have no very coherent concept of a person underlying our everyday talk and behaviour. If we do not take the Parfit line, then the most attractive alternatives are either a brain-based theory of personal unity or an account that starts from the position that personal identity is primitive or basic. I have already given reasons for doubts concerning this last position. We are left, then, with two promising models for developing the concept of a person, each with distinctive problems.

Given the general approach urged earlier to problems of identity, it is hardly surprising that I should tackle the issue of personal identity by thinking of us as *structured* Humean bundles of perceptions, experiences, and the like. After all, any account of bodily identity would, in my view, have to give an account of the survival of body stages, and this would involve discussing the structure, matter, and causal connections among body stages. It is perhaps surprising that those who might be seen as modern successors of Locke—Parfit and Wiggins, for example—have found themselves in difficulty when dealing with even so straightforward a case as amnesia. However, attention to the issue of psychological structure and matter will give us the means in the next chapter to avoid some of the difficulties these theorists have made for themselves. Again, the simple distinction between *production* and *copying* processes sheds light on some of the issues that baffle us when we think about persons.

This talk of developing a range of concepts of the person must not, however, lead us to believe that we will get to a *correct* answer in the end about the nature of persons. There may be occasions when conceptual development can lead to our selecting one developed concept as being, for certain purposes, the best one to use. But I will not be making this claim for the concepts developed here. If this result is disappointing, it is at least not depressing. For any progress that is made in getting clear about the issues involved in conceptual development and about the range of concepts open to us for deployment is dependent on the prior acceptance of the case I am making. It will be sufficient, then, if I can at least convince the sceptical reader that there are alternative *concepts* of the person, without going on to argue the merits of one particular development over any other.

One further peculiarity of my treatment should be noted. As is well known, mental phenomena are not well understood: we have no satisfactory, generally agreed, theory of *mind*. Further, the whole question of *content* is puzzling, whether we are thinking about the content of sentences or the content of mental states. Even those who deny dualism may therefore be reluctant to do what I do: this is to speak in *causal* terms about psychological states and their relationship to other psychological states and to physical things. Causality itself is an odd notion, and certainly not one about which we can be ultimately very comfortable. However, it is undeniably *useful*, and it seems to have a use for us here in providing a convenient way of regimenting, for example, the discussion of amnesia that follows.

9

Amnesia and Other Problems

As I have suggested, Parfit, like other neo-Lockeans, may be regarded as *developing* a concept of the person. It will not be argued that this concept is a better development than its nearest rival. What can be shown, however, is that there is the possibility of developing a concept like Parfit's in a consistent way. Thus, this chapter will deal with certain problems that have been thought to arise for the neo-Lockean, and the conception will be saved from certain potential inconsistencies. A study of the problems of amnesia shows how it is possible to use our conditions on survival to yield a surprising answer to a well-known puzzle. Since unity-claims can be made in the absence of experience memory, it turns out that there is no real ground for maintaining that memory is constitutive of personal identity. However, we can still maintain a development rather like Parfit's while acknowledging this. This result concerning amnesia will therefore be welcome to those who accept the Parfit line, for it means that the case of amnesia need not be assimilated to the quite different case of fission.

In the rest of the chapter, I turn to the consideration of the problem which seems to me to provide the greatest obstacle to developing any useful theory of the person. Although we are used to thinking of persons in dual terms, as somehow being both mental entities and physical things, there is another dualism which also infects our attitude to persons. For ease of labelling, I call this a type-versus-token dualism.

On the type theory of persons, a different story about bodies is given from that given by defenders of the token theory. In the end, the issue of the causal connections between selves is, I think, what is of real importance for survival. This issue cannot be resolved, however, as long as our notions about persons remain poised between the two kinds of theory identified. This means in particular that we cannot give any real support to Parfit's development of the notion of the person.

We have already noticed that the term 'continuity' is used in a somewhat strange way by some authors. In the Hollywood sense of the term, a series of episodes is continuous when each one goes on where a previous one left off, even if the episodes are separated in time. It is important to bear in mind that this is *not* the kind of continuity I intend when dealing with psychological continuity. Rather, let us forget—just for the moment—problems about episodic objects. Thus we can make sense of psychological continuity in the following way. Suppose that the mind is a structured bundle of thoughts, desires, hopes, wishes, intentions, fears, ambitions, memories, and so on. Now such a bundle could show either weak or strong continuity in the sense identified by Hirsch. If the bundle were weakly continuous, then this is compatible with its history's having 'jumps'. Recall Hirsch's example of the tree (Chapter 2). Although we may lop a very large branch from a tree, and the tree thus has a discontinuous history, the tree none the less shows a weak continuity in its history (provided its trunk and other branches do not have episodic existence). Likewise, some of my thoughts may vanish quite rapidly, and some new fears, hopes, and wishes be acquired in a rush. None the less, these rapid changes may be associated with underlying continuities that show only gradual change. So, for instance, habits of response, procedural skills, and sense of humour may all be relatively unaffected by even quite gross and sudden changes elsewhere in my psyche.

Now this way of thinking about a continuous mental life is in sharp contrast to the sort of thing said by some authors. Think, for example of David Lewis's remarks:

. . . what I mostly want in wanting survival is that my mental life should flow on. My present experiences, thoughts, beliefs, desires and traits of character should have appropriate future successors . . . Change should be gradual rather than sudden, and (at least in some respects) there should not be too much change overall . . . Such change as there is should conform, for the most part, to lawful regularities concerning the succession of mental states . . .[1]

This looks very much like an appeal on behalf of strong continuity. But some form of weak continuity looks very much more plausible when it comes to describing the features of the mind over time.

[1] Lewis [3]. The quoted passage appears on p. 17 of Rorty [1].

Sleep, for example, is not accompanied by 'that consciousness' Locke mentions, which—as already remarked—is absent too when we day-dream, lose ourselves in absorbing tasks, and so on. During all such occasions, we lack a certain co-consciousness between that part of our mental life and its neighbouring stages. Notice again, that this talk of stages is *not* meant to suggest that our mental lives are discontinuous in time.

It is important to recognize that Lockean self-consciousness may come and go, even if our mental lives are continuous in time. Even sleep, death's half-sister, does not interrupt the continuity of our mental lives, for we will register sounds, vibrations, and other disturbances while asleep and—of course—we also have dreams (whatever they are). We could say, then, that it is only from the point of view of my inner story that I appear to be strongly continuous. However, it is plausible, at least, to suggest that the history of my mind may involve only Hirsch's weak sort of continuity.

Now Parfit recognizes that some of our mental episodes are connected with others (as a memory is to a past experience, or the formulation of an intention to its subsequently being acted on). These direct psychological connections bind or tie one mental episode, conceived as a psychological bundle, in an appropriate way to another such episode. What Parfit means by psychological *continuity* is nothing other than overlapping chains of such connectedness, that is, continuity is simply the ancestral of the relation of connectedness. Both connectedness and continuity of Parfit's sort will admit of degrees. This distinguishes Parfit not only from Locke, but also from a neo-Lockean like Wiggins, for both of whom co-consciousness seems to be an all-or-nothing matter.[2] On Parfit's account, we can quite sensibly inquire to what degree some earlier psychological bundle is connected to some later one.

Let us now think of two stages in the psychological history of one person. In terms of the diachronic unity problem (as described in the last chapter), these stages can be thought of as bundles of psychological states connected, let us suppose, to some degree. If we imagine such connections being very dense, then we may find, for example, an abundance of memories in the one caused by

---

[2] I have in mind Wiggins's discussion in Wiggins [7] and in the final chapter of Wiggins [9].

experiences in the other. In this case, what *matters* is—for Parfit— the richness of connectedness. As we have seen, it should not really worry us if there are, for a given earlier stage, two later stages that are equally richly connected. For although identity may be impossible to determine in such a case—or even be settled by stipulation—what *matters* is the psychological connectedness (with some appropriate cause) between the earlier stage and the later ones.

Now the further apart any two stages are in time, the less rich the direct psychological connections between them are likely to be. Not only do memories fade, and intentions get forgotten, but even the relatively stable aspects of the personality show some change. For Parfit, we can have psychological 'continuity' between two such remote stages simply in virtue of the overlapping chains of connectedness among these and intermediate stages. In fact, he qualifies this. For he suggests that what we are likely to want, if we are to capture what is important in my survival, is that sequential episodes show *strong connectedness*. And this means that, let us say, half of the connectedness that *normally* holds between neighbouring psychological episodes, or that hold over every day in the life of the normal person, still hold.[3] Of course, strong connectedness is not transitive. But its ancestral is—and this is, as we have seen, simply 'continuity' in Parfit's sense.

Parfit here is using the term 'continuity' in a way akin to the Hollywood sense already identified. This time, one later episode is not continuous with an earlier episode because it goes on just where that earlier one left off (for it may be very much later than the earlier one). Rather, it is continuous with the earlier one because it is linked to it by means of a chain of episodes, each of which went on (to a high enough degree) where its predecessor left off. Now it will be useful if we introduce a term that captures some of what Parfit is after by his talk of continuity, but which differs from it in two ways. First, we do not take it that the episodes in a person's psychological life are continuous in time. And, second, we allow that the kind of psychological connections we are interested in may amount to more than the sort which Parfit describes. Thus we count in personality

---

[3] See Parfit [4], § 78. It is interesting to note that Parfit is not consistent in his use of the term 'continuity'. The present, and the following, section will show him operating with the term in distinct, ableit related, ways.

characteristics, skills, capacities, dispositions, modes of processing, and the rest, as well as memories, intentions, and the like. Let us continue to use Parfit's term 'connectedness' in preference to 'co-consciousness', only taking it now in the wide sense which embraces all the conscious and unconscious elements of a person's psychological states. And let us coin the new term 'coherence' to apply to the ancestral of the connectedness relation, noting that this means again that coherence can involve not just states of which we are consciously aware but the whole repertoire of our skills and capacities as well. Under this proposal, even if it turns out that persons are episodic in the way our hill of Chapter 3 was, we can still think of their persistence as *coherent* particulars.

What I now want to show is that there is apparently a severe problem facing this kind of approach. For if Parfit wants to use connectedness and coherence in identifying what matters when we discuss personal survival, then he seems to fall foul of a dilemma. On the one side, it seems that disordered experiences satisfy his constraints on what matters even where the degree of disorder is enough to make us worry about attributing unity of person. And on the other, we can apparently think of cases where his constraints are not satisfied, yet we naturally want to talk of there being one unified person in their absence. Both sorts of problem are revealed by a study of amnesia.

9.2. AMNESIA

Amnesia seems to give rise to two different problems. First of all, it gives us examples of coherence where there is a real puzzle over whether we have personal identity or unity. Consider, for example, the case of temporal lobe amnesics, as described in Iversen's well-known study.[4] These unfortunate people apparently have reason-

---

[4] In Whitty and Zangwill [1]. The effects of encephalitis may, in rare cases, produce even greater disorders than those described by Iversen. One case reported recently involved a patient whose memory-span extended no further than a few minutes. Although able to apply concepts, play instruments, and even conduct choirs in complicated motets, his own view of his life was that he had just awoken from an anaesthetized state—a view he repeats regularly. Along with this loss of even short-term memory is a recurrent panic, which adds considerable distress to the patient's predicament—a distress he is able to experience afresh every few minutes. The referential practice of those involved with this patient, as well as the references

ably normal cognitive abilities—they can converse, apply concepts, describe situations, and so on. Additionally, they are able to acquire some motor skills, like the ability to carry out tracking tasks, and they will even improve these skills with practice. However, they do not have anything other than short-term memory abilities. Thus someone they have been introduced to one day would be greeted as a stranger the next.

How, then, can they improve on motor skills with practice? Since they lack long-term memory, such patients themselves will be quite unaware that they are improving their skills, for on each new session of practice, they act as if the whole thing is quite new to them. However, those who are treating and working with such patients can make the observation that the motor skills are improving with practice. Moreover, such people show a high degree of psychological connectedness from moment to moment; for their short-term memory capacities are not impaired. It is quite frightening, however, even to contemplate what life must be like for such impaired people. It is as if one's whole life is lived like a journey through scenery which vanishes forever as soon as one passes it. Others tell us that we have been at this point in the journey before, or that a particular piece of scenery is something with which we are already familiar. But to us, each experience can only be retained for a short time. In an analogy I have used elsewhere, think of a day in the life of such an amnesic as like a chalk line being drawn across a blackboard, with a duster an inch behind erasing all but the line's immediate past.

In Parfit's terms, here is a clear case of psychological continuity, and so such an amnesic has a life which is *coherent* in our terms. Indeed, we can easily imagine that such an amnesic has a genuinely continuous psychological life (although my official position is one of agnosticism on this issue). Processing mechanisms can, as we have already noted, continue functioning despite sleep, day-dreaming, and even loss of memory. Yet there seems to be a real puzzle over how unified such a life can be. It might seem that the sameness of body displayed by a temporal lobe amnesic in some way compensates for their psychologically fragmented experience. More to the

to *him* throughout this note show that we can operate with a notion of personal identity which is not tied to the subject's own retention of past experiences, nor to coherent attachment to certain intentions, loyalty to friends, or any of the other high-level properties so important to the neo-Lockean.

point, however, we may argue that what is missing here is any high degree of certain forms of connectedness over time—something that Locke himself took seriously. Of course, the amnesic has had many experiences the day, or the week, before. But the inability to recall any of these to consciousness is what is striking. By contrast, the case with motor skills and cognitve abilities is not so very different from the norm. If we each have a distinctive cognitive style, a way of approaching problems, a characteristic style of describing things around us, then we can expect a temporal lobe amnesic to display just such a characteristic style over time as well. In the next section, I will in fact argue that, even without the aid of the body criterion, we can use these kinds of psychological coherence to support a notion of personal unity in such cases.

A second and quite distinct problem that studies of amnesia provoke concerns the possibility of unity without coherence. Suppose that we consider a fictionalized case of amnesia where we imagine that a serious infection has caused someone to lose all memories of the illness and those extending back to some time before the illness as well. This is a case of what is known as *retrograde* amnesia. We can depict such a case diagrammatically, using the labels *a*, *b*, and *c* for extended psychological stages (Fig. 20). Let us suppose that common sense inclines us to allocate each of *a*, *b*, and *c* to just one person, Pamela. After t_2, Pamela is unable to recall any of the events experienced in her *b*-phase, though she shows normal recall for events belonging to the *a*-phase. During her *b*-phase, however, and even during her illness itself (which, according to our story, occurred towards the end of that phase), she had normal recall of her *a*-phase. Thus there is connectedness between her *a*-phase and her *b*-phase, and between her *a*-phase and her *c*-phase. What is missing, and would be found in the normal case, is any connectedness between her *c*-phase and her *b*-phase.

Now Parfit, and other theorists, assimilate the unfortunate Pamela's case to what is, in my view, a rather different one.[5] Taking seriously the view that Pamela's life after t_2 is lived as if the *b*-phase has not occurred, they suggest that this sort of amnesia is rather like branching. In a branching case, of course, we would have to tell a rather different story. We would have to suppose that Pamela this

5 This is explicit in Parfit [4], ch. 13, and in Elliott [1].

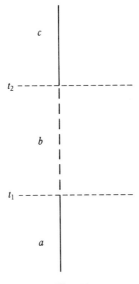

Fig. 20.

time underwent brain surgery of the sort already imagined in our
earlier discussion of fission. Before surgery both halves of her brain
were, let us imagine, brought into the same informational state. A
donor body becomes available shortly afterwards, the hemispheres
of her brain are separated, and the right hemisphere is transplanted
into the new body. Her left hemisphere stays in Pamela's body.
However, an infection proves disastrous, and this combination dies
not long afterwards. However, the right hemisphere flourishes in its
new body and this combination goes on to live for some
considerable time. We can depict this kind of fission in the same way
as we have done it before (Fig. 21). The diagram depicts only
psychological relationships. This time, segment *b* represents the
psychological history of the left hemisphere, while the more
sucessful right hemisphere has its history shown by the *c*-phase on
the diagram. Now, looking at this case, we can start to see why Parfit
and others want to assimilate amnesia to branching. Think of the *b*-
phase as a *branch-line*, as Parfit puts it, while the *c*-phase continues
Pamela's *main-line*. The branch-line is connected to the main-line
to the extent that *b* is connected to *a*. But *c* is also connected to *a*,

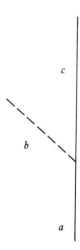

Fig. 21.

while failing to be connected to *b*. The logical relations thus seems to be the same in this as in the previous case.

Parfit gives a nice example of the assimilation of amnesia to the branch-line case. Notice, by the way, his explicit use of the term 'continuity' in its Hollywood sense. He writes:

Certain actual sleeping pills cause *retrograde* amnesia. It can be true that, if I take such a pill, I shall remain awake for an hour, but after my night's sleep I shall have no memories of the second half of this hour. . . . Suppose that I took such a pill nearly an hour ago. The person who wakes up in my bed tomorrow will not be psychologically continuous with me as I am now. He will be psychologically continuous with me as I was half an hour ago. I am now on a *psychological branch-line*, which will end soon when I fall asleep.[6]

If this is along the right lines, then we have a serious problem. For it does not seem plausible to maintain that the phases *a*, *b*, and *c* in our second case constitute the psychological history of a unified person. By contrast, there is real plausibility in the claim that we might make in the amnesia case that Pamela is—despite her amnesia—a unified person. Looked at in this light, we have unity without coherence.

[6] Parfit [4], § 97.

The problem that emerges here is fascinating. If we can have unity without coherence, then there seems to be no good reason why we should not count the phases *a*, *b*, and *c* in the branching case as episodes in one unified life. But this looks absurd. For, in the branching case, while the *b*-phase exists, we surely have two people before us, namely the original-body person and the new-body person. And it is quite likely that they will not share all their experiences. Indeed, they may converse with each other, seeing each other from quite different points of view, explaining that each has different feelings from the other and so on. This assimilation of branching to amnesia threatens to make nonsense of that fact that although Pamela has, for a time, survived the fission surgery twice over, she has survived as *different* persons.

By contrast, if we try to assimilate amnesia to branching, as suggested in the passage from Parfit, we seem to face an equal difficulty. For now, we have to count the *b*-phase in the amnesia case as being like the existence of a separate person within a larger life. But this means that what looks like the life of one person—including an episode with respect to which the person later has amnesia—is more properly regarded as the life of more than one person. This result strikes me as odd, to say the least.

As a last, desperate attempt to salvage something from the comparison of the two cases, we might try to insist that there really is either connectedness or coherence, *of the same sort*, in both cases. Thus we might try to say that in both cases the *b*-phase is connected with the *c*-phase, via the *a*-phase. In the amnesia case, for example, there are memories in the *b*-phase of the *a*-phase. Likewise there are memories in the *c*-phase of the *a*-phase. So the *b*-phase is in some way indirectly connected with the *c*-phase![7] But then, we can claim this indirect sort of connection for the *b*-phase in the branching case as well. This, however, looks like a desperate recourse compared with what I shall argue is the most plausible way of dealing with our puzzle. For this involves simply separating the two cases. They are not, despite the similarities mentioned here, to be assimilated at all.

---

[7] Thus Elliot, of precisely this sort of case: '(take) three slices of the one person, *P*1, *P*2 and *P*3. *P*1 is standardly, psychologically continuous with *P*3 and *P*2. *P*2 and *P*3 are not standardly, psychologically continuous. However, since *P*2 and *P*3 are both standardly, psychologically continuous with *P*1, we can regard them as indirectly psychologically continuous with each other.' (Elliot [1].)

9.3. WHY AMNESIA IS NOT A PROBLEM

If we recall our general conditions on survival, we can investigate whether they apply equally well to the fission case and to the amnesia one. Our question is to decide, then, whether the relation among the stages a, b, and c in each case is one of survival.

Starting with the branching case, we note that in terms of our conditions it seems reasonable to claim that a survives as b and that a survives as c. However, b does *not* survive as c. The reason for this is quite simple. Although c will—to begin with at least—show both structural and material similarities to b, these depend, causally, on a's prior possession of that structure and matter, but not in any way on b's prior possession of any such feature.

Of course, to write in the way I have done here and earlier of structure and matter is perhaps to be guilty of overbold metaphor. Not everyone will agree that we can even begin to think properly about psychological phenomena as long as we persist in using analogies with ordinary physical things. One response to this is to point out that theory must be served. If we are to give survival theory a run for its money, then we must not cavil over this admittedly crude treatment of the psychological. And we may find, to our surprise, that we can go much further using this metaphor than we might at first have expected. However, in a more conciliatory vein, I might also point out that we need not think of the issue in terms of structure and matter, but simply in terms of deploying psychological analogues of the notions of structure and matter. We may have no idea what such analogues are; but this should not inhibit us from thinking about them. Nor, incidentally, is my usage here a great departure from common sense. If we do think—as neo-Lockeans tend to—of the human mind as like the software that perhaps runs on the body and the brain as its hardware, then we can reflect that the software notions like *program*, *data*, *array*, *loop*, and so forth are all easily subsumed under our labels.

If we then return to our branching example, it is clear that the *causal* condition is the important one here. The brain transplantation operation, after all, used a procedure which involved copying the features of one of Pamela's hemispheres into the other. And it is this intitial copying that makes plausible the claim that a survives both as b and c. We thus have a causal dependency of both b and c on *a*, but no more relation between *b* and *c* than we expect to find in the products of a production process. Thus *b* does *not* survive as *c*.

By contrast, we find that the amnesia case is very different indeed. In fact, there is not just *one* amnesia case, but rather a range of cases which we could imagine, We will select some samples from this range, and find that in all of them there is something which differentiates amnesia from fission. Suppose, first of all, that we take it that Pamela's *c*-stage is not connected *at all* with her *b*-stage, using the term 'connected' in Parfit's narrow sense. Thus we have connectedness of memory and intention from *a* to *b* and from *a* to *c*, but no connectedness from *b* to *c*. It looks at first sight here that we can have no grounds for a survival claim: just as in the fission case, *b* fails to survive as *c*.

But we need to be careful here. Our *causal* condition requires that one stage survives as or in another stage provided the structure and matter of the later stage is causally dependent, in an appropriate way, on the structure and matter of the earlier one. But we can now see a dissimilarity between our two cases. For it is precisely the effect of the imagined infection that shows up in the amnesia about her *b*-stage typical of Pamela's *c*-stage. Her amnesia with respect to those parts of her life that occurred in stage *b* is causally dependent on things that happened *to stage b*.

There is a complication here. For the infection that was imagined as bringing about Pamela's problems is not itself a psychological phenomenon. However, we can suppose that, since it has psychological effects, there will be some way of characterizing its impact on her psychological components, and their structures. Pamela's psychological bundle, at the time of the infection, would—let us suppose—consist, among others, of a number of complex monitoring, storing, and searching devices standing in various relations to each other and to devices linked to perceptual and central processing mechanisms. In functional terms, her memory devices would be responsible for *consolidating*, *encoding*, and thereafter *retrieving* information handled by the cognitive part of the bundle.[8] Suppose, then, that the infection somehow interfered with the

---

[8] I am simply using—quite uncritically—the kind of model of memory assumed by the authors writing in Whitty and Zangwill [1]. Nothing of importance hangs on the question of whether this model is, ultimately, satisfactory. The important point to bear in mind is that any *functional* model of mind is likely to use notions to which the vocabulary of *structure*, *matter*, and *cause* is applicable.

mechanisms responsible for encoding information so that it could later be retrieved. In her c-phase, then, Pamela has no way of 'reading' the garbled material processed by her damaged encoding mechanisms. It is precisely this damage, though, that is causally responsible for her amnesia. The structure and matter of her c-phase, then, *is* dependent on the structure and matter (including the malfunctionings) of her b-phase.

Notice that in this case we are imagining less by way of dramatic structural and material changes than in the case, say, of the episodic hill. Quarrying at one hill episode, for example, could produce extremely impressive changes in later stages. Persons are living things, and since their psychological states, like their physiological states, *change*, then we might expect amnesia to involve rather more than just the usual sort of change. If perceptual and other processing skills remain unaffected, then amnesia will leave much of the perceptual and cognitive machinery of the subject unaffected. In Pamela's case, we have supposed that information is entered in the b phase, albeit in an unreadable form, so it seems safe to assume a pretty high degree of survival of psychological matter and structure from the b-phase to the c-phase.

Here, then, we see a real difference between amnesia and fission, even when we imagine that there is no high-level connectedness between the stages in the amnesia case. But, as has already been suggested, the situation is likely to be rather different when we consider connectedness of a broad enough kind. For even though Pamela is not conscious during her c-phase of things done and experienced during her b-phase, due to the amnesia, there may well still be many features of her later psychological structures that are causally dependent on modifications to these during the b-phase. Take, for instance, her procedural skills. As was noted in the case of temporal lobe amnesics, skills will persist and improve even though the amnesic has no recollection of acquiring or practising them. Thus suppose that Pamela was keenly practising the piano just before her infection struck. In the c-phase, she can no longer recollect practising a certain new piece, but she can—none the less—play it much better than she would have had she not been pactising it during her b-phase. Thus, although hidden from her own 'inside' story, we external observers can note this kind of further dependence of psychological structure and matter between the two phases.

Obviously, this last kind of information makes it rather clear that there is likely to be a real ditinction between fission and amnesia. It would be entirely surprising if, in the fission case, skills practised on the branch-line were to be transferred to the main-line. Of course, we could try to make some arrangment whereby this came to pass. For example, we could wire in tiny transmitters and receivers that would put the two separated hemispheres back in touch with each other. Or we could imagine that, rather like the children in *The Midwich Cuckoos*, anything that one of the separated hemispheres learns is also known to the other, perhaps due to some telepathic phenomenon that operates in such cases. As soon, however, as we make this move, we immediately change the fission story. It is now quite unclear what to say about the relation between the main-line and the branch-line persons. The very factors that made it seem so obvious that they were distinct persons are no longer present.

In the light of my suggestions in this section, it follows that Parfit, Wiggins, and other neo-Lockeans need not worry about amnesia. Moreover, the application of our conditions to this case is so pleasantly natural that we seem to have found good reason for having a certain confidence in them. That they work so well on the psychological case, delivering a result that is congenial to good sense, suggests that they ought to be taken very seriously indeed. Even if we still maintain that our employment of the notions of structure and matter is metaphorical, the metaphor has proved useful. We might indeed want to claim that we now have good reasons for thinking that a chain of non-branching survival relations can underpin personal identity. Now, although it would not be wrong to argue thus, and perhaps some readers will want to make this very use of the conditions, my own preference is to stay agnostic. If we recall Parfit's arguments about *what matters*, we would be wise to stick with the more modest conclusion that Pamela's stages show appropriate degrees of survival in the amnesia case. Thus *a*, *b*, and *c* merit being described as a series linked by the survival relation, the relation that matters.

As well as complicating the amnesia story by imagining unconscious links between stages, we can also think of the impact of the body criterion. There seems little doubt that, from the outsider's viewpoint, Pamela's experiences, however disordered, can all be associated with one body (forget, at least for the time being, problems about the identity of bodies). It may be that, for all we know, hamsters are incredibly amnesic. Each day may bring, from their interior viewpoint, radically new experiences uncontaminated by memory. But a child's pet hamster has, for all that, a clear identity—at least in the eyes of the child! The body condition seems to be what makes it clear in the case of fission that the mainline and the branch-line do not belong to one and the same person. For we have a great reluctance to allocate more than one body to a person at a time. Bodies do seem to loom pretty large in our everday notions of personal identity. However, the concept of a person that is yielded by development in favour of a body criterion is no more privileged, no more likely to be the right one, than any other. In the following section, I will make some suggestions about the weakness and strengths of the body approach.

For the moment, let us observe how we have fared in dealing with the dilemma facing Parfit. As was noted in the first section, Parfit's constraints on connectedness and coherence seemed to permit highly disordered experience to be coherent. Extreme amnesia, where not even motor skills nor modes of response show preservation from day to day, would be an example of highly fragmented psychology that might none the less display connectedness over short times. But high connectedness over short periods, along with high loss of material and consequent structural changes over moderately short times, does not constitute the kind of coherent experience we assocate with a persisting person. So the first of the problems we identified in Parfit's position has not so far received a satisfactory solution. The fact that the disordered experiences are temporally continuous in no way forces us to count them as *unified*. We will therefore have to bear in mind, as an outstanding problem, the question of what to say in a case where this kind of disorder is present.

What is more likely, of course, in a real amnesia case, is that we encounter conceptual skills that are able to develop, motor skills that can go on improving, but a poor degree of experience memory. Life for someone in this position is not so highly disordered as in the case just discussed. Rather, our extending of Parfit's notion of connectedness to embrace modes of response, skills and so forth, allows us to view this kind of life as showing connections among episodes—even episodes remote in time. The lack of conscious acknowledgement of these connections on the subject's part is perhaps not so important as the existence of the connections themselves. Thus, from an outsider's viewpoint, at least, there are grounds for saying that we have enough psychological unity to talk about what matters being preserved. Failing fission and other oddities, we have something here close to a plausible account of personal identity of a kind.

The other horn of the dilemma facing Parfit was that experience that failed to satisfy his constraints none the less could be described as unified—as constituting episodes in one life and being continuous in time. Our separation of amnesia from the case of branching has helped here. Within a unified life, as we have seen, it is perfectly possible for there to be little connectedness of memory, intention, and the like over even fairly short periods of time. We are all of us amnesics to a great or lesser extent, for few of us can recall more than a minute portion of our past experience. Some of those who are amnesics in the clinical sense will fail to satisfy Parfit's connectedness constraints while still leading lives that are continuous and unified to a degree. By broadening the scope of connectedness and including what we might call 'low level' connections, we have given an apparently satisfactory solution to this part of the dilemma facing Parfit.

9.4. BODIES AGAIN

It was observed earlier that one development of our concept of a person involved associating persons straightforwardly with bodies. Although in this chapter we have been looking primarily at the prospects for defending Parfit's and Wiggins's forms of Locke's position, we have found once again that bodies are very much a part of our everyday notions about personal identity. Maybe, though, this reflection is not important. For, as we saw in the last chapter, Parfit has a very powerful case against taking the notion of personal *identity* as important at all. Since identity is liable to depend in some cases on essentially trivial facts, what matters is bound to be something different from identity.

The liberation from concern with identity as the thing that matters need not, however, be a liberation from a concern with bodies. Although we can make sense of the neo-Lockean's concern with psychological relations between me now and other experiences and happenings in the future, we can also make sense of an equal concern that what matters may be certain relations between my body now and some body in the future. Williams, as we have already seen, mentions the question of *love for a body*. This he sees as a 'grotesquely misleading' way of describing one's love for someone, rather than as anything that might be philosophically mistaken. Bodily identity will, if Parfit is right, depend on trivial facts. But even if what matters when we are talking about the lives of persons is not identity, it may still be that what matters has some relation to bodies.

Bodies have the useful property of being accessible to the outsider's view. Whatever it is really like to be *me* may be something that forever eludes elucidation or any sort of characterization in language. It may be an inexpressible thing—although none the less real enough for all that. But at least as far as my family, friends, and enemies are concerned, the existence of a living body with certain characteristics is pretty important to the persistence of me. As we have already noted, 'what it is like' to be Pamela, in either the amnesia or fission cases, may, when viewed from the inside, be pretty well the same in each case. But from our outside point of view, the association of memories, experiences, and behaviour with certain bodies is likely to be significant in our judgements either about identity or about what matters.

We need to be clear that there really is something to be said here by those who oppose the neo-Lockean view—that they are not entirely silly to maintain that what matters might be possession of a certain kind of body, capable of doing certain things. One thing we should remember is that the very skills that persist through Pamela's amnesia might depend for their manifestation on her possession of certain bodily features. If she is a fine pianist, then she will have the muscle tone and other physiological characteristics that make good performances on the piano possible. If she plays the trumpet, she will have breathing control and diaphragm development that is different from the average.

If these seem essentially trivial points, then we must remember that not everyone places equal stress upon the more psychological or intellectual aspects of personhood. It makes perfectly good sense to maintain that we like someone because they remind us of one of our friends by virtue of the way they speak, smile, walk, lisp, drink coffee, and so on. To the response that such liking is of an essentially inferior kind, as based on essentially inferior features of persons, we have to ask what the standard is by which 'inferiority' is to be measured. Even if we were to concede that such matters are of less consequence than the more lofty—perhaps psychological—traits displayed by persons, we would at least have to admit that as a matter of fact people very often fall in love, set out on projects, face risks, and act in many other ways largely in response to their perception of such 'inferior' traits.

It is not, in my view, implausible to maintain that we are torn two ways in our account of what matters because we do not know to what extent we value the physical and to what extent we value the non-physical aspects of personhood. This is not, as might at first appear, because we are confused about *values*, although I am sure we are. Rather, it is because we have no clear conception of what a person is—and we are therefore at the mercy of somewhat inconsistent expectations. A body theorist can develop a consistent account, by pointing out that what matters to us is the existence of a body and the association with that body of certain behaviour. The same theorist can say that psychological characteristics matter only to the extent that they are responsible for the production of the behaviour which we recognize as typical of the person in question. Such a theorist, then, need not deny the existence of psychological or mental phenomena. Nor is the theory committed to viewing bodies as relatively unchanging, passive particulars. Rather, bodies matter to us by virtue of some of their individual features and the history that as tokens they carry; but the behaviour of the person we care about is also expressed via the body. To *behave* in the way persons do is to act intentionally, rationally, foolishly, cleverly, or whatever, and such action requires the possession of both mind and body.

We can make some headway on this by reflecting again on the matter of *daffodils*. As we argued in Chapter 4.8, daffodils have the interesting feature of producing remarkably similar blooms each year. We can thus value a particular daffodil because it is a production process, or at least houses such a process. Each year, this process results in the production of blooms which we admire, savour, and enjoy. Likewise, our imagined body theorist might maintain that what we value in a person is their ability to produce certain kinds of behaviour, certain responses to situations, certain jokes, certain cheering words, and so on. What we call their psychological states are simply some of those properties in virtue of which they are able to make the responses they do to the situations around them. Of course, being the sort of thing that can develop a repertoire of interesting behaviour typically involves having experience memory, ambitions, intentions, and all these other psychological states that the Lockean deems so important. For our imagined body theorist, however, these are only incidentally important—important as a means to *producing* those pieces of behaviour that are unique to and typical of persons, and for which they need to have bodies.

Now the idea that persons are, or house, production processes, has far-reaching consequences. And it need not be regarded as the sole prerogative of the body theorist. There is, I think, a certain truth in the underlying insight. We do care about people's behaviour, and we do think of that behaviour as typifying them, as—in some way—individuating them. Thus, although we may mourn the death of an old friend, we are pleased to see some survival of that persons's integrity, humour, or courage in the behaviour of one of their children. Now imagine that experience memories were passed on from parent to child. How much would we count the parent as surviving in the child? The degree of survival would not be as much, I conjecture, as it would be if the child also reproduced the parent's *way of talking, mode of gesticulation* and other behavioural characteristics—like the ones just mentioned above. Recall that, in our earlier speculations on the survival of parents in children, we were able to build our case on precisely such behavioural commonalities.

However, the body theorist should not build too much on the insight regarding behaviour. It is true that with a different face I could not smile one of my typical smiles or scowl one of my typical scowls. It is also true that with only one leg I could not cycle the way I currently do, and so on. But much of our behaviour is not body specific. Many different bodies would do for the production of gestures, the mimicking of accents, the waggling of eyebrows, or whatever. So although what matters, for the body theorist, might be the existence in future of a certain kind of body with a certain range of behaviour open to it, it is not clear that the theorist I have described here would be able to insist that what matters is the existence of some particular body.

Indeed, in response to Williams's observations on the matter of *loving a body*, Parfit cites Quinton's view that obsession, or lust, for a body is usually directed at a body *type*, not a body *token*. In what

Parfit thinks to be the normal case of infatuation of this sort, the obsession is easily transferable to a replica (even an approximate one) of the original body. By contrast, love normally is—according to Parfit—concerned with the continuously changing mental life of the loved one. Furthermore, love develops and grows over time, involving a shared history, and thus memories as well as bodies.

Moreover, Parfit, and other neo-Lockeans, are not maintaining any kind of commitment to disembodied existence. If what the body theorist is really getting at is that what matters for my persistence is the existence of some body, then this may well be acknowledged by all the software theorists. For without hardware to run it, software is peculiarly useless. In thinking about conceptual development, then, I will be taking at least this much on board from the body theorist. But this does not mean that the concepts of the person we will discuss are concepts of bodies.

9.5. SLEEP

We have seen so far how the neo-Lockean can deal with continuous and unified experience which is not linked over time by high-level connections. This is the experiential situation of the amnesic who is not so highly disordered as to lack coherence of a broad kind. In fact, our introduction of the broad notion of connectedness has made the position of Parfit rather stronger than it might first have appeared. Wiggins's position, however, is not so clear, for Wiggins uses the notion of co-consciousness in very much Locke's way. Thus Wiggins seems to be interested mainly in connections among episodes that are clearly *conscious* episodes. There is nothing, of course, to stop a defender of Wiggins dropping this requirement and operating instead with the broad conception of connectedness I have urged here. But this would be a substantial departure from Wiggins's expressed views.

However, one more problem still remains for Parfit's position. As we noted, a high degree of connectedness from moment to moment, coupled with large losses of cognitive material and structure over slightly longer periods, would give us a set of experiences that seem to satisy even Parfit's modified unity constraints while raising doubts about whether we really do have unity. Suppose there are people so disordered that, although each day their recall of the previous day's witnessings, learning sessions, and so on is close to normal, this ability declines rapidly over the space of just a few days. By Friday, their memory of what happened on Monday has almost entirely disappeared, although their recall of Thursday's happenings is perfectly normal. Likewise, although skills learned on Thursday can be improved on Friday, those acquired on Monday are apparently lost forever and need to be learned anew.

It seems highly unlikely that people born with these defects would ever be able to acquire language or learn to operate with concepts at all. However, injury and disease bring about the most peculiar conditions sometimes, and we can perhaps imagine that the patients in question have suffered some accident in adult life which has brought about the sorry state of affairs just described.[9] The nature of the disorder, then, is such that a victim of it can still communicate and deploy concepts to some extent, though since the accident no new skills have been gained nor knowledge acquired. Such a person no longer seems to have a coherent life, despite the connectedness from day to day. Put another way, it is hard to see why we should really talk of one person persisting since the accident, rather than of a series of short-lived persons who have existed since then.

The notion that we are confronted in this case by a series of persons might be further supported if, along with the other symptoms so far described, the patient displayed radical changes in personality, behaviour towards others, moral views, and so forth. It is clear that, faced with this kind of dislocation of behaviour, our broadening of the notion of connectedness does not help resolve the problem. In fact, in terms of our broad notion of connectedness, the patient clearly lives a disconnected existence. It seems to me that there are two things we might say about such a case. On the one hand, we might appeal to the continuity (or at least the *persistence*) of the person's body to support a claim of identity along with an admission of lack of unity. On the other, we might want to admit to an inability to settle the identity issue here at all. Whatever line we took, however, we would, if inclined to Parfit's position, maintain that in terms of what matters, we are not now confronting a unified

---

[9] Our a priori notions about how the components of our minds relate to each other tend to be flung into disarray when confronted by clinical accounts of actual psychological disasters. For some relevant case histories, see Sacks [1].

person. Yet again, there would be a gap between our decision on identity and our decision on what matters.

We can see just why the Parfit-minded would take this line if we think of a fictional community. In this community, rather like ours, people generally go to sleep at night and wake up the following morning. However, their scientists have discovered that sleep for these people does genuinely interrupt their psychological lives. Their psychological lives are best thought of as sequences of episodes interrupted by sleep—in the way that some of us think that our conscious life of experience is interrupted by sleep. Now what would a coherent life for such people be like? The answer is that it would be very like the lives we lead. Each morning, just like us, they wake able to go on with projects laid aside the day, or the week, before, recalling their lunch-dates, fulfilling their teaching commitments, writing letters to their friends, and so on. In our case, we may think that—despite the episodic nature of consciousness—we have psychologically continuous lives. At least, I assumed this to be so earlier in the present chapter. But our imagined folk have no grounds for holding any such belief.

So on what grounds can they maintain coherence of experience and of psychology in general? There seems to be four features which show their lives to be coherent in our sense. There are, first of all, our three features of survival. Each episode in the lives of such people survives in or as its neighbours. Their lives are thus built up out of a chain of episodes in just the way our flickering hill persisted as a sequence of causally connected hill episodes. Again, we can only take this position if we permit ourselves to talk of psychological structure and matter, but I am hopeful that what has been argued in this chapter so far makes such a mode of speaking not seem too outrageous, But a fourth feature, on which we have so far been silent, would also be important. Put negatively, this condition would insist that our imagined people do not behave like the disordered patient described above. Or, in positive terms, psychological episodes relatively remote in time must show sufficient connectedness (as opposed to coherence) in order for them to be allocated to one persisting person.

Lewis makes this sort of point about survival by referring to the fact that in a single, unified life there should not be too much change overall. However, Parfit is able to make much the same point—as we might expect—without making implicit or explicit reference to identity. As he puts it:

On my proposed way of talking, we use 'I', and the other pronouns, to refer only to the parts of our lives to which, when speaking, we have the strongest psychological connections. When the connections have been markedly reduced—when there has been a significant change of character or style of life, or beliefs and ideals—we might say, 'It was not *I* who did that, but an earlier self'. We could then describe in what ways and to what degree we are related to this past self.[10]

I would suggest that if we take 'connections' in the above passage in the broad sense identified already, then we obtain the most plausible version of the view.

Of course, I am assuming here that our imagined people really are different from us. Our psychological lives very probably are continuous—although I am prepared to allow that this is not a question on which philosophy has the resources to pronounce. For us, only our *conscious* lives are episodic in this way. But it is clear that we can make the point about connectedness over time whether we are dealing with a continuous or a discontinuous phenomenon. Continuity is not, after all, the issue. Rather, what we are facing is a problem about the *degree of change* which is compatible with the persistence of a single, unified set of Humean bundles, Parfitian self, or whatever. Like all other living things, human beings change as they grow and age. Some of our structures are relatively unaffected by these changes—for example, our gene complement. Others change in the lawful and regular way that is typical of humans—males lose their hair, all of us gain wrinkles. Our psychological matter and its structures likewise change. But there must be preservation of some structural invariances for there to be (and hence for us to recognize) persistence of the same human body.[11] Likewise, there must be preservation of structural invar-

---

[10] Parfit [4], § 101.

[11] McCabe shows this point clearly by reference to simplified drawings of a face, and her article contains many references to the psychological literature: see McCabe [1]. The reader may quickly become convinced by spending a few moments with pen and paper. Draw some simple object like a house, a sailing dinghy, or a stick figure, using lines. Now redraw the figure using crosses, small circles, or any other variant, in place of some of the lines used in the original drawing, but being sure to keep the relative configuration of the parts. Compare the result with another drawing in which the original lines are preserved as far as dimensions are concerned, but are located quite differently with respect to one another. Whereas the drawing that

iances for there to be persistence of the same psychological bundle, or self. We noted already that there must be principles of change and of conservation for any kind of thing, these principles differing according to the sort of thing in question. What we have now discovered is that the same is true of psychological as well as of physical phenomena.

9.6. TYPES AND TOKENS

So far, this chapter has defended a position rather like Parfit's. The intention has been to show how a neo-Lockean position, with appropriate modifications, can give an account of personhood that is interesting, and develops some of the features to be found in our normal ways of thinking about persons. Adding complications, we noticed that Parfit's own account was an account of *what matters* in some of our thoughts about persons and thus can be given in the absence of a decision on personal identity, or even where the decision on identity has favoured a candidate other than the one identified by the *what matters* criterion. Thus, even if we decide that our highly disordered patient of the last section is one person, this decision need not involve admitting that the patient therefore possesses the unity that matters, the unity of psychological history that we normally think accompanies personal identity. By contrast, if we decided that our imagined people with episodic psychological states really were new people each morning, this should not inhibit us from noting that these separate people display an important unity of psychological history.

In this section and the following one, I want to conclude the treatment of Parfit by showing that some problems remain for his view, despite its evident attractions. In the next chapter, we will consider whether a modification of Parfit's view will enable us to develop a concept of *person* that is genuinely neo-Lockean, and associates personal identity with what matters. Such a development would be greeted with some relief for those who find it a great strain

---

maintains structure will clearly be a representation of the same thing as the original, the drawing that maintains the lines but places them in a new configuration will either represent some different thing or be a mere pattern of no particular significance.

to bear in mind that what matters has to be kept separate from the identity question.

The current neo-Lockean position has treated selfhood as being rather like software, while denying that there is any way in which we can make sense of the existence of disembodied selves. What is important to the unity of self in normal situations is the survival of one psychological bundle in later ones, allowing for that degree of change that is appropriate to persons, or selves. In the unusual cases, we may not be able to talk of unity of self or person, but we can still recognize that different bundles—even when belonging to different persons—can show the connectedness and coherence that counts.

We need to recall that the view is reductionist. Personal identity is not some deep or primitive fact to be argued about even after all reasonable information-collecting steps have been taken. It is for this reason, after all, that Parfit is able to disentangle the issue of identity from the question of what matters. If Parfit is right, then there are important consequences that follow from accepting his reductionist views. Take the example of death. Death is less terrifying, perhaps, if we recognize it as no more than an extreme case of the loss of connectedness and coherence characteristic of normal life. On the positive side, I can be consoled by the thought that after my death there will be Humean bundles whose matter and structure is rather like the matter and structure of *my* bundle. If enough of my enthusiasms, obsessions, hobbies, and projects are still going on, then I have, to some extent, survived.

Parfit writes extremely eloquently in favour of the reductionist view:

When I believed that my existence was such a further fact, I seemed imprisoned in myself. My life seemed like a glass tunnel, through which I was moving faster every year, and at the end of which there was darkness. When I changed my view, the walls of my glass tunnel disappeared. There is still a difference between my life and the lives of other people. But the difference is less. . . . After my death, there will be no one living who will be me. I can now redescribe this fact. Though there will later be many experiences, none of these experiences will be connected to my present experiences by chains of such direct connections as those involved in experience-memory, or in the carrying out of an earlier intention. . . . My death will break the more direct relations between my present experiences

and future experiences, but it will not break various other relations. . . .
Now that I have seen this, my death seems to me less bad.[12]

Is Parfit right to be so optimistic? We an only assess this point, I
think, if we give further consideration to the nature of the
connections between my life and the lives of others.

Let us think back to the case of Beatrice discussed in Chapter 3.5.
Recall that she had an adventitious replica in some distant star
system, a replica, that is, who was not obtained from Beatrice by any
copying process. Now, when Beatrice died, she did not survive in or
as her replica; for she played no *causal* role in the creation of that
replica. We deferred further consideration of the case at that point,
noting that we apparently had no good theory of types and tokens
that could be given purely in terms of the theory of survival. It is
time, though, to think again about the problem raised by the
Beatrice case, for it can help to illuminate Parfit's larger claims.

Thinking back to the distinction between production and
copying processes, we will recall that both processes can yield
tokens of the same type. However, in the case of copying processes,
we were able to give a reduction of type-token talk as simply
shorthand for what we could more lengthily state in terms of our
survival conditions. But we had not at that point considered the
feature about persons drawn to our attention by the body theorist of
section 4 of the present chapter. We noted there that one reason for
valuing persons was as items that housed certain production
processes, whose products we value. One of my friends regularly
cheers me, let us suppose, by virtue of a behavioural repertoire
which is invariably optimistic, humorous, and caring. My friend
can be regarded as carrying around a set of recipes for behaviour: it
is the behaviour that we value, of course, and the recipes (usually
what we call the person's 'nature', or personality) are valued just to
the extent that they produce this very behaviour.

If we stick, for a moment, with this admittedly crude picture, we
can start to make some sense of something that Parfit may be after.
For, in the passage just quoted, his suggestion seems to be that the
lack of connectedness between me and some future persons is not
the only thing to think about when considering my death. Maybe
we should think also about the continued existence of recipes, or of

[12] Parfit [4], p. 281.

behaviour produced according to recipes. The fact that there will in future be certain experiences and pieces of behaviour that might have been causally connected with my present experiences and behaviour may give us grounds for some consolation. In terms of our Beatrice example, maybe we should say that although Beatrice does not survive in her replica, her personality, or modes of behaviour, are at least reproduced in her replica. And although Beatrice's death is a bad thing, the existence of the replica makes it not quite as bad as we thought.

If I am right in taking this interpretation, we have to consider just how to make the claim plausible. For, looked at another way, the fact that there is no *causal* connection of the right sort between Beatrice and her replica, or between me and some future person who has certain similarities to me, is precisely what makes the critical difference. We can get clearer on this by going back to the issue of q-remembering. Recall that both Parfit and Shoemaker hold that it is possible to q-remember the experiences of another. Memory thus displays the duality of token and type: I and another person can both share q-memories of some third person's experiences. We thus each have our own tokens of the same memory type. Now, in introducing the concept of q-memory, I suggested that we might supply some appropriate causal story to link my possession of the q-memory with the original experience. Thus we imagined machinery that copies information from one brain to another.

Now does q-memory, as envisaged in this way, hold out prospects for the survival of the person having the original experiences? Jones, let us say, underwent a whole host of experiences many years ago which I am now able to q-remember. Q-memory is thus a boon for me: it enables me to extend my knowledge and experience in the same vicarious way that I can by going to the movies or by reading a book. But does it do anything for Jones? Perhaps our response is to say that it enables Jones to survive to the same extent that an author can survive through a book. The analogy, indeed, looks quite close. If it makes sense at all to say that authors survive through their books, then it makes just as much sense, apparently, to suggest that Jones survives through my presently q-remembering his or her experiences.

We can contrast this kind of situation with the following one. A machine is devised for enhancing our range of experiences in a world where real variety of experience is increasingly difficult to obtain. This machine 'writes' into the brain just the appropriate structural modifications that will make the subject appear to have memories of a whole range of things that the subject has never in fact experienced—climbing Mount Everest, piloting Concorde, giving birth, or any of a thousand other things. Using this machine, I find myself in the same state, qualitatively speaking, as I would have been in had I been given some of Jones's memories. That is, there would be no discernible difference from my point of view between having the ability to q-remember bits of Jones's past and having been broadened by the experience enhancer. But this is purely chance. Jones played no part in the programming of the experience-enhancing machine. Yet if I have used it to obtain these apparent memories, is there any sense in which Jones has survived?

The response of someone attracted by Parfit's line here might well be to suggest that in this latter case, unlike the former, Jones has *not* survived. But, at the same time, the adventitious occurrence of things in me that are very like q-memories of Jones's past means that Jones's fate is not so bad as we might have thought. Just as in the Beatrice case, things are not so bleak as we might at first have been inclined to think. Beatrice did not survive in her replica, and Jones has not survived thanks to the experience enhancer. But there are connections between Beatrice and her replica and between Jones's experiences and my new apparent memories. These are not direct causal connections. But maybe the lack of causality here is perhaps not the most important thing. Let us call the apparent memories put into me by the experience-enhancer *e-memories*. Then Beatrice and her replica are two of a type, and your q-memories of Jones's past and my e-memories of parachuting over Senegal are tokens of the same type. And maybe this reflection might make us feel closer to others, and less concerned about death.

9.7. DEATH, DUALISM, AND VALUE

We can now attempt to bring the discussion of the last section and section 4 into clearer focus. There seem to be at least two dualisms at work in our account of what is important, or essential, to persons. First, there is the traditional duality of the mental and the physical, and second, the duality we might want to describe in terms of types and tokens—although, as we shall see in a moment, this may not be the best way of describing it.

If we think of a simple case involving an artefact, we can get some grasp of what the type–token duality involves. If I lose my old, dog-eared copy of *Word and Object*, my distress is to some extent mitigated by the fact that other copies of this book are readily available. Although these are not copies of my copy, they possess something that was *distinctive of*, although not *unique to*, my copy. This is the ability to convey Quine's ideas on language, modality, and ontology. My copy's marginal notes and coffee stains were not doubt not only distinctive of it but also unique to it.

A book type, then, can survive the destruction of some tokens of it provided other tokens continue to exist. Notice, however, that the term 'survive' was not used in the last sentence in the technical sense we have given it. Moreover, as we have already seen, our reference in some context to 'Quine's book' or to 'the book I am now holding' may be indeterminate between reference to a type or to a token. Suppose, then, that there is a duality not unlike this possible with respect to our talk about persons. To make a crude simplification, let us think about our reference to someone's typical smile—a piece of behaviour distinctive of that person in certain circumstances. Is this smile unique to that person, or simply distinctive of them without being unique? Let us associate with what we will call the *type theory* the claim that smiles may be distinctive of people without being unique to them. And with the *token theory* we will associate the contrary claim—that a person's smile is unique to them even although other persons may smile extremely similar smiles in similar circumstances. Let me emphasize again the point about terminology here. I am not saying that the distinction between the two theories really is best put in terms of types and tokens: the terminology is meant to be suggestive rather than accurate.[13]

What goes for smiles may be thought of as applying to all the rest of a person's behavioural repertoire. So we can have a dual view

---

[13] Basically, the type theory, as I here call it, is congenial to some of Parfit's and Quinton's views on bodies: that, for example, to become obsessed with someone's body is to become obsessed with a body type. The token view takes the person as very much grounded in their body as, in Descartes's phrase, 'constituting one whole' with their body.

about the whole complex of behaviour and response typical of—or characteristic of—someone. Notice that this is not to be confused with the duality of mental and physical. It is very likely the case that the kind of behaviour that is characteristic of persons as opposed to other things is dependent on their possession of various kinds of psychological structures. We will see later how one version of dualism attempts to associate all such structures with the possession of a brain. But this is not our prime concern here. The kind of dualism we are dealing with here is something completely different.

The defender of the *type theory* would maintain that although persons have bodies, and thus concern with the health, looks, and other characteristics of these bodies is perfectly proper, it is only the association of this body with a particular person that gives us any grounds for caring about this rather than about some fairly similar body. The body is no more than the medium through which the person acts. Consider a person as having a set of production processes associated with them—recipes, as it were, for the production of behaviour, recipes which are responsible for their loves and hates, passions and hobbies, values and deeds. It is this behaviour which, in the end, is important. This body which I now have is, on this view, rather like the token copy of *Word and Object*, one item through which my production processes or recipes work to produce my characteristic behaviour. But if these recipes and pieces of behaviour could be associated with a quite different body, then *I* would be associated with that body.

By contrast, the *token theory* denies all this. On that account, the type theory simply begs the question. What makes behaviour *mine*, after all, if it is not just its association with this very body, *my* body? Notice that the token theory is not a token theory of behaviour. For someone attracted to this line can readily understand the claim that the same behaviour (type) can occur on different occasions. Rather, it is a token theory of the person. What makes two tokens of the same behaviour type both pieces of *my* behaviour is, on this account, their association with my body. The ownership of the recipes, then, is determined by the identity of the body realizing the recipes which are made manifest through behaviour. There is no way normally, in which these recipes and their associated behaviour can survive in a different body. One qualification to be made here is that the brain theory of the person (to be discussed in Chapter 10.3) gives some account of how I could come to have a different body, while still asociating my identity quite firmly with possession of one particular lot of physical stuff, namely my brain.

It is interesting to note, then, that what I have called the 'type theory' is not committed to either of two famous doctrines. It is not committed to Cartesian or Lockean dualism about the mental, nor is it committed to the new version of this dualism, central-state materialism. Parfit, as a representative of the type theory, shows how it is possible to maintain that view while avoiding precisely these commitments.

Any attempt to say we are dealing with a *dualism* about persons here is therefore using the term 'dualism' in a heavily modified sense. Now we might think that if the type theory does not involve some kind of dualism of the traditional sort, then it has little chance of impinging significantly on our views about what is important in life or what is significant about death. Getting to grips with this issue is of extreme importance to Parfit, for he maintains that his theory is capable of making a radical impact on our view of death and of what is of moral value.[14] If the type theory is correct, then there are possible worlds in which my present body (perhaps thanks to teleclone machines) is only the body of one of my tokens. Moreover, even in this world, connectedness between me now and what we normally think of as our past and future selves is a matter of degree. In some cases, the degree of connectedness is so low that we can think of me now and that self then as tokens, so to speak, of different types.

Continuing along these lines, we can start to consider the issue of what degree of connectedness and coherence with some later self is necessary for the survival of my present self. In crude terms, my present self is no more than a complex of recipes associated with my responses, interests, desires, passions, loves, obsessions, and so forth. Now is what I want, in wanting the survival of my present self, that it should contribute in some causally appropriate way to the existence of some future such complex or bundle? If we are inclined to answer this question in the affirmative, we need to go on to consider just why the *causal* contribution of this present self is of any importance.

The loss of one copy of *Word and Object* was not the loss of the book. And maybe the loss of this bundle of recipes is not the loss of

---

[14] See, e.g., Parfit [4], §§ 102–8.

these recipes. Other persons—whether causally influenced by me or not—are custodians of recipe complexes too. Some of them will display behaviour that in some respects is very like mine. If we value behaviour, passions, pursuits, and responses of certain sorts, then the world will not be without the ones I manifest simply because the world is without me.

Further, there are many ways that the world could in future be without me as I am now, only some of which involve my death. It may be that I change greatly through time. My current self may fail to survive to a very high degree in any future self because I have changed. We do not normally regard such changes in personality and behaviour as death, but maybe we need to revise our way of thinking here. Imagine one of my future selves, as we would normally think of it. It may have lost much, although certainly not all, of its connectedness with my present self. What relates it causally to this present self are the intervening overlapping chains of connectedness which I have called *coherence* and which Parfit calls *continuity*. Maybe there is nearly as much causal connection between me now and me then as there is between me now and some of my present students as they are then. In studying with me, they have acquired some of my passions and interests, and over time these have flourished. Causal connections, then, can hold between me and future selves that we would not normally allocate to me. This seems, then, to give us some means of thinking about survival as holding between me now and others then.

We can thus come to wonder, finally, if the matter of causal connections can *really* be so important. We have already raised this issue in connection with the cases of Beatrice and Jones. If what we value are the recipes and the behaviour, then can we not, as type theorists, think of my relations to future persons with even more detachment than we have done so far? Think of it like this. I do not value the existence of future selves pursuing interests and caring about certain things because I have played a causal part in bringing about the existence of such selves. On the contrary, I may try to play some part in bringing about the existence of such future selves because I value the pursuits and interests themselves. But now, why should I care about the future existence of *my* students any more than I care about the future existence of other students? Is not what really matters, when I think about the future, the existence of people with the interests and concerns that matter most to me?

Such a way of thinking has certain virtues no doubt. It may give us the ability to view our own deaths with a certain detachment, and it may lead us to think more optimistically about the future. But I do not think that such a view really has anything to tell us about personal survival. For the very severing of the causal connection severs the link that is crucial in considering *my* future survival. If death seems less evil on this view, it is not because there are better prospects for my survival than we thought. In a sense, something distinctive of me can be thought of as surviving; but—as pointed out already—this would not be a case of survival in our technical sense at all.

What we can get out of Parfit's view by way of claims about our own survival depends very much, I would argue, on the issue of the *causal* connection between my present self and certain future selves. But I think there is overwhelming evidence to suggest that the degree of survival between our own past and our own future selves is, for the normal person, far higher than the degree of survival that can hold between ourselves and others. This is hardly surprising, after all, if we consider that our recipes and behaviour are themselves at least in part influenced by things like our gene complement, a complement that is probably unique to each person. Our histories are also unique to us: even identical twins differ in their doings virtually every day. So to the extent that our recipes and behaviour evolve in response to our changing surroundings, our past experience, and the impact of others on us, we will each show much higher degrees of survival over our own stages than any of these stages are likely to show to stages of others.

It would be satisfying, perhaps, to conclude this development of the Parfit arguments by recognizing some sort of survival relation as holding between some of our stages and at least some of the stages of others. But we have only been able to go along the developmental lines above by taking the type theory very seriously. We have so far found no reason for thinking that the type theory captures either all of, or whatever is most central to, our concept of the person. For we are forced back again to the problem facing us at the end of Chapter 8.2. We noted there that our everyday attitude to persons involved vacillation between the type and the token theories. On the one hand, we can see attractions in the claims of those who emphasize behaviour and recipes as being what matter. On such a view, as we then noted, it is hard for us to be sure we survive even to a degree in our children. More accurate, for all we know, may be the view that our children simply preserve and manifest features which have been previously manifested in us. The real survivor on this view is culture, the society, the gene pool, the moral code, or whatever.

If, by contrast with this view, we think of the other things we say about persons, we find that they are regarded as intensely individual items which can act on, and transform, their environment and themselves. To be a person on this account is to be more than simply a manifestation of various cultural, genetic, and other values. On this view, we can think of ourselves perhaps surviving to a degree in our children and in our books, but only to a most attenuated degree compared to the real thing—our survival through the changes and vicissitudes affecting these tokens here and now. As long as we are caught between these very different views, then we have no principled means of resolving the difficulties faced in this chapter. We can develop a Parfitian concept. But we cannot be sure that it is proper to apply it. The gloomy conclusion, then, is that we are as yet unable to give an entirely satisfactory account of what we value in life or of what is lost by death.

10
Concepts of the Person

In the last chapter we did our best to develop a concept of the person along Parfit's lines. It turned out that the enterprise was only moderately successful. However, we ended up giving an account of certain important relations rather than an account of personhood itself. The reason for this was simple. On Parfit's own account, what matters when we think about our future survival is not always identity.

In this section, I want to give brief consideration to the prospects for developing a concept of the *person* based on Parfit's ideas. In order to do so, we need to consider two different possible worlds. First, we take a world where there is no fission, that is, where survival never takes a branching form. Secondly, we will look at a world which permits fission and thus gives rise to the problems associated with having more than one replica of some original around at a time.

In the first case, we can imagine that telecloning of persons takes place regularly, but always serially. That is, no original survives entering the teleport chamber, nor does the machine ever produce two copies of the original. Alternatively, like Nagel, we can imagine a world in which people, after their thirtieth birthdays, go for regular annual replication in order to maintain their youthfulness. The scanning replicator destroys the brain and body of the person who enters it, but produces subsequently a body which is exactly similar to the original, except that no ageing has taken place.[1] The resulting replica is also psychologically connected to the original in all the right ways. If we call such persons *series persons*, then we might wonder whether series persons would have all the important features of persons as we know them in this world. For Parfit, they have. Indeed, Parfit goes further than this and argues that this world, as we know it, actually contains series persons: it happens

---

[1] See Parfit [5], § 98.

that, the way things are here, the series persons and persons as we normally think about them are exactly the same.[2]

It is hardly surprising that Parfit should take this line. We can go further, and argue that in the possible world described, the series persons are nothing other than persons, according to an easily developed concept. Using our conditions on survival, we can claim that each series person consists of a number of stages, each of which survives to an extremely high degree as its successor. Of course, the scanning replicator will introduce slight discontinuities into the history of the persons in the imagined world. But this need cause us no more trouble than the discontinuities in the hill described in the fourth chapter. If a sequence of episodes linked by the survival relation constituted one hill in that case, then the sequences of episodes linked by the survival relation in our new case constitute persons. This development of the concept of a person is not only in keeping with Parfit's constraints on *what matters*; it is also highly natural given our earlier account of survival.

It might seem a bit more puzzling to know what to say in the case where replication is able to take a branching form. Suppose we imagine, then, a world in which person fission occurs. In such a world, the teleclone devices allow existence of the original while still producing replicas. Perhaps only one replica can be produced from an original at a time. Thus, the history of certain individuals can be represented in a binary tree, as shown in Fig. 22. Here each labelled segment of the tree represents an extended person-stage, and our problem is to see if we can answer the question: How many persons are represented by the tree? At each fission point, only one of the successive stages is actually a copy of the preceding stage: the other stage simply continues that predecessor stage's history.

We might think that this fact settles the matter. If c, for example, is just a spatio-temporal continuation of stage a, then we might say that $a + c$ constitutes one person (by the usual body criterion), while $a + b$ is no doubt a mereological individual, but hardly a person. This, though, would hardly do justice to the Parfit-like concept we

---

[2] 'No phoenix has ever existed. But there are many series-persons. These sentences are being typed by a series-person, me. They are also being typed by a person: old-me ... I, the series-person, started to exist when Old-I the person started to exist. And it is very probable that both will cease to exist at the same time. This is very probable because it is most unlikely that, within the lifetime of Old-I, teletransportation will become possible.' (Parfit [4], § 98.)

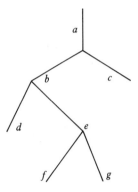

Fig. 22.

are trying to develop. For stage b is, after all, related just as strongly to stage a by the relation that matters—connectedness and coherence—as is c. In terms of survival, a survives as b to no greater or less a degree than as c. Further fission, indeed, affects the replica stage, for stage c, as the diagram shows, was not very long-lived and has no successors.

A natural move here, if we really are attracted by Parfit's account, is to take survival as supporting, indeed as constituting, identity. A *branch*, or maximal path, on the tree is any route starting from the original segment and finishing at the end of a stage to which no more stages are subjoined. Let each such branch represent the history of just one person. Then the tree above would represent the history of *four* persons, and each of these persons is no more than a maximal sequence of stages related by the survival relation. We might, to take account of Lewis's point about there not being too much overall change, add to the characterization. The addition would reflect the importance of connectedness over reasonable lengths of time. As well as stage collection $a+b+e+g$ being a maximal S-related sequence of stages, for example, there would also have to be sufficient connectedness between a and g in order for the collection to constitute one person.

This proposal may seem a bit drastic when it comes to the matter of knowing how to count, or speak about, persons. We usually think that if we count the number of person-stages present in a room at a time, then we have counted the number of persons in the room. But under the present proposal, this would not be true. If we imagine a time when stages *b* and *c* are alone in a room together, we would be making a mistake to claim that there were only two people in the room. For although stage *c* is unique to just one person (namely *a* + *c*), stage *b* is shared by three branches of our tree. However, in a world in which fission was commonplace, we might well have to get used to speaking in a slightly different way about persons. David Lewis makes some interesting suggestions about how we should do this using the notion of tensed identity (which is not any form of real identity).[3]

If we assume that we could find some way of being comfortable about describing this world of fissioning persons, then we might also consider a new solution to our old case of Theseus' ship. In our earlier discussion of this case and of the 'only *x* and *y*' principle, we were happy to allow that the world might contain the mereological individual consisting of the original ship-stages together with the stages produced by the plank-hoarder. The present suggestion about persons, however, goes further by suggesting that in a world in which fission is commonplace we might even come to regard that individual as itself a *ship*. This would mean allowing that two different ships could have shared a common set of stages—not really very much more dramatic a suggestion than the one made about mereological individuals sharing stages.[4]

However, even making these moves may seem not to give us, in the end, a concept of personal (or ship) identity that captures what matters. For although we are allowing a maximal aggregate of appropriately connected stages to be one person, it does not follow from this that psychological connectedness will on its own constitute identity. Even though we now have a means for determining that our diagram above shows the history of four separate persons, it might none the less be argued that the survival relation can hold between *different* persons.

Some abbreviations will help in the discussion of this issue. Let us designate the relations that constitute personal survival 'the survival relation'. The survival relation is thus a relation between

---

[3] See Lewis [3].
[4] Of course, we might be happier about wearing the complications of counting by tensed identity for *individuals* in the technical sense, than about doing so for everyday things. Individuals, unlike everyday particulars, are not, after all, generally of *sorts* or *kinds*.

stages where one survives—according to our conditions—in or as the other to a suitably high degree. Now, as just proposed, a maximal set of stages connected by the survival relation and with not too much change overall will constitute the history of one person. Let us call, by contrast, that relation holding between stages only when they are stages of one same thing the 'identity relation'. In the paper cited in note 3 of the present chapter, Lewis argued that the survival relation is the identity relation. But that conclusion does *not* follow from anything we have said so far. Indeed, Parfit has argued in response to Lewis that even if we allocate personal identity as suggested in this section, we are still forced to recognize that the survival relation can hold between different people.[5] So if the survival relation is the one that matters, then we will find that *identity* and *what matters* are still separate.

It is important to get to the heart of this disagreement, for although we have encountered several cases where identity and survival diverge, it is not clear that every case of fission needs to be added to the list. To get clear on Parfit's argument, let us think about the person in Fig. 22 constituted by stages a, b, and d—P_1 for short—and the person consisting of $a + c$—P_2 for short. Now P_1 and P_2 are distinct by our identity criteria, although they both share the common stage, a. If the survival relation were just the identity relation, Parfit claims, then we would get the following absurd result. P_2, during the shared a stage stands in the survival relation to stages c and b. But if the survival relation were the identity relation, a, b, and c would then have to be stages of some same person. But they are not. For whereas a and c are stages of P_2, a and b are stages of the different person P_1.

So—according to Parfit—it does *not* follow from the fact that a person is a maximal aggregate of survival-related stages that identity coincides with survival and thus with what is important. However, in his later defence of the coincidence of the two relations, Lewis denies, in effect, that survival is ever a relation between distinct persons. With certain reservations, mainly about the nature of the branching envisaged, I have to side with Lewis here. On my

[5] This was originally claimed in his response to Lewis [3], published in Rorty [1] as 'Lewis, Perry and What Matters'. In a new postscript to 'Survival and Identity' (found in Lewis [4]), Lewis has subsequently defended the claim that survival is constitutive of identity. It is this claim which I support in the present section—although only subject to certain rather large provisos.

official view, survival is a relation between *stages*, and as long as we stick to this official view it is hard to see how to formulate the very claim that Parfit wants.

His claim is that P_2 survives both as P_2 and as P_1. The grounds for this claim are that stage a is common to both persons. Now suppose that during that very stage P_2 (and hence also P_1) had a thought along the following lines: 'I want to go on living.' There is an immediate difficulty about attributing this thought to any one person (stage a is, after all, shared by four persons). Any argument to the effect that one of them had the thought shows equally well that another of them had it too.

So in a world where fission is commonplace, we not only have to count by tensed identity, in the style of Lewis, but we also have to engage in radical reinterpretation of desires and other shareable states. Suppose, however, we agree that stages, while not themselves persons, can have desires. Then we can construe the thought above as indicating a desire on the part of stage a to be such that *some* person of which it is a stage should persist. We can try to put the matter, equivalently, in terms of persons. What P_1, P_2, and the other stages share is the desire that *at least one* of them should persist. If we accept these proposals by Lewis, then we do have a way of preserving the claim that the survival relation is the identity relation, and hence saving the insight that survival is constitutive of identity.

Of course, Lewis does not give my analysis of survival. So I have been foisting my account of survival on to him in giving the above paraphrase of his debate with Parfit. Even so, it cannot be argued that in a world where fission occurs survival would reasonably be constitutive of identity. In the case just studied, we have made a big assumption, namely that the branching is equal, in the sense that each immediate successor of a given stage has as good a claim as any other to be the survivor of the stage above it. But this notion of equal branching would only be applied to the case described for Fig. 22 by someone who accepted psychological connectedness and coherence as what matters. For someone who was impressed by the persistence of the body through stages a and c, the branching would appear to be unequal, despite the close psychological relations between a and b. It is precisely our inability to pronounce on what matters for personal identity that drives a wedge between identity and survival. Likewise, faced with the intractable problem of artefact identity, we were still able, in virtue of our three conditions, to say sensible things about survival (for example, that one artefact had survived as a different one). So the endorsement of Lewis's position requires major provisos. Provided equal branching occurs in a world of fissioning particulars, there is at least a theoretical possibility that survival in my sense is constitutive of identity.

In a world without fission, but containing replication, the situation is, as we have seen, rather different. In such a world, our Parfit-inspired concept of a person is a natural development. That we are engaged in developing a concept in the case is shown by the fact that authors like Nagel would prefer to use a different terminology—namely that of *series person*—to describe just the same state of affairs. To the extent, then, that our world has in it analogues of replication and fission, we can talk about developing a concept of person, and an associated concept of survival, for its description.

10.2. HIGHER- AND LOWER-LEVEL CONCEPTS

It has already been suggested that we can develop concepts of the person at various levels. The kind of concept developed along Parfit's lines has been of an *intermediate* level. Although what counted as *important* in developing such a concept were psychological relations, these were of a very broad sort—on our modification, at least, if not in Parfit's original account. The relata of the survival relation, in other words, are, on such an account, psychological states, episodes, and data conceived as having structure and being capable of entering into causal relations with other such states and episodes.

In this way, our conceptual development so far has avoided working up any really high-level concept of the person, though it seems clear that both Locke and Wiggins are interested in just such a concept. For them, with the emphasis on co-consciousness, the relata of the survival relation are *conscious*, or even *self-conscious*, episodes, which are in communication with each other thanks to memory, intention, and other high-level psychological operations. Such a high-level conception, of course, ensures that persons are *episodic* for, as we already noted, consciousness and self-consciousness come to us only periodically, with gaps introduced due to sleep, absorption in fascinating tasks, day-dreaming, and so on. However invisible these gaps are to our inner viewpoint, it is not hard for us to realize that they exist. We are aware of having 'lost ourselves', as we put it, in some interesting activity, or of losing our bearings when we drift off to sleep in the middle of a tedious meeting.

On this high-level conception, one conscious episode survives as another, when connected to it by memory, intention, character, and so on, to a high enough degree. Notice immediately that such a refined conception of the person has two consequences. First, that it does not matter what changes there may have been in the structure and matter of the body that supports these conscious states. What is important is the functional relationship of items constituting the conscious states. Indeed, in an extreme case, we could even imagine reading off all the information concerning a conscious episode, loading this into a massive computer and then getting the computer to produce further episodes linked to this one. Here, we would have changed the entire physical means of producing such mental episodes. But for the functionalist operating with such high-level concepts of the person, such manipulations would be of consequence only if they destroyed important functional relationships.

The notion that my present stage might survive (thanks to some elaborate recording and computing) as a stage of consciousness of some machine is not unique to the Lockean. On the intermediate account, developed from Parfit's, we could make sense of the same phenomenon, as long as the computer program provided survival for enough of my subconscious psychological states and traits as well. Indeed, any conception that takes psychological features as being what matter for identity or survival, and which avoids mystical appeals to the existence of a soul or spiritual essence, will be able to make sense of my surviving in or as a computer program. For the psychological account of the person is the software account. However, it is in considering this software account of the person that we see the real implausibility and weakness in the Lockean account.

On the very high-level conception, not only is it possible to think of psychological states surviving physical rearrangements of the body, or transfer of the psyche to magnetic tape, the conception is also indifferent to changes in the individual's psychological configurations as well. Think of our characters, personalities, modes of response, memories, intentions, and so on all as the products of production processes. These processes manifest their existence by our characteristic forms of speech, behaviour, and action. Now, for all that I or you know, the psychological matter and structure that support such processes may be able to undergo massive changes, while still supporting processes which produce just the same product! Just as the same conscious episodes could be supported by differently configured bodies, so too they might be supported by differently configured minds.

A certain kind of *operationalism* about mental states—emphasizing the way Dennett does the critical links between mind and behaviour—would no doubt find all this quite congenial. So long as the nature of the conscious episodes experienced seem unchanged to me, so long as the behavioural repertoire of my successive stages changes only gradually and along clearly intelligible lines, then my identity need not be bound up with any sameness either of bodily structures or of psychological structures either. What is wrong with this approach is, quite simply, that it flies in the face of our everyday experience and our whole method of approaching the explanation of behaviour. We do not theorize about persons on the basis proposed. On the contrary, we try to find diagnoses of personality disorders by looking for disease or injury affecting specific portions of the body; we recognize that after drinking too much alcohol, someone's reflexes will be impaired, and his or her judgement affected. These are not trivial aberrations about explanation on our part. Rather, they reflect a deep-seated conviction that our mental states and behavioural responses depend on quite specific production processes, any change in which will have significant consequences for our mental life and behaviour. This is not, of course, to deny that different creatures from us might enjoy similar mental lives and behavioural repertoires supported by quite different processes. But the evidence all around us is that the possession of the mammalian nervous system, the operation of systems controlled by the glands, and the development of the brain to a certain degree is precisely what gives the higher animals with which we are familiar their sophistication of response, and whatever inner mental life they may have.

The Lockean conception's weakness, then, is that it stands in a certain tension with our other current views about the nature of explanation in the life sciences. This is not, obviously enough, a knock-down argument against the position. Nor would we expect any respectable philosophical position to be open to knock-down objections in any case. But these considerations do suggest that lower-level conceptions of the person, although they may do less justice to what seems important on the 'inside' view of personal identity, are likely to be more in keeping with our general style of approach to explaining the world we live in. So let us now descend lower than the intermediate conception of personhood in order to explore the prospects for developing a low-level conception of the person. Bearing in mind Williams's remark that our response to other persons (particularly our emotional response) reflects a deeply body-based situation, we might expect to find that some low-level concept of the person would reflect this situation. Surprisingly, however, it turns out that the most plausible of these low-level concepts still fails to do justice to this feature.

The simplest low-level proposal about personal identity makes use of our old intuitive idea of *continuity*. Provided we have continuity of enough of a living human body, we have sameness of person. Thus persons are nothing other than living human bodies. This conception has at least administrative convenience on its side. In the psychiatric or neurological ward, where there are patients with dreadfully disordered lives, we can still apply such a criterion of personhood. We can thus count as one person a patient who suffers from multiple-personality syndrome, or one of our unfortunate amnesics with no long-term memory. Of course, there will be problems aplenty in deciding just how much of the body has to continue, or how much damage to the body can be tolerated, for identity to be sustained. But, to some extent, these problems are no worse for human bodies than they are for other living things. And our survival conditions can be brought into play here, for they do not simply apply to the case of episodic objects. From day to day, we should be able to find a high enough degree of survival of one body-stage in its successor in order for there to be continuing sameness of living body.

This administrative concept of the person does do some justice to our body-based situation. To the extent that our concern for others is a concern for them as individual tokens, we will be concerned for the fate of their bodies (however odd this way of putting the point sounds). But concern for others as tokens does scant justice to that other dimension of concern we have for persons, namely our concern for those aspects of them which could be supported by other bodies. Nor is it clear that, in the case of multiple personality, amnesia, or other unusual conditions, we are right to follow the body condition. Telecloning fantasies only raise in an extreme form some of the problems associated with these real-life cases. However, there is a slightly different account of personal identity which we can offer here, which keeps some of the administrative virtues of the simple body theory while maintaining a conciliatory attitude to the claims on behalf of the importance of psychological relations. This is the version of the body theory that allows the brain, or the brain and certain other parts of the nervous and regulatory systems of the body, to be the components of greatest significance in establishing identity.

We noted that daffodils, just like other living things, have components that are extremely significant for their identity, and others that are not. The loss of a leaf or of a blossom is not destructive of the identity of a daffodil. Likewise, the loss of a finger, or even an arm, however much of a handicap it might prove, is not destructive of the identity of a person. Just as the bulb seemed to have a crucial role for the daffodil's survival, so the brain, and other central controlling systems in the body, seem to have crucial roles. Moreover, the identification of the brain as the crucial component in survival has a further virtue. Our best scientific theories of the nature of personality, memory, perception, concept-use, and so on associate all these faculties with the brain. Without a brain, I would not have those characteristics so important to my being a person. Moreover, it seems plausible to maintain, at least if we incline towards materialism, that as we change and mature, so there are related changes in the matter and structures of our brains.

Notice that this focus on the brain as the important thing does not go all that far towards capturing what is important as far as the Lockean is concerned. If the identity of the person is associated with the persistence of his or her brain, then the best we can do towards characterizing fantasies about the migration of minds is to engage in fantasies about the transplantation of brains. This is— from the point of view of those attracted by high-level accounts— only a bit better than the crude body account. It does, however, give us a way of constructing something like Locke's puzzle case. For we can, if we allow ourselves to speculate about brain transplantation, make some sense of the same person acquiring a new body. If materialism is true, then the focus on brains as the crucial thing, as being the things that matter, neatly welds together physical and psychological accounts of personhood.

Such a materialist account gives us a dualism that is modified with a vengeance. The duality of mental and physical is reduced simply to the duality of different physical things. Notice, though, that the duality of brain and body should not be confused with the duality—noted in the last chapter—between behaviour and body, where behaviour is a repeatable, type phenomenon, and the body is a unique biological token. On the latter duality, brains are as much tokens as any other physical particular and as much as any other parts of the body.

Brains are not only thought of as supporting very high-level conscious episodes. They also, so we think, support all the mundane processing, co-ordination, and problem-solving that any intelligent creature engages in, whether aware of this happening or not. So there looks to be a happy *rapprochement* possible between this version of the body concept and the broad psychological account deriving from our version of Parfit. It may well be—and I am not here trying to deny this for a moment—that in the end, our most useful concept of a person is to be developed along precisely these kinds of lines. Such a development would explain why it is, as we have seen in the last section, that the important survival relation can hold between two *different* people. For if brain hemispheres can be brought into similar informational states, then we could transplant one hemisphere into a new body and that body would then produce behaviour distinctive of—but no longer unique to—the original person. In fact, this procedure for bringing about person fission has already been suggested earlier. In using it, I was tacitly appealing to a view rather like the one now being canvassed, in the expectation that most readers would be prepared to consider as a case of fission one where the obvious carrier of identity (the brain) itself is split, and in so doing carries what matters (psychological connectedness) to a new body.

I have previously identified two kinds of concern we have for others, and for ourselves. One is the concern with phenomena of a *type* (behaviour, moods, styles of response, feelings, and so on), while the other is concern with *token* phenomena (our bias towards specific bodies). Now it would be convenient if the notion of a person as individuated by the brain were to reconcile these two perspectives. That is, it would have helped our conceptual development a great deal if our concern with persons as tokens could be properly described as a concern with their brains. But this, very clearly, is not the case. The trouble with our dual concern is that to talk, for example, of our love for someone, our urge to be with them, our desire to touch and hold them, and so on is not readily translated into talk of love for a brain, or a desire to touch and hold a brain. On the contrary, our interest in bodies is far more closely tied to external features of the body. If we had to choose one bodily feature, it is probably true to say that most of us would find the *face* by far the most important, and significant part, of another person's body. It is not only grotesque, but also definitely misleading, then, to imagine the brain as being in any way the focus of our interest in others as tokens.

Since it is relatively easy to imagine brain transplantation that moves the brain of someone we love into a body of a different sex, age, shape, and so forth, it is clear that the brain-based concept of personhood, like the higher-level concepts, captures some of the things we believe and think about persons without capturing all of this.[6] By contrast, the low-level body account does justice to our response to persons as tokens, admittedly, but only at the cost of ignoring our interest in persons as producers of types of behaviour and response. But notice that the duality of type and token persists even when we give a materialist account of the mind. It is the existence of behaviour, of action (including language), of mood, and so on which gives rise to our difficulty. We value persons not only for what they are as bodies but for what they are as producers of behaviour. None of the concepts so far developed do justice to this duality. Yet it is the very existence of such a duality that leads us into some of the hardest puzzles about personal identity (to the extent that these are different from puzzles about artefact and animal identity).

Our everyday talk about persons can now be viewed in the light of what has just been argued. We normally operate with a concept of personhood that is unexamined. It is used variously to apply to very different kinds of situations—situations in which we talk about our feelings for others, situations in which we discuss our beliefs about the differences between humans and animals, situations in which

---

[6] See, e.g., Puccetti [1] and the response in Brennan [1]. Needless to say, my views on persons have changed greatly since writing Brennan [1].

we ascribe responsibility for actions, and so on. One part of the web of rules, associations, and inferences associated with this concept is that persons are rational beings, endowed with high-level abilities, like memory, the ability to intend, to reason, to be aware of some of their own inner goings-on, and the ability to speak in highly sophisticated ways. Another part of the same web associates value with the possession of person status: persons are not only different from other animals, but they have rights and duties which the other animals do not. Persons are also proper objects of caring, love, and regard—but this time, we admit that other creatures can also be objects of these things. The difference is more one of degree than kind. What may seem to have emerged from our argument so far is that no one thing can possibly satisfy all these desiderata. So our everyday concept of the person is perhaps confused, or vague, or indeterminate.

In such a situation, can we wonder that no development of the concept of the person meets all the constraints we want to put on it? For these constraints themselves apparently derive from everyday confusion—not to put too fine a point on it. Is there then not something to be said for pressing ahead with what seems the most sensible form of conceptual development? Maybe, for example, we should give up our view that the object of my love—as object of love—is a person, reserving the concept of *person* for items that are rational and possessors of a special sort of value. But the people I love are rational, and possessors of a special sort of value. I also love things other than people. I love certain bits of nature, and certain books. But this does not confuse me. I do not think the natural things I love are rational items (I am sure trees are not rational), nor do I confuse the value of books with the value of my friends and loved ones. We cannot, in other words, press ahead with the most sensible form of conceptual development simply because we have as yet no grasp on the question of which development of the concept of a person is more *sensible* than any other.

Such a conclusion is not meant to undermine the efforts of the Lockeans, or Parfit, or even the body theorists. It is important, after all, that theorizing goes on. For in a situation of confusion, we are naturally driven to seek clarification. My conclusion, then, should be read as an interim one. In the present situation, we have several developments of the concept of a person available. These are in competition with one another. But none is yet worthy of commendation over its rivals. Much more theorizing and exploration in conceptual development may be necessary before we can get any further in the area.

10.3. NAGEL'S BRAIN

Given the attractions of the brain theory of personal identity, it is not surprising that some theorists have spent some time arguing for its plausibility. As with all conceptual development, they are on firm ground here. For the problem of development is not whether we can work up plausible concepts, but rather whether these concepts are more useful than their rivals. However, in the spirit of contributing to the theorizing that is essential to this area. I will look briefly in this section at one aspect of a brain theory. This is Nagel's unpublished account, discussed by Parfit in an appendix to his book.[7]

Nagel defends a reductionist account of personal identity. Where he differs from Parfit is by holding that I am *essentially* my brain, and that the identity of my brain is what matters. It follows, on Nagel's account, that destruction of my brain is the destruction of what matters. Thus I am unable to survive a process which involves destroying my brain. Now, as must be clear, Parfit is bound to disagree with this. What I want to show in the present section is simply that we can defend the view that I can survive the destruction of my brain, while staying closer to Nagel's view than to Parfit's. The reason is that Nagel has not noticed the importance of our three conditions on survival. Indeed, the case that Parfit introduces in order to undermine Nagel's account is one which need not be described as the destruction of the brain at all.

Parfit is concerned to show that the identity of the brain need not be what matters when it comes to the survival question. Instead of directly discussing Nagel's account of telecloning, he takes two cases which differ by less than the difference there is between destruction of the brain (and production of a replica by telecloning) on the one hand and ordinary continuation of the brain on the other. Parfit imagines that all his brain cells have a defect which, in time, would prove fatal, but which can be rectified by surgery which

---

[7] See Appendix D of Parfit [4].

replaces each defective cell by replicas which lack the defect. He considers the following cases:

In *Case One* the surgeon performs a hundred operations. In each of these he removes a hundredth part of my brain, and inserts a replica of this part. In *Case Two*, the surgeon follows a different procedure. He first removes all the parts of my brain and then inserts all of their replicas.

He then describes the difference between these two cases in the following terms:

In Case One, each of the new parts of my brain is for a time joined to the rest of my brain. This enables each new part to become part of my brain. . . . In Case Two, things are different. There are not times when each new part is joined to the rest of my brain. Because of this, the new parts do not count as parts of my brain. My brain ceases to exist.

Unfortunately, things are rather more complicated here than Parfit suggests. He wants to go on to argue that the cases pose Nagel a problem. Since the first case does not involve destruction of my brain, while the second does, Nagel is forced into defending the view that I survive in one case but not in the other. And this cannot be right:

Can *my* fate depend on the difference in the ordering of removals and insertions? Can it be so important, for my survival, whether the new parts are, for a time, joined to the old parts? . . . He [Nagel] suggests both (1) that identity is what matters, and (2) that he is his brain. . . . When I consider Cases One and Two, I find it impossible to believe both (1) and (2).[8]

But although we might at first be inclined to agree with Parfit here, we will come to a different verdict if we go back to think about simple cases involving replication.

As we saw earlier, there are great problems about artefact identity. Indeed, our notions about artefacts make it very difficult to come up with a decent theory of identity for them. At least some of the time, we allow that quite massive replacements of an artefact's parts may not interfere with its identity. Recall the case of the car enthusiast described in Chapter 6.3. All sorts of part replacements were put down to the processes of 'modifying' or 'hotting up' the original car. Maybe Parfit has this sort of case in mind when he

---

[8] These, and the previous quotations from Parfit, all come from Appendix D to his book.

writes that the gradual replacement of parts results in the new parts becoming part of the original object. Hirsch suggests, rather optimistically in my view, that so long as we replace no more than a third of an artefact's parts at one time, then we do not destroy the artefact.[9] So I can replace a third of my car's parts on Monday, another third of them on Tuesday and the final third on Wednesday without having destroyed my car.

Now what we need to distinguish in this sort of case is the difference between replacing old parts with *new* parts and replacing parts with *replicas* copied from the old parts. We saw before that there were a number of different things covered by our use of the term 'replica'. Thus we distinguished replicas produced by *copying* both from *adventitious replicas* (produced by chance) and from replicas produced by *production* processes. So let us make clear here just what the difference in this context amounts to. If I am to replicate by copying the shock absorber that has just been removed from my car, I need to engage in a manufacturing process that uses the original shock absorber as its prototype. My process, then, involves a *copying process* as part of it. Indeed, to produce an exact replica, I will have to construct my new shock absorber out of old parts, or artificially age the components I use so as to replicate the exact condition of the old shock absorber. Now, if my replacement of my car parts is of this sort, it is arguable (modulo doubts on a general theory of artefact identity) that my car will stay the same throughout the replacement of a great many of its parts (and let us ignore the question of *how many* a great many is).

By contrast, if I am replacing old shock absorbers by new ones which are not modelled on the old ones, we find ourselves in a difficulty. Of course, it might be—to take the closest case to the one just discussed—that our new shock absorbers have been produced by the same production process that produced the original ones. They will thus be new tokens of the same type as the original. But, since they are not modelled on the original, the original does not, according to our previously defended position, *survive* in or as these new shock absorbers. Such a consideration is not, of course, fatal to the car's identity. A change in one or two components does not seem to affect the identity of the larger artefact, even where the original components have been replaced by ones of a different design. And

---

[9] See Hirsch [2], ch. 7.

in this case, what Parfit says seems to be true. The new parts, even if they do not match the originals, become *part* of the larger artefact simply by fitting into the overall structure of the larger item. So long as the process of replacement is gradual, we feel no violence done to our intuitions by the claim that the artefact has retained its identity (though this is still being said with due caution, in view of our general worries about artefact identity).

Telecloning, on our account, is rather different from this last kind of case. For in telecloning, the original plays an important *causal* role in the production of the replica. It is because of the causal role, together with the satisfaction of our structure and matter conditions, that it seemed so natural to maintain that items can survive the teleclone. Now what Parfit has not mentioned in the case of the two operations is the causal role played by the original brain cells. But, in keeping with our earlier conclusions, it should now be clear that this is a matter of some importance.

How, after all, is the surgeon to go about replacing my brain cells with non-defective replicas? Presumably, if I am to survive the process, then either there is a bigger difference between the two cases than Parfit mentions, or they are similar in respect of causality. First consider the latter. If I am my brain, then presumably certain structures in my brain will be distinctive of me, and would need to be preserved in order for me to be preserved. It may even be that certain structural features of my brain cells would need to be preserved in order for me to be preserved. Let us assume that this is so. Parfit, then, is assuming that the surgeon's intervention retains these structural features of my cells that are distinctive when putting in replicas of my cells. The replicas will keep those features of structure, and be in those structural relations to other cells, that are distinctive of me.

But if this is how the case is meant to be understood, then there is no difference, as Parfit indeed says, between the two cases. But Nagel need make no difference between them either. For what happens in Case One *and* in Case Two is that my brain cells play a crucial causal role in the production of their replicas. Thus my brain cells, individually, survive as the new cells. And thus my brain survives as the new brain. Of course, it is an open question whether we should now associate this case with the case of the episodic hill in Chapter 4. In the latter case, the chain of surviving stages were all allocated to the one hill. And Nagel would certainly be able to say of both Parfit's cases that what has happened is that my brain has persisted despite the changes in cells between stages. The survival of the damaged cells as their replicas would underpin this very identification.

Let us suppose, for the sake of the argument, that Nagel did indeed take such a line. Then the claim that I am my brain does not need to be modified in the light of the Parfit example. By contrast, suppose that, somehow or other, my existing brain cells play no causal role in the production of the non-defective cells inserted by the surgeon. This time we can imagine, perhaps, that new brain cells can be grown in some appropriate culture or medium, and that one health brain cell is pretty well like another. But now there would seem to be a real difficulty in understanding how I could survive both operations. Maybe what happens is like this. What makes me the person I am are certain brain structures and certain electro-chemical states and changes in my brain. Any old brain cells could support such structures and so the gradual replacement of my brain cells does not threaten its identity. As each new cell is inserted, it gets organized into certain overall structural patterns, and receives appropriate chemical messages which in turn modify its responses to other electro-chemical signals.

In this sort of case, it would be a matter of some importance whether my cells are replaced gradually or all at once. For, in order to be incorporated into the right structures and be responsive in an appropriate way to electro-chemical signals, new cells have to be associated with the existing arrangement of old ones. The sudden replacement of all my brain cells would involve the destruction of that brain, for it would involve destruction of the structures that were distinctive of it. In this case, then, Parfit's two operations have very different consequences. Indeed, we would readily understand it if Nagel chose to maintain that I do persist through the one operation, but cease to exist given the other.

In fact, these two cases are simply drawn from a whole spectrum of cases which could be considered. But, whatever kind of case we chose to discuss, much would depend on the *copying* question. Survival requires the participation of an original (stage, or item) in the causal process, that results in the existence of the item or stage in which the original survives. Of course we can argue about the relation of survival to identity, as we have been doing all through this book. But Parfit's two cases do not pose the fatal dilemma for the brain theorist that he imagines. The brain theorist may, or may not, be committed to the view that identity is what matters. But what such a theorist has to be committed to is the view that the identity, or the survival, of the brain is what matters for a person's identity or survival. If anything, the attractiveness of the brain theory is increased by the way it responds to the cases imagined by Parfit.

10.4. FORENSIC CONCEPTIONS OF THE SELF

In exploring various developments of the concept of a person, we have repeatedly come up against the same difficulty. Although a paticular development commends itself as plausible, we seem to be unable to marshal considerations that can decide for us whether this development is more useful or productive than any of its rivals. We do not know how to assess values the concept may have in these cases. But why should we be faced with such a difficulty?

One reason for this may be that we have no idea how to set about testing one particular development against its rivals. Consider, by contrast, the case in the sciences. Although writers like Quine have suggested that there is no hard and fast theory–observation distinction, we regularly do make such a distinction.[10] Even if we admit, with Quine, that the boundary between them is not fixed, we can make some distinction between theory, as that which is set up for test, and observational data, as desiderata against which the theory is to be tested.

But in the case of our theories of the person, we have no clear idea of what the body of testing data would be. We are dealing, after all, with *intuitions*, notions that we have in advance of all our conceptual analyis and development. Unless we can find some principled way of weighting these pre-theoretic intuitions, we can have no principled way of settling upon some as data against which our theory of the person is to be tested. Of course, we could settle, in some given case, for some intuitions to be held constant, so to speak, and use these as the testing-bed of theory. Indeed, this seems to be how philosophers often proceed. But these intuitions may them-

---

[10] Hence his ability to treat ordinary particulars as posits of theory (in, e.g., Quine [2] ch. 1): see ch. 7, n. 8.

selves be challenged by some other development of the concepts we are studying. In some cases, we may claim that *general agreement* settles which intuitions are the most central. But the literature alone on personal identity bears witness to the fact that there is no such agreement in the case of our concept of a person.

We can point up the difficulty very clearly by reflecting on the role of the concept in moral philosophy. Locke puts the moral and legal role of persons in the following terms:

Where-ever a Man find what he calls *himself*, there I think another may say is the same *Person*. It is a Forensick Term appropriating Actions and their Merit; and so belongs only to intelligent Agents capable of a Law, and Happiness and Misery. . . . whatever past Actions it cannot reconcile or appropriate to that present *self* by consciousness, it can no more be concerned in, than if they have never been done: And to receive Pleasure or Pain; i.e. Reward or Punishment, on the account of any such Action, is all one, as to be made happy or miserable in its first being, without any demerit at all. For suppose a Man punish'd now, for what he had done in another Life, whereof he could be made to have no consciousness at all, what difference is there between that Punishment and being created miserable?[11]

There seems to be a certain force in Locke's observations. Yet the difficulty with this forensic concept is knowing whether we should reject theories that permit one person to be responsible for the deeds of another, but which make sense of Parfit-style survival, or whether, by contrast, we should take Locke's own passage here as developing a theory of the person which itself can be tested against our other views.

We can think briefly, then, about what to say on the legal issues posed by the forensic concept when taken in conjunction with what we know about amnesia. Studies of various amnesias show that certain patients are genuinely afflicted with loss of memory. Is it right, then, to try such a patient for an offence which the patient cannot now recall committing (although there is psychological coherence, let us suppose, between the person committing the offence and the patient before us, as well as bodily continuity). If the law is not to be an ass, then it must make the tests for the presence of amnesia very stringent. And even Locke noticed that there may be such a difficulty here that amnesia is no more of an excuse than drunkenness.

[11] Locke [1], II. 27.

Gibbens and Hall Williams give attention to the question of whether, in the case of an absolutely genuine amnesia, there would be a problem about the accused's fitness to plead. They point out: 'Many trials proceed in the absence of a witness whom the accused considers essential for his defence, or without the assistance of the evidence of the accused himself. Amnesia would therefore not appear to be relevant on this preliminary issue . . .'[12] But the Lockean would here object to the use of the comfortably vague term 'the accused'. If they mean that the accused may be the same person as did the criminal deed, although now genuinely amnesic with respect to that deed, then they are simply operating with a different concept of the person from Locke's one. They are begging the question against the Lockean.

If, however, the issue of the accused's identity with the perpetrator of the criminal act is still open, and depends on the accused genuinely remembering doing the deed, then the problem is not one of fitness to plead. Rather, on Locke's view, the wrong person is being accused of the crime, for the person who did commit it no longer exists.

It might now be argued that we were wrong to take this difficulty in the first instance as being a difficulty about theory and observation. An objector might want to say that the problem concerns, rather, the collision of two different theories of the person. Such an objection does not take us very far, even if we were to concede some of its force. For when two theories collide, we are able to check them for coherence with the rest of our body of theory, and also to test both of them against some shared observational evidence. After all, if there were no such shared observations or predictions common to both theories, what sense could we make of their rivalry?

Applying this to the case in hand, we then have to take the forensic conception, and—let us say—the body conception, as two rival theories which we must test against our other other intuitions, taken as data. We also have to think about other areas of theory— moral theory, our theories about other objects and their identity, and so forth—with which we are to make our theory of the person cohere. But again, I would argue, the hope for progress is doubtful. Duhem's thesis that hypotheses can be indefinitely retained even in

---

[12] In Whitty and Zangwill [1], p. 260.

the face of adverse data hits us with a vengeance.[13] For we are operating in an area of great conceptual indeterminacy. We cannot look to our theories of the identity of other kinds of things, nor to our theory of morality, for the kind of definitive test that would settle the issue for or against the Lockean. Instead, as Quine has so forcefully argued in other contexts, we are faced with the possibility of making compensatory adjustments else where to accommodate whatever theory of the person we choose to fix on.[14]

The progress of science is slow. If I were a good Quinean, then I might be consoled by the thought that at least some of the theorizing in this book may itself have contributed to the development one day of a theory of the person within some appropriate branch of science. But anyone who is that much of a Quinean ought also to be sceptical enough to recognize that the indeterminacy in the concept of a person, like other conceptual indeterminacies, is liable to be around for some time. Early in my treatment, I pointed out that the notion of conceptual indeterminacy I am using is not meant to be the same as Quine's notion of translational indeterminacy or the associated notion of inscrutability of reference.[15] That point still stands. But the weaker thesis I have defended here, namely that our everyday notions about persons are vague, probably confused, possibly inconsistent, and capable of development in a variety of ways, is still alive and well. Persons, as we might have suspected all along, have proved to be somewhat more complicated objects than hills or lakes. So our modest success at developing an account of identity, based on survival, for other particulars has not carried over to the case of persons.

---

[13] See Duhem [1] and Quine's repeated defence of this position.

[14] One of Quine's classic statements of this position is in 'Two Dogmas of Empiricism': 'The totality of our so-called knowledge or beliefs, from the most casual matters of geography and history to the profoundest laws of atomic physics or even of pure mathematics and logic, is a man-made fabric which impinges on experience only along the edges. A conflict with experience at the periphery occasions readjustments in the interior of the field. Truth values have to be redistributed over some of our statements. Reevaluation of some statements entails reevaluation of others, because of their logical interconections . . . But the total field is so underdetermined by its boundary conditions, experience, that there is much lattitude of choice as to what statements to reevaluate in the light of any single contrary experience.' (Quine [1], pp. 42–3.)

[15] See the title essay of Quine [7].

10.5. PROSPECTS AND RETROSPECTS

The present chapter opened by making one last attempt to develop a useful concept of the person along Parfit's lines. This time, a way was shown of making survival in our sense constitutive of personal identity. The enterprise was moderately sucessful, and can be applied to cases of equal and of unequal branching.

However, a new difficulty with developing a concept of the person was then identified. According to it, there are different levels at which the concept can be developed. Our normal thinking about persons does not give any guidance about which is the preferred level of development. In combination with the type–token problem, this threatened to spell the end of conceptual development in this area.

One way of tackling the new difficulty involved taking a materialist stand, and letting the identity of the person be associated with the identity of a brain. Although the materialist account brings us no nearer to solving the type–token problem it does survive what Parfit puts forward as a 'fatal' dilemma for it. A brief consideration of the forensic conception of the person again pointed up the difficulty faced by those engaged in conceptual development. This time, we have to notice the difficulty of deciding what counts as data against which to test our theory of the person.

In an attempt to disarm one part of my negative pronouncements on the problem of persons, it might be argued that the type–token dualism afflicting our thinking about persons is no worse than the ambiguity of dimensions afflicting our normal consideration of particulars. Perhaps persons can be viewed under either guise, just as particulars can be viewed as three-, four-, or even five-dimensional. The difference, as I will argue in a moment, between type and token notions of the person is not akin to a difference in dimension.

It may now seem hardly surprising that some theorists of the person are foundationalist or non-reductionist. Both body-based and connectedness-based theories looked promising, but have proved to have difficulties associated with them. If we return to Strawson's well-known argument that persons are essentially subjects both of predicates ascribing mental states and predicates ascribing physical states, this gets us out of some of our difficulties.[16] If the move is coupled, as it was in Strawson's original argument, with an appeal to the primitiveness of the concept of the person, then, as we have seen, the cost of the move is that it avoids the issue of saying in what the unity of a person consists.

It strikes me, however, that the case of persons is rather different from the earlier puzzle case involving artefacts. It was clear that certain very general difficulties make it unlikely that we could ever come up with a decent theory of artefact identity, even when applying the apparatus of survival theory. The chain theory will, certainly, give us some account of the unity of artefacts, but the relation of structure to function was too loose to enable it to apply to the cases where it was most needed—those where dispute is possible.

However intractable the case of artefacts, there is not a similar problem in the case of persons. For it is now clear that the chain theory can work on either a body-based account (where this account includes suitable reference to brains) or on a connectedness-based account. Our problem is in determining whether persons are best thought of in one or other of these ways. Taking the latter account first, it has been shown that neither amnesia, nor ownership, are real problems for the psychological account of unity. Rather, the real problem is that no psychological account will apparently do justice to our concept of persons as individual, body-based 'tokens'. Although Parfit and others have tried to show that our concern for bodies is not a concern for what is important, it is wrong, in my view, to dismiss our body-mindedness as mere bias. Rather, a good psychological theory will either find some way of doing justice to this aspect of our thinking or reveal clearly why it should be abandoned. As far as I can see, natural though the connectedness account is, it fails to deal adequately with this pre-theoretic attitude.

Even attaching a connectedness-based account to one part of the body—the brain—and arguing that we then have a *rapprochement* between materialism and psychological considerations does not do the trick. It is tempting to see a whole chain of reductions taking place here. First, the high-level psychological connections mentioned by Parfit are reduced to the interaction of variously structured mechanisms. These mental devices are reduced in turn

---

[16] See n. 33 to Ch. 8.

to interacting complexes of simpler mechanisms until we reach a point where we are comfortable about identifying the psychological with the physical. If I am still the same person I was ten years ago, then presumably my present states are connected to a suitably high degree with the states I had then. If we go along with the reduction, then this means that there is some appropriate causal relation between my brain structures now and my brain structures then—a relation that supports this psychological unity.

As we have seen, however, concern for, and care about, brains is no part of our usual concern for someone thought of as an individual, embodied token. But to go all the way and identify the person with the body (including brain, heart, liver, endocrine system, and everything else) ignores the plain fact that it is the doings, the experiencings, the desirings and strivings that matter to us just as much as the body which supports these things. Nor is it just the case that we value the actual doings as much as we value the body that does them. Recall, for a moment, the five-dimensional view of particulars. There is a double potential for persons, viewed as being either tokens or types, hardware or software. I could be the same, in a sense, while yet my body is (within limits) different. My body could be the same while yet my behaviour, styles of response, loves, and hates are (within limits) different. There is, after all, a sad truth in the observation that sometimes we love people for what they might have been as much as for what they are. The 'might have been' for persons ranges over the two domains which are at the root of our problem.

There are yet further complications in the story about persons that have not even been mentioned. We might wish to talk of persons as systems in which certain production processes, recipes for behaviour, interact with the behaviour produced. But this would be a feeble attempt at giving the ecology of persons. For it would ignore two things, already familiar in some philosophical traditions, but ignored in recent analytical work. Dewey, for example, would protest that we spend too little time in explaining how the individuality of a person is at least in part a function of involvements with others; for action involves location within a community of persons, and individuation requires different involvements in different groups. He would also remind us of the need to take account of *growth*—the process which involves the continuous interpretation and reconstruction of experience.[17] Any account of psychological connectedness informed by Dewey's insights would allow that my view of what I was doing *then* is to some extent coloured by the position I am in *now*. Such considerations are familiar to students of literature, but the subtleties of a Proust, for example, are ignored by the thin accounts of memory and experience given in books like this.

So if we were tempted to explore the ecological dimension of personal unity, we would have to give due weight to the dynamics of the person, and the relation of the person to other persons and the rest of the environment. An exploration along these lines might well model itself on the ecology of daffodils; for they too contain recipes for behaviour—the pushing up of shoots and bursting into annual bloom—and are affected by their environments. But I am personally sceptical about the prospects for any such investigation. The dual nature of our conception of the person is, I suspect, likely to be as great a stumbling-block for the systems theorist as for the hardy analyst.

Before succumbing to a sense of failure in the face of these reflections, they can be put into perspective by considering the gains that have been made so far. Although we do not have a comprehensive theory of unity for every conceivable sort of thing, a general framework is available for approaching unity or identity questions. Take, for example, a case not so far considered. Biologists commonly talk of species as staying the same through countless generations. In other cases, however, a current species is classed simply as a descendant of an earlier one. It looks

---

[17] The central theme of the early chapters of Dewey [1] is that growth, or self-renewal, involves living things in interaction with their environment. The environment itself is what promotes, stimulates, inhibits, or hinders the characteristic activities of living things. For human beings, a *social* environment is an indispensible condition of the realization of the individual's tendencies. Famously, Dewey's conception of growth is linked to particular development he makes of the concept of education. The school, according to his theory, should be a special growth-promoting environment, which simplifies the complexity of the wider social environment, eliminates less worthy features of it, and overcomes limitations of the social groups into which individual persons were born. The growth and reconstruction associated with living and with education go on throughout each person's life, according to Dewey. Moreover, if his association of types of life and growth with the nature of democratic society is correct, it would follow that different social organizations would produce different kinds of persons. For more on Dewey, and on conceptual development in eduction, see my 'Analysis, Development and Education' in the *British Journal of Educational Studies*, 24 (1986).

overhwelmingly plausible to suggest that we can best regiment discussion of the cases involved by thinking of the matter in terms of the survival of species. To do so, we would have to investigate just what constitutes the matter and structure of a species—an issue that the modern systematists have already studied. For them, a species is a superindividual, a breeding population, whose components are the particular plants or animals.[18] Then we would need to consider the nature of causal connections between stages of a species, to try to distinguish these cases where there is survival of a high enough degree for unity from those where there is survival without identity.

The applicability of the conditions to this case is not surprising. After making a case early on for the utility of the general framework, its subsequent application to the problem of discontinuity and to the quite separate problem of amnesia and branching amply confirms its value. That the general framework of survival theory stands in close relations to plausible psychological models of how we latch on to structures in the world gives it, in my view, further credibility. The rejection of what was called the 'extensionalist myth' thus seems well founded, even if, in these matters, there is no possibility of conclusive refutation.

A number of other results have been established, including some that discredit well-known strategies in metaphysics and the theory of identity. Spatio-temporal continuity has been shown to be fairly worthless in giving an account of the identity of anything; given the difficulties in making precise just what our intuitive notion of continuity is meant to embrace, this result is fortunate. In the case of the concept of *sortal*, I have argued that it is less primitive than the concept of structure, and can mislead us if used in the theory of survival. Survival, after all, can be a relation between different sorts of things. Our recognition of survival is thus more closely in touch

[18] The conception of species as individuals is a response of sorts to Ghiselin and Hull's arguments that species are not natural kinds. For discussion and references see Sober [1]. The case of species is just one of many that might have been mentioned. For other examples, consider the claims that can be made about societies, or cultures. Like species, cultures can develop, change, grow, decline, or thrive without losing their identity. Only by examining these sorts of cases in detail could we get to grips with the Eusa problem and produce a decent account of the metric of change. For in all cases, retention of identity, I suspect, will depend on there not being too much change in matter and structure between stages remote in time. Apart from the denial that limits to change are sortal relative, I am conscious of not having suggested so far any positive theory of change.

with the genuine similarities and differences in the world than our recognition of sorts.

It is against this background, I think, that we should view our problems about personal identity. No doubt it would have been pleasant to find some overwhelming support for the 'token' theory of the person, for this comes closest to expressing my own pre-theoretic beliefs. But to adopt this account would be impossible unless I were to close my eyes to the persuasive arguments that support the 'type' theory. It is necessary, then, to recognize virtues in both accounts, and to voice, therefore, the suspicion that we are systematically ambiguous in our references to, and our thinking about, persons. The ambiguity isolated may simply be one of many that afflicts our reflections on this topic. Considering the matter thus in terms of ambiguity might give us some hope that the situation is not so bad as I have been making out. After all, it was argued in Chapter 5 that particulars are not 'really' three-, or four-, or even five-dimensional. So might it not be suggested that the ambiguity about persons is no worse than this: persons are not really tokens or types, but can be viewed now in this, and now in that, way.

The ambiguities, however, are not similar, and even this last hope of comfort has to be set aside. It is entirely understandable that we do not switch vocabulary when switching our attention from one dimension to another. So any exploration of different dimensions is bound to bring in its train the kind of ambiguity isolated in the fifth chapter. But nothing similar to switching dimensions is taking place when we think about persons. Rather, if my diagnosis has been correct, there is something of which we are not normally aware when we refer to persons. This is that we bring two very different, and irreconcilable, kinds of assessment to bear when we consider the question of their unity.

To put the disanalogy between the two kinds of case in a crude way, we might say that the point about dimensions applies to items that are one and the same, whatever level we are using to describe them. A particular like my desk is the same particular whether I am describing it in three-, four-, or five-dimensional terms. The ambiguity in our thinking about desks is thus not an ambiguity about the number of objects being described: there is *not* a three-dimensional desk in my office sharing space—but not time—with a four-dimensional particular. By contrast, our difficulty with the mode of describing and responding to persons is precisely a difficulty about the object of our attention. If recipes and behaviour make a person, then a person is a different sort of thing from an individual token. If I am right about our different modes of response to persons, then the situation is like one where two different things compete for our attention, evaluation, and care. When we try to focus our analytical gaze on persons we cannot escape a kind of double vision.

At the risk of emphasising the obvious, let me repeat that the duality in our view of persons discussed here and at the end of Chapter 9 is not the familiar duality of the mental and the physical, though it is easily confused with it. The discovery of this duality is, to my mind, one of the most important outcomes of the discussion in the last three chapters. The result is not just a limitation on survival theory, but a problem for any account of persons, however reductionist or non-reductionist it is. It should also be clear by now that my own commitment to reductionism is not of great eliminative significance.

My own view on the issue of reductionism is quite simple. A complex artefact is a collection of parts, but has properties that its individual parts lack. None the less, we can explain the properties of the whole item by reference to properties of its parts. A scientific account of the powers and capacities of whole natural objects will likewise explain what their features consist in by appeal to the features of the parts and their relations to each other. Just so is it, in my view, with the property of unity or identity. In saying that the unity of a particular consists in certain causal relations among its spatial or spatio-temporal parts, we only in a sense reduce that particular to its parts.

To insist that a broad particular is no more than a sum of spatio-temporal parts would be like maintaining that a complex, structured item is simply an aggregate of matter. Certainly there is a limited way in which this is true. One problem with taking the latter line, as we have seen, is that things like statues become indistinguishable from mere lumps of clay. This would be reductionism with a vengeance, and would involve an implausible impoverishment in our descriptions of the universe to which I have no commitment. But just as a statue is clay with structure, so a particular thought of in terms of its spatio-temporal extent is a sequence of stages with structure—this structure being defined at least in part by the survival relation as I have described it. No doubt this crude way with the issue of reductionism leaves many questions unanswered, but these can be left for exploration in other places.

If I were now to start on the project of the book, knowing what I now know, and armed with the discoveries, hunches, and arguments that are scattered through the preceding pages, the result—I hope—would be a clearer, more focused account of problems involving identity. However, the same major themes would be stressed in much the same order. The claims of the survival account over any elucidation in terms of spatio-temporal continuity, the dimensional ambiguity of particulars, the theory of real possibility, the rejection of the extensionalist myth, the denial of the importance of memory to self-identity, and the seemingly irresolvable duality in our thinking about persons as types and persons as tokens—these would all have a central place in any revised version. As it is, any reader stimulated by what is written in the present version will, I hope, be able to approach the study of identity aware of some of the pitfalls to be avoided and of the problems yet to be solved.

Bibliography

The bibliography, although selective, is meant to be relatively comprehensive and lists several works that are not cited in the main body of the book.

Ackermann, R. [1]. 'Sortal Predicates and Confirmation', *Philosophical Studies*, 20 (1969).

Adams, R. [1]. 'Primitive Thisness and Primitive Identity', *Journal of Philosophy*, 76 (1979).

Albritton, Rogers [1]. 'On Wittgenstein's Use of the Term "Criterion" ', in Pitcher [1].

Ames, L. L., jun. [1]. 'The Genesis of Carbon Apatite', *Economic Geology*, 54 (1959).

Anderson, A. R., and Belnap, N. D. [1]. *Entailment* (Princeton: Princeton University Press, 1975).

Anscombe, G. E. M. [1]. 'The Principle of Individuation', *Proceedings of the Aristotelian Society*, Suppl. Vol. 27 (1953).

Aristotle [1]. *The Works of Aristotle*, ed. W. D. Ross (Oxford: Oxford University Press, 1929–52).

Aschkenasy, Jeannie, and Odom, R. D. [1]. 'Classification and Perceptual Development', *Journal of Experimental Child Psychology*, 34 (1982).

Ayer, A. J. [1]. *Philosophical Essays* [London: Macmillan, 1954).

—— [2]. *The Problem of Knowledge* (Harmondsworth: Penguin, 1956).

—— [3]. *The Concept of a Person, and Other Essays* (London: Macmillan, 1964).

—— [4]. 'Identity and Reference', *Philosophia*, 5 (1975).

Ayers, Michael R. [1]. 'Individuals Without Sortals', *Canadian Journal of Philosophy*, 4 (1974).

Barcan (Marcus), Ruth [1]. 'The Identity of Individuals in a Strict Functional Calculus of Second Order', *Journal of Symbolic Logic*, 12 (1947).

—— [2]. 'Interpreting Quantification', *Inquiry*, 5 (1962).

—— [3]. 'Essential Attribution', *Journal of Philosophy*, 68 (1971).

Benacerraf, Paul [1]. 'What Numbers Could Not Be', *Philosophical Review*, 74 (1965).

Bennett, Daniel [1]. 'Essential Properties', *Journal of Philosophy*, 66 (1969).

Bennett, J. [1]. *Kant's Analytic* (Cambridge: Cambridge University Press, 1966).

Bertalanffy, L. von, and Rapoport, A. (eds.) [1]. *General Systems Theory* (Ann Arbor: 1962).

Black, Max [1]. 'The Identity of Indiscernibles', *Mind*, 61 (1952); reprinted in Loux [1].

Borst, C. V. (ed.) [1]. *The Mind-Brain Identity Theory* (London: Macmillan, 1970).

Bradley, M. C. [1]. Critical Notice of Wiggins, *Identity and Spatio-Temporal Continuity*, in *Australasian Journal of Philosophy*, 47 (1969), 69–79.

Brennan, Andrew [1]. 'Persons and Their Brains', *Analysis*, 30 (1969).

—— [2]. 'Personal Identity and Personal Survival', *Analysis*, 41 (1982).

—— [3]. 'Survival', *Synthese*, 59 (1984).

—— [4]. Critical Study of E. Hirsch, *The Concept of Identity*, in *Nous*, 18 (1984).

—— [5]. 'Amnesia and Psychological Continuity', in Copp, R. and McIntosh, J. J., *New Essays in the Philosophy of Mind* (*Canadian Journal of Philosophy* Suppl. Vol. 11, 1985).

Brody, Baruch [1]. 'Locke on the Identity of Persons', *American Philosophical Quarterly*, 9 (1972).

—— [2]. 'Why Settle for Anything Less Than Good Old-Fashioned Aristotelian Essentialism?', *Nous*, 7 (1973).

—— [3]. *Identity and Essence* (Princeton: Princeton University Press, 1980).

Burge, Tyler [1]. 'A Theory of Aggregates', *Nous*, 11 (1977).

—— [2]. 'Belief De Re', *Journal of Philosophy*, 74 (1977).

—— [3]. 'Mass Terms, Count Nouns and Change', *Synthese*, 31 (1975).

Butler, J. [1]. 'Of Personal identity' (first dissertation to *The Analogy of Religion*), printed in Flew [3] and in Perry [5].

Care, N. and Grimm, R. H. [1]. *Perception and Personal Identity* (Cleveland: Ohio University Press, 1969).

Carnap, R. [1]. *Meaning and Necessity* (2nd edn.; Chicago: Chicago University Press, 1956).

Carter, W. R. [1]. 'On Contingent Identity and Temporal Worms', *Philosophical Studies*, 41 [1982] 213–30.

Cartwright, Helen M. [1]. 'Quantities', *Philosophical Review*, 79 (1970).

—— [2]. 'Heraclitus and the Bath Water', *Philosophical Review*, 74 (1965).

—— [3]. Review of Wiggins. *Sameness and Substance*, in *Philosophical Review*, 92 (1982).

Cartwright, Richard [1]. 'Identity and Substitutivity', in Munitz [1].

—— [2]. 'Scattered Objects'. in Lehrer, K. (ed.), *Analysis and Metaphysics* (Dordrecht: D. Reidel, 1975).

—— [3]. 'Indiscernibility Principles', *Midwest Studies in Philosophy*, 4 (1979).

Castañeda, Hector-Neri [1]. 'Identity and Sameness', *Philosophia*, 5 (1975).

Chandler, H. S. [1]. 'Wiggins on Identity', *Analysis*, 29 (1968/9).
—— [2]. 'Constitutivity and Identity', *Nous*, 5 (1971).
Chappell, V. C. [1]. 'Sameness and Change', *Philosophical Review*, 69 (1960).
—— [2]. 'Stuff and Things', *Proceedings of the Aristotelian Society*, 71 (1970/1).
Chisholm, R. M. [1]. 'Identity Through Possible Worlds', *Nous*, 1 [1967].
—— [2]. 'The Loose and Popular and the Strict and Philosophical Senses of Identity', in Care and Grimm [1].
—— [3]. 'Parts as Essential to their Wholes', *Review of Metaphysics*, 26 (1972/3).
—— [4]. 'Problems of Identity', in Munitz [1].
—— [5]. *Person and Object* (London: Allen & Unwin, 1976).
Clark, E. V. [1]. 'What's in a Word?' in T. E. Moore (ed.), *Cognitive Development and the Acquisition of Language* (New York: Academic Press, 1973).
Clarke, D. S. [1]. 'Mass Terms as Subjects', *Philosophical Studies*, 21 (1970).
Cornman, James W. [1]. 'Types, Categories, and Nonsense', in Rescher [1].
—— [2]. 'The Identity of Mind and Body', in Borst [1].
—— [3]. *Materialism and Sensations* (New Haven: Yale University Press, 1971).
Darwin, Charles [1]. *The Origin of Species* (London: Murray, 1900).
Davidson, D., and Hintikka, J. (eds.) [1]. *Words and Objections* (Dordrecht: D. Reidel, 1969).
Dawkins, R. [1]. *The Selfish Gene* (Oxford: Oxford University Press, 1976).
Dennett, D. [1]. *Brainstorms* (Hassocks, Sussex: Harvester, 1979).
Descartes, R. [1]. *Philosophical Works*, tr. Haldane E. S. and Ross G. R. T. (Cambridge: Cambridge University Press, 1969).
Dewey, John [1]. *Democracy and Eduction* (New York: Macmillan, 1916).
Duhem, P. [1]. *The Aim and Structure of Physical Theory* (Princeton: Princeton University Press, 1954).
Dummett, M. A. E. [1]. *Frege: Philosophy of Language* (London: Duckworth, 1973).
—— [2]. 'Does Quantification Involve Identity?', in Lewis, Harry, and Saarinen, E. (eds.), *Peter Geach: A Profile* (Dordrecht: Reidel, forthcoming).
Elliot, R. [1]. 'How to Travel Faster than Light', *Analysis*, 41 [1981].
—— [2]. 'Going Nowhere Fast?', *Analysis*, 42 [1982].
Enç, Berent [1]. 'Numerical Identity and Objecthood', *Mind*, 84 (1975).
Evans, Gareth [1]. 'Identity and Predication', *Journal of Philosophy*, 72 (1975).

—— [2]. 'The Causal Theory of Names', in Schwartz [1].

—— [3]. 'Vague Objects', *Analysis*, 39 (1978).

—— [4]. *The Varieties of Reference*, ed. John McDowell (Oxford: Clarendon Press, 1982).

Flew, A. [1]. 'Locke and the Problem of Personal Identity', *Philosophy*, 26 (1951).

—— [2]. ' "The Soul" of Mr A. M. Quinton', *Journal of Philosophy*, 60 [1963].

—— (ed.) [3]. *Body, Mind and Death*, (New York: Macmillan, 1964).

Fodor, Jerry [1]. *Psychological Explanation* (New York: Random House, 1968).

Forbes, G. [1]. 'Origin and Identity', *Philosophical Studies*, 37 (1980).

—— [2]. 'Thisness and Vagueness', *Synthese*, 54 (1983).

—— [3]. *The Metaphysics of Modality* (Oxford: Clarendon Press, 1985).

Fraassen, Bas C. Van [1]. 'Essence and Existence', *American Philosophical Quarterly Monograph* (1977–8).

Frege, Gottlob [1]. *The Foundations of Arithmetic*, tr. J. L. Austin (Oxford: Blackwell, 1950).

—— [2]. *Grundgesetze der Arithmetik* (Jena: Verlag Hermann Pohle, 1883, 1903), partly translated as *The Basic Laws of Arithmetic*, with introduction, by Montgomery Furth (Berkeley: University of California Press, 1967).

Furth, Montgomery [1]. 'Transtemporal Stability in Aristotelian Substances', *Journal of Philosophy*, 75 (1978).

Gale, R. M. (ed.) [1]. *The Philosophy of Time* (Hassocks, Sussex: Harvester, 1978).

—— [2]. Review of Eli Hirsch, *The Concept of Identity*, in *Journal of Philosophy*, 80 (1983).

Garner, W. R. [1]. *Uncertainty and Structure as Psychological Concepts* (New York: John Wiley & Sons, 1962).

—— [2]. *The Processing of Information and Structure* (Potomac: Laurence Erlbaum, 1974).

Geach, P. T. [1]. *Reference and Generality* (Ithaca: Cornell University Press, 1962).

—— [2]. 'Some Problems About Time', *Proceedings of the British Academy*, 1965.

—— [3]. *Logic Matters* (Oxford: Blackwell, 1972).

—— [4]. 'Ontological Relativity and Relative Identity', in Munitz [2].

—— [5]. 'Names and Identity', in Guttenplan [1].

Geach. P. T., and Black, Max (eds.) [1]. *Translations from the Philosophical Writings of Gottlob Frege* (Oxford: Basil Blackwell, 1952).

Gibbard, A. [1]. 'Contingent Identity', *Journal of Philosophical Logic*, 4 [1975].

Gibson, J. J. [1]. *The Ecological Approach to Visual Perception* (Boston: Houghton Mifflin, 1979).

Goldstein, L. [1]. 'Quotation of Types and Other Types of Quotation', *Analysis*, 44 (1984).

Goodman, N. [1]. *Fact, Fiction and Forecast* (New York: Bobbs-Merrill, 1965).

—— [2]. *The Structure of Appearance* (New York: Bobbs-Merrill; 2nd edn., 1966).

—— [3]. *Languages of Art* (New York: Bobbs-Merrill, 1968).

—— [4]. *Problems and Projects* (Indianapolis: Bobbs-Merrill, 1972), Pt. IV.

Grice, H. P. [1]. 'Vacuous Names', in Davidson and Hintikka [1].

Griffin, Nicholas [1]. 'Ayers on Relative Identity', *Canadian Journal of Philosophy*, 6 (1976).

—— [2]. *Relative Identity* (Oxford: Clarendon Press, 1977).

——, and Routley, R. [1]. 'Towards a Logic of Relative Identity', *Logique et Analyse* (1979).

Guttenplan, S. (ed.) [1]. *Mind and Language* (Oxford: Clarendon Press, 1976).

Hacker, P. M. S. [1]. 'Substance: The Constitution of Reality', *Midwest Studies in Philosophy*, 4 (1979).

Hacking, Ian [1]. 'On the Reality of Existence and Identity', *Canadian Journal of Philosophy*, 8 (1978).

Hampshire, Stuart [1]. 'Identification and Existence', in Lewis, H. D. (ed.), *Contemporary British Philosophy* (London: Allen & Unwin, 1956), 3rd Ser.

Hempel, Carl G. [1]. *Aspects of Scientific Explanation* (New York: Collier Macmillan, 1965).

Hirsch, Eli [1]. 'A Sense of Unity', *Journal of Philosophy*, 75 (1978).

—— [2]. *The Concept of Identity* (Oxford: Clarendon Press, 1982).

Hobbes, Thomas [1]. *De Corpore*, in Molesworth, William (ed.), *The English Works of Thomas Hobbes* (London: John Bohn, 1839–45), vol. i.

Hofstadter, D. R. and Dennett, D. [1]. *The Mind's I* (Brighton: Harvester, 1981).

Hull, David [1]. 'Units of Evolution: A Metaphysical Essay', in Jensen and Harré [1].

Hume, David [1]. *A Treatise of Human Nature*, 1739 (Oxford: Clarendon Press, 1978).

—— [2]. *An Enquiry Concerning Human Understanding*, 1748 (Indianapolis: Bobbs Merrill, 1955).

Ishiguro, H. [1]. *Leibniz's Philosophy of Logic and Language* (London: Duckworth, 1972).

Iversen, S. D. [1]. 'Temporal Lobe Amnesia', in Whitty and Zangwill [1].

Jensen, U. J., and Harré, R. (eds.) [1]. *The Philosophy of Evolution* (Hassocks, Sussex: Harvester, 1981).

Kant, Immanuel [1]. *Critique of Pure Reason*, tr. Norman Kemp Smith (London: Macmillan, 1964).

—— [2]. *Prolegomena to Any Future Metaphysics*, 1783; tr. P. G. Lucas (Manchester: Manchester University Press, 1953).

Kaplan, David [1]. 'Transworld Heir Lines', in Loux [2].

Katz, Bernard D. [1]. 'The Identity of Indiscernibles Revisited', *Philosophical Studies*, 44 (1983).

Kemler, Deborah [1]. 'Exploring and Re-exploring Issues of Integrality, Perceptual Sensitivity and Dimensional Salience', *Journal of Experimental Child Psychology*, 36 (1983).

Kirwan, Christopher [1]. 'How Strong are the Objections to Essence?', *Proceedings of the Aristotelian Society*, 71 (1970/1).

Kitcher, Patricia [1]. 'Kant on Self Identity', *Philosophical Review*, 91 (1982).

Koffka, Kurt [1]. *Principles of Gestalt Psychology* (New York: Harcourt, Brace and World, 1935).

Krecz, C. A. [1]. 'Parts and Pieces', *Philosophy and Phenomenological Research* 46 (1986).

Kripke, S. [1]. 'Identity and Necessity', in Munitz [1].

—— [2]. *Naming and Necessity*, rev. edn. (Oxford: Blackwell, 1980).

Leibniz, G. W. [1]. *Discourse on Metaphysics*, translated by P. Lucas and L. Grint (Manchester: Manchester University Press, 1952).

—— [2]. *Philosophical Papers and Letters*, tr. and ed. Leroy Loemker (Dordrecht: D. Reidel, 1969).

Lewis, David [1]. 'Counterpart Theory and Quantified Modal Logic', *Journal of Philosophy*, 65 (1968), reprinted in Loux [2].

—— [2]. *Counterfactuals* (Oxford: Basil Blackwell, 1973).

—— [3]. 'Survival and Identity', in Rorty [1]; reprinted with postscript in Lewis [4].

—— [4]. *Philosophical Papers* (Oxford: Oxford University Press, 1983).

—— [5]. 'Individuation by Acquaintance and by Stipulation', *Philosophical Review*, 92 (1983).

—— [6]. *On the Plurality of Worlds* (Oxford: Basil Blackwell, 1986).

Linsky, Leonard [1]. Critical Notice of Geach, *Reference and Generality*, in *Mind*, 73 (1964).

—— [2]. *Referring* (London: Routledge and Kegan Paul, 1967).

—— [3]. *Names and Descriptions* (Chicago: University of Chicago Press, 1977).

Locke, John [1]. *An Essay Concerning Human Understanding*, 2nd ed., 1694; ed. P. Nidditch (Oxford: Clarendon Press, 1975).

Lockwood, Michael [1]. 'Identity and Reference', in Munitz [1].

Loux, M. J. (ed.) [1]. *Universals and Particulars* (Garden City: Anchor Books, 1970).

—— (ed.) [2]. *The Possible and the Actual* (Ithaca: Cornell University Press, 1979).

Lowe, E. J. [1]. 'On the Identity of Artifacts', *Journal of Philosophy*, 80 (1983).

—— [2]. 'Instantiation, Identity and Constitution', *Philosophical Studies*, 44 (1983).

Lucas, J. R. [1]. *A Treatise on Time and Space* (London: Methuen, 1973).

Luschei, Eugene C. [1]. *The Logical Systems of Lesniewski* (Amsterdam: North-Holland, 1962).

Lycan, W. Gregory [1]. 'Noninductive Evidence: Recent Work on Wittgenstein's "Criteria" ', *American Philosophical Quarterly*, 8 (1971).

McCabe, V. [1]. 'The Direct Perception of Universals', *Synthese*, 52 (1982).

MacDonald, G. F. (ed.) [1]. *Perception and Identity* (Ithaca: Cornell University Press, 1979).

MacLeod, R. B., and Pick, H. L., jun. [1]. *Perception: Essays in Honor of J. J. Gibson* (Ithaca: Cornell University Press, 1974).

Madell, G. [1]. *The Identity of the Self* (Edinburgh: Edinburgh University Press, 1981).

Margolis, Joseph [1]. 'Dracula the Man: An Essay in the Logic of Individuation', *International Philosophical Quarterly*, 4 (1964).

—— [2]. 'Nature, Culture and Persons', *Theory and Decision*, 13 (1983).

Martin, C. B., and Deutscher, M. [1]. 'Remembering', *Philosophical Review*, 78 (1969).

Mellor, H. [1]. 'On Things and Causes in Spacetime', *British Journal for the Philosophy of Science*, 31 (1980).

—— [2]. *Real Time* (Cambridge: Cambridge University Press, 1981).

Mendelsohn, Richard L. [1]. 'Rigid Designation and Informative Identity Sentences', *Midwest Studies in Philosophy*, 4 (1979).

—— [2]. 'Frege's Begriffsschrift Theory of Identity', *Journal of the History of Philosophy*, 20 (1982).

Millar, Alan [1]. 'What's in Look?', *Proceedings of the Aristotelian Society*, 86 (1985–6).

Moore, G. E. [1]. 'Identity', in *The Commonplace Book of G. E. Moore*, ed. Casimir Lewy (London: George Allen & Unwin, 1962).

Moravcsik, J. M. E. [1]. 'The Discernibility of Identicals'. *Journal of Philosophy*, 73 (1976).

Morris, T. V. [1]. *Understanding Identity Statements* (Aberdeen: Aberdeen University Press, 1985).

Munitz, Milton K. (ed.) [1]. *Identity and Individuation* (New York: New York University Press, 1971).

—— (ed.) [2]. *Logic and Ontology* (New York: New York University Press, 1973).

Nagel, Thomas [1]. 'Brain Bisection and the Unity of Consciousness', *Synthese*, 22 (1971) and in Nagel [2].

—— [2]. *Mortal Questions* (Cambridge: Cambridge University Press, 1979).

Nerlich, G. [1]. 'What Can Geometry Explain?', *British Journal for the Philosophy of Science*, 30 (1979).

Noonan, H. [1]. 'Wiggins on Identity', *Mind*, 82 (1973).

—— [2]. 'Sortal Concepts and Identity', *Mind*, 87 (1978).

—— [3]. *Objects and Identity* (The Hague: Martinus Nijhoff, 1980).

—— [4]. 'The Necessity of Origin', *Mind*, 92 (1983).

—— [5]. 'Wiggins, Artefact Identity and "Best Candidate" Theories', *Analysis*, 45 (1985).

—— [6]. 'The Only *x* and *y* Principle', *Analysis*, 45 (1985).

—— [7]. 'A Note on Temporal Parts', *Analysis*, 45 (1985).

—— [8]. 'The Closest Continuer Theory of Identity', *Inquiry*, 28 (1985).

Nozick, R. [1]. *Philosophical Explanations* (Oxford: Clarendon Press, 1981).

O'Connor, D. J. [1]. 'On Resemblance', *Proceedings of the Aristotelian Society*, 46 (1945/6).

—— [2]. 'The Identity of Indiscernibles', *Analysis* [1954]; reprinted in Loux [1].

Odegard, Douglas [1]. 'Identity Through Time', *American Philosophical Quarterly*, 9 (1972).

Parfit, Derek [1]. 'Personal Identity', *Philosophical Review*, 80 (1971).

—— [2]. 'On "The Importance of Self-Identity" ', *Journal of Philosophy*, 68 [1971].

—— [3]. 'Personal Identity and Rationality', *Synthese*, 53 [1982].

—— [4]. *Reasons and Persons* (Oxford: Clarendon Press, 1984).

Peacocke, C. [1]. 'Are Vague Predicates Incoherent?', *Synthese*, 46 (1981).

—— [2]. *Sense and Content* (Oxford: Clarendon Press, 1983).

Peirce, C. S. [1]. *Collected Papers*, ed. C. Hartshorne, P. Weiss, and A. W. Burks (Cambridge, Mass.: Harvard University Press, 1933).

Penelhum, Terence [1]. 'Hume on Personal Identity', *Philosophical Review*, 64 (1955).

—— [2]. *Survival and Disembodied Existence* (London: Routledge & Kegan Paul, 1970).

Perry, John [1]. 'The Same F', *Philosophical Review*, 79 (1970).

—— [2]. Review of Wiggins, *Identity and Spatio-Temporal Continuity*, in *Journal of Symbolic Logic*, 35 (1970).

—— [3]. 'Can the Self Divide?', *Journal of Philosophy*, 69 [1972].

—— [4]. 'Personal Identity, Memory, and the Problem of Circularity', in Perry [5].

—— (ed.) [5]. *Personal Identity* (Berkeley and Los Angeles: University of California Press, 1975).

—— [6]. 'The Problem of Personal Identity', in Perry [5].

—— [7]. 'The Importance of Being Identical', in Rorty [1].

—— [8]. Review of Williams, *Problems of the Self*, *Journal of Philosophy*, 73 (1976).

—— [9]. 'The Essential Indexical', *Nous*, 13 (1979).

Piercy, M. F. [1]. 'Experimental Studies of the Organic Amnesic Syndrome', in Whitty and Zangwill [1].

Pitcher, G. (ed.) [1]. *Wittgenstein: The Philosophical Investigations* (London: Macmillan 1968).

Plantinga, Alvin [1]. *The Nature of Necessity* (Oxford: Clarendon Press, 1974).

—— [2]. 'World and Essence', in Loux [1].

—— [3]. 'The Boethian Compromise', *American Philosophical Quarterly*, 15 (1978).

Price, M. [1]. 'Identity Through Time', *Journal of Philosophy*, 74 (1977).

Prior, A. N. [1]. 'Report on the Analysis "Problem" No. 11', *Analysis*, 17 (1957), 122–3.

—— [2]. 'Opposite Number', *Review of Metaphysics*, 11 (1957/8).

—— [3]. *Time and Modality* (Oxford: Clarendon Press, 1957).

—— [4]. *Formal Logic* (Oxford: Oxford University Press; 2nd edn; 1962).

—— [5]. 'Time, Existence and Identity', in *Papers on Time and Tense* (Oxford: Clarendon Press, 1968).

—— [6]. 'Things and Stuff', in *Papers in Logic and Ethics* (London: Duckworth, 1976).

Puccetti, R. [1]. 'Brain Transplantation and Personal Identity', *Analysis*, 29 (1968).

Putnam, Hilary [1]. 'It Ain't Necessarily So', *Journal of Philosophy*, 59 [1962].

—— [2]. 'Is Semantics Possible?', *Metaphilosophy*, 3 (1970).

—— [3]. 'Meaning and Reference', *Journal of Philosophy*, 70 (1973).

Quine, W. V. [1]. *From a Logical Point of View* (New York: Harper Torchbooks; 2nd edn., 1961).

—— [2]. *Word and Object* (Cambridge, Mass.: MIT Press, 1960).

—— [3]. *Set Theory and its Logic* (Cambridge, Mass.: Harvard University Press, 1963).

—— [4]. Review of Geach, *Reference and Generality*, in *Philosophical Review*, 73 (1964).

—— [5]. *The Ways of Paradox* (New York: Random House, 1966).

—— [6]. 'Natural Kinds', in Rescher, N. (ed.), *Essays in Honour of C. G. Hempel* (Dordrecht: Reidel, 1969) and in Quine [7].

—— [7]. *Ontological Relativity and Other Essays* (New York: Columbia University Press, 1969).

—— [8]. Review of Munitz, Milton K. (ed.), *Identity and Individuation*, in *Journal of Philosophy*, 69 (1972).

—— [9]. *The Roots of Reference* (La Salle: Open Court, 1974).

—— [10]. *Theories and Things* (Cambridge, Mass.: Belknap Press, 1981).

Quinton, A. M. [1]. 'The Soul', *Journal of Philosophy*, 59 [1962].

—— [2]. *The Nature of Things* (London: Routledge & Kegan Paul, 1972).

Ramsey, Frank P. [1]. *The Foundations of Mathematics and Other Logical Essays*, ed. R. B. Braithwaite (Totowa, NJ: Littlefield, Adams, 1965).

Reid, Thomas [1]. *Essays on the Intellectual Powers of Man* (1784), Ch. 4, 'Of Memory', reprinted in Perry [5].

Rescher, Nicholas (ed.) [1]. *Studies in Logical Theory* (Oxford: Basil Blackwell, 1968).

——, and Urquhart, Alasdair [1]. *Temporal Logic* (New York: Springer Verlag, 1971).

Roberts, M. [1]. 'Lewis's Theory of Personal Identity', *Australasian Journal of Philosophy*, 61 [1983].

Robinson, D. [1]. 'Reidentifying Matter', *Philosophical Review*, 20 [1982].

Rorty, A. O. (ed.) [1]. *The Identities of Persons* (Berkeley: University of California Press, 1976).

Rosch, Eleanor, Mevis, C. *et al.* [1]. 'Basic Objects in Natural Categories', *Cognitive Psychology*, 8 (1976).

Routley, Richard, and MacRae, Vera [1]. 'On the Identity of Sensations and Physiological Occurrences', *American Philosophical Quarterly*, 3 (1966).

Russell, Bertrand [1]. *The Principles of Mathematics* (London: Allen & Unwin; 2nd edn., 1937).

—— [2]. 'The Philosophy of Logical Atomism', in *Logic and Knowledge*, ed. Robert C. Marsh (London: George Allen & Unwin, 1956).

—— and Whitehead, Alfred [1]. *Principia Mathematica* (Cambridge: Cambridge University Press; 2nd edn., 1925/7).

Sacks, H. [1]. *The Man Who Mistook His Wife for a Hat* (London: Duckworth, 1985).

Salmon, N. U. [1]. *Reference and Essence* (Oxford: Blackwell, 1982).

Sanford, David H. [1]. 'Locke, Leibniz and Wiggins on Being in the Same Place at the Same Time', *Philosophical Review*, 79 (1970).

Scheffler, S [1]. 'Ethics, Personal Identity and Ideals of the Person', *Canadian Journal of Philosophy*, 12 (1982).

Schlesinger, G. [1]. 'Spatial, Temporal and Cosmic Parts', *Southern Journal of Philosophy*, 23 (1985).

—— [2]. *The Intelligibility of Nature* (Aberdeen: Aberdeen University Press, 1985).

Schwartz, S. P. (ed.) [1]. *Naming, Necessity and Natural Kinds* (Ithaca: Cornell University Press, 1977).

Schwartz, Stephen P. [1]. 'Natural Kinds and Nominal Kinds', *Mind*, 89 (1980).

Scott, Dana [1]. 'Existence and Description in Formal Logic', in *Bertrand Russell: Philosopher of the Century*, ed. Ralph Schoenman (London: George Allen & Unwin, 1967).

Shoemaker, Sydney [1]. *Self-Knowledge and Self-Identity* (Ithaca: Cornell University Press, 1963).

—— [2]. 'Wiggins on Identity', *Philosophical Review*, 79 (1970).

—— [3]. 'Persons and Their Pasts', *American Philosophical Quarterly*, 7 [1970].

—— [4]. 'Identity, Properties and Causality', *Midwest Studies in Philosophy*, 4 (1979).

—— [5]. 'Personal Identity: a Materialist's Account', in Shoemaker and Swinburne [1].

—— [6]. *Identity, Cause and Mind* (Cambridge: Cambridge University Press, 1984).

—— [7]. Critical Notice: Parfit, *Reasons and Persons*, *Mind*, 44 (1985).

—— and Swinburne, R. G. [1]. *Personal Identity* (Oxford: Blackwell, 1984).

Shorter, J. M. [1]. 'More About Bodily Continuity and Personal Identity', *Analysis*, 22 (1961/2).

Simons, P. [1]. 'Token Resistance', *Analysis*, 42 (1982).

Slote, Michael [1]. 'Causality and the Concept of a "Thing" ', *Midwest Studies in Philosophy*, 4 (1979).

Smart, B. [1]. 'How to Reidentify the Ship of Theseus', *Analysis*, 32 (1972).

—— [2]. 'The Ship of Theseus, the Parthenon, and Disassembled Objects', *Analysis*, 34 (1973).

—— [3]. 'Diachronous and Synchronous Selves', *Canadian Journal of Philosophy*, 6 (1976).

Smart, J. J. C. [1]. 'Spatialising Time', *Mind*, 64 (1955).

Sober, E. [1]. 'Sets, Species and Evolution', *Philosophy of Science*, 51 (1984).

Stalnaker, R. [1]. *Inquiry* (Cambridge, Mass.: MIT Press, 1984).

Stevenson, Leslie [1]. 'Relative Identity and Leibniz's Law', *Philosophical Quarterly*, 22 (1972), 155–8.

—— [2]. 'A Formal Theory of Sortal Quantification', *Notre Dame Journal of Formal Logic*, 16 (1975), 185–207.

Strawson, P. F. [1]. *Individuals* (London: Methuen, 1959).

—— [2]. 'Particular and General', *Proceedings of the Aristotelian Society*, 54 (1954), 233–60.

—— [3]. *The Bounds of Sense* (London: Methuen, 1966).

—— [4]. 'Chisholm on Identity Through Time', in Kiefer, H. E. and Munitz, Milton K. (eds.), *Language, Belief, and Metaphysics* (Albany: State University of New York Press, 1970).

—— [5]. 'Entity and Identity', in Lewis, H. D. (ed.), *British Contemporary Philosophy* (London: Allen & Unwin, 1976), Vol. IV.

—— [6]. 'May Bes and Might Have Beens', in Margalit, A. (ed.), *Meaning and Use* (Dordrecht: Reidel, 1979).

Stroll, Avrum [1]. 'Faces', *Inquiry*, 28 (1985).

Swinburne, R. G. [1]. *Space and Time* (New York: St Martins Press, 1968).

—— [2]. 'Personal Identity', *Proceedings of the Aristotelian Society*, suppl. vol. (1973/4).

—— [3]. 'Personal Identity: the Dualist Theory', in Shoemaker and Swinburne [1].

Tarski, Alfred [1]. 'The Semantic Conception of Truth', in *Logic, Semantics and Metamathematics* (Oxford: Oxford University Press, 1956).

Thomason, R. H. [1]. 'A Semantic Theory of Sortal Incorrectness', *Journal of Philosophical Logic*, 1 (1972).

Thomson, J. J. [1]. 'Parthood and Identity Across Time', *Journal of Philosophy*, 80 (1983).

Tichy, Pavel [1]. 'Kripke on Necessity A Posteriori', *Philosophical Studies*, 43 (1983).

Travis, C. [1]. 'Vagueness, Observation and Sorites', *Mind*, 44 (1985).

Tye, Michael [1]. 'The Puzzle of Hesperus and Phosphorus', *Australasian Journal of Philosophy*, 56 (1978).

Unger, P. [1]. 'I Do Not Exist', in MacDonald [1].

Vision, Gerald [1]. 'Essentialism and the Senses of Proper Names', *American Philosophical Quarterly*, 7 (1970).

Wallace, John R. [1]. 'Sortal Predicates and Quantification', *Journal of Philosophy*, 62 (1965).

—— [2]. 'On the Frame of Reference', in Davidson, D. and Harman, G. (eds.), *The Semantics of Natural Language* (Dordrecht: D. Reidel, 1971).

White, Alan [1]. 'Mind-Brain Analogies', *Canadian Journal of Philosophy*, 1 (1972).

White, Roger [1]. 'Wittgenstein on Identity', *Proceedings of the Aristotelian Society*, 68 (1978).

Whitty, C. M. and Zangwill, O. L. (eds.) [1]. *Amnesia*, 2nd edn. (London: Butterworths, 1977).

Wiggins, D. [1]. 'The Individuation of Things and Places', *Proceedings of the Aristotelian Society*, Suppl. Vol. 37 (1963).

—— [2]. *Identity and Spatio-Temporal Continuity* (Oxford: Blackwell, 1967).

—— [3]. 'Identity-Statements', in R. J. Butler (ed.), *Analytical Philosophy*, Second Series (Oxford: Blackwell, 1965).

—— [4]. 'Reply to Mr Chandler', *Analysis*, 29 (1968/9).

—— [5]. 'On Being in the Same Place at the Same Time', *Philosophical Review*, 77 (1968).

—— [6]. 'Essentialism, Continuity and Identity', *Synthese*, 23 (1974).

—— [7]. 'Locke, Butler and the Stream of Consciousness', in Rorty [1].

—— [8]. 'The Concern to Survive', *Midwest Studies in Philosophy*, 4 (1979).

—— [9]. *Sameness and Substance*, (Oxford: Basil Blackwell, 1980).

Williams, B. A. O. [1]. 'Personal Identity and Individuation', *Proceedings of the Aristotelian Society*, 57 (1956–7).

—— [2]. 'Bodily Continuity and Personal Identity', *Analysis*, 21 (1960).

—— [3]. 'Persons, Character and Morality', in Rorty [1].

—— [4]. 'The Self and the Future', *Philosophical Review*, 79 (1970), and in Williams [5].

—— [5]. *Problems of the Self* (Cambridge: Cambridge University Press, 1973).

Wilson, I. R. [1]. 'Explanatory and Inferential Conditionals', *Philosophical Studies*, 35 (1979).

Wilson, Ian [1]. *Engineering Solids* (London: McGraw Hill, 1979).

Wilson, N. L. [1]. 'Space, Time and Individuals', *Journal of Philosophy*, 52 (1955).

Witggenstein, Ludwig [1]. *Tractatus Logico-Philosophicus*, translated by D. F. Pears and B. F. McGuinness (London: Routledge & Kegan Paul, 1961).

—— [2]. *The Blue and Brown Books* (Oxford: Blackwell, 1958).

—— [3]. *Philosophical Investigations*, translated by G. E. M. Anscombe (Oxford: Blackwell, 1953).

Woodger, J. H. [1]. *The Axiomatic Method in Biology* (Cambridge: Cambridge University Press, 1937).

Woods, John [1]. 'Essentialism, Self-Identity and Quantifying In', in Munitz [1].

—— [2]. ' "Non in Particular" ', *Canadian Journal of Philosophy*, 2 (1973).

—— [3]. 'Identity and Modality', *Philosophia*, 5 (1975).

Woods, M. J. [1]. 'The Individuation of Things and Places', *Proceedings of the Aristotelian Society*, Suppl. Vol. 37 (1963).

—— [2]. 'Identity and Individuation', in Butler, R. J. (ed.), *Analytical Philosophy* (Oxford: Blackwell, 1965); 2nd ser.

Zemach, E. M. [1]. 'In Defence of Relative Identity', *Philosophical Studies*, 26 (1974), 207–18.

Index

continuant 12, 86, 88, 96, 136, 193
continuity
  compositional 38–9
  closest continuer theory 41–2,
    115–16
  Hollywood 41–2, 59, 94–5, 293
  psychological 293–6, 297
  spatio-temporal 11–13, 37–45, 97–9,
    105–6, 125–6, 136, 295, 335,
    353
  theory 12, 15, 58–9, 137, 185, 193–4
  see also connectedness; discontinuity
Coolidge, C. 1
copying processes 75–9, 112, 168, 174,
  244–5, 317, 342–4
Corbett, J. 204 n.
correlational structure 188–9, 219, 227,
  228–32, 234–6
cosmic parts *see* parts
counterparts 131–4, 158, 159 n.,
  162–4, 165–6
Craig, W. 106
criteria 87, 96, 245, 251–5, 262
critical realism 220
crystal structure 104, 136, 172, 179–80

Dawkins, R. 175, 244 n.
death 316–17, 322
deferred ostension 195–6
Democritus 170–1
Dennett, D. C. 59, 65, 82, 181, 334
Descartes, R. 258, 320 n.
design 181–3, 203
Deutscher, M. 250 n
Dewey, J. 352
diachronic identity 87
diachronic relations 146–8, 269–70,
  277–9, 297–300
differentiation 213, 219, 221–2, 225–7
dimensions 218–21, 223–5, 232
discontinuity 43–4, 91–5, 97–9, 136,
  304, 332–3
  functional 92, 95–6
  spatial 98, 113
disembodied existence 240–1
dualism 257–9, 320–1, 337
Duhem, P. 104, 347–8
Dummett, M. 164 n.
Dumyat (example) 93–9, 107, 109–14,
  127

Elliot, R. 301 n.
episodic objects *see* discontinuity

epistemology 51, 146–8, 167, 176, 205,
  217, 272
essence 150, 155, 159–61, 165–6, 170,
  190–1, 193, 202
eternal sentences 135
Euclidean distance 223
Eusa problem 62–5, 85, 126, 147, 197,
  353
Evans, G. 279–82
events 151–2
existence
  contingent vs. necessary 163 n.
  see also metaphysics
experience 51, 59–61, 140
explanation 101, 109–10, 144
  D–N model 101–4
extension 209–11
extensionalist myth 207–11, 215–17,
  228, 232–4
extensionalism 164 n, 212–15, 229, 231

family resemblance 233
fifth dimension 133, 261, 354–5
  see also parts, cosmic
figure and ground 220–1
fission 254 n., 262–7, 299, 304–5,
  328–9
Forbes, G. 121 n., 123 n., 159 n., 163,
  164
foundationalism 58 n., 285–6
Frege, G. 40 n., 209–10, 252 n.
function 181–3, 184–7, 188–90
functional discontinuity 21, 38–9, 41,
  92, 95
  see also parts
functionalism 257–8
Furth, M. 209 n.
fuzzy logic 163–4

Garner, W. R. 218–32 *passim*
Geach, P. T. 192 n.
genes 137, 168, 175, 201, 224
Ghiselin, M. T. 353 n.
Gibbard, A. 52, 53 n., 88–90
Gibbens, T. C. N. 347
Gibson, J. J. 188–9, 218
Goldstein, L. 77 n.
Goodman, N. 35, 97, 102, 109 n., 149,
  211 n., 212 n., 234
gravity 100, 106–7
Griffin, N. 7 n., 10 n., 192 n., 193 n.
growth 198
Guy Fawkes (example) 115–16, 262–5

haecceitism 159–66
Hall Williams, J. 347
Hanson, N. R. 189
Hempel, C. G. 101–3
Heraclitus 5, 11
Hirsch, E. 7 n., 38, 43–4, 47–8, 52,
　55 n., 91, 94–6, 115, 119, 180,
　214, 293–4, 342
histories 23, 54, 110, 145, 149, 160,
　199
Hoban, R. 63
Hobbes, T. 11
Hofstadter, D. R. 65
Hull, D. 353 n.
Hume, D. 23, 25, 48, 85, 91, 99–100,
　103–7, 137–8, 154, 207, 212,
　214–15, 261–2, 268–70

identification-free judgements 279–81
identity 136, 191–9, 260–1, 266, 282–4
　conditions of 5–32 *passim*
　and importance 122
　of indiscernibles 10
　necessity of 116, 119, 155
　primitiveness of 40, 51–8
　qualitative *see* similarity
　relative 192–3
　reflexivity of 9
　see also personal identity; similarity;
　　survival
ideology 136
indeterminacy 9, 22–3, 290, 347–8
indiscernibility
　principle of 9
　theory 11, 13–17
individuals 34–6, 98–9, 118–24, 149,
　157–8
infatuation 310–11
information 218–19
innateness 6, 48, 221
integrality *see* dimensions
intension 209–10
Ishiguro, H. 10 n.
Iversen, S. D. 296

Kant, I. 138, 269–70, 272–3, 275
Kaplan, D. 131 n.
Kemler, D. 213 n., 222, 226 n.
kinds *see* natural kinds; sortals
Koffka, K. 218 n., 232 n.
Köhler, W. 232 n.
Krecz, C. 260 n.
Kripke's disc (example) 45–51

Kripke, S. 34, 37, 43–53, 114, 150,
　155, 157 n., 163 n.

larvae 191
legal persons 243
Leibniz's Law 9, 10 n.
Leibniz, G. W. 129
levels 218
Lewis, D. K. 56 n., 95, 99, 131 n.,
　149 n., 157 n., 293, 313, 328–32
life histories 53–4, 55, 90, 160
Locke, J. 64–5, 68–9, 126, 170, 188,
　201, 246–9, 254, 258, 272, 290,
　298, 332, 346–7
Lorenz, K. 216
Lot's wife (example) 194–5
love 271, 308–11
Lowe, E. J. 52 n., 124 n.
Lucas, J. R. 56 n.

Martin, C. B. 250 n.
materialism 257–8
materials 179–80
matter 27, 29, 68, 99, 107–9, 168, 170,
　179–80, 302–4, 352–3
maximal sequences 137–8, 147
McCabe, V. 107 n., 176, 314 n.
Measor, N. 56 n., 57 n., 87
Mellor, H. 53–6, 86 n., 150–2
Melsen, A. van 171
memory 246, 248–51, 263, 265, 274–5,
　279–82, 296–301
　see also co-consciousness;
　　connectedness
Mendel, G. 102
mereological fusions *see* collections
mereology 34, 97, 109, 113–14, 118,
　121
　see also individuals
metamorphosis 191, 197, 203
metaphysics 51, 59–60, 88, 167, 205
Millar, A. 140, 280 n.
Minkowski, H. 87
modifications 185, 187
Moore, G. E. 116 n.
Morris, T. V. 40 n.

Nagel, T. 326, 332, 340–5
names 135, 160
　see also rigid designation
Napoleon (example) 155–6, 157 n.
natural kinds 8 n., 147–8, 201, 242–4
　see also sortals

natural selection 213
natural vs. human 241
natural vs. philosophical 212
nature *see* essence
necessity 155, 160, 163
  see also identity; origin
Nerlich, G. 53 n., 56 n.
nominalism 35
Noonan, H. 53 n., 116–18, 120, 143,
  145, 155 n.
nouns
  and concepts 8, 191 n.
  count *see* sortals
Nozick, R. 2, 41, 95, 114–15, 118

Odom, R. D. 213 n.
'only *x* and *y* rule' 66, 114–20, 187, 262
ontological parasites 276, 282–4, 289
ontology 135–7, 148
  see also metaphysics
organisms 168, 181, 197–8
  unitary vs. modular 30–1
origin 155, 166–8
overdetermination 140
overextension 222, 226 n.
overlap 42–4, 94
ownership 275–9

Parfit, D. 17–20, 22, 65 n., 69, 95, 121,
  199, 238, 240 n., 241 n., 247–9,
  254–68 *passim*, 275, 278, 281, 288,
  290, 292, 294–300, 305–8, 310–19,
  322, 324–5, 326–8, 330–2, 340–5,
  350
particulars 12, 24, 33–4, 53, 84, 88,
  136, 138, 145–6, 147, 149–50, 159,
  166, 181, 193, 208
  abstract vs. concrete 34, 88, 92, 96–7
  basic 287
  cosmic particulars 89–90, 133
  episodic Ch. 4 *passim*
  as four dimensional 85–6, 89–90,
    151–2
  scattered 97, 149
  as short lived 111–14
  as three dimensional 86–8, 90
  see also parts; persistence; stages
parts
  cosmic 133, 159, 165–6
  functional 181–2
  spatial 52, 133, 142–6, 149–50
  temporal *see* temporal parts
  and wholes 143–4

Pascal, B. 104 n.
Peirce, C. S. 10
Penelhum, T. M. 240 n.
perception 107, 176
Perry, J. 40 n.
persistence 105, 148, 153–5, 160–1,
  200, 266, 308
personal identity 336–9
  and branching 327–31
  and what matters 290, 294–5, 305,
    307, 312–13, 326–7, 329–31
persons 9, 141, 167 238–9, 304, 326–7,
  338–40
  primitiveness of concept of a person
    287–8, 349–50
phenomenalism 48, 205, 215, 276–7
phenomenology 285
philosophy 136
  and analysis 2–4
  and theory construction 1–2, 33–4
  and thought-experiments 82–3
Plantinga, A. 132, 133
posits 47–8, 138
  see also theoretical entities
possible
  entities 97
  possibilities 156–7, 166
predicates 135
prediction 101–2
Price, M. 16 n.
primitives 138, 153, 194
  see also persons; theory
production processes 79, 112, 127,
  151, 167, 202–3, 244–5, 309–10,
  317, 333–4, 342–3, 351
proper parts 139
properties 6, 58, 153–4, 208–11, 232,
  234–6
  high- and low-level 94
  indexed 131–5
  and time 132, 153
propositions 131 n.
prototypes 71–2, 228
pseudomorphism 80–2, 174, 195–6
pupation 197–8, 200, 203
Putnam, H. 147, 202 n., 242

q-memory 250 n., 264–5, 280–1,
  318–19
quality spaces 213–16
Quine, W. V. 3, 6, 10 n., 23, 47–9, 96,
  135, 137–8, 149, 164 n., 188,
  195–6, 207, 212–17, 345, 348